No Trail to Follow

ALSO BY MICHAEL E. LASALLE

*Emigrants on the Overland Trail:
The Wagon Trains of 1848*

No Trail to Follow

The First Wagon Party to California, 1841

Michael E. LaSalle

COVERED WAGON PRESS || WISCONSIN DELLS, WI

Copyright © 2018 Michael E. LaSalle
All rights reserved.

ISBN: 978-0-692-17294-0
Library of Congress Control Number: 2018954788

Printed in Illinois by Versa Press, Inc.

Design and production by BW&A Books, Inc.
First edition, first printing

Covered Wagon Press
P.O. Box 41
Wisconsin Dells, WI 53965

Cover painting: "Ever Westward," oil on canvas by E. S. Paxson, 1910.
Courtesy of painting owner, Ken Guddal, and of photo image,
Jackson Hole Art Auction.

Title page photo: Ruby Mountains, Nevada, by the author.

In Memoriam

*For Yvonne, my late wife
and travel companion*

Contents

Introduction   1

Roster of the 1841 Company   8

Prologue   11

1 Dreams of High Adventure   15

2 The Gathering at Sapling Grove:
   May 6 to 12, 1841   31

3 From Sapling Grove to the Kansas River Crossing:
   May 12 to 17, 1841   44

4 Organizing and Departing: May 18 to 20, 1841   55

5 Across a Sea of Grass: May 21 to 31, 1841   69

6 Along the Platte River: June 1 to 15, 1841   94

7 Fort Laramie and Beyond: June 16 to 30, 1841   132

8 Crossing the North Platte and Up the Sweetwater:
   July 1 to 15, 1841   167

9 Over South Pass and On to the Green River:
   July 16 to 31, 1841   194

10 Along the Bear River: August 1 to 15, 1841   219

11 Across the Great Salt Lake Country:
    August 16 to 31, 1841   246

12 Languishing North and West of Salt Lake:
   September 1 to 15, 1841   267

13 Ignorant Wanderings: September 16 to 30, 1841   281

14 Will the Humboldt Ever End? October 1 to 15, 1841   315

15 Struggling over the Sierra Nevada Mountains:
   October 16 to 31, 1841   341

16 The Journey Ends: November 1 to 4, 1841   386

   Epilogue   401

   Notes   407

   Bibliography   423

   Acknowledgments   428

   Index   429

   About the Author   440

"We were now thrown entirely upon our resources. All the country was to us a veritable terra incognita, and we only knew that California lay to the west."

—JOHN BIDWELL

Introduction

A LONG TIME AGO, a group of people gathered at a remote place called Sapling Grove, about ten miles southwest of today's downtown Kansas City, Missouri. It was Friday, May 7, 1841. Their covered wagons were parked on a grassy knoll just north of a small spring that was bordered by a grove of young hickory trees. People stood in small groups, engaged in lively conversation. Others tended their livestock on the grassy slopes, while down in the grove a few children gathered wood to fuel their campfires.

In many respects, they were ordinary people assembling at an ordinary place. They were, for the most part, unremarkable as to education, wealth, and station in life. Nothing extraordinary appeared to be going on. But in truth something was. They were assembling for a purpose that was anything but ordinary. As expeditions go, it would be a small one, but its size belied its significance. The group was about to begin a new age in the nation's history, an important milestone in the nation's settlement of the Far West. Later called the Bartleson-Bidwell party or the Bidwell-Bartleson party, it would have the distinction of being the first organized group of emigrants to attempt a wagon journey from Missouri to far-off California. They would open a new phase in the expansion of a nation that would eventually stretch from one ocean to the other.

Various forces and conditions had been pushing American settlers westward for over two hundred years, but there was something significantly different about this expedition. It would not be a gradual step, with ready support from settlements just a stone's throw away. Rather, it would be a gigantic leap of two thousand miles across mysterious country where there would be no support from the civilized world. Since it had never been done before, it would serve as a useful dress rehearsal for a massive pageant of wagon trains that would lumber westward to Oregon and California in the years to come.

The following table shows how western migration to the Pacific Coast started as a trickle, then slowly mounted until the Gold Rush transformed the movement into a flood. During the twenty years after 1841, it is estimated that about 300,000 brave souls tramped across these trails to Oregon, California, and Utah.[1]

Number of Emigrants per Year, 1840–1850

	to California	to Oregon	Total
1840	0	13	13
1841	34	24	58
1842	0	125	125
1843	38	875	913
1844	53	1,475	1,528
1845	260	2,500	2,760
1846	1,500	1,200	2,700
1847	450	4,000	4,450
1848	400	1,300	1,700
1849	25,000	450	25,450
1850	44,000	6,000	50,000

Source: John D. Unruh Jr., *The Plains Across: The Overland Emigrants and the Trans-Mississippi West, 1840–1860* (Urbana: University of Illinois Press, 1993), 119–20. Curiously, Unruh's table fails to reflect the twenty-three-member Rowland-Workman party that traveled to southern California in 1841 by way of the southern route.

When the Bartleson-Bidwell party neared Fort Hall, in today's Idaho, it divided into two groups, one going to California and the other to Oregon. This division is shown in the table above.

While most historians have called Bartleson-Bidwell a party of emigrants, it included only three families—men with wives and children—who were planning on putting down roots and staying. Most of the rest, however, were young, single men, many of whom had no intention of remaining in the West. They just wanted to see California and were looking forward to experiencing high adventure. That is not to say that none of them would remain as permanent settlers in California, because many of them did. Young men like John Bidwell, Charles Weber, and Josiah Belden would remain there and carve out bright futures, while many of the others, having satisfied their adventuresome appetites, would not stay and would return east.

This book will reveal what a special breed the members of this expedition were. We will observe how they handled the difficulty of their struggles and will come to appreciate their courage and fortitude. We will marvel at the remarkable human spirit it took to subdue and defeat the hardships and obstacles that were thrown in their path. We will reach the inescapable conclusion that the West could not have been settled by the weak or fainthearted.

Few in the party would bequeath to us a detailed, contemporary account of the journey, but we are fortunate that two day-by-day accounts survived—those of John Bidwell and James John. These two young men would witness and narrate this pivotal moment in the nation's history. Their daily entries are treasures that cannot be overestimated. Rather than paraphrasing their entries or using snippets, I have included them in full and verbatim. Let the diarists speak for themselves and let us hear their voices. Let us experience their unique personalities and be amused by their writing quirks. After all, they were reporting what they saw and did each day. Their entries were written when memories were fresh and not when dimmed or distorted by the passage of time.

It is remarkable how these two young diarists were such faithful recorders, exercising unfaltering discipline in dragging their journals out at the end of each day to jot down a few lines, even when they were exhausted or when conditions were miserable. Their entries tended to be brief, often maddeningly bereft of detail. There was undoubtedly more to the story than what they recorded, but given their fatigue, it is understandable. It would be unreasonable to expect more. They rarely offered a glimpse into what was going through their minds. We can only guess at their thoughts and feelings. There would be days when they must have been terribly distressed, angry, discouraged, or frustrated, but we rarely hear them complain. Perhaps the culture of the times considered it unmanly to complain too much about hardships and discomfort.

All that survived of Bidwell's journal is found in a printed pamphlet in the possession of the Bancroft Library. The pamphlet was a reproduction of a lengthy letter that Bidwell sent back to Missouri after he arrived in California. It contained an abridged version of the journal he kept on the trail. Dated March 30, 1842, five months after his arrival in California, his letter began: "Owing to circumstances I am compelled to abridge my Journal, and likewise a description of the Country so far as I have been able to travel. By perusing the following pages you will learn more of the particulars of all my travels since I left the United States."[2] Since Bidwell's original journal is lost, it is unknown what details he may have left out.

There are two copies of James John's journal. First, there is a fragile, 4-inch-by-6-inch notebook in the possession of the Oregon Historical Society (OHS) in Portland. The entries begin on May 17 and end on August 20, 1841. It appears to be the journal that John carried on the trail, since the entries appear to be in his hand, a hand that deteriorated as time went by. The second is a 2¾-inch-by-6⅛-inch notebook consisting of seventy-nine pages and covering the time period from May 16 to October 31. It is in the possession of the Rosenbach Museum and Library in Philadelphia and is a perplexing document. While its first few pages appear to be in John's handwriting, the rest appears to be written in the hands of two others, suggesting that the second notebook is a copy of the first one, although the wording in many of the entries for the same date differs slightly. I use the OHS journal entries until they end on August 20. From then on, all entries come from the Rosenbach notebook.

Another member of the expedition, Nicholas Dawson, did not keep a daily diary in the traditional sense, but he left something else of value. He kept a log in which he recorded his estimate of the miles the party traveled each day and a brief description of each campsite. His entries were made in a small booklet that is in the possession of the Bancroft Library. His log is especially useful to compare with Bidwell's and John's estimates of distances.

Besides these priceless documents, some recollections and memoirs were written many years later by some of the members of the expedition. People such as Nicholas Dawson, Josiah Belden, Robert Thomes, Nancy Kelsey, Joseph Chiles, and Bidwell produced some memoirs as well.[3] These recollections provide some information not contained in Bidwell's and John's daily journals, but not much more. Often short and sometimes inaccurate, the memoirs frequently suffered from their authors' failing or faulty memories. They tended to understate the hardships and privations, which is to be expected since time tends to soothe the sting.

INTRODUCTION

This book contains photographic images of a few members of the expedition. Photographs depicting them at the time of their trip, when they were young, are lacking, since photography was in its infancy in 1841. Most of the portraits in the book were taken many years after their journey, when the subjects were much older. As the reader follows the expedition, it will be difficult to avoid visualizing the subjects as they are portrayed in their older state.

Throughout the book, the location of the trail and the estimated location of the expedition's campsites are described in reference to today's roads, highways, and towns. We all are indebted to an earlier generation of trail scholars, people like the late Dale Morgan, Paul Henderson, Charles Camp, Irene Paden, Aubrey L. Haines, Merrill Mattes, and Gregory M. Franzwa. These devoted people pored over countless trail diaries, interviewed local ranchers, walked the landscape looking for ruts, swales, and other physical evidence of the trail, and published books confirming what they found. Franzwa, for example, published a particularly helpful book in 1982, entitled *Maps of the Oregon Trail*. It includes an extensive collection of detailed modern maps developed by the National Park Service on which were imposed the precise route of most of the trail. The trail routes are shown, mile by mile, in relation to present-day roads, highways, and other terrain features. Franzwa updated and supplemented the maps in a 1990 edition. While the route of the trail did change slightly in places with the passage of time, these maps, for the most part, show where the 1841 expedition traveled between Independence, Missouri, and Soda Springs, Idaho.

Beyond Soda Springs, the Bartleson-Bidwell party left the established trail and struck out on its own, stumbling blindly westward. Much of the route they took to eventually reach California would not be followed by others in the years to come—and for good reason. But we can ascertain their path with some degree of confidence by studying Bidwell's and John's descriptions of the terrain and by considering the geography and their estimated mileages.

Any account of an expedition like this would be disappointing and incomplete if insufficient attention were paid to the terrain through which they traveled and to the vegetation and animal life they encountered. Bidwell's and John's journal entries fail to provide much description regarding these matters. Fortunately, there are others to whom we can turn who give an additional feel of the trail experience. Rufus B. Sage, for example, wrote about his experiences on the same trail when he traveled with a fur trading caravan in the fall of 1841. Lt. John C. Frémont, in charge of a detachment from the U.S. Army's Corps of Topological Engineers, kept detailed notes when he and his expedition traveled the trail to South Pass in 1842. Two exceptionally gifted writers recorded their journeys west in 1846: Edwin Bryant, a newspaper editor, who had decided to take a sabbatical trip to California, and J. Quinn Thornton, an emigrant bound for Oregon. Whether it was 1841, 1842, or 1846, much of the landscape these people described had not changed. Their observations are relevant and illuminating, and I will incorporate some of them from time to time.

The reader is urged to drive along the route of the Oregon Trail as well as the route that the Bartleson-Bidwell party took once it left the trail west of Soda Springs. For those who are interested in following the route as closely as possible, we highly recommend Gregory M. Franzwa's *Maps of the Oregon Trail* (1982). Traveling the trail can be an exhilarating and rewarding experience. In places, old wagon ruts and other evidence of the trail can still be seen, although the tour should be taken before any more of these trail remnants are erased from the landscape. We are grateful for the dedicated efforts of the Oregon-California Trails Association and Trails West, two important organizations that promote and publicize the trails and continue to fight endless battles to preserve and protect what is left.

Even where there is no present evidence of the trail, one can still see the lay of the land and the physical environment through which these early travelers passed. There is much to appreciate. There is nothing like the pungent scent of sagebrush at dawn, the bracing smell of dust kicked up by a sudden downpour, and the odor of stagnant water standing along the fringes of a small stream.

The reader is encouraged to use Google Earth while reading the book. It is a remarkable modern resource that will help the reader follow the progress of the wagon party across the West. Google Earth is a mosaic of high-resolution aerial images from which the reader can see in astonishing detail the country across which these wagons lumbered. In some places, especially in Wyoming, one can discern the faint line of the trail that the passage of time has not yet completely erased.

The era of the Oregon Trail evokes romantic images of long lines of ox-drawn covered wagons rumbling over a sage-covered plain while engulfed in clouds of choking dust. Sadly, we live in a country that is in danger of losing interest in its historic past. Our youth seem more concerned with matters of the present and future, and a dwindling percentage of our country's residents are descendants of the brave pioneers who settled the West. A growing number of people living in the United States have come from somewhere else and, understandably, may have limited interest in how or why our nation developed into the country that it is today.

The settling of the Far West is still a great story. Those who study how our nation was built will recognize that the Bartleson-Bidwell party was an important step in that process. Celebrating landmark events in our nation's history should never go out of style. It is said that history, like love, tends to portray its heroes with excessive virtue. I have worked hard to avoid this trap and have endeavored to reveal the story's principal characters as they really were, and not as we would like them to be. The story is about courage and self-reliance and about people who had very little to fall back on but themselves and their fortitude. It is hoped that the book will play a small part in stimulating renewed interest in the fascinating age when covered wagons lumbered along the Oregon and California trails and when they became an enduring symbol of the conquering of the Far West.

Michael E. LaSalle
HANFORD, CALIFORNIA

Roster of the 1841 Company

Missionary Party and Associates

Pilot: Thomas Fitzpatrick
Jesuit Priests: Pierre Jean De Smet, Nicholas Point, Gregory Mengarini
Jesuit Brothers: William Claessens, Charles Huet, Joseph Specht
Teamsters: L. Boileau, E. Chaussie, L. L. Coing (or Coviong)
Professional Hunter: John Gray
Trappers: James Baker, William Mast, and Piga
Sightseers: Amos E. Frye, Mr. Rogers, W. G. Romain (Englishman)

Bartleson Party
THOSE WHO WENT TO CALIFORNIA

John Bartleson
Elias Barnett
Josiah Belden
William Belty
John Bidwell
Henry L. Brolaski
David W. Chandler
Joseph B. Chiles
Grove C. Cook
Nicholas Dawson
V. W. Dawson
Paul Geddes, also known as Talbot H. Green
George Henshaw
Charles Hopper
Henry Huber
James John (Jimmy John)
Thomas Jones
Andrew Kelsey
Benjamin Kelsey, his wife, Nancy A. Kelsey, and young daughter
John McDowell
Nelson McMahan
Samuel Green McMahan
Michael C. Nye
Andrew Gwinn Patton
Robert Rickman
John Roland
John L. Schwartz
James P. Springer
Robert H. Thomes
Ambrose Walton
Major Walton
Charles M. Weber

THOSE WHO WENT TO OREGON

Mr. Carroll
Augustus Fifer (Pfeiffer)
Richard Fillan (or Phelan) and wife, Mrs. Gray, and her daughter by a previous marriage
William Fowler
Charles W. Flugge
David F. Hill
J. M. Jones
Samuel Kelsey, his wife, and five children
Isaac Kelsey (sometimes Zebidiah)
Edward Rogers
James Ross
Richard Williams, his wife, and daughter (daughter married Isaac Kelsey during the journey)
Reverend Joseph Williams

MEMBERS WHO DEPARTED THE COMPANY DURING THE JOURNEY

Elisha Stone, turned back at the Platte River
George Shotwell, died in a gunshot accident on the North Fork of the Platte
George Simpson, turned back at Fort Laramie
William Mast, left the party at Fort Laramie, purportedly to begin trapping
John Gray, Amos Frye, Mr. Rogers, W. G. Romain, Henry Payton, and J. M. Jones, turned back at the Green River
James Baker, and perhaps Piga, left the party at the Green River to begin trapping

Prologue

To put the Bartleson-Bidwell party into historical context, it is helpful to provide a brief overview of what had been happening west of the Missouri River prior to 1841. The first white men to intrude into the vast prairie lands and mountains beyond the Missouri were the Spanish explorers of the 1500s and 1600s. In the 1700s, part of this enormous region was traversed by French fur trappers and traders who could travel from Quebec to St. Louis and from St. Louis to New Orleans, and never leave French Territory. All that began to change in 1804, the year of the Louisiana Purchase. Having bought an immense expanse of land sight unseen, Jefferson did not know what he had acquired. But he was determined to find out. He sent Meriwether Lewis and William Clark with their Corps of Discovery to explore and report on what he had added to the nation. The expedition opened a new age of discovery that revealed the great riches existing in the streams and creeks of the Upper Missouri River Basin and the western mountains. It launched an age of American fur companies and their trappers.

Brigades of mountain men, working for various fur trading companies, soon began crisscrossing the mountains of the West, trapping or trading with the Indians for beaver pelts. At the apex of the trapping era, it is estimated that as many as twelve hundred of these rugged men ranged throughout the western mountains.[1]

One of the great innovators in the fur business was William Ashley. In 1822, Ashley began employing brave young men to venture into the Rockies to pursue these valuable furs. Most of the legendary names in the mountain trade—Jedediah Smith, William and Milton Sublette, Hugh Glass, Robert Campbell, Thomas Fitzpatrick, Jim Bridger, James Clyman, and Black Harris—started out as Ashley engagés. They were the earliest and truest of the mountain men and became important mentors to many who would later take up the profession.

Ashley pioneered a new way of conducting the fur business. There would be no fixed trading posts. Rather, goods and supplies would be transported by pack mules over land routes up the Platte River, through the Sweetwater River Valley in today's Wyoming and over South Pass to a predetermined summer rendezvous. The scattered fur trappers and scores of Indians would assemble at the rendezvous for a couple of uproarious weeks, where conviviality, debauchery, and trading would flourish. After exchanging goods and supplies for furs and buffalo skins, the supply trains would return east. The era of the rendezvous had a glorious run, but beaver were becoming depleted to the extent that the days of the wide-ranging brigades could no longer be sustained. In 1839, trapper Robert "Doc" Newell wrote: "times is getting hard all over this part of the Country beaver Scarce and low all peltries are on the decline."[2] By then, the days of the big trapping brigades were over, although fur trapping would continue for a few stubborn trappers unwilling to give up their hardy lifestyle of freedom and solitude. The trading companies did not die either. Rather, they had already begun shifting their business from beaver pelts to buffalo hides. In terms of value, the trade in buffalo skins had already exceeded beaver pelts as early as 1833.[3]

Apart from the fur trade, American settlers had been steadily moving westward since the days of the colonists. It was a process of conquering and subduing a vast wilderness, a process that was often painful and deadly. The character of the American pioneer and settler couldn't have been more aptly described than when Lord Dunmore, the Virginia governor, wrote in the 1770s: "Americans . . . do and will remove as their avidity and restlessness incite them. They acquire no attachment to place. But wandering about seems engrafted in their Nature; and it is a weakness incident to it, that they should forever imagine the lands Further off, are still better than those upon which they are already Settled."[4]

As settlers began filling in the spaces in Kentucky, Ohio, Indiana, Illinois, Arkansas, Wisconsin, and Iowa, they also began moving into Missouri. However, America's steady migration, which had heretofore been unstoppable, stalled at Missouri's western border in 1834. That was the first year that settlement further west was blocked due to the federal government designating the lands beyond Missouri's border as Indian Territory.[5] The Territory was a vast expanse that the government declared would be the exclusive domain (sort of) of the tribes that lived there. It would be off limits to white men unless they had acquired Indian trading licenses from the government or were missionaries, army personnel, or travelers passing through.[6] Some of the tribes had lived there for ages, tribes like the Kansa, Pawnee, Arapahoe, Crow, and Shoshone. Others, like the Cheyenne and Sioux, had migrated to the Plains in recent decades. Still others, like the Delaware, Shawnee, Wyandotte, Sac, Fox, Kickapoo, and Potawatomie, had been uprooted from their former homes in Ohio, Indiana, Illinois, and Iowa. having been induced by the government to give up their homelands in exchange for replacement land in Indian Territory. They were also given annual cash annuities and provided with technical assistance from agriculturists who would teach them modern farming practices.

In 1822, traders began departing Missouri settlements to travel to Santa Fe for the purpose of trading American goods to the Mexicans for furs, mules, and silver. During the rest of the 1820s and during the 1830s, the Santa Fe Trail became a heavily traveled road, with long caravans of freight wagons leaving from Fort Osage and Franklin, Missouri. These caravans would later depart from the newer and more westerly Missouri settlements of Independence and Westport.

Another movement began to stir in the early 1830s. It was the evangelizing of the Indians west of the Missouri River. Religious organizations began sending ministers into Indian Territory to save souls. The Methodists and Baptists were the most active, establishing missions among the Kansa, Delaware, Shawnee, Kickapoo, Otoe, and Pawnee tribes.[7] In 1833, William Walker, a well-educated Christian Wyandotte Indian, exhorted his fellow Methodists to further expand their missionary efforts in a piece he published in the Methodist *Christian Advocate*: "Let the Church awake from her slumbers and go forth in her strength to the salvation of those wandering sons of our native forests."[8] Jason Lee, a Methodist minister, was one of the first to answer the call, and he set out in 1834 to convert tribes in the "Oregon country."[9] Two years later, in 1835, the Presbyterians' American Board for Foreign Missions sent Doctor Marcus Whitman and the Reverend Samuel Parker to the Oregon Territory to evaluate setting up a mission among the Nez Perce tribe. After returning from his exploratory trip, Dr. Whitman traveled back to Oregon the following year with his new wife, Narcissa, and with the Reverend William Spaulding and his wife. The Spauldings established a mission among the Nez Perce, while the Whitmans made the fateful decision of establishing their mission near Walla Walla among the Cayuse Indians. Tragically, the Cayuse would massacre both of the Whitmans in 1847.[10]

The Catholics had been less active missionaries west of the Missouri River. While the Jesuits had occasionally sent a priest into today's Kansas during the late 1820s and the first part of the 1830s, they had not established any permanent missions west of the Missouri River until 1836, when they established one among the Kickapoo.[11] In 1840, however, the Jesuit bishop of St. Louis sent Father Pierre-Jean De Smet, a Belgian priest, to begin work among the Flathead Indians in the Bitterroot Mountains of today's Montana. De Smet traveled with an American Fur Company supply train of pack mules to Pierre's Hole in present-day Idaho, where the 1840 rendezvous was being convened. Met there by a delegation of Flatheads, he was escorted to their villages. That fall, De Smet returned to St. Louis to begin forming a large missionary party that would return to the Flathead homeland in the spring of 1841.

As will be seen, both the fur trade and missionary movements will play a significant role in the settlement of the West. The fur trapping era had laid down important foundations from which the first emigrants to the Far West would benefit. The fur companies, and the mountain men who worked for them, opened up the middle of the country, blazed the trails, developed amicable relationships with the Indians, and acquired the skills needed to survive. Moreover, the business produced the men who would serve as the guides needed to lead the earliest emigrant wagon trains west. One of these former mountain men, Thomas Fitzpatrick, was hired by Father De Smet to pilot his missionary party west in the spring of 1841. These two men will play important roles in the fortunes of the Bartleson-Bidwell expedition. If it were not for De Smet and Fitzpatrick, it is possible that the party would never have made it to California. At least that is what John Bidwell would later claim.

Chapter 1

Dreams of High Adventure

JOHN BIDWELL is a principal character in this story. Although the expedition to California has been called the Bartleson-Bidwell party and the Bidwell-Bartleson party, we will eventually see that Bidwell's role in the venture, and his influence over it, were overblown by most historians, and perhaps by Bidwell himself. This does not diminish Bidwell's importance. Besides being one of two members of the party whose daily journal accounts survived, this determined and talented young man had talents and a resolve that would serve the party well during the trip. Indeed, it will eventually be shown that if Bidwell had not been in the party, there is a great chance that the group would not have survived.

Years later, Bidwell would play a significant role in the development of early California. He would become a large landowner and farmer, would found a town, and would become an active politician in the state's future. In 1841, however, he was little more than a green, audacious youngster determined to seek adventure in the Far West.

Bidwell's journal entries did not begin until May 18, weeks after his odyssey began. But his memoirs described how he came to be at Sapling Grove in the spring of 1841.[1] He explained that he was not a contented youngster, but rather aspired to "see the great prairies of the West." Like many young people of the time, he grew up fast, and became independent, self-actuated, and self-reliant at an early age. He was only twenty years of age when he left his home in Ohio in 1839 with only $75 in his pocket. He traveled to Cincinnati, boarded a steamer, and traveled down the Ohio River to the Mississippi.[2] He got off the boat at Burlington, Iowa, but quickly discovered that the area was plagued with malaria—what was called "fever and ague" in the parlance of the day. Deciding that this was not the place, he moved on. By the summer of 1840, he had come to rest in what became Platte County, Missouri. In what was called the Platte Purchase, the federal government had purchased two million acres on the east side of the Missouri River in 1836 from a few Indian tribes and made it available for white settlers.[3] Bidwell decided to make the area his home, describing the country as "lovely, rolling, and fertile, wonderfully productive, beautifully arranged for settlement, part prairie and part timber. . . . Nearly every place seemed to have a beautiful spring of clear cold water. The hills and prairie and level places were alike covered with a black and fertile soil."[4]

Young Bidwell got a job teaching school near Weston, a tiny, three-year-old settlement built on the east bank of the Missouri River. It was just across the river from Fort Leavenworth. Bidwell took out a homestead claim on 160 acres. He left his claim to travel to St. Louis for supplies, but when he returned, he found that a "squatter" had jumped his claim. Describing the man as a "scoundrel" and a "bully" whom "everyone was afraid of" because he had killed a man, Bidwell decided against challenging him.[5] Since settlers had been pouring into the area for some time, Bidwell complained that the other good sites were already taken. "There being no possibility of getting another claim to suit me," he explained, "I resolved to go elsewhere when spring [1841] should open."[6]

Bidwell recounted in one of his memoirs that in the winter of 1840–41 "a man came to the settlement [Weston] by the name of Rowbadeaux [Robidoux]. He was an Indian trader and brother to the famous Joseph Rowbadeaux."[7] The man was probably Antoine, a younger brother of Joseph.[8] The Robidoux brothers came from a distinguished family of French traders. Joseph operated an Indian trading post on the east bank of the Missouri River, twenty-five miles north of Weston, and would found the town of St. Joseph there in 1843. St. Joseph would soon prosper and become a major jumping-off point for emigrants going to Oregon and California. Antoine, on the other hand, had spent many years in New Mexico and Colorado as a trader, and had made an overland trip to California in 1837.[9] Because "Rowbadeauz described California to us in glowing terms," Bidwell explained, he was invited to come to Weston to talk about this golden paradise. Robidoux described California "as one of perennial spring and boundless fertility," with "countless thousands of wild horses and cattle."

The desire for a more healthful environment was no trivial issue. Malaria was a scourge along the Missouri River, and peoples' interest in "fever and ague" was genuine. At the time, no one knew that mosquitoes were responsible for transmission of the disease. The swamps and wetlands along the Missouri River bottoms spawned hordes of malaria-bearing mosquitoes that would share the virus with anyone who would let them alight. Few would escape the affliction. In 1835, Charles Murray, a Scottish visitor, noticed "the wan and unhealthy appearance of all settlers on the banks of the Missouri between the Fort [Leavenworth] and St. Louis" and that the disease seemed to have struck every family he saw.[10] So it was natural that someone asked Robidoux if California had fever and ague. Robidoux scoffed, declaring that "there was but one man in California that had ever had a chill there, and it was a matter of so much wonderment to the people of Monterey that they went eighteen miles into the country to see him shake."[11]

Indeed, the Far West, especially California, was acquiring the reputation as a place where one could restore one's health. Robidoux's story was not the only tall tale that would make the rounds about the healthfulness of California. Other yarns would be concocted in the years to come, such as the one mentioned by Edwin Bryant in 1846. In explaining why he decided to go to California, Bryant related that he had heard about a man living there who had attained the advanced age of 250 years. The aged man had grown tired of life and wished to die. Yet, life stubbornly clung to him. To be granted his wish, he was advised that he would have to leave California. So he moved to another country, where he promptly took sick and died. Well-meaning friends thought he would have wanted to be buried in his former abode. No sooner had his body been interred in the California earth than its life-giving qualities invaded his corpse and he burst from the grave, alive and fully restored to vitality.[12]

Stories such as these were part of the California mythology that proliferated during those times. While people must have enjoyed a good laugh, knowing that these tales were nothing more than ludicrous hyperbole, the stories may have resonated just a little with people who hoped that a germ of truth lurked behind their outlandishness.

Robidoux's presentation had undoubtedly planted intoxicating visions in the heads of his audience, because Bidwell and others immediately organized the Western Emigration Society. To further bolster enthusiasm, Bidwell explained that the society obtained "a letter from Dr. Marsh, an American living in California, to a friend in Jackson County, Missouri." They had his "glowing account" of California published.[13]

Bidwell claimed they had no trouble getting five hundred people to sign a pledge that was "binding each one to dispose of his property, purchase a suitable outfit and rendezvous at Sapling Grove in Kansas Territory on the ninth day of the following May, ready for crossing the plains." According to Bidwell, "we pledged to each other our lives, our fortunes, and our sacred honor."[14]

But had Robidoux made it clear that California was a foreign country where you were subject to arrest if you did not have a passport when you arrived? Had he also warned that the Mexican authorities would accept American settlers only if they agreed to become Mexican citizens and convert to Catholicism? Judging by the large numbers signing the pledge, it does not look as if he had.

The Weston town merchants were in a panic about the prospect of suddenly losing so many valued customers. "[D]etermined to defeat the movement," Bidwell explained, the merchants "argued against it, denounced it, and ridiculed it."[15] They claimed that "it was the most unheard of, foolish, wild-goose chase that ever entered into the brain of man for 500 people to pull up stakes, leave that beautiful country, and go away out to a region that we know nothing of."[16] While their warnings may have been prompted by their self-interest, their admonishments were quite justified.

The merchants seemed to be making very little headway until they heard of a recent letter by Thomas Jefferson Farnham, a Peoria, Illinois, lawyer. He had arrived in California in 1839, in time to witness the Mexican authorities arresting and jailing a number of Americans suspected of threatening an American-led insurgency. When Farnham returned east, he published a couple of letters in New York newspapers, one of them excoriating the oppressiveness of the native Californios toward the handful of Americans living there. When the Weston merchants learned of the letter they had it "republished in all the papers of the frontier," including one in nearby Liberty, Missouri.[17]

Discussions, some heated, must have raged through the homes of those who had signed the Emigration Society's pledge to go to California. By the time the debates had run their course and the initial clarion call waned, minds had changed. The flames of enthusiasm had been doused. According to Bidwell, the Farnham letter had dealt a mortal blow. "Our party soon fell to pieces," he lamented, "notwithstanding our pledge was as binding as language could make it. . . . [I]t overthrew our project completely. . . . When May came I was the only man that [was] ready to go, of all who had signed the pledge."[18] Perhaps Bidwell had exaggerated the letter's effect. The passage of time has a way of tranquilizing feelings. Once the members' overheated enthusiasm had returned to room temperature and they had properly weighed the pros and cons, it must have finally occurred to them that this venture was terribly rash and unlikely to have a good ending. California was a foreign country where the obtaining of free land by American intruders was probably a far-fetched notion. Besides, there was plenty of free land still available in Missouri. There was no need to tear the family away from its snug and secure moorings. It was probably best to pass on the idea.

In coming to their senses and changing their minds, these five hundred people had probably averted a horrible catastrophe. The terrain that such an expedition would have to cross was harsh and unforgiving. A group as large as this would have very likely been sentenced to a sad and terrible fate.

It looked as though another of Bidwell's plans had been annihilated. Twice he had been faced with adversities from which he retreated—fever and ague in Iowa, and the dangerous, claim-jumping bully in Missouri. But for some reason, this appeared to be a turning point in Bidwell's personality. Rather than concede another defeat, he wrote that he took steps to prevent the collapse of his luminous dream. In one of his memoirs, he said he had heard of men in Jackson County, Missouri (in which Independence was located), "who were talking of going to California."[19] In another memoir, he described himself as a principal force behind the Jackson County men, saying that during the winter, "to keep the project alive," he "made two or three trips into Jackson County, Missouri . . . to see the men who were talking of going to California."[20] While he did not identify them, it is probable that they included Colonel John Bartleson and William Baldridge, both residents of Jackson County.

Determined to go, Bidwell "purchased an outfit which consisted of a wagon and some provisions, a rifle, and ammunition."[21] He de-

*John Bidwell, 1850. Call No. 2007-0008.
Courtesy of California State Library.*

scribed his preparations: "I laid in one hundred pounds of flour more than the usual quantities, besides other things. This I did because we were told that when we got into the mountains we probably would get out of bread and have to live on meat alone, which I thought would kill me even if it did not others. My gun was an old flint-lock rifle, but a good one. Old hunters told me to have nothing to do with cap or percussion locks, that they were unreliable, and if I got my caps or percussion wet I could not shoot, while if I lost my flint I could pick up another on the plains."[22]

Bidwell admitted that he lacked the money to complete his outfit. He was unable to buy a team to pull his wagon. To make matters worse, the man who was to go with him backed out. Things were looking bleak until a well-dressed man from Illinois named George Henshaw appeared. According to Bidwell, Henshaw was "old, quite an invalid, and nearly helpless." But he was a godsend. Not only did he agree to go but he allowed Bidwell to trade his splendid black horse for a team of oxen to pull Bidwell's wagon, along with a one-

*Robert H. Thomes, circa 1870. Neg. #22,264.
Courtesy of California State Library.*

eyed mule that Henshaw would ride. Bidwell did not explain the nature of Henshaw's health problems, but the man did make it to California alive despite the hardships. In addition to Henshaw, four others from Weston would also go with Bidwell: Robert H. Thomes, a wagon maker, Michael Nye, the son of a local merchant, and two other young men Bidwell did not identify.[23]

At the same time, things were happening in Jackson County. The activity there had its beginnings with a man by the name of John Marsh. Arriving at Independence in the fall of 1833, Marsh had opened a store and bar in the bustling settlement. Catering to the needs of Santa Fe freighters, fur trade suppliers, and the trappers and traders who were passing through, Marsh did well at first. During this time, he became friends with local residents John Bartleson, William Baldridge, and Michael Nye. For reasons unknown, Marsh's businesses began to fail. By 1835, he was bankrupt. To escape his clamoring creditors, Marsh left town in the middle of the night for Santa Fe. By 1836 he had made it to California. Shortly, the ambitious Marsh purchased a rancho on the eastern slopes of Mt. Diablo. He began sending letters to his friends in Independence. Joseph Chiles, a resident of Independence and a friend of Baldridge, recalled that "[Baldridge] had been corresponding with Dr. Marsh, whose descriptive letters of Cal and its climate and resources, had awakened in him a great desire to see the country. They at once set about making a company of venture[some] persons to seek the far off shore."[24] As mentioned earlier, one of Marsh's letters had been published by the Western Emigration Society in Weston to encourage people to join its expedition. One of them purportedly contained directions to California.

On February 1, 1841, a meeting was held in Jackson County, probably in Independence since that is where the principal promoters lived. The meeting did not escape the attention of the press.[25] The March 8, 1841, issue of the *Western Atlas and Saturday Evening Gazette*, a St. Louis newspaper, ran an article that conveyed genuine excitement about the formation of an expedition to California and Oregon:

FOR CALIFORNIA AND THE WEST. —We see by several of the newspapers of the upper Missouri, that there is in that quarter, quite an excitement on the subject of emigration to California and Oregon. At a very large and spirited meeting held recently in Jackson county, a company was formed, consisting of 58 gentlemen, 19 of whom have families, which they will take with them. This company invites all who wish to join them, as emigrants to California, to rendezvous at the Sapling Grove on the old Santa Fe route, about nine miles west of the Missouri State line, against the 10th of May next.

A Resolution was passed appointing a committee of correspondence consisting of Messrs. R. Rickman, A. Overton [indexed as William Overton], and Hensley, to give information to enquirers in regard to the expedition. The following Resolutions were also passed, and show that they have begun the thing in the right way:

Resolved. That all persons either single or having families shall be provided with a sufficiency of provisions and other necessaries to insure them against want, till they reach the buffalo region.

Further Resolved. That no person shall be permitted to take any spirituous liquors except for medicinal purposes.

The country to which they propose to emigrate is described as exceedingly eligible in all points of view—whether commercial or agricultural. The climate is salubrious and delightful—the soil rich—the natural productions various—and all the means of a pleasant and comfortable subsistence afforded in abundance. A glorious era is, no doubt, dawning on those regions so favored by nature; and they who first take possession have all before them where to choose. To the young, the buoyant, and the enterprising the field is full of promise. They may grow rich by skill, industry and perseverance, but achieve the splendid fame of laying deep and broad the foundation of an empire.[26]

The Jackson County meeting sounded remarkably similar to the one that had been held in Weston, including the date and place decided upon for the rendezvous. This reinforces the notion that Bidwell's trips to Jackson County had been for the purpose of coordinating with these people. Historians have generally credited Bidwell with playing a major role in forming the expedition, and while there is no doubt he played a role, it may have been less significant than some have portrayed. These Jackson County men seemed independent and resolute, and it appears that they would have proceeded with their venture even if Bidwell had never appeared on the scene.

The Jackson County promoters discovered, much as Bidwell had, that the initial fervor to go to California would cool considerably in the months to come. As May approached, most of the original fifty-eight had renounced their intention to go.

The *Western Atlas and Saturday Evening Gazette* had not forgotten about the expedition and published a follow-up article in its May 1, 1841, issue, a few days before people began gathering at Sapling Grove:

EXPEDITION TO CALIFORNIA.—We have chronicled the movements in the upper Missouri, on the subject of emigration to the gulf of California, just as we should any other matter of interesting information. The project of such an emigration has been agitated; and the scheme has been, and probably is now, that men shall go out with families consisting of wives and children. By the latest dates from Independence we see, however, that some of the original agitators have "drawn back." No doubt, this is all very well. For men, with families perhaps of young children to say nothing of women, to join any such expedition as has been set on foot in the upper Missouri, is, in our opinion, absurd. Nothing but the most fatal disasters will be in store for such emigrants.

But there is no serious objection to young men, full of life, spirit and energy, starting off upon an expedition to the Pacific Ocean. Let them take good mules and stout trappings, rifles and knives with store of ammunition, and doubtless they can get up as pretty a bit of romance as turns up in real life at this late age of the world. They can hunt buffalo, fight Indians, [and] get into frays with Mexicans.

Nicholas Dawson, 1902. Call No.: Dawson, Nicholas-POR, 10/19/1902. Courtesy of Bancroft Library.

The newspaper was singing a different tune this time, now expressing second thoughts about taking a family so far and on such a hazardous venture. As for the young men, let them have their adventure, it opined. But the article went on to wonder why anyone would feel compelled to go to a "foreign jurisdiction, to a country perfectly wild of which really little is known." Missouri was a "vast territory," it argued, with the "cheapest and richest soils." Therefore, people ought to "stay at home and improve the vast and as yet undeveloped resources" of their own country. The piece concluded: "[W]e go for peopling Missouri, not California."[27]

Although most of the original pledgees from around Independence had dropped out, some were still undismayed. One was Nicholas Dawson, who, like John Bidwell, was single and educated, had recently taught school, and was only twenty-two years of age. Like Bidwell, he had itchy feet, claiming in his 1894 memoirs that he had an "overweaning desire to travel."[28] Dawson left his teaching job in Arkansas and came to Independence in the early spring of 1841,

*John Marsh, circa 1860. Neg. #6525.
Courtesy of California State Library.*

where he "should most likely find a company going to Oregon."[29] He further explained, "Learning here that a company was soon to go to California and Oregon, I stopped with a man by the name of John Bartleson, who was preparing to go. I soon decided to make one of the company, and remained with Bartleson until the crowd should be made up." Dawson traded his "horse for an old mule and bought an interest in Bartleson's wagon and team," and added, "When this and my share of provisions were paid for, I had seventy-five cents left."[30]

Dawson reported that when the group got ready to leave they formed a "mess" consisting of himself, John Bartleson, Charles Hopper, Gwinn Patton, and Talbot Green. He described Hopper as a noted hunter, Patton as a young relative of Hopper's, and Talbot Green as "a young man of evident culture and very pleasing address." He also mentioned that Talbot was taking a large quantity of lead with him on the journey.[31] What Dawson did not mention, probably because he did not know it at the time, was that Talbot was an alias.

Josiah Belden circa 1875. Courtesy of Clyde Arbuckle Collection, California Room, San Jose Public Library.

His real name was Paul Geddes, a fugitive from the law. He had embezzled money from a bank and invested the ill-gotten funds in lead. Dawson also mentioned that Grove Cook, a brother-in-law of the famous Sublette brothers, "joined us after we had started, and begged to be allowed to pay his way by driving our wagon, as he could furnish nothing."[32]

A few others from Independence and Jackson County joined the expedition, although Dawson did not mention them as part of their "mess." They included Robert Rickman, William Overton, and the Kelsey families.[33] William Baldridge, one of the men who had been communicating with John Marsh, would not be going. He had to stay behind because he was committed to building a number of flour mills in the Independence area. It would be Bartleson who would carry the Marsh letter that allegedly contained the famous directions for "Marsh's route."[34]

Twenty-six-year-old Josiah Belden, another single man, would also go. His memoirs, written years later, explained that he grew up restless and infected with an intense desire to travel, much as Bidwell and Dawson had. He said that he wanted "to see something of a wild country, of buffalo hunting, and to have some adventures among the Indians."³⁵ Belden recounted that after he arrived in St. Louis he became acquainted with Henry Brolaski, David Chandler, and George Shotwell. From them, he learned about "an expedition that was being got up to go to California." Understanding that it was being formed in Independence, Belden and his friends bought a wagon and provisions, loaded them on a steamboat, and traveled up the Missouri River to Independence.³⁶

ALTHOUGH THIS STORY is not about Father Pierre De Smet's missionary party, it cannot be ignored. Its involvement with and influence on the Bartleson-Bidwell party would be significant. The two groups would travel together for the first one thousand miles under the guidance of the missionary's hired pilot, Thomas Fitzpatrick. The story leading up to this missionary party had its beginnings in about 1816, when a small group of Iroquois left the Montreal area and headed west, looking for a better place to live. They ended up in the Bitterroot Mountains of today's Montana and settled among a band of Flathead Indians. The Iroquois were converts to the Catholic religion, having been taught by the Jesuits, whom they called "Blackrobes" or "Blackgowns." They urged their new Flathead friends to obtain the services of "a Blackgown to conduct them to heaven."³⁷ In many cases, the Indians were not so much interested in being "saved" as they were awed by the white man's powerful magic or "medicine." They suspected that his impressive powers must come from his Great Spirit and they wanted access to it. In 1831, the Flatheads and Nez Perce sent a delegation to St. Louis to inquire about getting a Blackrobe.³⁸ Not only did the delegation fail to achieve their goal: none of them made it home alive. They all died of disease or at the hands of enemy warriors.³⁹ Three more delegations were sent in ensuing years, the final one consisting of two Iroquois who met with the Jesuit bishop of St. Louis in 1839. The bishop promised he would send someone, and the following year sent Father Pierre De Smet, a Belgian priest, to assess the situation. De Smet left Westport in April 1840 and traveled with an American Fur Company supply train. It was bound for the fur trappers' summer rendezvous that was to be held in the Green River Valley that year. In the meantime,

Father Pierre-Jean De Smet, S.J. Courtesy of Jesuit Archives, Central United States, St. Louis.

the Flatheads sent a delegation to greet De Smet at the rendezvous and to escort him to their villages in the Three Rivers area of today's Montana. After spending the summer with the Flatheads, De Smet left but promised he would return. He and an escort made their long and arduous return trip, traveling beside the Yellowstone River and then the Missouri River until they finally reached St. Louis on December 31, 1840.[40]

De Smet immediately began making preparations to return the next spring to the Flatheads. Needing funds to outfit and support the expedition, he contacted the bishops of Philadelphia, New Orleans, and other places and asked them to take up collections from their congregations. The response was good and provided enough to make the trip possible.[41] By spring, De Smet was ready to go. His party included Father Nicholas Point (a French Jesuit priest), Father Gregorio Mengarini (an Italian priest recently arrived from Rome),

Thomas Fitzpatrick. Portrait painted by Waldo Love, 1936. Accession # H.6130.27, Scan # 10027099. Courtesy of History Colorado.

and three Jesuit brothers: Brother William Cleasons (a Belgian blacksmith), Brother Charles Huet (a Belgian carpenter), and Brother Joseph Specht (a German tinsmith). In addition, the party employed two French Canadian wagoneers and a half-Iroquois professional hunter by the name of John Gray. Most importantly, De Smet hired the experienced mountain man, Thomas Fitzpatrick, to be their pilot.[42] De Smet's experiences traveling with the fur company's supply train in 1840 had impressed upon him the importance of using a knowledgeable trail guide.

De Smet's party included a few men not connected to the church. There were three fur trappers on their way to the Rockies to try their luck: James Baker, William Mast, and Piga, a French Canadian. Three others were on nothing more than a sightseeing excursion: Amos Frye, Rogers (first name unknown), and a young English aristocrat named W. G. Romaine.[43] Altogether, the De Smet party amounted to seventeen men.

The missionary group was taking a small wagon and four two-wheeled carts, commonly referred to as "Red River carts."[44] The carts were usually made of hard oak, including the wheel hubs and axles. Grease was rarely used, causing them to produce an annoying creak when the wheels turned.

The *Daily Missouri Republican*, a St. Louis newspaper, had been keeping its eye on the De Smet party. On April 20, 1841, it ran a story about the party leaving St. Louis:

EXPEDITION TO THE OREGON.— We understand that a portion of a party under command of Mr. Fitzpatrick leaves to-day for the Rocky Mountains and the south of the Columbia, the remainder of the party will leave in a few days, and the whole expedition will rendezvous at Independence on the 10th of May next, immediately after which they will take up their march for the Mountains. The company consists entirely of volunteers, and is not filled to the extent to which it has been limited. Persons desiring to go out can, by immediate application to Father De Smiat [sic] at the St. Louis University, to obtain a place in it.

The Rev. Father De Smiat, who accompanies the expedition, has been for some time past a Missionary among the Flat Head Indians, whom he left a short time since and came down the Missouri, having traveled the entire distance with one companion. Being pleased with his Missionary labors and the results attending his exertions and satisfied that the field of usefulness may be extended, he returns in a few days accompanied by several other gentlemen who will also contribute to the spread of the Gospel and the amileration [sic] of the condition of the Indians. . . .

The party will be under the command of Mr. Fitzpatrick, who has been twenty odd years in the Indian country, is perfectly familiar with their character and habits and is well known as not only an efficient hunter but a skillful commander.

The party is also accompanied by Mr. Romain, a young gentleman from England, who has crossed the Atlantic for the sole object of making this interesting tour. . . .[45]

Chapter 2

The Gathering at Sapling Grove

MAY 6 TO 12, 1841

AFTER 1840 CAME TO A CLOSE and the dull, gray skies of winter gave way to the warmer days of spring, the ice in the Missouri River began breaking up and the river opened to another season of steamboat traffic. It was time for those intending to assemble at Sapling Grove to begin heading toward their designated rendezvous.

John Bidwell and his five companions left Weston in early May 1841. Although most of the people in the Weston area were experiencing a change of heart about going, Bidwell's memoirs claimed that many of them showed up to say goodbye: "The people of Weston, notwithstanding their failure to make good their pledge and in spite of the breaking up of the company, evinced their good feeling toward us by following us out in great numbers and bidding us goodbye two miles from town."[1]

The Bidwell group traveled south approximately forty miles and crossed the Missouri River.[2] They could have crossed the river eleven miles further upstream at Westport Landing because it would have placed them closer to Sapling Grove. But Robert Thomes, traveling with Bidwell and his companions, claimed in his memoirs that they left Independence on May 6, likely meaning that they crossed the river at Independence Landing instead.[3] It suggests that Bidwell and his friends planned on meeting up with John Bartleson and his group in Independence before going on to Sapling Grove.

The old Independence Landing is on the south bank of the Missouri River and north of downtown Independence. In later years, the name would be changed to Wayne City Landing. To see the location of the landing, travel north from Independence along North Sterling Avenue to East Kentucky Road. Then turn right and proceed east a

Wayne City Landing, 1842. *Oil on canvas by John Stobart, image 1977. Courtesy of Kensington Galleries, Salem, Mass.*

short distance. Turn left on to North Vermont Street, a road that descends the bluff to the river bottom. Travel down the road 1.6 miles to the landing.

Steamboats had been chugging up and down the Missouri River since 1819, connecting the western settlements along the river to St. Louis and beyond.[4] Steamers coming from St. Louis would stop at Independence Landing after a four-hundred-mile journey up the winding river to unload or take on passengers and freight. At the landing, the Bidwell party should have encountered boatmen, bullwhackers, merchants, buckskin-clad trappers, and ornately dressed Indians. Kegs, crates, sacks, and other freight would have been piled beside the docks, waiting to be hauled into Independence. From the landing, a road ascended a crease in the steep bluff that followed the same path as today's Wayne City Road. One can enter Wayne City Road on the south from East Kentucky Road, where there is a Historic Trails interpretive site, but travel beyond that point is closed to the public.

Upon gaining the top of the bluff, the road from the landing into Independence generally followed today's River Road south. Following a ridge higher than the surrounding terrain, the road wound

*Independence Courthouse and Square.
Courtesy of Kansas State Historical Society.*

three and a half miles through a tangle of trees, vines, and underbrush to Independence, the center of which stood on a high hill.

First established in 1827, Independence was intended as a more westerly staging and outfitting point for trading caravans going to Santa Fe. For many years, long trains of heavy freight wagons, sometimes pulled by as many as ten to twelve yoke of oxen, had been leaving Independence in the spring and headed for Santa Fe. According to John Townsend, a distinguished ornithologist who passed through Independence in 1832, the settlement was ideally situated: "The site of the town is beautiful, and very well selected, standing on a high point of land, and overlooking the surrounding country."[5] A number of springs provided the community with an ample supply of water. Blacksmith shops, wagon shops, saddle shops, dry goods stores, inns, and taverns lined the streets on all sides of the Courthouse Square. There were stables and dealers who sold horses, mules, and oxen. Indeed, one could find just about anything needed by the Santa Fe freighters and suppliers of the Rocky Mountain fur trade. The current Courthouse Building, constructed in 1933, stands in what was once the Courthouse Square.

The scene greeting Bidwell and his companions when they entered town is easy to imagine. A large caravan of wagons was getting ready to depart for Santa Fe in a few days.⁶ The streets must have been abuzz with men, horses, mules, oxen, and wagons. Merchants were probably hustling sales of livestock and provisions. The sounds of cracking whips, creaking wagon wheels, and cursing bullwhackers would have animated the air, while the sharp hammering of iron upon iron resounded in the blacksmith shops.

Travelers heading west could take one of a couple of trails out of Independence. One branch, commonly referred to as the old Santa Fe Trail, left the square and headed almost due south for about six miles before turning southwest. Another branch, called the Independence-Westport Road, left the square along today's Lexington Street. Since the objective of the Bidwell and Bartleson parties was to rendezvous at Sapling Grove, it seems logical that they would have taken the Independence-Westport Road. First established in 1837, this road headed in a winding but generally westerly direction toward Westport, about ten miles away. The road to Westport crossed the Blue River about one-half mile north of where today's Interstate 70 crosses the river, and entered the tiny settlement of Westport at today's intersection of Westport Road and Broadway Street in downtown Kansas City, Missouri.

Westport was first established in 1834, and by 1841 it was beginning to siphon off a good deal of Independence's business as the preferred jumping-off point for the West. Freighters taking the trail to Santa Fe or pack trains supplying the fur brigades in the Rocky Mountains could depart from Westport by taking a road heading south until it joined the Santa Fe Trail. Or they could take a road that headed southwesterly toward Sapling Grove. Two miles after leaving Westport, the latter road crossed the Missouri state border into Indian Territory. The road then passed the Shawnee Indian Mission a mile west of the state border.

Methodist missionary Thomas Johnson had established the Indian Mission in 1830 to educate children of the nearby Shawnee and Delaware Indian tribes. Johnson built the westerly structure in 1839 and commenced construction of two more buildings in 1841. All three buildings can still be seen at the southeast corner of Mission Road and West 53rd Street, Fairway, Kansas.⁷ A contagion had swept through the mission the previous summer, resulting in a number of deaths, mostly Indian children. One hundred Shawnee and Kansa Indian students were reported to be residing at the Mission in 1842.⁸

Beyond the Shawnee Mission, the road continued southwesterly another six miles before reaching the Sapling Grove campground. Since Robert Thomes claimed that they left Independence on May 6, it is probable that the Bidwell and Bartleson groups passed through Westport sometime later that day, likely arriving at the Sapling Grove campground late that afternoon.

Father De Smet's letter to his father provincial reported that he and most of his party disembarked from a steamboat at Westport Landing on May 7, following a seven-day, four-hundred-mile journey up the Missouri River from St. Louis.[9] After losing two horses and one of his wagons to fire while aboard the steamboat (perhaps from sparks from the smokestacks), they temporarily "took refuge in an abandoned little cabin" near Westport.[10] During the next three days, Father De Smet got his party assembled and organized. He then reported that they departed Westport on May 10.[11] Father Point recalled their departure:

> On May 10, we left Westport, taking with us all the supplies for our dear mission in five two-wheeled carts driven by two Canadians who were excellent wagoners, and three of our brothers, still novices at that difficult art. The three priests rode horseback.[12]

After passing the Shawnee Mission, De Smet's party emerged from a forested area and entered an open prairie, a treeless domain that was now clad in a spring carpet of soft, green grass.[13] Father Point seemed moved:

> On quitting Westport, which is separated from the river by a stretch of woods about two or three miles wide, we before us saw what the inhabitants of the region call the Great Prairie. What a beautiful perspective for a missionary! But especially for me, who for twenty years have seen nothing but the walls of a college. At the sight of the azure distances, so pleasing to the eye, I thought I could perceive what is most attractive about the beautiful ideal of the apostolic life. The verdure of the earth and the thousands upon thousands of small spring flowers helped support the illusion.[14]

In the years to come, others would be similarly struck when first encountering the prairie. Edwin Bryant, for example, penned his description of the open prairie after he had emerged from the wooded areas just south of Independence in May 1846:

> *The vast prairie itself soon opened before us in all its grandeur and beauty. I had never before beheld extensive scenery of this kind. The many descriptions of the prairies of the west had forestalled in some measure the first impressions produced by the magnificent landscape that lay spread out before me as far as the eye could reach. . . . the illimitable succession of green undulations and flowery slopes, of every gentle and graceful configuration, stretching away and away, until they fade from sight in the dim distance.*[15]

Since the Sapling Grove campground was only nine miles from Westport, the missionaries probably reached it by the evening of May 10. Its grass, wood, and water were why the campground was a favorite place for caravans to assemble and organize before beginning their long journeys to Santa Fe or the Rockies. George Sibley, a government surveyor, noted in his 1827 field notes that one would find at Sapling Grove "an excellent fountain Spring, a very good place to camp."[16] Dr. F. A. Wislizenus, an adventurer and sightseer traveling with an American Fur Company supply train in 1839, wrote, "Our first camp, Sapling Grove, was in a little hickory wood with fresh spring water."[17]

Sapling Grove was just west of the intersection of today's Grant Street and West 82nd Street, in Overland Park, Kansas, and is about a half-mile east of Interstate 35. The party likely assembled on the knoll where the present-day Comanche Elementary School now sits. There is a set of historical markers in a small park adjacent to the creek and school. The spot overlooks the creek below, which was then bordered by a grove of young hickory trees

The dates for the organizers to rendezvous at Sapling Grove were not selected capriciously. For years, caravans heading to Santa Fe or the Rockies had waited until the new spring grasses poked through the dead vegetation of the previous year. In most years, there would have been plenty of new grass by May 10, likely explaining why the date was selected for people to assemble. Caravans consisting solely of horses and mules could sometimes leave earlier because horses and mules have protruding front teeth, allowing them to nibble on very short grass. Oxen are not similarly endowed, meaning that a wagon party with oxen would usually have to wait longer to let the grass grow.

Bidwell's memoirs described what happened at Sapling Grove when they first arrived on May 6 or 7: "When we reached Sapling

Modern-day view of site of Sapling Grove campground. Author's photograph.

Grove, the place of the rendezvous, in May, 1841, there was but one wagon ahead of us. For the next few days one or two wagons would come each day, and among the recruits were three families from Arkansas [the Kelsey and Williams families]."[18]

The members of the party were probably lingering at Sapling Grove because they knew of others who were coming but had not yet arrived. The expedition would be traveling through the land of the Plains Indians, horse-mounted warriors who were skilled buffalo hunters and reputed scalp lifters. Rumors of Indian hostilities, true or not, usually made the rounds each year. It was common wisdom, learned from years of experience on the trails to Santa Fe and the Rocky Mountains, that a party needed to "travel strong." That is to say, it was advisable to travel through Indian Territory with sufficient numbers of well-armed men so that Indian raiding parties would not be emboldened to try their luck. Young braves were courageous, but not stupid. They were much less likely to molest a party if they perceived that the travelers were heavily armed and had the upper hand. Nicholas Dawson's memoirs expressed this concern: "Some doubt existed as to whether a sufficient number would congregate to make it safe to go."[19]

Bidwell had previously described the provisions he purchased for himself in Weston. Josiah Belden was the only other member of the party who commented on the subject, recalling: "We took as much provision as we could haul and carry, to last us until we should get into the buffalo country, when we expected to supply ourselves by hunting."[20] Other than Bidwell and Belden, there are no other accounts by members of the party as to how they had provisioned themselves.

The people assembling must have been apprehensive and uncertain, not only as to what lay ahead, but as to the people with whom they would be traveling. It is easy to imagine them beginning the early stages of acquaintance. It must have been awkward, since they were being thrown together with others they did not know. They probably eyed each other with probing eyes, trying to take their measure. Sticking out their hands and introducing themselves, they probably engaged in uneasy conversation, while they wondered if they could trust their safety, even their lives, with these people they knew nothing about.

Since so many had changed their minds and decided to stay at home, one wonders why these few people were showing up. Undoubtedly, each was looking for something—not necessarily the same thing—but certainly something. It is significant that most of those going were young, single men. Belden, Bidwell, and Dawson fell into this category and they freely admitted in their memoirs that they were drawn to an opportunity for adventure. It is likely that many of the other single men were looking for adventure as well. Some may have had fathers and grandfathers who had participated in the American Revolution, the War of 1812, or any number of Indian conflicts. This venture would provide these young men with an opportunity to test their mettle and earn their own laurels. For the most part, they did not look upon themselves as emigrants. Rather, they just wanted to see California.

Only three families were going: brothers Samuel Kelsey and Ben Kelsey were each taking a wife and children. Then there was Richard Williams, who was accompanied by his wife and daughter. Though few in number, these families were the true emigrants. They were planning on establishing permanent homes in that distant land. It is not surprising that the expedition involved so few families. Most men had the good sense not to uproot their wives and children from a snug and cozy home and take them on a journey that promised so much uncertainty and danger.

Benjamin Kelsey, circa 1870. Neg. # 8105a. Courtesy of California State Library.

Nancy Kelsey, circa 1870. Call No. 2012-0353. Courtesy of California State Library.

It appears that a few married men were going to California without their families to see if it was a suitable place to bring them later. Nicholas Dawson's memoirs mentioned them:

> It was a very mixed crowd. There were heads of families going out first to find a spot to bring their families to, and heads of families taking the families along to share whatever fortune might bring. There were many adventurous youths like myself, and John Bidwell, . . . who wanted nothing but to see and experience. There were gentlemen seeking health, and an English lord, Lord Romain, going out with a half-breed hunter, John Grey [this occurrence indexed under Gray, John], to shoot buffalo.[21]

When Father Point described the group's composition, he made the intriguing comment that a few were going to unburden their families:

> [T]he travelers were a composite of all ages, languages and denominations. Some were traveling in pursuit of material interests, others for pleasure, and still others, of the age of the prodigal son, only to relieve their families of their unfortunate presence.[22]

Some of those congregating at Sapling Grove may have been looking for fame, drawn to a chance for some sparkling glory. They were probably aware that they would be making history by participating in an important milestone in the conquering of the West. A wagon expedition to California had never been attempted before. No one even knew if wagons would hold up over such a long distance. To think that they might get a convoy of wagons all the way to the Pacific Coast. Now that would be something. It would surely make the country sit up and take notice.

These people lived in an age of discovery, in a country that admired exploration and that celebrated its explorers. Lt. John C. Frémont, for example, would lead an expedition to the Rocky Mountains in 1842. Afterwards, he and his wife published his "discoveries," which became a best-seller and made him a national celebrity. For his ventures he was labeled the "Great Pathfinder," although the sobriquet was misleading because he was guided in most of his travels by frontiersmen who knew the country and who usually led him along already established trails.

Bidwell recalled in one of his memoirs that "all were enthusiastic and anxious to go."[23] But was he remembering excited faces that had been put on as a way of concealing their nervousness and anxiety? After all, it was going to be a journey of over two thousand miles, the last half of which would involve groping blindly across uncharted and unmapped country, devoid of established trails, and without the benefit of a knowledgeable guide. They were setting out in almost complete ignorance of what lay between them and the Pacific Coast. It would be a monstrously risky venture and a reckless throw of the dice.

One of the reasons these people appeared willing to throw caution to the wind and to march off across such a vast wilderness with few resources was that they were beguiled by a false reality. What they imagined was largely cobbled together from embellished tales and wishful dreams. Their perception of the lands through which they would have to travel—the distances, threats, risks, and privations—was incomplete, inaccurate, and distorted. They did not fully fathom how far it was, nor how harsh and tragic the calamities might be. It is chilling how unimaginably naïve and unprepared they were. Like being unaware of the need for passports. Indeed, one wonders whether they would have joined such a venture if they had accurately perceived the magnitude of the unknown and their chances for disaster.

While most must have sensed in some undefinable way that the trip involved danger, they lived in a time when people faced danger every day as a matter of course, whether one ventured into the wilds or stayed at home. Life could be fleeting. Illness could suddenly strike down young and old alike. One could catch a cold and die of pneumonia in even the most civilized and comfortable settings. Perhaps this was why letters of that day often began with inquiries about the recipient's health, followed by assurances that the writer's own health was good. Most understood that this journey would not be easy, but hardship and discomfort were common conditions in those times and it rarely acted as a deterrent.

In the end, for whatever their reasons, these people were here at Sapling Grove. They had closed their accounts and were prepared to leave polished civilization behind. They were setting out on an adventure of a lifetime, and it would become one of the great stories in the settlement of the Far West.

The most serious problem confronting those at Sapling Grove was the lack of something or someone to guide them all the way. As of 1841, the trail from Independence and Westport to the Rockies was well known to the men who had led supply pack trains to the annual summer fur trappers' rendezvous. A wagon route from the Bear River in present-day Idaho to California was a different story, however. It had not yet been blazed. A few American trappers had made it all the way to the Pacific in earlier years, but they had not taken wagons. There were no published maps—at least accurate ones—that depicted the enormous expanse or the roughness of the geography. Even if you could have found someone who had made it all the way, it is unlikely he could have recalled and diagramed each important detail of the route—every critical turn, bend, canyon, creek, and pass. Besides, much of his route would have been impassable for wagons. In truth, no one knew for sure if any route existed that would allow wagons to make it all the way.

The people arriving at Sapling Grove did not know how to get to California, but they probably thought that someone here would. As they arrived and began to get acquainted, they might have asked about who would be leading them. John Bartleson was probably assuring people that he had Dr. Marsh's letter of directions. One of these letters had been sent to his friend Michael Nye, whom Marsh had urged to travel "over the Rockies and Sierras to California, and to come to [my] rancho."[24] But Marsh had not traveled to California by this route. He was simply relying on what he had heard regarding the trips made by trappers Jedediah Smith (1827), Peter Ogden (1827), and Joseph Walker (1833).[25] The Marsh instructions, if you could call them that, were laughably inadequate and uninformative. It was something that most of the people assembling at Sapling Grove did not know at the time.

Bidwell had been given a flawed map by his friend Elam Brown, but he admitted in his memoirs years later, "Our ignorance of the route was complete. We knew that California lay west, and that was the extent of our knowledge."[26] He further elaborated:

> *No one of the party knew anything about mountaineering and scarcely anyone had ever been into the Indian Territory, yet a large majority felt that we were fully competent to go anywhere no matter what the difficulties might be or how numerous and warlike the Indians. We heard before starting, however, that a party of Catholic missionaries from St. Louis going to the Flathead Indians under the auspices of Father De Smet were soon expected and that they had for their guide the experienced Captain Fitzpatrick. . . . The more prudent advised waiting for the missionary party and finally with much persuasion they prevailed on the others to wait.*[27]

Bidwell made the point again in another of his memoirs:

> *[N]o one knew where to go, not even the captain [Bartleson]. Finally a man came up, one of the last to arrive, and announced that a company of Catholic missionaries were on their way from St. Louis to the Flathead nation of Indians with an old Rocky Mountaineer for a guide, and that if we would wait another day they would be up with us. At first we were independent, and thought we could not afford to wait for a slow missionary party. But when we found that no one knew which way to go, we sobered down and waited for them to come up; and it was well that we did, for otherwise probably not one of us would ever had reached California, because of our inexperience.*[28]

It is clear from Bidwell's memoirs that the Bartleson and Bidwell groups were already at Sapling Grove when they first learned of the missionary party and its guide, Thomas Fitzpatrick. They must not have encountered the missionary party when they passed through Westport. One cannot but wonder why a "large majority," as Bidwell claimed, thought they did not need a knowledgeable guide. Fortunately, good sense prevailed after the "more prudent" persuaded the others to wait at Sapling Grove for De Smet's party. Even though the people may have been comforted by the notion that they would now be guided by Fitzpatrick, it is unclear whether they understood at the time that he would only be leading them halfway. How many understood that when the missionary party separated from them near Fort Hall they might be on their own?

Chapter 3

From Sapling Grove to the Kansas River Crossing

MAY 12 TO 17, 1841

May 12

After De Smet's party had joined the California-bound people at Sapling Grove on May 10, the entire group remained in camp a few more days as they waited for more "stragglers." But by May 12, the expedition had waited at Sapling Grove long enough. It was time to go. Anyone still coming would simply have to catch up. Bidwell in his memoirs recalled, "five days after my arrival we were ready to start."[1] Nicholas Dawson was the only member of the expedition who expressly recorded the date on which the California-bound group and the missionary party departed from Sapling Grove. His memoirs reported, "The whole crowd rendezvoused, until all was ready, at Sapling Grove, a few miles from West Port. . . . On May 12, 1841, we set out, Fitzpatrick in the lead."[2] His daily log solidified the date by also reporting that the party left Sapling Grove on May 12.[3]

When the combined missionary and Bartleson parties, having pledged to travel together, pulled out on the morning of May 12, they commenced an epic era in American history. The two parties were now linked, their consolidation benefiting each other. The Bartleson-Bidwell group would profit from Fitzpatrick's knowledge and experience; the missionary party, from traveling with additional armed men.

When the carts and wagons pulled into line and lurched uncertainly forward, the caravan probably stretched over a half-mile, perhaps more, from front to back. The road leaving Sapling Grove had been heavily traveled and was well defined. Dr. Wislizenus wrote in 1839 that when his party left Sapling Grove, it "marched over the broad Santa Fe road, beaten out by caravans."[4]

Bidwell was likely the one driving his ox-pulled wagon. He may have been too mentally engaged at first to contemplate the significance of the historic moment. But once the cavalcade settled into a steady pace, with each vehicle following the one ahead, he may have been able to relax and reflect on the day, considering how it represented the culmination of everything he had worked for. He must have been experiencing a great deal of excitement. For good or bad, the expedition had finally come together and was on its way. How could he not have been moved by feelings of pride, relief, and satisfaction?

Despite the landmark significance of the expedition, the public would only be provided with an indifferent report of the event. On May 19, 1841, a week after the company had pulled out of Sapling Grove, the *Daily Missouri Republican* published a letter from its correspondent in Independence. Almost hidden among the other news was the following unremarkable item:

> To-day the Oregon and Calafornia [sic] Companies rendezvous at Sapling Grove to make arrangements for their departure, and judging from appearances, we think there will be a considerable number who intend going out—some five, six or ten families among them. Mr. Fitzpatrick is expected to be elected Captain, and to take the superintendence of both parties for some distance.[5]

Bidwell did not commence making entries in his journal until May 18. As a result, he did not describe their journey between Sapling Grove and the Kansas River crossing—a distance of about seventy-five miles. We have Nicholas Dawson's log, however. He recorded that the party traveled ten miles after leaving Sapling Grove on May 12 and that they stopped to camp that afternoon at what he called "McLeans branch." This campsite was probably what was later called Indian Creek Campground. The location is where a tiny branch of Indian Creek passes beneath today's West 103rd Street, east of its intersection with Noland Road, Lenexa, Kansas, and is about one half-mile east of the present-day interchange of Interstate 35 and Highway 435.

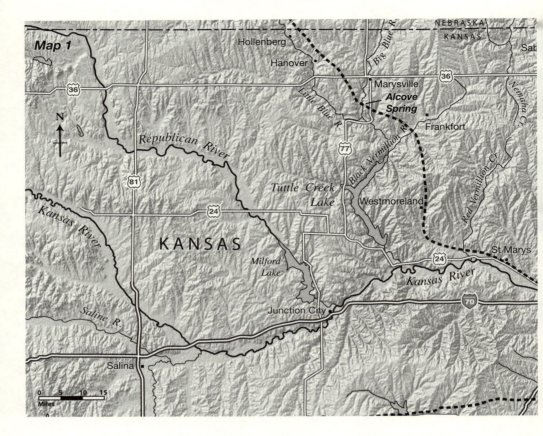

May 13

Dawson recorded that the group traveled eight miles on May 13, and that they camped that night at Elm Grove, another frequently used campground. The site is in the woods just south of the present-day Cedar Creek bridge on Old 56 Highway, three miles west of its intersection with Interstate 35, and near Olathe, Kansas. About twenty-one miles from Westport, Elm Grove consisted of a small grove of elm trees, which, like Sapling Grove, was another desirable place to camp because of its wood and water.

The route of the trail through here, and for much of the next few weeks, was determined by a fundamental rationale, an inherent logic. It tended to follow the ridgelines and divides. The higher ground would not be low and swampy and readily drained after

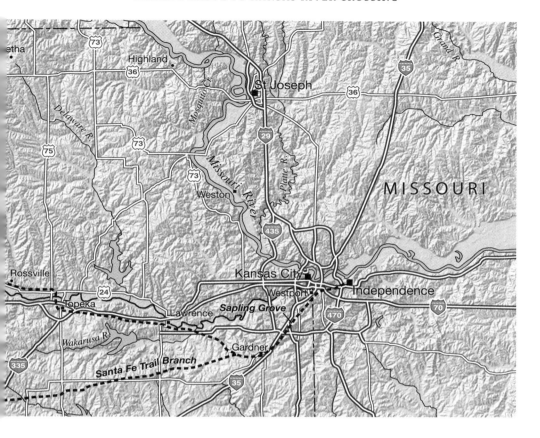

storms. More importantly, such a route minimized the crossing of swales, hollows, ravines, and creeks. The problem with the creeks and ravines was their steep banks. Heavily laden wagons were difficult to ease down and pull up the sharp inclines on the other side. It was best to avoid them whenever possible.

May 14

According to Dawson's log, the party did not travel on May 14, but stayed at the Elm Grove campground for an extra day. It suggests that they were purposely dragging their feet to give late-comers a chance to catch up.

May 15

The long train of wagons and carts returned to the road on May 15. From Elm Grove, the road continued southwesterly another seven miles, then struck the Santa Fe Trail coming in from Independence. After traveling west on the Santa Fe Trail for about two miles the party would have come to a fork in the road. Caravans going to Santa Fe took the left-hand fork. It had been heavily traveled by hundreds of heavy freight wagons and thousands of animals every year since it was established in the early 1820s. Parties heading to the fur country of the Rockies or on to Oregon, however, took the more recently established and much less heavily traveled right-hand fork.

In the winter of 1826–27, William Sublette and "Black" Harris, members of a William Ashley trapping brigade, left the Rocky Mountains and headed east on a frigid, fifteen-hundred-mile journey to St. Louis. Thinking that they could find a shortcut, they left the Platte River near Grand Island and headed in a generally southeastward direction across uncharted country. The distances were immense and the terrain had a maddening sameness. They kept to the higher ridges, periodically adjusting their route whenever they sensed that they needed to head more eastward or southward. Upon reaching St. Louis in March, Sublette immediately headed back to the mountains, this time leading a pack train of supplies across his new route. Given the thick carpet of grass, it is incomprehensible how he could have detected his earlier tracks. Later that summer, Sublette sent a large shipment of furs back to St. Louis, and he assigned James Clyman the task of guiding it. He somehow explained to Clyman the route to follow. It is even more incomprehensible how Clyman was able to find his way, but he did. This new route would become known as "Sublette's Trace."

Unlike the Santa Fe Trail, Sublette's Trace was principally used between 1827 and 1840 by infrequent pack trains carrying supplies to the annual fur trade gatherings during the summers, and for bringing back the year's harvest of pelts and buffalo skins. Wagons rarely used it.[6] Such light traffic caused the trail to remain vague and indistinct in many places. Dr. Wislizenus complained in 1839 that the path was so difficult to detect that "our leader at times lost it."[7] It was only two years later, in 1841, and the trail was still faint. Only one emigrant family had traveled it so far on their way to Oregon. They accompanied a fur trade supply train in 1840. A few years after 1841, after a number of large emigrant parties had used the route to travel to Oregon, a crude sign was planted at the fork that read, "Road to Oregon." Someone quipped that never has such a humble sign announced such a long journey.[8] This was when people began referring to Sublette's Trace as the Oregon Trail. During the trail's glorious career between 1840 and 1860, it is estimated that over three hundred thousand people would use it to reach Oregon, California, and Utah.[9]

There is a National Historic Trails site at the junction of today's West 183rd Street and Highway 56, Gardner, Kansas. It marks the splitting of the Santa Fe and Oregon trails. While this may have been where the trails parted in later years, the right-hand fork to the Rockies left the Santa Fe road farther west as of 1841. Jesse Applegate recorded in 1843 that his party left the Santa Fe Trail just beyond Bull Creek, which is west of where the creek crosses today's West 183rd Street and east of its intersection with Dillie Road. This is a mile and a half farther west than where the Oregon Trail forked in later years.

Upon leaving the Santa Fe Trail, the Oregon road headed north about seven miles to about where the former Sunflower Munitions Works was located, then headed northwest. Dawson recorded that after leaving Elm Grove on the morning of May 15, his group traveled twenty miles before stopping to camp. Unfortunately, his entry identifying their campsite that night is illegible. But his mileage estimate would suggest that the party camped on a small stream called Coleman Creek today. The estimated camp location would be on the west side of where the creek crosses today's N 1100 Road, about one half-mile west of E 2400 Road (County Line Road) and two miles southeast of the community of Eudora, Kansas.

May 16

Dawson's log specified that the party traveled twenty-five miles on May 16. Five miles beyond their Coleman Creek camp, they would have crossed the Wakarusa River. The crossing was about one mile southeast of the junction of today's Highway 10 and E 1900 Road, and a few miles southeast of Lawrence, Kansas. The Wakarusa was not big, but it had steep banks and was a challenge to cross. In 1846, Edwin Bryant described their crossing of the Wakarusa: "The banks of the eastern side are so steep, that the wagons were let down by ropes, and the teams were doubled, sometimes quadrupled, in order to draw them up on the other side."[10]

In 1846, J. Quinn Thornton described the country on the west side of Wakarusa Creek: "We all crossed the Wokaruska Creek, and encamped for the night in a most beautiful piece of woods, which skirted both sides of the stream." Beyond the creek, he wrote, there stretched "as far as the eye could reach, a plain, broken into gentle swells, and covered with a heavy coat of grass. A green carpet spotted with flowers, covered the hills."[11]

Leaving the Wakarusa behind, the road traveled northwesterly, continuing to travel upon the highlands just south of the Kansas River. At the end of the day on May 16, Dawson reported camping on a "Prairie branch," his mileage estimate suggesting that their day's travel ended near today's Big Springs, Kansas. Between the Wakarusa crossing and Big Springs, the trail roughly followed the route of present-day Highways 10 and 40.

May 17

From Big Springs, the trail traveled twelve miles to what was eventually called the "lower crossing" of the Kansas River. In 1846, J. Quinn Thornton described the terrain between these two points:

> *The country over which we passed during the day was a beautiful, rolling, fertile, limestone prairie, covered with a rich and luxuriant coat of grass; in some places rising almost into hills. A few small oaks and tall quivering asps [aspen] were seen near at hand in ravines. In the distance larger groves were seen skirting the horizon.*[12]

One mile before reaching the Kansas River, the trail crossed the steep-banked Shunganunga Creek, which is now channeled through the city of Topeka. Shortly after crossing the creek, the expedition would have passed through what Thornton described as "a beautiful woodland of oak, ash, walnut, sycamore, quivering asp, hazle [sic], grape vines, and a variety of under-growth, which skirts both sides of the Kansas river, about half a mile on either side."[13] Emigrants often complained about its steep southern bank compelling people to let their wagons down to the riverside with ropes. On the other side, the northern shore was more accommodating. It was broader and flatter, making it easier to move away from the river.

An 1843 emigrant described the Kansas River here as "about two hundred yards wide, with a rapid, turbid and deep current."[14] There were times, however, when the river could be much more daunting. For example, the spring of 1844 was suffering through an exceptionally wet period when James Clyman described the river as spreading "8 or 10 miles wide." He may have been exaggerating, but embellishment or not, it was a monstrous river that year which dramatically delayed the crossing of his wagon company.[15]

Nicholas Dawson's log showed that the expedition arrived at the Kansas River crossing on May 17. The river's lower crossing is believed to have been where today's NW Topeka Boulevard Bridge crosses the river in the city of Topeka.

When the party crossed the river, they were in territory belonging to the Kansa tribe. Its lands stretched along the northern bank of the Kansas River, commencing about sixty miles west of the river's mouth with the Missouri River. Fool Chief, head of the nearest Kansa village, had been aware of the coming of the missionaries and had sent two of his warriors to the river crossing to greet the priests. After helping the party cross, one of the braves raced off to inform Fool Chief of their arrival. The chief arrived soon thereafter. After a conference, followed by a smoking of the pipe, the chief took his leave. According to De Smet, Fool Chief left the two warriors as guards for the "three days and three nights that we had to wait the coming up of the stragglers of the caravan."[16]

Prior to 1841, wagons, baggage and people had to be floated across the Kansas River, while the livestock were made to swim. A number of authorities claim that the Papin (or Pappan) brothers, Joseph and Louis, first established a ferry there in 1843 or 1844 and used two pirogues (dugout canoes), lashed together with poles, to transport wagons, cargo, and people.[17] The Kansas Historical Society claims, however, that the two brothers began their ferry in 1841. There are two accounts that could be evidence that the Pappan ferry was not yet operating when the party arrived at the river. Nancy Kelsey, one of the women traveling with the party, recalled that "[t]he Indians towed us across the river in rawhide boats made of buffalo skins. Our oxen crossed the river with the empty wagons."[18] Father Point reported that when they arrived at the river crossing, "[t]here we found two men who had transported part of our baggage by water, and two relatives of the great chief of the Kansa [Indian tribe] who had come to meet us. While one of them aided the pack animals in crossing the river by swimming ahead of them, the other announced our arrival to the first of the tribe awaiting us on the other side."[19] As can be seen, neither Kelsey nor Point mentions a ferry. In contrast, Josiah Belden recalled, "We traveled to the Kansas River, and were ferried across."[20] Even more specifically, Father De Smet wrote, "Our baggage, wagons and men crossed in a piroque, or hollowed tree trunk."[21] These last two descriptions, especially De Smet's, suggest that the Historical Society may have been correct in claiming that the Papins were ferrying across wagons, baggage, and people with their piroque as early as 1841.

After crossing the river, John Bidwell said that the party proceeded another two miles before encamping for the night. De Smet wrote that they camped that night on Soldier Creek. Although sections of the creek have been rerouted in modern times, the above allows us to fix the approximate location of their camp as south of today's Highway 24, about two miles west of its intersection with NW Topeka Boulevard. When J. Quinn Thornton's party camped beside Soldier Creek in 1846, he described the abundant deer and strawberries nearby, and complained about the sounds of croaking frogs, chirping crickets, and howling wolves disturbing the tranquility of the night.[22]

It is not clear, but some sources indicate that Robert Rickman and Henry Payton, starting late, did not catch up to the company and join it until just after it had crossed the river.[23]

DESPITE THE PARTY'S waiting at Sapling Grove for five days, and at Elm Grove for a day, there were still some who could not seem to make the original May 10 rendezvous date. On May 16, when the main body was about sixty miles to the west and drawing near the Kansas River, Joseph B. Chiles, Charles M. Weber, and James John left Westport and hurried to catch up. Why this party of three was late is unknown. One of them, James John, was our other diarist, and he recorded that they encamped four miles east of Sapling Grove on the night of May 16.[24]

Joseph Chiles was a six-foot-four-inch thirty-one-year old. He and his wife had moved from Kentucky to Jackson County in 1830 and took up farming. But Chiles's wife had died in 1837 and he was left with four young children. He would have been one of the men men-

(clockwise from top left)

Joseph B. Chiles, circa 1880. Neg. # 22,223. Courtesy of California State Library.

James John, "Jimmy John," circa 1875. Courtesy of Old Oregon Historic Photos.

Charles Weber, circa 1855. Neg. # 22,261. Courtesy of California State Library.

tioned by Nicholas Dawson who was leaving his family behind while he assessed what California had to offer. Yet, Chiles claimed in his memoirs that he joined the expedition because he was restless and under the spell of a "love of adventure." His biographer proclaimed that Chiles yearned to see "strange lands, strange people."[25] Leaving his four young children with relatives, Chiles began the journey with a wagon pulled by a team of Missouri mules, and took a yoke of oxen, just in case.²⁶ Weber and John were young, single men. Weber, twenty-seven, was a recent German immigrant, and James John was a thirty-one-year-old wanderer, admittedly beset by restlessness.²⁷ Since James John was a tricky name to remember, Bidwell dealt with it by always referring to him as Jimmy John. From this point forward, this book will also call him Jimmy John.

Chapter 4

Organizing and Departing

MAY 18 TO 20, 1841

May 18

In the early morning hours of May 18, a gray mist hung over the bottom of the Kansas River. The travelers were beginning to stir in their Soldier Creek camp. It would prove to be an important day. This recently thrown together collection of people had to figure out where everyone fit. There was no pre-existing hierarchy as to who would give orders and who would follow them. For all practical purposes there was no law beyond the settlements, so they needed to adopt a set of rules. It was time to hold an organizational meeting.

Their meeting would be one of the first episodes of organizing an emigrant wagon train, and it would become a classic template, an exercise of democratic principles that would be held by most wagon parties in the years to come. John Bidwell described their meeting in this, his first journal entry:

> *May. T. [Tuesday] 18th 1841. Having waited at this place (2 miles W. of Kanzas river) 2 days, and all the Company being arrived, except these heretofore mentioned [the Chiles group], the Company was convened for the purpose of electing a Captain and adopting rules for the Government of the Company; when T. H. Green was chosen President—and J. Bidwell, Secretary. After the Rules were read and adopted, J Bartleson was elected Captain; it will be understood that Fitzpatrick was Capt. of the Missionary Company and Pilot of the whole—Orders were given for the company to start in the morning, and the meeting broke up.*

Bidwell did not express any adverse opinion about John Bartleson in his first journal entry. He did not yet know what he would later learn about the man. He would grow to revile the man and his leadership as the journey unfolded. In one of his later memoirs, Bidwell offered his candid opinion of the man, and it was not flattering. "[Bartleson] was not the best man for the position," he wrote, "but we were given to understand that if he was not elected captain he would not go; and as he had seven or eight men with him, and as we did not want the party diminished, he was chosen."[1] Bidwell's recollection of being pressured into electing Bartleson as their captain is perplexing. Of the "seven or eight men with him," a few, such as Nicholas Dawson, had just joined Bartleson's group. They hardly knew the man. Since these seemed determined to go to California, it suggests that their allegiance to Bartleson would have been weak. Even if Bartleson had acted upon his threat to pull out, it seems they would have remained with the expedition anyway. Besides, it was a large group and it seems odd that the threat of losing a few men would have been enough to sway the election.

Father Point's appraisal of Bartleson was markedly different from Bidwell's. "Only on May 18 the American element assembled," Point recalled. "The most remarkable traveler among them was Colonel Bartleson, whom the Americans made their leader in the search for fortune to the much-vaunted territory of California. This man, already advanced in years, calm in temperament but enterprising in character, was kind to us during the whole trip."[2] Despite acknowledging their differences in religious beliefs, the priest added that "[n]evertheless, through the maintenance of mutual respect, the most perfect concord reigned between him [Bartleson] and us right up to the end."[3]

May 19

Now that the formalities of electing a leader and adopting a few rules were behind them, the expedition set sail the next morning. Bidwell recorded their departure from their Soldier Creek camp:

> *W. 19th. This morning, the wagons started off in single file; first the 4 carts and 1 small wagon of the Missionaries, next 8 wagons drawn by Mules and horses and lastly, 5 wagons drawn by 17 yoke of oxen. It was the calculation of the company to move on slowly till the wagon of Chiles*

overtook us. Our course was West, leaving the Kanzas no great distance to our left, we traveled in the valley of the river which was prairie excepting near the margin of the stream. The day was very warm and we stopped about noon, having traveled about 12 miles. This afternoon we had a heavy shower of rain and hail. Several Kanza Indians came to our camp; they were well armed with bows and arrows, and some had guns, they were daily expecting an attack by the Pawnees, whom they but a short time ago had made inroads upon, and had massacred at one of their villages a large number of old men, women and children, while the warriors were hunting buffalo.

As the freshly organized party began its march, it is estimated to have contained seventy individuals. There were seventeen in the missionary party, including the three trappers and three sightseers. There were fifty-six in the California-bound party, including three wives and six young children. Five others, starting late, would catch up and join the expedition in the next few days.

The people would now belong to each other for a long time. Father Point recorded his belief that everyone in the party understood the need to adhere to good discipline: "[A]ll agreed on one point, namely, that they must try not to perish on the journey. This kind of agreement facilitated the establishment of good discipline."[4] But discipline might not be easy for those who were independent by nature and used to acting on their own impulses. Accustomed to going about their daily business at their own speed, they would now be traveling with others and would have to adjust their pace. For some, it would be to speed up, for others to slow down. The expedition would hopefully benefit from the knowledgeable and steadying hand of Fitzpatrick and the sanctifying influence of the priests. Perhaps there was the belief that a few weeks of traveling together would foster a spirit of amity and unselfishness, something similar to what J. Quinn Thornton observed when his party set out for Oregon in 1846:

> *We were nearly all strangers, and there was manifestly an effort on the part of each, to make the most favorable impression he could upon every other. All were obliging and kind; and there was even an extraordinary absence of selfishness. Suffering, want, and privations; mental anxiety, hardship, and exhausting labor, had not yet blunted the moral perceptions of any, excited cupidity and selfishness, or dried up the fountains of the heart's best and purest affections.*[5]

Father De Smet expressed satisfaction in one of his letters with his decision to travel with this California-bound group, although he believed its members were making a mistake in seeking "their fortune in the too highly boasted land of California."[6]

The company's fourteen wagons and four carts strung out in single file along the trail. For the most part, the wagons were probably farm wagons weighing about a thousand pounds empty, and were covered with white canvas stretched over a series of wooden bows. It must have been an impressive sight. Many of their wagons and carts would have been new and clean, with their livestock strong and fat. In a later memoir, Bidwell recounted how Fitzpatrick would take the lead, followed by his missionary party and their carts. The California party followed. If danger was anticipated, Bidwell explained, they would travel in a more compact body, but during relaxed times the caravan could stretch out for a half-mile or more.[7]

Bidwell's memoirs boasted that he was a principal promoter and organizer of this bold new venture, and his writings described the prominent role he claimed to have played in getting matters to this point. He also reported that he was elected secretary of the company. If his claims were all true, he would have been justified in experiencing pride and satisfaction that the child he helped conceive had finally been delivered. His mind and senses must have tingled with excitement. But if he had experienced these emotions, he failed to express them in his journal.

Long convoys of wagons had been traveling to and from Santa Fe since the early 1820s, so the relative advantages and disadvantages of using teams of oxen versus horses and mules should have been well known. Horses and mules tended to be quicker, traveling at about four miles per hour. On the other hand, oxen were excruciatingly slow, plodding along at about two and a half miles per hour. Oxen were big steers, having been allowed to grow into big, strong bulls before being castrated. While horses and mules had the advantage of speed, oxen had superior endurance and could pull heavily loaded wagons weighing two to three thousand pounds all day long. And oxen were cheaper—considerably cheaper. A "yoke," consisting of two oxen, would cost about $20 in the early 1840s. In contrast, a good pair of wagon-pulling horses or mules cost from $100 to $150.[8] Mules may have been speedy, but they were not without their problems. Harness them together and interesting things could happen. Their personalities could be as varied as those of people. Some were passive and cooperative, while others could be obstinate and obstreperous, even malicious. They could bite, kick and bray loudly. They could also be stubborn, giving rise to the time-honored phrase "stubborn as a mule." Generally, oxen were more stoic and less excitable than mules. As would become evident later in the trip, they were ruminants that were better able to digest the tough, fibrous plants growing in the arid deserts of the West.[9] Importantly, people discovered that they were less hesitant to eat their oxen if their food sources ran out. The fact that more wagons in the expedition were being drawn by mules and horses than by oxen demonstrates that the debate between the two options had not yet been settled. Each wagon owner's decision was based on his own circumstances, preferences, and biases.

According to Bidwell, the party only traveled twelve miles on May 19, following the trail west along the north side of the Kansas River bottom. They stayed just south of the bluffs and north of the band of thick timber and undergrowth that grew on both sides of the river channel. Bidwell said they traveled through "prairie," meaning grassy terrain. Their route that day would have been parallel to and in close proximity to today's Highway 24. They did not travel far that day, Bidwell acknowledging that they knew about Joseph Chiles and his late-starting party. They were trying to make it easy for them to catch up.

Approximately twelve miles west of their Soldier's Creek camp, they stopped to encamp on the afternoon of May 19 on the west side of Cross Creek where it now passes under Highway 24, and just west of the present-day community of Rossville, Kansas.

As Fitzpatrick led the party along the trail on the morning of May 19, Fathers De Smet and Point did what one would expect Indian missionaries to do. Together with their English companion, Lord Romaine, the two priests left the caravan and traveled to visit Fool Chief at his village just north of the Kansas River, about six miles west of where the expedition had camped on Soldier Creek.[10] This places the Kansa village just south of Highway 24, near its intersection with NW Huxman Road. De Smet described the village as a group of twenty "wigwams" resembling "large stacks of wheat." Each hut was large, timber-framed, and earth-covered, about forty feet in diameter and capacious enough to shelter thirty to forty persons. He estimated that the village contained between seven and eight hundred members, noting that the entire tribe consisted of approximately fifteen hundred members, divided between two villages.[11] The Kansa had once been a much larger tribe, but in 1831–32 many tribes in Indian Territory, including the Pawnees, Shawnees, Delawares, and Kansa, had suffered catastrophically from a smallpox epidemic that swept through their villages and killed large numbers. The white man's contagions were extraordinarily lethal to Indians, and another epidemic of smallpox ravaged these tribes in 1837–38, decimating their numbers even more.[12] Only after this did the government conduct vaccination programs to protect the tribes. These tragic losses could have been avoided since vaccinations against smallpox had been available for many years. In fact, the U.S. Government began vaccinating its troops as early as 1777.[13]

Father Point described the fierce-looking Kansa warriors as "quite tall and very well shaped."[14] They shaved their heads except for a tuft of hair on top, and adorned themselves with colorful face paint, necklaces, bracelets, and other ornaments and baubles.[15] The priests did not describe Fool Chief, although James Clyman, when passing through here in 1844, described a Kansa chief as "tall lean wrinkld faced Filthy looking man with a forehead indicating deceet Dissimilutoin and intriegue."[16]

De Smet believed that "religious sentiment is deeply implanted" in the souls of the Kansa, adding that Fool Chief held the Blackrobes in "profound esteem."[17] Both priests acknowledged that the Kansa had a dark side as well, knowing that they could be cruel toward their enemies. De Smet wrote that they were inclined to take "many a scalp from their enemies, or to rob them of many horses."[18] As Bidwell mentioned in his journal entry for May 19, they had learned that a Kansa war party of sixty-five warriors had descended upon a Pawnee village during the previous December, when its men were away hunting buffalo. The Kansa massacred and scalped over seventy women, children, and old men that day, and took six women and five children as prisoners.[19] The tribes of the plains had been sending raiding parties against each other for a very long time, even before the white man appeared on the scene. It was an integral part of their culture and value system. Stealing horses, counting coup, and taking scalps demonstrated courage and skill. But their culture also demanded revenge and retribution. Every affront deserved a reprisal. Scores were rarely settled, and the process tended to go on ad infinitum. Given the Pawnees' notorious reputation for attacking their neighbors, the 1840 massacre may have been payback by the Kansa for an earlier Pawnee depredation.

The Reverend William Johnson had been a Methodist missionary among the Kansa tribe since 1831. In a letter dated January 31, 1841, he complained that the braves returning from the massacre spent so much time in unending celebrations that little was being done to provide for the needs of the tribe. "Since the Indians came in," he wrote, "the war song and scalp dance constitute their daily employment. All other matters . . . are laid aside. . . . The village near the mission are so elated with their past act of bravery, that they have done little else than dance."[20] In February, just three months before the priests came through, a detachment of U.S. Army soldiers arrived at the village and demanded the Pawnee prisoners. Taking them, the soldiers returned the Pawnees to their people.[21]

Although the young Kansa warriors were jubilant about their raid, the tribe was nervous, knowing that the Pawnees were not going to let the Kansa massacre go unavenged. It was just a matter of time.[22]

Despite how the Indians' traditional beliefs and values conflicted with Christian teachings, De Smet expressed optimism, citing the Iroquois as an example of how a ruthless race had successfully been converted to a Christian way of thinking.[23] The priest's optimism was a trait for which he would become well known. Years later, Bidwell paid tribute to De Smet, praising his gift of dealing with difficulties in a positive way: "[De Smet] was a genial gentleman of fine presence, and one of the saintliest men I have ever known, and I cannot wonder that the Indians were made to believe him divinely protected. He was a man of great kindness and great affability under all circumstances; nothing seemed to disturb his temper." When a cart toppled down a hill and broke into pieces, Bidwell recalled that "De Smet would just be the same—beaming with good humor."[24]

When the two priests concluded their visit with Fool Chief, the warriors escorted them back to the trail, passing through what De Smet described as a vast, desolate field, "which the United States had cleared, enclosed, and sown for them."[25] Beginning in about 1827, the government had assigned farmers to help the tribes learn modern farming techniques. When a Methodist missionary, the Reverend Jason Lee, traveled to Oregon in 1834, his party passed a Kansa village and recorded that "they raise an abundance of good corn; potatoes and other vegetables are also plentiful." But the Kansa stubbornly clung to the ways of their forefathers. They were not farmers; they were hunters and warriors. A year later, in 1835, the Reverend Thomas Johnson, from the Shawnee Mission, visited the Kansa and lamented that the tribe had turned its back on the government's aspirations:

> I never saw any part of the human family in so wretched a condition.... They cultivate only a small portion of ground, done chiefly by the women. They do not plough.... Their only dependence for meat is on the chase, and the deer have entirely disappeared from their prairies. They have to go 250 miles, or farther, to find the buffalo and then are frequently driven back by their enemies.[26]

The Kansa remained impervious to change. Eleven years after Johnson wrote the above, Edwin Bryant's emigrant party passed through a Kansa village near here in 1846. Their condition had not improved much. Bryant was astonished at their condition, chastising them for being "the most unblushing and practiced beggars." He could not understand why they "gave no attention to agriculture," writing that they "have not the smallest appreciation of the great natural wealth of the country over which they roam." In his mind, it made no sense for them to cling to their ancestral ways when they could rid themselves of their poverty by grazing cattle on the boundless prairie and raising crops in the fertile river bottoms.[27] Bryant's attitude was typical of many white men at the time: if the Indians would simply adopt the white man's ways, they would prosper and have more than enough to eat. It was for this reason that many whites held the view that the Indians had far more land than they needed and that much of it should be made available to white settlers.

By the end of the day on May 19, the priests had overtaken the expedition's encampment on Cross Creek. Their two Kansa warrior escorts stayed the night with them, but would travel no farther because of their fear of encountering Pawnee war parties looking for revenge.[28]

When Father De Smet had traveled west with an American Fur Company pack train the previous year, he saw the importance of having a skilled trail guide. In Thomas Fitzpatrick, he had probably hired the best. The expedition could not have been more fortunate than to have the forty-two-year-old as its guide. As of 1841, Fitzpatrick was already a legend, having been involved in many important events in the opening of the West.

Like many of the young men he would pilot this year, Fitzpatrick was born restless, having emigrated from Ireland when he was only seventeen. In 1822, at the age of twenty-four, he had joined one of William Ashley's early fur trapping brigades, and in the ensuing years he prowled the remote Rocky Mountains, learning the craft of the mountain man. He would be in the company of other young trappers who would go on to achieve legendary status as well, mountain men like Jedediah Smith, Jim Bridger, William Sublette, Milton Sublette, and James Clyman. Fitzpatrick was part of the 1824 Ashley party that "rediscovered" South Pass. Besides being an explorer, a trapper, and a leader of trappers, Fitzpatrick was one of the partners who formed the Rocky Mountain Fur Company in 1834.

Fitzpatrick had attended the University of the Wilderness, graduating summa cum laude with advanced degrees in all of the uncommon arts needed to live and survive in the mountains. Because of weakness, stupidity, carelessness, or just plain bad luck, many trappers did not survive for long. Those who did were, by that fact alone, considered exceptional. Fitzpatrick was no ordinary mountain man, having made it nineteen years in the business. The late Harvard history professor Bernard DeVoto once proclaimed that Fitzpatrick was "as expert a mountain man as ever lived; he was at the head of his profession."[29]

Mountain men were a tough breed, perhaps the toughest. Fitzpatrick's bravery and toughness were widely known, especially among the Indians. In 1834, when only thirty-five, he was involved in one of the more astonishing survival stories in the folklore of the American West. While traveling alone, he stumbled upon a hostile war party of Gros Ventres. Riding hard to escape them, his horse gave out and he had to continue his flight on foot. He concealed himself among some rocks. After combing the area, the Indians finally gave up their search and left. Fitzpatrick struggled forward on foot and survived a harrowing two-week ordeal while subsisting on roots, buds, and berries before finally stumbling into a camp of his friends. Because his hair was reputed to have suddenly turned pure white after the ordeal, some tribes called him "White Hair" or "White Head." Other tribes called him "Broken Hand" because an exploding rifle had left him with a mangled hand. The Indians' respect for him would serve him well, as it would for anyone who traveled with him.

The fur trade era was about washed up by 1841. But men with a résumé like Fitzpatrick would be in high demand as trail guides for the reasons set forth above. Just because someone had been a former mountain man, however, did not mean he would be desirable as a trail guide. Indeed, there were some whom you would not want to lead you through your own backyard. But Fitzpatrick was not one of those. He knew the wilderness and knew the trail—at least to Fort Hall. He was keen-sighted, quick-minded, and in his physical prime. Although he was muscular, no one ever described him as tall and imposing. Dr. Wislizenus met him in 1839 and wrote that "[h]e has a spare, bony figure, a face full of expression, and white hair; his whole demeanor reveals strong passions."[30]

The costume of the mountain man was fairly standard. It was that of the Indian. Typically, mountain men were shaggy, bearded, long-haired men who wore greasy buckskin shirts and leggings, knee-length moccasins, and a furry cap. They typically cradled a long-barreled Hawken rifle in their arms while stowing a tomahawk and skinning knife in their belt. Unfortunately, no one bothered to record how Fitzpatrick was dressed. It would have also been nice to read whether anyone found him loquacious or taciturn, flamboyant or dull, charismatic or colorless. Unfortunately, very little was written that revealed the nuances of his personality.

After this assignment in 1841, Fitzpatrick would later be selected as a trail guide for men like John C. Frémont and Colonel Stephen Watts Kearney. He would then be appointed as Indian agent responsible for the Plains Tribes. Fitzpatrick died in 1856 at the fairly young age of fifty-seven. Ironically, not from an arrow while guiding an emigrant train wagon in the wilderness, but from pneumonia in a hotel in Washington, D.C., as a government bureaucrat delivering his report to the Bureau of Indian Affairs.

Prior to 1841, Fitzpatrick had led a number of pack mule trains over the trail, managing groups of crusty, testy, foul-mouthed mule-skinners. This would be the first time he would lead a wagon company of wet-behind-the-ears greenhorns, people who were inexperienced in trail life. Some might be difficult to manage because of their independent nature, used to self-governance, indifferent to authority, and resistant to taking orders. This could be problem in a wagon party. People needed to work together, much like a hive of bees or a colony of ants.

While the party generally consisted of strong and hardy young men, they were also raw and untested, ignorant of the knowledge and skills needed to travel along a western trail. That was where Fitzpatrick came in. He knew where the water was and where to stop and camp. He knew how to bag game, how to read the weather, and how to read the mind of the Indian. It would be his responsibility to act as their wet nurse, showing them how to camp, how to guard livestock, ford rivers, survive the mountains and deserts, and deal with Indians. As a tough and hardened man, Fitzpatrick would have had little sympathy for weak or soft people. He would not coddle them. No doubt, his patience would be tested. How long would it be before he would tire of being asked, "Hey, Fitz, how much further to the next crick?"

Fitzpatrick's many years of leading supply pack trains over this trail had schooled him in the importance of having a well-regimented, well-disciplined camp with strict routines and safeguards. Nicholas Dawson described some of these routines:

> *A little before night, he [Fitzpatrick] would gallop on ahead and select a camping place. When the camping place was reached, the wagons were placed in a hollow square, leaving a space between each two for tents and campfires. The horses were grazed outside until night, when they were picketed inside, and a guard kept outside all night.*[31]

Father Point penned his own description of their routines as well:

> *Wherever possible, camp was pitched on the wooded bank of some river so there would be no lack either of drinking water or wood for cooking. First, the captain would mark a spot for our tent; then the vehicles would be arranged one beside the other in a circle or a square, more or less regular according to the nature of the terrain, but always in such a manner as to provide the pack animals a secure enclosure for the night. For added security, everyone picketed his own animals at a sufficiently great distance from the others and on tethers long enough to permit them, without doing injury to themselves, to supplement by grazing what they had been fed in the evening. From the moment when the camp retired until the break of day, all the travelers, including the priests, stood watch according to roster in order to guard against surprise attack.*[32]

Bidwell's memoirs also recalled them drawing their wagons and carts into a square at the end of each day's travel. He remembered picketing their horses and mules inside the square, and how they cooked during daylight and were allowed no campfires at night.[33] Fitzpatrick divided the expedition into "messes," small groups who would cook and eat together, a practice employed for years by the Army and by the pack trains supplying the fur trade. Since the trail had been mostly used by pack trains, seeing very little wagon traffic to date, improvements along the trail were needed for their wheeled vehicles. Bidwell reported that they were compelled to periodically fill in gulches and remove stones.[34]

Bidwell fully recognized the value of Fitzpatrick's services, recalling years later that "[i]t was well that we did [wait for Fitzpatrick], for otherwise probably not one of us would ever had reached California, because of our inexperience."[35]

It is possible that at some point Bartleson, the elected captain of the California party, asked Fitzpatrick how far he could guide them. Would he be available to lead them all the way to California? Fitzpatrick would have surely made it clear that he was obligated to get De Smet and his missionary party to the Flathead Indian homeland in today's Montana. But he had never ventured further west than the Great Salt Lake country. It is likely that Fitzpatrick would have mentioned that there were a few mountain men who had traveled to California and back. The most prominent was Joseph Walker, who had led a brigade of trappers to California in 1833. Walker would be a good prospect, and there was a chance they would run across him somewhere between Fort Laramie and Fort Hall. As we learn more about Bartleson's personality, it seems increasingly possible that he believed a guide beyond Fort Hall to be unnecessary, because the Marsh letter he carried, coupled with his own leadership skills, would be sufficient to get the company the rest of the way to California.

IN THE MEANTIME, Joseph Chiles, Charles Weber, and James John (Jimmy John) were struggling to catch up. While the main party had left Sapling Grove on May 12, Jimmy John's journal explained that he, Chiles, and Weber left Westport on the morning of May 16, and camped four miles east of Sapling Grove on their first night out. By that time, the main company was already four days' travel ahead of them.[36]

The following day, May 17, the Chiles group made good time. Jimmy John reported that they camped eleven miles east of Waukarusa Creek. They reached the creek and crossed it at noon the next day. During the night of May 18, Jimmy John recorded, "one of our oxen strayed and we did not get him until 10 o'clock in the morning." By the end of the day on May 19, the day on which the main party departed its Soldiers Creek camp, Jimmy John reported that they "camped at a spring 20 miles from the Canzas [Kansas] river [probably Big Springs]." At this point, the Chiles group was about thirty-four miles behind the main party, but they were closing the distance.

May 20

Bidwell's entry:

> *T. 20. The day was tolerably pleasant. Our road was interrupted by small streams which crossed our course in every 2 or 3 miles during the day. The land was prairie, except the narrow groves which accompanied every stream—timber principally, bur-oak, black walnut, elm, and white hickory. Traveled this day about sixteen miles and encamped in a beautiful grove of timber through which meandered a small stream.*

The day's travel, like that on May 19, was along the flat and grassy Kansas River bottom. "Prairie" is how Bidwell described it—except for the band of trees growing beside the small creeks flowing into the Kansas. The trail followed the present route of Highway 24 passing where the small town of St. Mary's, Kansas, stands today. The Jesuits would establish a Catholic mission there in 1848 to serve the Pottawatomie Indians and called it St. Mary's.[37] At St. Mary's turn north on 8th Street, then turn west on to Durink Street, which then becomes Oregon Trail Road as it heads west out of town. The trail continued westerly along the foot of the river bluffs, following the path of today's Oregon Trail Road. Based upon Bidwell's estimated mileage, the party probably camped the night of May 20 at Lost Creek, near the intersection of today's Oregon Trail Road and Lost Creek Road, and about six and a half miles west of St. Mary's. Their campsite was likely on the west side of the creek because it was a common practice for trail masters to cross their party to the far side of a creek so that if runoff from an upstream rainstorm arrived during the night, the high-running creek would not delay them.

Bidwell mentioned that the groves along the stream included hickory trees. Emigrants in later years often mentioned them along here because they prized hickory wood for its flexible, yet resilient, properties. It was ideal for fashioning the curved, wooden bows over which they stretched their canvas wagon covers.

JIMMY JOHN REPORTED on the progress of his Chiles party on May 20, as they tried to overtake the main company:

> *May 20—This morning we set out for the crossing place. We had not gone far before we [met] two of the company coming back to meet us. They told us that the rest of the company had gone on ahead. They helped us to push on and we got to the river at three o'clock, and got all our bagage and wagon animals, etc, across the river at sunset. The indians were very active in helping us across. They floated the baggage over in buffaloe hides, swimming and pushing them before them.*

The Chiles group, now about twenty-eight miles behind the main party, were closing the gap. But where was the Papin brothers' "pirogue" that Father De Smet said helped them cross the river? With the main body having crossed on May 16, perhaps the Papins had shut down their ferry and put their pirogue in "dry dock" for the rest of the year.

Chapter 5

Across a Sea of Grass

MAY 21 TO 31, 1841

May 21

Bidwell:

> F. 21st. Our oxen left us last night, and it was 9 o'clock before we were all ready to start, passed a considerable stream called Vermillion, a branch of the Kanzas. On its banks was finer timber than we had heretofore seen, hickory, walnut &c, &c. The country was prairie, hilly and strong; we passed in the forenoon a Kanzas village, entirely deserted on account of the Pawnees, encamped by a scattering grove, having come about 15 miles.

Because of starting late on the morning of May 21 due to tracking down strayed oxen, the company had traveled only four miles when it came to what Bidwell called the Vermillion. This was Red Vermillion Creek, also known as the Little Vermillion. The company crossed about three miles east of the present-day community of Louisville, Kansas, and just west of where the creek presently flows under Oregon Trail Road. They probably camped in the vicinity of the giant elm tree, which is now gone. Bidwell did not describe the difficulty of their crossing, but it was a famously deep-cut channel that many future emigrants excoriated because of the difficulty of letting their wagons down and hauling them up its nearly perpendicular banks. Even today, travelers will be amazed at the depth of the channel and the steepness of its banks. It is a wonder how parties managed to get their wagons across. Finally, in 1847, Louis Vieux erected a wooden

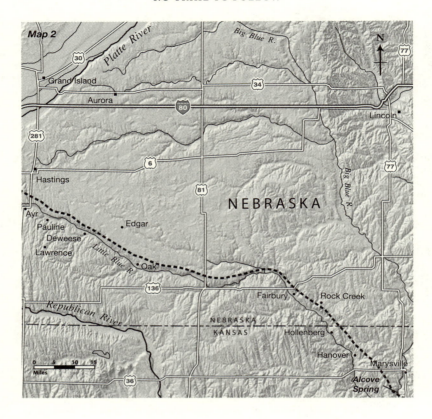

toll bridge across the channel and charged one dollar per wagon, which most wagon owners were delighted to pay.[1]

While the company kept its horses and mules inside the square corral formed by the wagons at night, the oxen were allowed to spend the night grazing and resting near the encampment. It was early in the journey and the oxen had not yet adjusted to the idea of spending each night in a new and strange location. Many emigrants arriving by steamboat understood that it was cheaper to purchase wagons and teams at the settlements rather than paying the steep price of bringing their own on the boat. Therefore, it is assumed that some or many of the oxen teams had been purchased in Independence. There are no journal entries covering the days before May 18, so we have no accounts of whether any oxen had strayed prior to that date. It was common to have difficulty with animals at the beginning, especially those purchased at Independence or Westport. They tended to be less bonded to their new owners and were animated by a strong natural homing instinct. They were more inclined to want to return to the corral, pasture, or stable from which they had recently come. In 1846, Edwin Bryant wrote that it was a nettlesome problem: "Emigrants cannot be too watchful of their cattle and horses when first starting out on this journey. They are more or less disposed to stray and return to the settlements."[2]

In addition to preventing a surprise Indian attack, it was the night guards' job to keep an eye on these restless creatures. Night guard duty was a crucial but detestable job. It was essential for the guards to stay awake, listen, keep their eyes open, stare into the darkness, and be alert to any movement, sound, or sign that that did not belong to the ordinary. In addition to making sure no oxen wandered off in the darkness, they needed to be sensitive to any change in an animal's behavior, such as an ox suddenly lifting his head, cocking his ears, and sniffing the air. Or a dog beginning to bark. There is nothing like an animal to tell a man if something strange is out there. Given what happened, the guards appeared to have slept on the job. They were going to have to do much better.

Bidwell mentioned a vacant Kansa village, blaming its desertion on the Pawnees. The following year, during the summer of 1842, Frémont and his exploring party encountered "a huge but deserted village" at the same location. He reported that it had been attacked by a Pawnee war party just a few months earlier.[3] After crossing the Kansas River in 1846, Edwin Bryant wrote about a recently burned-out Kansa village only three miles southwest of Soldier Creek.[4] This suggests that the Pawnees were still exacting revenge more than five years after the 1840 massacre.

Just beyond the Red Vermillion crossing, the trail changed course and began angling in a northwesterly direction. Leaving the Kansas River bottom behind, the trail began to climb, forcing the mules and oxen to strain as they pulled their heavy burdens up the slopes. Through here, the trail traveled roughly parallel to and about one mile east of today's Highway 99.

The trail was now taking the party across high prairie country. Once again, the path followed the ridgelines and divides to avoid the steep banks of creeks, gullies, and ravines wherever possible. The long procession of wagons and carts must have been an imposing sight, resembling a string of dull-colored pearls slowly lumbering along the gently curving trail, rising and falling with the contours of the land.

By traveling along the high ground, the travelers could often see great distances in all directions. The prairie scenery was pleasing, rolling, and undulating. The expanse was treeless, except for narrow bands of timber growing in the creases where the water channels ran. The winds and breezes, unimpeded by obstacles, could blow with perfect freedom. Now deep into spring, the slopes were carpeted with fresh, green grass about a foot high. The air was thick with the prairie's sweet smells. The spring wildflowers were beginning to bloom, their rapturous colors, textures, and smells teasing the senses. Honeysuckle and wild roses were tucked along the ravines and watercourses. As the spring progressed, tulips, larkspur, buttercups, daisies, pink verbenas, wild indigo, coreopsis, blue flax, leadplant, stiff goldenrod, primrose, spiderwort, violet, dovesfoot, and cowslip, each in its own time, opened their dazzling petals and perfumed the air. The company was passing through here before peak bloom. That may have been why Bidwell did not bother to mention them.

This was classic tallgrass prairie country, a vast ecosystem of grasses where the Big Bluestem predominated. These tall grasses were just stretching their legs now, and would not reach their full height until summer. In addition, there was switch grass and Indian grass, each grass species finding its own niche, each occupying a different place, a different height, and a different role. Together, the grasses would produce a dense, thick mat of vegetation that swarmed with countless varieties of birds and insects.[5]

Grassland prairies were partly caused by lower precipitation, but fire played a key role as well. In the fall, when the grasses were mature and dry, fires would periodically be ignited by lightning strikes or by Indians who had learned that new grass did better if it emerged from fire-scorched earth. New tree seedlings would perish in the hot flames. Only the larger, established trees growing along the waterways survived. The role of fire in preserving grasslands can be seen today. With prairie grass fires largely a thing of the past, many of today's uncultivated parcels, when left alone, have become overgrown with trees.

The prairie was usually a quiet, lonely place, with soft and gentle sounds—the chirping of birds, the buzzing of insects, and the whisper of breezes rustling through the grasses. When the long procession of wagons and livestock rolled into view, the voices of men, the creaking of wagons, the jingling of chains, and the heavy breathing of the mules and oxen would have disturbed the tranquility. When they had passed, the quiet returned.

Today, for the most part, the scene is different. While some of it, mostly the pasturelands, has retained some similarity in appearance, the rest has been altered with farmsteads, cultivated fields, and large wooded parcels invading the former grasslands.

Bidwell did not mention it, but a wagon party usually "nooned," near midday. They would stop to eat and give the livestock a short rest. Not wanting to take the time to build fires and cook, they usually ate something that had been prepared that morning. It was nothing fancy, the vanities of life having been left behind. The oxen were unhitched but not unyoked and were allowed to crop a few mouthfuls of grass. After eating their noon meal, some of the men might have stretched out on the grass, after checking for snakes. Those troublesome snakes seemed to be everywhere, and they had the unnerving habit of crawling into a man's warm bedroll during the night. Soaking up the warm sun and sedated by the fragrances of the wildflowers, it was difficult for the men not to slip off into a short nap.

Bidwell said they encamped at a "scattering grove" on the afternoon of May 21, about fifteen miles beyond their previous camp at Lost Creek. Since the prairie was treeless except near a source of water, his use of the term "grove" indicates that it was near a small creek. Assuming Bidwell's estimate of traveling fifteen miles that day was close to accurate, it suggests that they camped near a small fork of Boxelder Creek. To reach their estimated camp location, take Highway 99 out of Westmorland and travel southeast about four and a half miles to Boxelder Road. Then proceed 2.8 miles east to Wheaton Road and turn right. Their camp location is about one mile south, near the creek.

Between May 21 and June 3, when the company arrived at the Platte River, it would have traveled approximately 190 miles and crossed a number of small streams and creeks. Bidwell and Jimmy John either did not mention them or, when they did, did not identify them by name or by their correct name. This is not surprising. The era of emigrant parties using the trail was just beginning. Perhaps some of these smaller streams had not yet been named. If they had, their names were not yet widely known. Fitzpatrick would have been the most likely person to know, but we see little evidence that Bidwell or Jimmy John had bothered to ask him.

In trying to determine the location of each of their campsites, the first resource was Gregory Franzwa's 1982 edition of his *Maps of the Oregon Trail*. It is a great starting place. The maps in his book are the result of years of devoted study: the consulting of hundreds of emigrant diaries and recollections of "old timers" and of looking at the physical evidence that remained. The next step was to consider the mileages estimated by our diarists. Bidwell's estimates between two known points were often close to correct. Nicholas Dawson's log was useful, but his estimates between two known points were inconsistent, sometimes overestimating and sometimes underestimating. Either way, their estimates were rarely off by more than about 10 percent. Sometimes Bidwell's and Dawson's mileage estimates agreed, and sometimes they were different.

In the end, the geography usually provided the final answer. Although the trail generally traveled along the backbone of the prairie during the day to avoid crossing ravines and watercourses, the importance of camping near wood and water meant that they needed to end their day beside a wooded stream or creek. Fitzpatrick knew the trail. He had traveled it many times. He knew what was ahead and how far it was. He would stop the caravan early in the day if the next suitable camping spot was too far, or he would push them forward in a long travel day if the next stop was within reach. In short, even if the diarists failed to name the creek or even if they incorrectly named it, the route of the trail, the mileage estimates, and the locations of the wooded streams or creeks are what identified their likely campsites,

IN THE MEANTIME, on May 21, the Chiles group was about two days' travel behind the expedition. Jimmy John reported that five members from the main company appeared shortly after they had taken to the trail that morning. The visitors said that they had come to escort them until they overtook the main party.

May 22

Bidwell:
> S. 22nd. Started at six o'clock this morning, travelled about 18 miles, high rolling prairie, encamped on a small stream, shaded by a few willows.

The camp stirred early on the morning of May 22, the sounds of human activity rudely disturbing the peaceful dawn. Although our narrators did not describe their morning routines, emigrants in future years would describe a typical morning's activity. Even before dawn, campfires would be started, and the mouthwatering smells of freshly brewed coffee and bacon sizzling on their cast iron frying pans would permeate the air. Tents and camp equipment were packed and loaded. Oxen were driven into the corral of wagons to be "caught up" and yoked. Once the oxen and mules were hitched to their wagons and carts amidst the sounds of jingling pull chains, the wagon master would give the signal, and shouts to get moving would echo up and down the line. The company would lurch forward and another day on the trail began.

Shortly, the company passed Scott Spring, although Bidwell did not mention it. The spring is on the west side of today's Highway 99, a mile south of Westmoreland. Its cold, refreshing water, seeping from a rocky ledge, was often mentioned by future travelers. Continuing northward, the trail traveled through where the middle of Westmoreland now stands, then drifted slightly westward and continued north roughly parallel to and about a mile west of Highway 99. After traveling eighteen miles that day, the company likely encamped beside the headwaters of Bush Creek.

To observe the location of their camp, head north from Westmoreland on Highway 99 about six and a half miles and then turn west on to Highway 16. After going only 0.2 miles west, turn on to Bucksnort Road and proceed west another 0.7 miles.

May 23

Bidwell reported that they awoke on the morning of May 23 and found themselves bedeviled by a recurring problem:

> *S. 23rd. All the oxen were gone this morning excepting nine, there was considerable complaint among the company, some saying at this slow rate of traveling we would have to winter among the Black Hills, and eat our mules &c. We however made a start about 9 in the morning, proceeded about 9 miles and stopped to wait for Chiles' waggon which overtook us about 5 PM; 14 Pawnees were seen by the wagons, well armed with spears &c. It was supposed they were on an expedition against the Kanzas.*

Bidwell had reported earlier that the company had seventeen yoke of oxen. With two oxen per yoke, this represented thirty-four oxen. Since he reported that nine stayed, it seems twenty-five had fled. It was another vexatious delay. Was it because the animals were still not trail broke and not yet adjusted to the routine of trail travel? Was it a case of oxen with unusually restless temperaments? Or was it poor night guarding? Had Fitzpatrick inadequately trained the night guards, or was it a matter of failing to enforce discipline?

Bidwell had mentioned that the line of wagons and carts had been toiling along at a slow, plodding pace, holding back to allow the Chiles group to catch up. Because some in the company were apparently concerned that they would not cross the western mountains before the snows came, the situation had occasioned some discord. The idealistic goal of traveling together in perfect harmony was now disintegrating. Forced companionship with strangers was going to be awkward even when things were going well. But when things were going awry, comity could easily unravel. In their home communities, people could pick their friends. Here, people were thrown together with strangers. Common sense suggests that the party was composed of a broad spectrum of personalities and temperaments, ranging from the gracious to the abrasive, from the congenial to the rancorous, and from the accommodating to the stiff-necked.

There was nothing like a stressful journey to give measure to a man. Stress and fatigue tended to magnify one's more unattractive traits. It was a perfect environment in which even the slightest provocations could cause people to erupt in anger. Edwin Bryant noticed the same thing early in his 1846 trip: "If a man is predisposed to be quarrelsome, obstinate, or selfish from his natural constitution, these repulsive traits are certain to be developed on a journey over the plains."[6] In any event, the problem of straying oxen needed to be solved.

Jimmy John's journal described his Chiles group finally overtaking the main company on May 23:

> *This day [23rd] we met 14 Pawnee Indian Warriors armed and equipped for battle. They shook hands with us and appeared to be friendly. One of the men gave them some tobacco which pleased them very much. We went on and encamped on a large creek called Blue. There we overtook the company who were waiting there for us. Here we caught some fine fish and stayed until morning.*

Neither Bidwell nor Jimmy John explained whether they crossed the creek, although it was a common trail practice to cross before setting up camp. Jimmy John erroneously called the creek the "Blue." Given the distances that Bidwell recorded since crossing the Red Vermillion, it is clear that they had stopped at Black Vermillion Creek on the evening of May 23. During his expedition in 1842, Frémont called it the Big Vermillion. He described its valley as one mile wide, one-third of which was occupied with timber.[7] Edwin Bryant described the Black Vermillion as bordered by thick stands of oak and elm about a quarter of a mile wide, and said it abounded with "good-sized catfish."[8] The landscape here has changed a great deal since 1841. The creek is narrower now, and much of the timber has been cleared and the land converted to cultivated fields.

To see the location of their camp on May 23, head west out of Frankfort, Kansas, on West Second Street. It becomes Highway 9 after it leaves town. Proceed four and a half miles southwest to 17th Road, then go south two miles to where it turns west. Their probable campsite would have been in the field to the south and on the north side of the Black Vermillion.

With the arrival of Joseph Chiles and his mule-drawn wagon, the company now boasted nineteen wagons and four carts. Chiles, Weber, and Jimmy John likely introduced themselves, exchanged news, and traded tales. Both Bidwell and Jimmy John recorded the appearance of fourteen Pawnee warriors, well-armed and obviously on the warpath. The Kansa chiefs were correct in their fears; they would soon be facing the wrath of a Pawnee raiding party. The appearance of the Pawnees confirmed that Indians could appear along the trail at any time and from anywhere. If anyone was sensitive to this, it would have been Fitzpatrick. During each day's travel, it is likely that he rode ahead of the column, his eyes constantly searching the distance. He may have assigned horse-mounted outriders to ride at the rear and along the flanks at some distance from the wagons, to keep a lookout for trouble. It may have been beautiful country, but it was dangerous, too.

The Pawnee tribe was once mighty and proud. Numbering as many as twenty-four thousand in the late 1700s, they were once regarded as the pirates of the plains.[9] The historical record is replete with accounts of Pawnee raiding parties ranging far and wide, taking horses and scalps from neighboring tribes such as the Comanche, Apache, Arapahoe, Kiowa, Cheyenne, Sioux, Kansa, Shawnee,

Osage, Arikara, Ponca, Otoe, and Omaha. In their heyday, the Pawnees were regarded as inveterate and arrogant troublemakers. They had no friends or allies, and did not feel the need for any. Then, in 1832, their fortunes changed, and their dominance over the prairie between the Platte and Kansas rivers began to decline. A smallpox epidemic hit them hard, killing thousands. Then the powerful Sioux made their appearance and began sending raiding parties against them. Failing to perceive their vulnerability, the Pawnees retaliated instead of seeking peace. For the next decade, the Sioux seemed dedicated to eradicating the Pawnees and mounted unremitting attacks on the Pawnee villages along the Platte River and on their buffalo hunting parties.[10] By 1840, a government survey reported that the Pawnee numbers had declined to about six thousand.[11] By 1848, another survey reported that only twenty-five hundred Pawnees were left.[12] As a broken and fast-dwindling tribe, the Pawnees would eventually become known as the beggars of the plains. Disheartened, they would loiter along the trail during the months of May and June, intercepting emigrant wagon trains, begging for food, clothing, and blankets, and often trying to steal anything not closely watched or guarded.[13] As of 1841, however, the Pawnees had not yet fallen into such a deplorable state.

Rufus B. Sage was a young adventurer who had hoped to join the Bartleson expedition. But he had arrived at Westport after the company had long departed. Sage hung around the settlement until fall, when he then joined a company of traders headed for the Rockies. He expressed apprehension in his memoirs about traveling through Pawnee country:

> *This section of the country is very dangerous in the summer and fall months, on account of the strolling Pawnees which infect it. The voyageur holds the latter in great dread, unless he chances to be accompanied by a sufficient force to bid defiance to their approach. A party, numerically weak and indifferently armed, meets with rough treatment at their hands while on the open prairies.*[14]

The journal entries of Bidwell and Jimmy John had not indicated any wariness toward the Pawnee warriors, perhaps because the Pawnees seemed focused on finding Kansa and inflicting revenge upon them. Indians were ordinarily careful and prudent, sensible enough not to molest a large and strongly armed company. But Fitzpatrick had probably warned everyone to stay close and not venture far from the wagons alone.

The section of trail the company traveled on May 23 ran roughly parallel to and about two miles west of present-day Highway 99.

May 24

May 24 would prove to be a tranquil day, with the prairie soft, gentle, and soothing.

Bidwell:
> M. 24th. Traveled about 13 miles to day over rolling prairies and arrived at the Big Vermillion, a branch of the Kanzas, here we were obliged to stop, the water being so high as to render it impossible to cross with the waggons.

Jimmy John:
> May 24—This day we arrived at another creek about one o'clock; it being very high, we were obliged to camp there until morning.

Bidwell reported on May 24 that they arrived at the Big Vermillion, but he incorrectly named the river. Having traveled thirteen miles after leaving their Black Vermillion camp, it was the Big Blue River that they had come to. Fitzpatrick should have known the correct name of the river. Led by Kit Carson the following year, Frémont had no trouble calling it the Big Blue. He described the river as 120 feet wide and running through a "well-timbered valley."[15] Edwin Bryant described it as bordered by very large oak, cottonwood, walnut, beach, and sycamore trees.[16] It is easily the largest river in the area, with a large watershed. Heavy rains north and west of here would cause the river to run high for a short period, pinning travelers, as it had here, on its eastern side until it receded.

As the company descended toward the river, it passed a spring that was given its name by Edwin Bryant in 1846. At the time, Bryant was traveling with the fated Donner party. He named it Alcove Spring and carved the name into a flat rock near a small waterfall below the spring.[17] James Reed, one of the principals in the Donner party, inscribed his name and the year 1846 on another flat rock near the waterfall. These inscriptions can still be seen today. Reed's ill mother-in-law, Sarah Keyes, died there and they buried her before moving on. Neither Bidwell nor Jimmy John mentioned the waterfall, which is not surprising since it is concealed in dense vegetation about a half mile from where they camped beside the river. Alcove Spring is on East River Road, about seven miles south of the present-day town of Marysville, Kansas. It is a picturesque spot along the trail.

May 25

Bidwell:
> T. 25th. Passed the stream without much trouble and made a stretch of about 20 miles when we encamped on the border of a beautiful forest where we found plenty of grass and water. The country, over which we passed, was similar to that of yesterday.

Jimmy John:
> May 25—We crossed the creek at 7 o'clock this morning. Here we caught some fish and some of the company seen a gang of elk. We encamped this night on a small creek.

The high water in the Big Blue must have receded during the night since, as the diarists explained, the party was able to cross it early the next morning. About twelve miles beyond the river the company passed a place that would later be called the "junction-of-the-ways." Joseph Robidoux would found his town of St. Joseph, Missouri, in 1843. The first wagon party of emigrants to depart from St. Joe left in the spring of 1847. After that, St. Joseph would gradually surpass Independence and Westport as the principal jumping-off point for wagon trains heading west. The St. Joseph trail, which headed almost due west until it joined the trail from Independence, had the advantage of bypassing the difficult crossings of the Kansas River, the Red Vermillion and the Black Vermillion. But most significantly, it shortened the trip by about sixty-five miles because of St. Joseph's more northerly location. Exactly where the Independence and St. Joseph roads merged is in dispute. Some claim it is in a field just west of today's County Line Road (1st Road) and three miles north of Highway 36 (eight miles west of Marysville). However, according to a granite marker near this site, the merger was one-quarter mile east of the marker's location.

The trail continued northwesterly until it crossed Cottonwood Creek about one and a half miles east of present-day Hanover, Kansas, on the south side of Highway 243 and west of where the creek crosses the highway. Years later, a pony express station was established there. It is now restored and includes a museum.

From here, the trail continued to follow the ridgeline east of and above the valley of the Little Blue River, a tributary of the Big Blue. As the trail continued to wind through elevated country, one could gaze in some places upon the river valley below. Edwin Bryant described the view in 1846: "Late in the afternoon, we reached the summit of a ridge, overlooking a valley through which winds a small rivulet, the banks of which are fringed with timber. The view from the ridge of the beautiful valley below appeared almost like a creation of enchantment."[18]

Dawson's log agreed with Bidwell that they traveled twenty miles on May 25. While Bidwell reported that they camped on the border of a beautiful forest, Jimmy John recorded that they camped by a small stream. These clues suggest that the group camped near a tributary of Bush Creek, approximately northeast of the intersection of today's Yankee Road and 27th Road, and about five miles southeast of the present-day community of Hollenberg, Kansas.

May 26

Bidwell:

> W. 26th. Two waggons were broke to day; about a dozen Pawnees came to camp, stopped to repair the waggons, having come about 15 miles. A deer was brought in by C. Hopper. A man by the name of Williams, a methodist preacher overtook the company this evening on his way to visit the Oregon territory: He had not arrived in time to start with the company from the settlements, and had travelled entirely alone, without any gun or other weapon of defence, depending wholy on Providence for protection and support.

Jimmy John:

> May 26—We left here at about 7 o'clock. One of the waggons broke down. Today we seen about 30 Pawnee Indians today. They were very friendly and were well armed with bows, lances and guns, prepared to meet the Caws [Kaws/Kanzas]. One of the mule teams ran away and broke the hounds of their wagon. This night we encamped at a small creek.

In a letter to his Father Provincial, Father De Smet also reported this encounter with the Pawnees on May 26. He claimed that the warriors were the same as those mentioned by Bidwell and Jimmy John on May 23. De Smet reported that the Pawnees had been traveling south on May 23 "in quest of Kansas [Indians]," and that they had achieved their goal and were returning north to their home village. Bidwell's and Jimmy John's accounts reveal no sense of alarm. Perhaps their youthful innocence blinded them to the danger, but De Smet was not so sanguine. He perceived the Pawnees' visit on May 26 as tense and unsettling, writing that one of the warriors "had a human scalp which hung from the neck of his horse." After the company fed them, the warriors refused to smoke the peace pipe and left abruptly. De Smet went on to explain his fears:

> [T]hey left us in a manner which indicated they were dissatisfied. The suddenness of their departure, their refusal to smoke the calumet [peace pipe] the unexpected return of their party, the neighborhood of their village, and their well-known love of plunder—in short, everything induced us to fear they had some design to make an attempt, if not upon our persons, at least upon the horses and baggage.[19]

Father Point's recollection of the incident was the same as De Smet's, expressing the same unease. He added that the warriors claimed they had not seen any Kansa, although he suspected they were lying: "What we beheld boded nothing good for the fate of our hosts [the Kansa]. But when the captain [Fitzpatrick] inquired about the results of their expedition, they informed us that they had not even seen the Kansas."[20]

The "small creek" where Jimmy John said they stopped would have been Rock Creek, six miles southeast of today's Fairbury, Nebraska. Dawson's log called it Missionary Creek. The next year, Frémont called it Wyeth's Creek, undoubtedly named after the fur trader Nathaniel Wyeth, who traveled west in 1834. Eventually, it was called Rock Creek, the name by which it is known today. The location where the trail crossed Rock Creek later became a pony express station and is now part of the Rock Creek Station State Park, operated by the Nebraska Game and Parks Commission.

This is the first we have read about any wagons breaking down. Bidwell and Jimmy John did not agree on whether it was one or two wagons. In later years, wagon owners often carried spare wagon wheels, axles, and tongues to provide for such emergencies. However, the lack of spare wagon parts was rarely catastrophic since wagon owners usually carried woodworking tools with which they could quickly fashion a replacement part from a dead tree or limb found near the trail.

Bidwell also mentioned the Reverend Joseph Williams catching up to the company. A sixty-four-year-old Methodist minister from Napoleon, Indiana, Williams had left home on horseback in April 1841, intending to preach in the Oregon Territory. When he arrived at Independence, he learned that the Bartleson-Bidwell party had already left and was about five days' travel ahead. Everyone he met discouraged him, telling him that it was too hazardous a journey for an old man, and they urged him to give it up.[21] Undaunted, Williams resolved to proceed anyway, trusting in God to protect him, even though he admitted he had a gun as well.[22] He left the Shawnee Methodist Mission on May 21 and crossed the Kansas River on May 24. That he managed to travel unaccompanied without being molested is extraordinary. In 1843, after returning to Indiana, he published an account of his journey. While he did not record an entry every day, he did make periodic dated entries. They are valuable in helping document the company's fortunes until he and others separated from the California-bound contingent at Soda Springs.

After setting out in pursuit of the expedition, Williams complained that he "could scarcely follow the wagon tracks, the ground was so hard in the prairie."[23] This not only confirmed that the company had been traveling during a dry spell, but also that the light wagon traffic in former years had heretofore failed to inscribe definitive marks across the prairie.

On his fifth night out, Williams said he encountered a whining dog where he camped, a dog he believed had been left behind by the company. But he never mentioned it again, suggesting that he may not have invited it to accompany him the next morning. In the years to come, dogs would become controversial. Most were great pets and companions, and most were excellent sentinels, quick to bark at night at the slightest strange sound or smell. Some were good with livestock. But others could be troublesome. These were usually the high-strung, impulsive, and quick-to-bark kind. While some oxen were docile, even-tempered, and difficult to alarm, others were skittish and easy to spook by a sudden or unexpected noise or movement. Oxen, like all animals, were heavily governed by an instinct to flee from a perceived threat. It did not take much to startle certain oxen and get them running. If one panicked, they all did. It was a trait inherited from their primitive ancestors and was deeply imbedded in their DNA. The last thing the company needed was a mass runaway ending in overturned or upended wagons. Such incidents did happen and dogs were often to blame. One wagon party in 1862 shot all of their dogs after they had caused a disastrous runaway of their wagons.[24]

Williams reported that when he caught up to the company he felt welcomed, even by "Mr. de Smidt [De Smet], who was extremely kind to me, and invited me to come and eat supper with him that night, and next morning brought me some venison. He appeared to be a very fine man."[25] Despite his welcome, Williams was soon complaining that he felt he had overtaken a group of gutter scum, finding himself "in the midst of an ignorant and hard-hearted people."[26]

Even though Bidwell reported that Williams appeared on May 26, the minister claimed that he overtook the company on May 28. Based on Williams's account of when he left the Shawnee Mission near Westport, and Bidwell's report of when he caught up to the expedition, it appears that the old man had traveled about 185 miles in only five days, an astonishing pace of thirty-seven miles per day. For a man of his age, it was an impressive feat of stamina and determination for both himself and his horse.

Williams claimed that when he joined the wagon train he was told that over two hundred Indians had been shadowing the wagons, with the intent of molesting those who fell behind. He was also told that four of the men had been robbed and left naked.[27] Miraculously, the minister had somehow managed to avoid them. Since neither Bidwell nor Jimmy John mentioned the matter, one wonders whether Williams had decided that the finer points of accuracy should take a backseat to a story that would better impress his readers.

May 27

Bidwell:

> *T. 27th. Started late, being detained at repairing the wagons, the day was warm, but the evening mild and pleasant, encamped in a commodious valley, well watered by a beautiful little stream which glided smoothly through the scattering grove, come about 15 miles.*

Jimmy John:

> *May 27—Left here early this morning. The route is a little broken today and the heat oppressive. Camped this night at a handsome little creek about 15 miles from the place where stayed last night.*

After breaking camp, the company returned to the trail. From Rock Creek, the trail angled northwest, tracing across a great rolling sea of green. About ten miles beyond Rock Creek (and about five miles north of Fairbury, Nebraska), the trail turned almost due west. For the next few days, the trail would travel north of and roughly parallel to the Little Blue River. Based on their estimated mileages from Rock Creek, they would have camped on the night of May 27 where the trail intersected Sandy Creek, near its mouth with the Little Blue. This location would be about six miles west of Highway 15 and where Sandy Creek crosses 717th Road, near its intersection with 561st Avenue.

May 28

Bidwell:

> *F. 28th. Started about sunrise, travelled about 5 miles and stopped to take breakfast. The heat was oppressive and we were compelled to go 20 miles farther before we came to either wood or water. The stream on which we encamped is a fork of the Kanzas and is well known to all mountaineers, by the name of Big Blue, an antelope was killed.*

Jimmy John:

> *May 28—Set out this morning early. Stopped and took breakfast at a beautiful creek of pure water at 9 o'clock. Left there at 10 o'clock and arrived at a creek called the Big Blue. There we encamped this day. One of the men killed one antelope. The heat was oppressive today. We have killed one antelope and a few deer and turkeys since we started for California and that is about all we have killed.*

Bidwell and Jimmy John had again misidentified the creek where they camped, calling it the Big Blue, when it was really the Little Blue.

Rising early on May 28, perhaps to avoid as much of the scorching heat as possible, the company followed the trail west, traveling a short distance north of the Little Blue River Valley. As they neared the end of the day, the trail returned to the Little Blue. Dawson, like Bidwell, estimated in his log that the party had traveled twenty-five miles that day. Assuming that their estimates were correct, their campsite that night would have been where the trail struck the north side of the Little Blue River, about where it crosses today's Highway 5, and about four and a half miles north of the present town of Deshler, Nebraska. Neither diarist described the Little Blue at this location, but a year later Frémont did, reporting that it was fifty feet wide and three feet deep.

As both diarists noted, they were now in pronghorn antelope country. Pronghorns are amazing creatures, with keen eyesight, sharp hearing, and an acute sense of smell. Frustrated hunters sometimes described them as faster than a streak of lightning. It was an exaggeration, of course, but they were unquestionably fast. Despite using the most careful stealth, it was difficult to approach them within rifle range. When a hunter was detected, the wary speedsters could depart the scene at sixty miles per hour.[28] Edwin Bryant commented in 1846 that he had never seen an animal "that could run with the apparent ease, speed and grace of these."[29] Any hunter who could bag one was uncommonly skilled.

Although the country was open and sparse, there was plenty of other wildlife. Besides antelope, emigrants in future years frequently mentioned seeing herds of elk and packs of wolves through this area. At night, the wolves would often be heard howling somewhere nearby, while a chorus of bullfrogs croaked down by the river. It was somewhere near here that James Clyman reported catching "two or 3 dozen of fine catfish."[30]

During its travels on May 28, the company would have crossed the 98th parallel about eight miles southeast of today's Deweese, Nebraska. The noted American explorer Stephen H. Long declared that the "Great American Desert," a region of markedly lowered rainfall, began at this meridian. As the company marched farther west, the members should have been noticing that the country was getting drier. The dry, clear air intensified the effects of the withering sun. The travelers' faces would have seemed redder and their lips more cracked and blistered. The dry air would have steadily sucked the moisture out of the wood in their wagons and carts. The wooden parts, no longer solidly joined, would cause the wagon boxes to rattle and the wheels to creak. The tire irons on the shrinking wheels were becoming loose and threatening to come off. Although neither Bidwell nor Jimmy John mentioned the issue, it was a common problem for future wagon trains at this point along the trail. Emigrants first tried soaking their wagon wheels in water at night. But it proved too much work and was only a short-term fix. The wheels would simply dry out again. Some drove wooden wedges as shims between the tires and wheel rims, but that fix would not last long either. Eventually, they learned to remove the tires, nail thin hoops on the wooden rims, and, after heating and expanding the tire irons, would slip them back on.

The drier country presented other changes as well. Frémont mentioned seeing cacti for the first time at his camp near here. Short buffalo grass, jackrabbits, and prairie dogs were also becoming evident. The area was the primary north-south corridor for migratory birds. The skies overhead should have been filled with V-shaped formations of Canada geese, snow geese, sandhill cranes, trumpeter swans, and other migrating waterfowl, all heading north to their summer nesting grounds.

Other than agreeing that the "heat was oppressive," Bidwell and Jimmy John had not commented on their mood or on the mood of the company. There had been no rain for over a week and the trail was dry. As the party lumbered westward toward a distant horizon shimmering under a scorching sun, we can imagine the wagons swallowed up in clouds of dust and covered in a thin veneer of grey powder. People coughed as they tried to clear the dust from their lungs. The oxen would have been laboring at their yokes, their sides heaving and their tongues hanging out. The sweating wagon drivers would have been slumped in their wagon seats while the men on horseback rocked listlessly in their saddles.

The expedition was traveling through a world of largeness and isolation. How were they weathering the tedium? Were they still in high spirits? They should have been. Besides enduring a few minor annoyances like straying oxen, broken wagons, high water, grumblings about slow progress, and some hot weather, the company's fortunes had been uncommonly good so far. There had been no reports of sickness. They had been lucky to travel without being pummeled by any violent lightning and thunderstorms for which the prairie was well known. Later years would not be so kind to emigrant wagon trains. Some years were terribly wet, when wagon parties suffered the effects of long, heavy rains, and the women and children in particular suffered from walking mile upon mile through thick and gummy mud in wet clothing and shoes, while being buffeted by chilling winds and then trying to sleep at night in wet bedding. For the most part, the company had been blessed with dry weather. How dare they complain about a little heat?

Some may have been sinking under the mind-numbing monotony of the journey. After all, they had been on the trail for over two weeks now, having traveled over 250 miles. Yet, they were still in the prairie's relentless grasp. Their eyes must have wearied from the changeless sea of grass. Each day had seemed the same; grass as far as the eye could see, interrupted only by the occasional strip of trees and brush hugging the occasional watercourses. No vague, jagged mountain range loomed in the distance. There was not much of any landmark other than a late afternoon sun pointing the way west.

The endless prairie, the dry conditions, and the faintness of the trail had left a lasting impression on Father Mengarini, compelling him to record his distressed feelings in his memoirs: "To lose the road and be in want of water had become such an ordinary matter as to be daily expected. But why speak of road when no such thing existed. Plains on all sides! Plains at morning, plains at noon, plains at night! And this, day after day."[31]

When the sun disappeared in the evening and twilight filled the western sky, it could be an especially melancholy time. Stepping away from camp to gaze westward toward a glorious sunset, some might have been struck by the profound solitude and seemingly endless distances. Were some worrying about how far they still had to go and what hardships and dangers awaited them? Were they fretting that the trip might be more than they had bargained for? Were they wondering if they had what it took to see the journey through? Were they regretting their decision to come?

May 29

Bidwell:

> S. 29th. We again started about sunrise and travelled not less than 22 miles. One antelope was killed—saw several elk.

Jimmy John:

> May 29—Started early this morning. Killed two antelope. Encamped on the banks of the Blue this evening, for we are traveling on the banks of

that stream. It rises eastward and we are going west. Encamped on same stream this night.

For most of the company's travel on May 29, the trail led west, then northwest, rarely more than a mile north of the Little Blue. About midday, the company squeezed through "the Narrows," a path threading between the Little Blue on the left and some high bluffs on the right. The Narrows can be seen by driving one and one-half miles west out of the small town of Oak, Nebraska, on Road S. Then turn onto Road 4300 and proceed north one mile. The Narrows is on the east side of the river channel about one-quarter mile away. Just beyond the Narrows, the trail shifted to a more northwesterly direction.

Bidwell estimated that the group traveled twenty-two miles on May 29, while Dawson reported that they traveled twenty-five miles. The most likely spot where they encamped is where the trail came close to the river approximately twenty-five miles beyond their previous camp. This would be on the eastern bank of the Little Blue, near where today's Highway 18C bends two-thirds of a mile northeast of Deweese, Nebraska.

May 30

Bidwell:

S. 30th. Nothing of importance occurred—distance about 15 miles—grass mingled with rushes, afforded our animals plenty of food of the best quality.—Game appeared to increase, though but one deer and one antelope were brought in.

Jimmy John:

May 30—Started early this morning at 7 o'clock. Killed one deer and antelope today. Stayed this night on the banks of the Blue.

A large wagon party like this needed a sizeable quantity of fresh meat. The company was fortunate to have good hunters such as Charles Hopper and John Gray. It is all the more impressive that someone was able to kill the wary, fleet-footed antelope.

About six miles north of leaving camp on the morning of May 30, the company would have crossed the Great Pawnee Trail. At about this location, James Clyman mentioned it in his journal in 1844:

"[A] little after noon passed the great Pawnee Lodge trail leading South."[32] The Pawnee Trail would have crossed the Oregon Trail on the east side of Pawnee Creek, about six miles northwest of Deweese and near the intersection of County Road D and County Road 305.

For untold ages, the Pawnees had left their earth-lodge villages on the Platte River in June or July and headed as far south as the Arkansas River for their summer buffalo hunt. When they moved, they traveled across country in a great mass.[33] Someone reported seeing the Pawnee nation on the move in 1835. They described a large camp, consisting of six hundred buffalo-skin lodges, four thousand people, seven thousand dogs, and thousands of horses.[34] This was when the population of the entire tribe was estimated at six thousand.[35] The dog numbers, though astonishing, were probably not exaggerated. The Pawnees, like many Plains tribes, used dogs as a traveling food supply that could be accessed when other food ran short. When the tribe returned to their Platte River villages in September they returned along the same trail. Hence, these great annual migrations left an unmistakable mark across the land, a wide swath of trampled grass and discarded items. Yet, neither Bidwell nor Jimmy John mentioned seeing any evidence of it.

After crossing Pawnee Creek, the trail moved across a narrow divide separating Pawnee Creek from the Little Blue. Bidwell says the group traveled fifteen miles on May 30, while Dawson said it was twenty miles. Jimmy John only said that they camped on the Little Blue. Given this information, it is likely that they stopped to camp beside the Little Blue about eight miles beyond Pawnee Creek. It is the same location where Frémont and his party camped the following year. It would be about three and a half miles northeast of the tiny community of Ayr, Nebraska, and about one and one-half miles west of Highway 62 on East Pony Express Road, near its intersection with South Palomino Road.

May 30 was Sunday and the Reverend Williams felt it was his professional duty to deliver a sermon. He complained that his offer to preach was met with resistance, however:

> *On Sunday, [May] 30th, I had a thought of trying to preach to the company. There were some as wicked people among them as I ever saw in all my life. There was some reluctance shown by the captain of the company [Bartleson or Fitzpatrick?]; others wanted me to preach to them.*

Williams bitterly fumed about traveling "in the midst of an ignorant and hard-hearted people." Righteousness seemed to be a strong trait in this man and he appeared to be in an exceptionally foul mood on May 30. He grumbled that Col. Bartleson, a fellow Methodist, was a "backslider," and he described Fitzpatrick as a "wicked, worldly man."[36] Unfortunately, he provided no details explaining why he felt that way.

May 31

Leaving camp the next morning, the company returned to a trail that was pointing northwest. The trail was leaving the Little Blue behind. It ascended out of the river channel and began to cross the high table-land that separated the Little Blue from the Platte River. About four miles after leaving camp, they crossed Thirty-Two Mile Creek, a narrow and meandering stream. After another four miles, the trail crossed an even smaller stream, the West Branch of Thirty-Two Mile Creek.

Bidwell:

> M. 31st. This morning about 10 o'clock we met six waggons with 18 men, with Fur and Robes on their way from Ft. Larimie, to St. Louis. Ft. Larimie is situated on Larimie's fork near its junction with the N. fork of Platte, and is about 800 miles from Independence. The waggons were drawn by oxen and mules—the former looked as though they received a thousand lashes every day of their existence! the rusty mountaineers looked as though they never had seen razor, water, soap, or brush. It was very warm, and we travelled till dark before we were able to reach water, and then it was not fit to drink, and then we could not procure any wood, grass scarce.

Jimmy John:

> May 31—Started early this morning at 7 o'clock. Met 5 waggons going from Fort Laramer [Laramie] to Independence. They said it would be 4 days before we would get to any buffalo. They were loaded with peltry, buffalo hides, etc. We traded with them for some buffalo meat and moccasins. We are about 4 hundred miles west of Independence, traveling through sandy but fertile plains. We are still traveling on the Blue. Left the Blue this morning and encamped on the prairie.

Given the boredom of the journey, an encounter with this dirty-as-hogs, eastbound group of bearded mountain men was bound to excite. They were likely free agent traders, unlikely to have been affiliated with the American Fur Company. They were returning from Fort Laramie, after trading supplies and other goods with trappers, hunters, and Indians for beaver pelts and buffalo hides.[37] There is a high probability that the goods taken earlier to the mountains by them had included copious amounts of alcohol. Traveling with a trading party later that fall, Rufus B. Sage expressed astonishment when he discovered that the traders he was traveling with carried *twenty-four barrels of alcohol*, much of it intended for the Indians. Despite it being against the law to transport alcohol into Indian Territory, with severe penalties, Sage observed:

> *Trading companies, however, find ways and means to smuggle it through, by the wagon-load, under the very noses of government officers, stationed along the frontier to enforce the observance of laws. I am irresistibly led to the conclusion, that these gentry are willfully negligent in their duty; and, no doubt, there are often weighty inducements presented to them to shut their eyes, close their ears, and avert their faces, to let the guilty pass unmolested.*[38]

Just as the missionary and Bartleson group found these swarthy traders entertaining, the traders were probably equally amused. After all, an emigrant wagon train would have been something quite new to the trail. After lingering together long enough to swap yarns and exchange news, the two parties continued on their separate ways.

As the company resumed its march, it followed the trail as it bore northwesterly for about another ten miles. The trail was traversing a naked landscape that was wide, dreary, and boring. Neither Bidwell nor Jimmy John estimated miles, but Dawson claimed that they had traveled twenty miles when they finally stopped to camp that night. This would suggest that their camp was where the trail again encountered the West Branch of Thirty-Two Mile Creek. The site is on Highway 74, one-half mile west of South Prosser Avenue, and about four miles west of the small community of Juniata, Nebraska. Out here, near the summit of the divide, the soil was sandy and the buffalo grass stunted and sparse. The stream was so small that it did not support trees. It ran intermittently, only after heavy rains. With the dry weather, it is no surprise that Bidwell groused about the bad water and scarcity of grass. But not all was dismal. Father Point was captivated by the wildflowers, what he called the *epinette des prairies*. He wrote that "The plains on which they bloom, when seen from a distance, seem to have no green at all; all is a yellow-gold, similar to the color of the narcissus in northern France."[39]

Bidwell and Jimmy John did not mention it, but the Reverend Williams reported passing some "Pawnee towns" after they had traveled six miles on May 31. This would have been near where the trail crossed Thirty-Two Mile Creek. If Pawnees were encamped nearby, it is surprising that no one reported being visited by them. While our diarists failed to express any alarm about their proximity, Frémont was worried about his expedition's safety when he crossed this divide in 1842. He described the area as the "range of the Pawnees, who were accustomed to infest this part of the country, stealing horses from companies on their way to the mountains, and, when in sufficient force, openly attacking and plundering them."[40]

Diarists in future wagon trains frequently expressed anxiety when they ran into small bands of destitute Pawnees who came forward to plead for handouts. But the emigrants were usually tight-fisted, reluctant to give away even a pound of flour, because they were unsure whether their food supplies would be enough to complete their journey. It could mean the difference between starvation and survival as they neared the end of their trip.

Chapter 6

Along the Platte River

JUNE 1 TO 15, 1841

June 1

About three miles beyond the company's May 31 camp, the trail led through a shallow basin in which a number of small pools of stagnant water were bordered by a few trees. Beyond, one could see a long, wavy line on the northern horizon. It was a narrow range of grass-covered sand hills. Over the ages, strong winds had been blowing enormous amounts of sand, grain by grain, out of the Platte River channel and depositing it along the border of the river valley. Upon reaching the summit of these sand hills, the company was greeted with a sweeping view of the Platte River Valley ahead. They could faintly see Grand Island, which was formed by the river dividing into two channels. The two channels created an elongated island almost fifty miles long and more than a mile wide. In the distance, the island appeared as a dark band because of the dense woods, mostly cottonwoods, that grew on it. The vegetation was protected from prairie fires by the channels on either side.

The Platte was unlike any river the travelers had ever seen. Father Point described it as "a river which, it is said, does not have an equal anywhere in the world."[1] Just upstream of Grand Island, before the river divided, the Platte was about a mile wide. But its waters were shallow and notoriously muddy, so muddy that some humorously described them as "too thick to drink and too thin to plow." Looking forward to a chance to get some laundry done, women in future years would frequently march to the edge of the river and then return in disgust, complaining that their clothing emerged from the murky river dirtier than when they had put it in.

The Platte was also a long river, originating deep in the Rockies. It emptied into the Missouri River below Council Bluffs and Bellevue. Here, it ran through a flat river valley that varied from three to four miles wide, and was about one hundred or more feet below the sand hills bordering it. Besides the wind, the valley had been scoured away over hundreds of thousands of years by the sluicing, meandering action of the water. The river pulsed, sometimes running high and wide when the winter snow packs melted or when there had been heavy rainstorms upstream. At other times, especially late in the fall or winter, the river flow would be greatly diminished, exposing countless sandbars and other broad sections of dry riverbed.

The travelers of the time would note how treeless the river banks were, although willows and small cottonwoods grew on the sandbars and islands within the main channel because they were protected from fire. As a result, wood was rarely available along the outside banks of the river. Anyone who wanted fuel for a campfire would have to wade over to a wooded island.

The wagon party descended from the sandy hills and lumbered across the wide river plain until it reached the banks of the south channel of the Platte near midday. Their encampment was about six miles northwest of present-day Kenesaw, Nebraska, and about where today's Road 42 crosses the south channel of the Platte River. When they set up camp on the afternoon of June 1, the company had been on the trail just short of three weeks and had marched 310 miles since leaving Independence.

Bidwell:

> *June, T. 1st. This morning we hastened to leave our miserable encampment and proceeding directly north, we reached Big Platte river about 12 o'clock—The heat was uncommonly oppressive. I here discovered the ground was in many places hoary with Glauber Salts, or at least I was unable to distinguish them by taste. This afternoon we had a soaking shower, which was succeeded by a heavy hailstorm. Wonderful! This evening a new family was created! Isaac Kelsey was married to Miss Williams, daughter of R. Williams. The marriage ceremony was performed by the Rev. Pr. Williams, so we now have five families if we include a widow and child.*

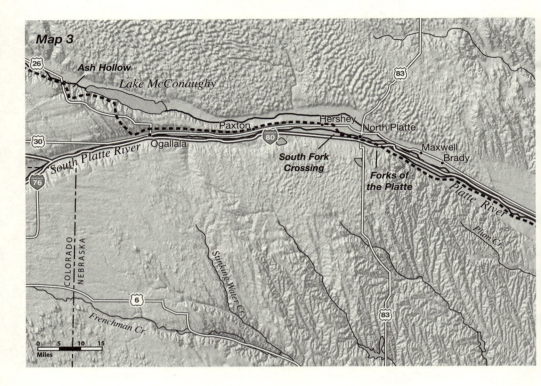

Map 3

The weary travelers had barely taken a deep breath upon reaching the Platte when unruly weather blew in from the southwest. A rainstorm, at last! Bidwell sounded delighted. It was refreshing and invigorating, and provided welcome relief from the "oppressive" heat about which he had been complaining. For the next week, the company would experience changed weather, and it would bring a different measure of discomfort and misery.

Jimmy John:

June 1—Left here. Encamped on the banks of the Platte at two o'clock. Here we encamped. There came up a small cloud, with the appearance of a light shower of rain. As it arose it grew darker. The thunder roared, the rain and hail came until the ground was covered with hail as large as partridge eggs, and some four times as large. The rain ceased a little while in the evening, but commenced again and rained nearly the whole

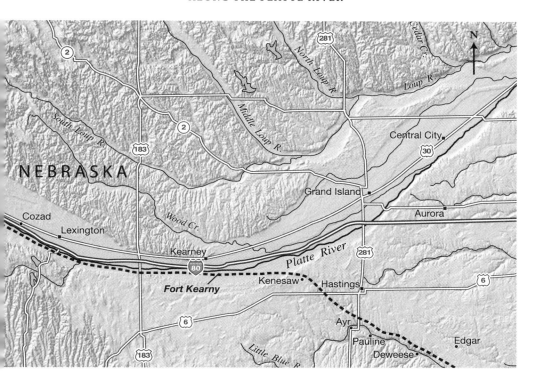

night. *The guards had a bad night for standing. All the baggage and every thing the rain could get at was in a dreadful condition in the morning, but as bad as the weather was there was a wedding in the camp this night—Mr. Kelsey to Miss Williams by Rev. Mr. Joseph Williams.*

It appears that a romance had been budding on the trail. The bachelor, Isaac Kelsey, had captured the affections of Richard Williams's daughter (not the Reverend Williams). Although the reverend had been called upon to join the couple in matrimony, his written account of the day did not focus on the ceremony. Rather, he was more interested in relating how the storm subjected them to a miserable night: "At 2 o'clock commenced a most tremendous bad storm, with wind, which blew down most of the tents, accompanied with rain and lightning and thunder almost all night. I slept but little, the ground being all covered with water. That night, dreadful oaths were heard all over the camp ground. O the wickedness of the wicked."[2]

June 2

Perhaps the discomforts of the storm had put people into a foul mood, because the morning of June 2 erupted in an outpouring of complaints that may have been festering for some time.

Bidwell:

> W. 2nd. This morning the company was convened for the purpose of taking a vote upon the question, whether the companies should continue to travel together? that some were complaining that the Missionaries went too fast; but the very thought of leaving Mr. Fitzpatrick who was so well acquainted with the Indians &c. &c. met, as it ought to have done, the disapprobation of all. We now proceeded directly up the river, making this day about twelve miles.

Oxen had their advantages, but speed was not one of them. Quick-stepping mules were capable of moving along at a brisk pace, while oxen tended to plod at about half their speed. As a result, wagons pulled by mules, including the missionaries' mule-drawn carts at the head of the caravan, could have easily pulled away from the ox-drawn wagons had they not been held back. Like a convoy of ships, a wagon train could only move as fast as the slowest. Those traveling in companies with ox-drawn wagons had to be patient, but patience has its limits. In future years, when a number of wagon companies were strung along the trail, slower-moving wagons often pulled over and waited for a company coming up from behind, while the fast-movers would hasten forward to join a company ahead. But in 1841, this solution was not available.

Despite the discord, Bidwell made it clear that everyone in his party was unwilling to separate from the missionary group because they did not wish to lose Fitzpatrick's services. His knowledge and experience, especially his way with the Indians, had clearly earned the respect of the company's members. Besides, Father De Smet was probably as reluctant to lose the protection of about fifty armed men as the Bartleson members were reluctant to lose the services of Fitzpatrick.

Jimmy John:

> *June 2—This morning a council was held for purpose of regulating the time of starting, which was agreed on to be at 30 minutes after six o'clock in the morning; but we did not [leave] early this morning on account of being so well drenched with rain and hail. The animals need no salt here. The ground is covered with salt for many places. We stopped today at noon near the head of Grand Island to dry our clothing. Went on about 12 miles and camped on the banks of the Platte.*

For the second day in a row, the trail traveled either across or near white beds of what Bidwell had called Glauber salts. They were likely patches of alkali or similar alkaline material. Under drier conditions, the finely powdered alkali would have been kicked up by hundreds of hooves and wagon wheels into suffocating clouds of dust that would have irritated the travelers' nostrils, lungs, and sweaty faces. However, the recent rain had suppressed the caustic dust.

If the company traveled twelve miles on June 2, as Jimmy John reported, they would have camped that afternoon at the head of Grand Island, where the Platte divided into its two channels. It was near here that Fort Kearny would be constructed in later years. The U.S. Army purchased the site from the Pawnee tribe for $2,000 in April 1848, and then commenced construction of the fort. Its purpose was to house a military garrison that would patrol this section of the trail and protect emigrant wagon companies from harassment by the Pawnees. Initially named Fort Childs, it was shortly thereafter renamed Fort Kearny (they misspelled it) to honor the recently deceased General Stephen Watts Kearney.[3] Restored and currently maintained by the State of Nebraska Department of Parks, Fort Kearny is well worth a visit.

Above the head of Grand Island, the Platte flowed as a single channel. In 1848, a young wagon driver by the name of William Anderson decided he would determine the river's width near here: "I had a curiosity to know something about the width of this river so I puled off my pants and waded to the opposite shore. In the deepest places I found it only about 3 feet deep. As I came back I steped it and found it to be over 2000 steps across [about a mile]."[4]

It was also near here that the trail from Council Bluffs and Bellevue crossed over from the north side of the Platte to join the Oregon Trail on its south bank. It was a good place to cross because of the river's uniformly shallow and firm bottom.

It is going to be difficult to identify the precise location of the company's campsites for the next six days. The Platte River Valley is flat and devoid of distinctive geographic features. Similar-looking sand hills border both sides of the river, with few significant creeks flowing into it. In addition, Bidwell and Jimmy John failed to record distances during four of these six days. Fortunately, Dawson recorded distances in his log for each of these days. Between striking the Platte on June 1 and passing the confluence of the South and North Forks of the Platte River on June 8, Dawson's log estimated they traveled 123 miles, while the actual distance between these two points is about 114 miles, meaning that he was overestimating his distances by an average of 8 percent.

June 3

Bidwell:

T. 3rd. Still continued up the river, traveled about 16 miles, rained in the afternoon.

Jimmy John:

June 3—This day went about 20 miles. Encamped on the Platte. There was another shower of rain today, and the air was cool.

All day the wagons and carts trundled steadily forward in close proximity to the Platte. Dawson's log and Jimmy John both agreed that they traveled twenty miles on June 3. Hence, it is likely that they camped about three miles east of today's Highway 183 and about a mile south of the present river channel.

Today, a traveler will see a changed landscape. While the area is quite beautiful, its appearance is different from what the emigrants of the 1840s and 1850s saw. What was once a flat, grassy river plain, interrupted by occasional alkali flats, is now irrigated farmland growing corn, alfalfa, and soybeans. Farmsteads, protected by lines of trees serving as windbreaks, stand between the broad fields. The once treeless bluffs are no longer treeless. Trees, often juniper, have gained a substantial foothold on the slopes because prairie fires have been suppressed during modern times. The river, once a mile wide, now usually spans less than a hundred yards because much of its waters are diverted upstream for irrigation and municipal uses and are held in check by a number of dams. Protected from regular fires, the riverbanks are no longer treeless, but are bordered by dense growths of cottonwood, willow, and underbrush. The old route of the trail ran close to the south bank of the old river, but because the river is so much narrower today, the route of the original trail averages almost a mile south of today's present channel.

June 4

June 4 would produce a memorable incident. After what seemed an eternity of boredom, the tedium would vanish in an instant. Nicholas Dawson was the precipitating character and he would relate the story from his perspective in his 1894 memoirs:

While we were in the Platte valley a little incident occurred that would give me a nickname for the rest of the journey. We were now in the country of hostile Indians, and Fitzpatrick had warned us to not stray beyond sight of the wagon train. But one day, curious to see the country that lay beyond a range of hills, I had ventured farther than usual, and coming upon a herd of antelope I, in my eagerness to get a shot at them, had followed them still farther. I was off my mule (I was riding "The Badger," one of our wagon mules) trying to creep near enough for a shot, when I was startled by an Indian whoop. I sprang upon my mule, but he perversely wheeled and ran toward the sound, I pulling desperately on the reins. Finally, I got his head in the direction I wanted to go, but no amount of urging could get that mule to hurry, and in an instant I was surrounded by Indians. One galloped by me and thrust a spear along my back, and motioned me to dismount. I did so. They seized my gun and knife, stripped me of my outer clothing, and taking my mule, left me. I hurried after our train, and overtaking it, told my story. The alarm spread along the line, and all was confusion. Fitzpatrick galloped back, calling out the horsemen as he came, and was off to find the Indians, and, if necessary, give them battle. I was very angry now and intent on vengeance, so hastily borrowing a horse and gun, I hurried after the party. I came on at full speed and was aiming at the first Indian within range, when I was stopped by some forcible language from Fitzpatrick, and perceived that Fitzpatrick and the Indians were engaged in a friendly powwow. It had proved to be a band of Cheyennes, friendly but thievish. They camped near us that night, and Fitzpatrick attempted to get back my property. He and I and the Indians sat around in a circle, and for every article to be returned, gifts of blankets, clothes, etc., had to be thrown down, a peace pipe smoked by all and much haranguing done. Fitzpatrick's patience gave out before all was got back, and declaring that I ought to be satisfied to have got off with my life, he refused to intercede further. I chaffed under my enforced friendliness, and after that, to distinguish me from another Dawson in the company known as Bear Dawson, I was called Cheyenne Dawson.[5]

What happened to Dawson was entirely his fault. He freely admitted that he had been warned against going off alone. Father Point's account confirmed that Fitzpatrick had frequently admonished everyone against it:

In spite of repeated warnings from the captain [Fitzpatrick], a young man of the party [Dawson] chose to go hunting for buffalo. He fell into the hands of a party of Indians who began by appropriating his gun and horse and ended by responding violently to his remonstrances. Very angry and chagrined by his misadventure, he returned to the camp and gave the cry of alarm. The campsite had already been chosen and the horses unsaddled when the cry reached our ears. In an instant, the horses were rebridled, resaddled, remounted, and ranged in a battle line. It was the colonel [Bartleson] who had ordered this maneuver. . . . The young man [Dawson] wanted to pounce upon the robbers without delay, killing everyone and smashing everything if his property was not returned. Already he had charged with raised gun and at such speed that he failed to notice that his hat blew off. Fortunately, he was pursued by our captain [Fitzpatrick], a man of good sense as well as of spirit, who had a great deal of experience behind him. By great good fortune, he was readily recognized by the Indians because of his white hair. And very soon there was no question of fighting, but only of friendship, provided restitution was made. Our young man learned that, even with Indians, calm reason accomplishes more than force or anger.[6]

In contrast to Dawson's and the priest's account, which were written fifty years and twenty years after the event, Bidwell's and Jimmy John's journal entries were contemporaneous.

Bidwell:

F. 4th. Half past six this morning saw us on the march, the valley of the river here was about 4 miles wide, antelope were seen in abundance—A young man (Dawson) was out hunting, when suddenly a band of Chienne [Cheyenne] Indians about 40 in number came upon him; they were pleased to strip him of his mule, gun and pistol, and let him go. He had no sooner reached the camp and related the news than the whole band, came in sight; We hastened to form a Carrel (yard) with our waggons, but it was done in great haste. To show you how it effected the green ones, I will give the answer, I received from a stout, young man (and he perhaps was but one of 30 in the same situation), when I asked him, how many Indians there were? he answered with a trembling voice, half scared out of his wits, there were lots, gaubs, fields and swarms of them!!!. I do really believe he thought there were some thousands, lo! there were but 40, perfectly friendly, delivered up every article taken, but the Pistol.

Jimmy John:

June 4—Today we started early. Traveled briskly along the banks of the Platte until in the afternoon, when some of our men scattered out from the Company to hunt antelope. One of them being alone, slipping along to get a shot at an antelope, was surrounded by a band of Shina [Cheyenne] Indians and robbed of his mule, gun and pistol. They tried to get his clothing off him, but he tore loose from them. He came up with the Company and informed the captain of the circumstance. Immediately part of the Company were sent back to recover the property. The Indians came, meeting them. The teamsters hastened to put their wagons in order [of] battle. Some were panic struck. They saw the Indians coming, 30 in number,—appeared to them to be an army of thousands. When, lo! 30 Indians came and brought the property and restored it to the Company. They were very friendly. They came to our camp, shook hands and smoked the pipe of peace and encamped about 50 yards from us this night.

Bidwell retold the story in his memoirs, recalling that Dawson ran up to the wagon train on foot "frightened to death," and crying that "there are thousands of them." Bidwell also recalled that everyone fell into a shameful panic:

Then commenced a general stampede for the Platte River, distant about three miles. The women and children were crying and screaming. Oxen and mules were put to the gallop and we all went pell-mell for the river. In this race for life, as we thought, no need was taken for the hindmost; it was each for himself. Captain Fitzpatrick did all that he could to stop the party. He [said] we were cowards, that if the Indians were hostile and should see us running, they would be sure to kill us. They ought to, he said, if we were such fools as to run. Up to this time, no one except Dawson, the scared man, had seen any Indians. On reaching the river, Captain Fitzpatrick had all the wagons formed into a circle with the animals securely staked inside. In the course of half an hour the Indians came in sight. They proved to be a friendly party of Cheyenne Indians.[7]

The company received a stern tongue-lashing from Fitzpatrick for their behavior, according to Bidwell. There was a correct way for a company to conduct itself when an Indian party approached, and the way this company behaved, especially how everyone "was each for himself," was both disgraceful and dangerous.

Bidwell added a few more details in one of his recollections: After the Cheyenne set up their own camp within a hundred yards of the wagon party, Fitzpatrick and the hunter John Gray went to them and communicated in sign language. The Cheyenne claimed that they did not intend to harm Dawson, but had to disarm him because he was so excited that they feared for their safety. Yet, no explanation was offered as to why they also relieved him of his mule and some of his clothing.

The foregoing accounts described a chaotic scene. After so many uneventful days, perhaps the company had been lulled into an attitude of security and complacency. When Dawson, missing some of his clothing, came running up with cries of "Indians," the people simply lost their composure. It suggested a lack of training about how to respond to a sudden Indian threat. Fitzpatrick may have been a good teacher, but his students appeared to have forgotten their lessons. It brings to mind what a famous boxer once said: "Everybody has a plan until they get punched in the mouth."[8]

Josiah Belden's memoirs recalled that "We saw a body of Indians coming up full charge in our rear as though intending to attack us."[9] After Fitzpatrick talked to their chief in sign language, Belden recalled that the chief called off the attack. Belden also thought that the war party numbered fifty to sixty and that they had been on the prowl for Pawnees. A number of sources related that Fitzpatrick began negotiating the return of Dawson's property. After mentioning that members of the company traded tobacco and beads to the Cheyenne, Belden did not explain what they received in trade. Perhaps it was nothing more than some of Dawson's lost property. The Cheyenne impressed Belden, who described them as "the finest looking body of men I ever saw for Indians."[10]

Nancy Kelsey, one of only three women in the party, related very little about the trip in her memoirs, but one of the few things she did mention was her condemnation of Dawson for racing back to the wagon train and thereby fecklessly leading the Cheyenne to the wagons. The only thing that had dissuaded the Cheyenne from attacking them, in her opinion, was the strength of the wagon company.[11]

Father Point described the Cheyenne, recalling that they carried bows, arrows, and a few guns. Their faces were painted blue, red, white, yellow, and black, and their hair was long, braided, and adorned with feathers. Their clothing was ornamented with glass beads and porcupine quills.[12]

Each account provided different details and perspectives, some in conflict. Bidwell described the Cheyenne as "perfectly friendly," and Jimmy John called them "very friendly." But Josiah Belden recalled that they were not friendly at all. How many were in the Cheyenne party? Was it 30, 40, 50, 60? Reverend Williams's account of the incident added nothing remarkable except that he thought they were "Sioux Indians." Differences like these make it difficult to separate fact from exaggeration or faulty recall.

There must have been an "I told you so" moment. After Fitzpatrick had repeatedly warned everyone to not stray far from the wagons alone, Dawson had defied the warnings anyway. It is difficult to offer much sympathy to the frequently warned Dawson. To make matters worse, the young man's overreactions were rash and potentially fatal. To make the situation even more explosive, Father Point recalled that Bartleson got the men mounted and "ranged in battle line." That, coupled with Dawson's hot-blooded charge at the Cheyennes, suggest that if Fitzpatrick had not been there, hot tempers on one side were bound to have been matched with equally hot eruptions on the other. The scene could have played out drastically different. Someone needed to take control and keep the situation from boiling over. Thankfully, it was Fitzpatrick. Better than most, he understood the importance of avoiding a fight, despite the emotions. It was not worth it, even if you prevailed, to have any of your own wounded or killed. Bidwell, in his memoirs, recognized Fitzpatrick's value. "[W]hen we came in contact with the Indians, our people were so easily excited that if we had not had with us an old mountaineer [Fitzpatrick] the result would certainly have been disastrous."[13]

This was Fitzpatrick at his best. His approach kept a combustible situation from getting out of hand. Negotiating with Indians was a delicate art. You had to know when to flatter and when to insult, when to advance and when to retreat, when to cajole and when to threaten. Fitzpatrick's far-flung reputation among the Indians probably helped as well. A lesser man than Fitzpatrick would have told Dawson that he deserved what had happened and would not have lifted his tiniest finger on his behalf. Despite having every reason to abandon Dawson to his losses, Fitzpatrick did what he could. The reputed harmonizer stepped forward to avert misunderstanding and hostilities, even if there was the suggestion that the recovery of some of Dawson's stolen property may have come at a cost equal to or exceeding the value of what was recovered. Fitzpatrick acted as a skilled mediator, balancing the injured feelings of an irresponsible hothead against an Indian culture that saw nothing dishonorable about relieving a careless fool of his possessions. The incident could not help bolstering Fitzpatrick's widely known reputation for handling tense Indian situations with aplomb, and would burnish his credentials as an "Indian whisperer."

Pack mule trains or a few wagons involved in supplying the fur trade had tramped along this trail only a couple of times each year. As of 1841, a company of almost twenty covered wagons and carts would have been unprecedented. It is likely that many of these Cheyenne braves were entranced, having never seen a spectacle such as this before.

Like the Sioux, the Cheyenne were not native to the Great Plains, having migrated from Minnesota many years earlier. Without the benefits of horses and guns, the Cheyenne had originally lived in Minnesota in permanent villages and subsisted on the crops they raised and the small game they bagged while hunting on foot with bows and arrows. In the 1700s, however, the nearby Chippewa tribe, supplied with guns by the French, began driving both the Sioux and Cheyenne tribes westward and out of Minnesota. By about 1780 the Sioux and Cheyenne had both migrated across the Missouri River and onto the open plains of the Dakotas.[14] By the early 1800s, both tribes had moved into the Black Hills of South Dakota and adapted to a new way of life. They had learned how to keep and ride horses. This allowed them to follow the buffalo herds and hunt them on horseback. This enabled them to transition from permanent, farming-based villages along rivers to classic nomadic camps in which they lived in movable, buffalo skin–covered tepees.

It is uncertain where this Cheyenne war party had come from. At the time, Cheyenne villages were known to have been located in and around the Black Hills of South Dakota, along the South Fork of the Platte River, and west of Fort Laramie.[15] It would not be surprising if the Cheyenne were looking for Pawnees. Like most other plains tribes, the Cheyenne had developed a malignant hatred of them. As an example of the especially incendiary nature of the Pawnee's deeds, they had once captured the Cheyenne tribe's sacred Medicine Arrows.[16] In another instance, they had captured a young Cheyenne girl and killed her as a human sacrifice to the Morning Star.[17]

The Dawson incident brings into sharp focus how the behavior of Indians toward whites was often dictated by the circumstances. While Fitzpatrick's reputation may have played a role in squelching any intent to attack, it is also possible that the warriors surveyed the circumstances and calculated that it would be unwise to attack a party of about seventy heavily armed men. So they put on their friendly, smiling faces. Had they thought they had the upper hand, their actions could have been different. Whether his opinion was valid or not, Oregon-bound emigrant J. Quinn Thornton expressed the view in his 1846 diary that relative strength was a huge factor in Indian conduct: "Indians are generally cowards; and they will seldom fight without a decided advantage in numbers, weapons or position."[18]

Fitzpatrick had a couple of Indian encounters the following year that shed further light on this phenomenon. He was at Fort Laramie in 1842 when Dr. Elijah White arrived with his Oregon-bound wagon party. Dr. White hired Fitzpatrick to escort his party as far as Fort Hall. While en route, near Independence Rock, a combined war party of about three hundred Sioux and Cheyenne intercepted the wagon train with the intent of killing all the whites. Fitzpatrick rode out to meet the leaders of the war party and somehow induced them to let the party resume its travels in safety. Was there any magic Fitzpatrick could not perform in dealing with Indians? But there is more to the story. After safely delivering Dr. White's wagon party as far as Fort Hall, Fitzpatrick began his return trip to Missouri, traveling with only one companion. Fitzpatrick later wrote to the superintendent of Indian affairs in St. Louis, describing his experiences. He acknowledged that the danger of traveling undermanned caused him and his friend to alter their route to avoid the Sioux and Cheyenne.

Yet, nearing home, they had pushed their luck too far and found themselves surrounded by a party of Pawnees. They were rudely relieved of their guns and possessions.[19]

It is ironic that Fitzpatrick, of all people, ignored the principle of traveling strong during his return trip in 1842. It appears that his esteemed reputation among the Indians protected him only so far. The outcomes may have been more dependent on how many well-armed men he had to back him up.

Given that the day had provided a terrible scare, it is understandable that both Bidwell and Jimmy John neglected to record how far they had traveled on June 4. We can thank Dawson, the young man who had been but one step away from disaster, for not ignoring the issue. His log estimated that they traveled fifteen miles that day. If he was correct, it would suggest that the company encountered the Cheyenne and camped near the intersection of today's A Road and 748 Road, about nine miles southeast of Lexington, Nebraska.

June 5

Upon returning to the trail early in the morning of June 5, the company continued up the long, wide Platte River Valley. About three miles after departing camp they crossed Plum Creek, a small, low-flow stream that entered the Platte from the south. The Reverend Williams described this stretch as traveling "along smooth banks, without any timber."[20]

June 5 would be another memorable day. They were now entering buffalo country and would spot their first buffalo herd roaming gloriously in the distance, even though it was on the north side of the river. In earlier years, one did not have to travel so far west to first encounter the great herds. In 1804, for example, Lewis and Clark spotted their first buffalo near where the Platte emptied into the Missouri River.[21] It was now thirty-seven years later, and the herds of the lower Platte River Valley had been effectively slaughtered into extinction. One would now have to travel up the Platte about two hundred and fifty miles before encountering the first significant herds.

Bidwell:

> S. 5th. Started early to get clear of our red visitors—descried a large herd of Buffalo on the opposite side of the river—saw several Boats descending the river, laden with fur, robes, &c, they belonged to the American Fur Company—one of our Company E. Stone returned with them—the latter part of the day was very inclement, high winds, dark clouds rushed in wild confusion around and above us, soon with amazement we saw a lofty water spout, towering like a huge Column to support the arch of the sky; and while we were moving with all haste lest it should pass over us and dash our wagons to pieces, it moved off with the swiftness of the wind and was soon lost among the Clouds—Rain & hail succeeded, the largest hail stones I ever saw, several were found, an hour after the sun came out bright & warm, larger than a turkey egg—9 of the Indians that left us this morning, returned this evening.

Jimmy John:

> June 5—This morning we set out before sunrise. Stopped at 7 o'clock for breakfast. We seen six flat bottom boats land a little below us on the river. Some of their crews came to us and informed us that they were from Fort Laramie, and that we were about 400 miles from that place. We seen numerous herds of buffalo today on the opposite side of the river from us, and have killed two antelope today. There came a tremendous hail and rain storm this afternoon. The wind blew very hard where we were, and on the opposite side of the river it blew tremendous. We saw trees flying in the air and water blowing up out of the river as high apparently as the clouds. After the storm had abated somewhat we traveled about a mile farther and found hail stones as large as geese eggs. We made a very lucky escape not to be in the midst of it, but there were some large hail where we were. We went on and encamped again on the banks of the Platte. We had not more than got our tent spread before another storm of the same kind came on and lasted until night, leaving the ground covered with hail. It drowned out all the fires in the camp, and wet most of our baggage, and left us in an unpleasant situation.

The Cheyenne war party had camped near the company the previous night. Although the previous day's experience with the Indians had ended well, members of the company must have still been nervous about the warriors' intentions and the fickleness of their moods. Wariness and suspicion must have hung over the camp during the night and it is likely that the night guards were more vigilant than usual. There was something about the Cheyenne party that prompted Bidwell to write on June 5 that the company "started early to get clear of our red visitors."

Bidwell might have written more about their first significant buffalo sighting if it had not been for the storm they experienced on June 5. The prairie was notorious for the fury and suddenness of its spring and summer storms. Described as fierce, with raging winds, egg-sized hailstones, and a terrifying tornado that raised a waterspout as it crossed the river, the storm left a lasting impression. Bidwell included an extensive description of it in his memoirs:

> On the Platte River, on the afternoon of one of the hottest days we experienced on the plains, we had a taste of a cyclone: first came a terrific shower, followed by a fall of hail to the depth of four inches, some of the stones being as large as turkey's eggs.; and . . . a waterspout—an angry, huge, whirling cloud column, which seemed to draw its water from the Platte River—passed within a quarter of a mile behind us. We stopped and braced ourselves against our wagons to keep them from being over turned. Had it struck us it doubtless would have demolished us.[22]

The tornado also made an impression on Father De Smet, because he described it in detail in a letter he wrote about a month after the event:

> A spiral abyss seemed to be suddenly formed in the air. The clouds followed each other into it with such velocity, that they attracted all objects around them. . . . The spiral column moved majestically towards the North, and alighted on the surface of the Platte. Then, another scene was exhibited to our view. The waters, agitated by its powerful action, began to turn round with frightful noise, and were suddenly drawn up to the clouds in a spiral form. The column appeared to measure a mile in height; and such was the violence of the winds which came down in a perpendicular direction, that in the twinkling of an eye the trees were torn and uprooted, and their boughs scattered in every direction.[23]

The second storm, less spectacular, arrived that evening. Rain came down in heavy sheets, and they spent a wretched night. Wet to the skin, miserably cold, and unable to find a dry place on the ground, they found it difficult to sleep.

It is unfortunate that not more was written about the company's encounter with the American Fur Company employees who were transporting pelts and skins down the Platte in six flat-bottomed boats. Fitzpatrick had once been a partner in the Rocky Mountain Fur Company, a former and failed rival of the cutthroat AFC. It seems certain that Fitzpatrick would have conversed with these men, and it would have been fascinating to listen in and see if they talked about old times and exchanged gossip about mutual acquaintances.

According to Dawson's log, they traveled eighteen miles on June 5, which, if correct, suggested that they camped about six miles west of Lexington, Nebraska, in the vicinity of Road 755, about one mile south of its intersection with Interstate 80.

June 6

Bidwell:

> S. 6th. This morning was extremely cool for the season, 25 more of the same Indians came up with us.

Jimmy John:

> June 6th—This morning we set out early, accompanied by 12 Indians, who encamped with us. They were of the Chian [Cheyenne] nation; they traveled and encamped with us perhaps for protection from the Pawnees. This day we killed 3 elk. The weather was cool until twelve o'clock; then it turned warm, and rained at night. We encamped this night on the banks of the Platte. The Indians left today.

While neither diarist estimated the distance they traveled on June 6, Dawson's log estimated that they traveled twenty miles that day. If that was true, the approximate location of their camp that evening would have been near today's Highway 47, about one mile south of its intersection with Interstate 80, and south of Gothenburg, Nebraska.

June 7

Bidwell:

> M. 7th. Three Indians continued with us, the wind blew very hard towards evening—3 buffalo were killed and part of their meat was brought to the camp.

Jimmy John:

> *June 7th—Started at 7 o'clock this morning. Travelled almost 20 miles today and encamped on the banks of a small creek. The hunters killed two buffalos today. The captain sends out a small party of men every day by turn for the purpose of killing meat for the company. We had another storm of rain and wind this evening, but not very much rain.*

Later emigrants often complained about huge swarms of mosquitoes and gnats that rose up from the grass bordering this stretch of river, but neither Bidwell nor Jimmy John mentioned them. The cool and windy weather undoubtedly suppressed the troublesome pests.

Based on Jimmy John's estimated miles, the company's encampment on the night of June 7 would have been near today's Fort McPherson National Cemetery on Highway 56A, about two miles south of the highway's intersection with Interstate 80.

According to Dawson's memoirs, Romain, the English gentleman who had joined the expedition to hunt wild game, had accompanied John Gray, the company's principal hunter, on his buffalo hunting excursions. On one occasion Romain managed to get himself lost in the trackless, featureless high plains. Since he had not returned by nightfall, Gray had to go find him.[24] Even though Jimmy John reported "small parties" of hunters venturing out to kill buffalo, it is likely that these parties were limited to the most experienced hunters, men such as Gray, Charles Hopper, and perhaps Romain. They only needed to kill a few buffalo to supply the expedition with an ample supply of meat. Killing more would have been for sport only. Buffalo hunting was a dangerous activity, and most of the members of the company were terribly unqualified to engage in such a perilous activity. If someone intended to hunt buffalo, he did it from his horse. A wounded buffalo tended to turn and charge and a horse was better able to escape than a man on foot. Furthermore, only certain horses had the aptitude and training required to gallop precariously beside a panic-stricken herd, and be alert and agile enough to avoid calamity if a buffalo suddenly wheeled on them. In addition, the plains were riddled with prairie dog burrows and creased with narrow gullies into which a galloping horse could stumble, break a leg, and throw its rider. Despite the possibility that many members of the company clamored for the opportunity to go on a hunting spree, Fitzpatrick may have prohibited it to keep these greenhorns from getting killed or injured.

June 8

Bidwell's entry for June 8 was unusually reflective and insightful:

> T. 8th. There were 8 or 10 Buffalo killed to day, but not one tenth of the meat was used, the rest was left to waste upon the Prairie. In the afternoon we passed the confluence of the N. & S. forks of Platte River & encamped, having come about 18 miles, many hundreds of Buffalo were seen at this place. The scenery of the Country on the Platte is rather dull and monotonous, but there are some objects which must ever attract the attention of the observant traveler; I mean the immense quantity of Buffalo bones, which are every where strewed with great profusion, so that the Valley, throughout its whole length and breadth, is nothing but one complete slaughter yard; where the noble animals used to graze, ruminate and multiply in uncounted thousands—but they are fast diminishing. If they continue to decrease in the same ratio that they have for the past 15 or 20 years, they will ere long become totally extinct. It has been but a few years since they left the frontier of Missouri, and are now fast retreating towards the Rocky Mountains. The Indians are anxious to preserve them, and it is said of them that they never kill as long as they have meat remaining, but behold with indignation that shameful and outrageous prodigality of the whites, who slaughter thousands merely for their robes and leave the meat, which is far more delicious than that of tame Cattle, to waste, or be eaten by Wolves & vultures.

Jimmy John:

> June 8th—This day we killed some four buffaloes and a few rabbits and encamped in the evening on the south fork of the Platte river. The buffaloes are very plenty here. We have seen several herds today consisting of perhaps some hundreds.

They were now approaching the "Forks," where the South Fork and North Fork of the Platte River joined. The immense grasslands of this region were where large buffalo herds of from five hundred to one thousand animals ranged. As beaver trapping declined, many fur trappers had become buffalo hunters to meet the growing demand for hides. Enormous numbers of buffalo were killed where only the hides and tongues were taken, while the rest of the carcass was left to the wolves and vultures. What the scavengers could not eat was left to rot. It was rare to see a herd of buffalo without also noticing one or more packs of wolves shadowing it, waiting to pounce on any lame, sick, or dead animal.

In his 1845 *Report*, Frémont mentioned that from 1834 to 1842, the hide-trading companies, which included the American Fur Company, had been hauling about 90,000 buffalo hides annually out of the plains. Frémont estimated that the hides were removed from only a third of the buffalo killed. If he was correct, it meant that the hunters were killing about 270,000 buffalo each year.[25]

Bidwell also described the "immense quantity of buffalo bones" found here as evidence of the slaughter that had been going on for a few years. In the future, innovative emigrants would leave messages to friends traveling behind them by scribbling notes on the foreheads of these bleached skulls and then mounting them on sticks driven into the ground beside the trail.[26]

Experts have estimated that there were still about 35 million buffalo roaming the West as of 1840, down significantly from earlier numbers.[27] An annual kill of 270,000 looks like a large number. But a harvest at that level might have been sustainable, given all of the offspring that millions of females would have produced each year. Despite Bidwell's fears, the vast buffalo herds in the area proved to be remarkably resilient for a number of years. During the 1840s, emigrant wagon parties trundling through here would hunt them for meat, but it was only during one month out of the year. The total killed by emigrants would hardly put a dent in the population. In 1842, when about forty miles east of the Forks, Frémont described buffalo as "swarming in immense numbers over the plains."[28] When James Clyman reached the Forks in 1844, he "found the Buffalo in great Quantities."[29] Perhaps with some exaggeration, Francis Parkman reported in 1846 that when his companions returned from a hunt in the Forks region they claimed that they had seen "millions of buffalo."[30] As late as 1848, one California-bound emigrant, Edward Smith, wrote in his diary that he saw "innumerable swarms of Buffalo" near their camp eighteen miles west of the Forks.[31] But it was the hordes of Gold Rushers who began streaming through here in 1849, and the large brigades of professional buffalo hunters who came later, that changed everything. In any event, Bidwell's worry that these immense herds south of the South Platte were eventually doomed was a farsighted perception that was impressive for someone so young.

While Bidwell was condemning the profligate hunting practices of the hide takers, it is ironic that the hunters of the Bartleson company were killing more buffalo than they needed. In one of his later memoirs, Bidwell reported, "[O]ur people began to kill them just to get the tongues and marrow bones, leaving all the rest of the meat on the plains for the wolves to eat."[32]

Bidwell recorded that the company traveled eighteen miles on June 8, passing the confluence of the two Forks that afternoon. He did not specify how many miles beyond the confluence they traveled before stopping to set up camp. Assuming that they traveled about three more hours before calling it a day, and traveling at a pace of about two and a half miles per hour, they would have stopped about eight miles upstream of the Forks. In that event, their camp on the south bank of the South Fork would have been just north of today's Interstate 80, and about five miles west of its interchange with Highway 83, near the current town of North Platte, Nebraska.

June 9

The next morning, just north of their camp, the company commenced fording the South Fork, perhaps not realizing at first that it would be an all-day endeavor.

Bidwell:

> W. 9th. Spent the day in crossing the S. fork of Platte—a Buffalo was killed from a herd that came within 300 yards of the Camp. We crossed the river by fording the water being sufficiently shallow—width of river here about ⅔ of a mile—its waters are muddy like those of the Missouri.

Jimmy John:

> June 9th—Today we crossed the river at the same place we encamped at last evening. The river being wide we occupied nearly the whole day in crossing. It is about 14 hundred yards wide here and has a sandy bed. The water is of the same culler [color] as that of the Missourie. We have seen, I believe, a thousand buffaloes today. We have killed 2 of them today. We forded the river with our loaded wagons, which were 19 in number. The bottom is so level that the water is about three feet deep nearly all the way across. We encamped this night on the opposite side to where we lay last night.

Neither Bidwell nor Jimmy John went into any detail regarding the crossing, even though it must have been a tense experience. To cross a river almost a mile wide, with sections of quicksand concealed beneath the muddy water, the drivers had to keep their mules and oxen moving briskly to keep them from being swallowed up.

Emigrants in future years would describe their South Fork crossing, often mentioning how the water was deep enough to swirl around the oxen's necks and make them nervous. It could seep through leaky wagon boxes and soak their supplies and bedding. The water could even get the wagons dangerously close to floating, something that needed to be avoided. Top-heavy and with canvas tops, covered wagons were susceptible to tipping over in a strong gust. One can picture frightened mothers clutching their children and praying that their unsteady wagons would not dump them into the river.

While Bidwell provided few details in his journal entry about the crossing, he had more to say about it later in his memoirs. "The ford was deep but only by putting our efforts on the top of the wagon beds that we managed to keep them dry."[33] He also explained that some teams and wagons, better at making the journey across, were called upon to make multiple trips to carry the freight that other teams and wagons could not or would not carry.

Father Point's account of the crossing explained in detail how they kept the wagons from tipping over:

> While the driver lashed away at the beasts from his seat, others, on horseback or wading on foot on either side of the wagon, shouted and whipped them, to keep the vehicle in motion as well as to prevent it from being turned aside. For greater security a number of ropes were tied to the top of the wagon and held taut by men placed at some distance in the river to help preserve equilibrium. The water and the cattle roared, the horses neighed, the men shouted in an earsplitting fashion. I have never heard such an uproar. Nevertheless, strange as it may seem, the crossing was made almost without mishap.[34]

It was here, when the company crossed the South Platte, that someone finally mentioned that dogs were traveling with the company. Father Point recalled: "The most sorely inconvenienced members of the expedition were the poor dogs. How they ran to and fro on the bank! How piteous they yelped! Most of them remained on the first bank. Finally, the most daring ones prompted the others to venture into the treacherous element and with great effort they all

Crossing the South Platte, *by William Henry Jackson. Catalog No. SCBL-23. Courtesy of Scotts Bluff National Monument.*

had the good fortune to be able to rejoin the camp."[35] It is curious that no one ever mentioned dogs again, making us wonder what happened to them and when.

Jimmy John had reported that nineteen wagons forded the South Fork, the same number reported when the Chiles party joined the company at Black Vermillion Creek. There had been no recent reports of breakdowns or abandoned wagons, so it appears that the wagons and carts had been holding up well. There had also been no reports of any oxen or mules being lost to injury, drowning, illness, exhaustion, or theft. Despite experiencing a few dangers recently, the company appeared to be traveling under the blessings of good fortune.

Since the crossing must have left the people and livestock exhausted, Jimmy John indicated that they set up camp immediately after crossing the river. Their camp would have been about five miles west of the present-day town of North Platte, Nebraska, and about a mile south of Highway 30 near where North Front Road turns into West Front Road.

There were many locations along the South Fork that were fordable, but in the early years, wagon parties tended to cross at or near where Fitzpatrick had crossed in 1841. James Clyman's diary of 1844 indicated that his wagon party crossed the South Fork near the same spot.[36] In 1845, Joel Palmer's party crossed about five or six miles above the Forks, also near the spot of the 1841 crossing.[37] In later years, wagon trains tended to travel farther up the South Fork and primarily used two crossing points. One crossing was about twenty miles above the Forks (four miles west of today's Hershey, Nebraska), the other about sixty-five miles above the Forks (four miles west of Brule, Nebraska).[38] The Brule crossing became the most heavily used, especially during the Gold Rush years. One of the better places to see evidence of wagon ruts and swales is just west of Brule. From Brule travel west four and a half miles on Highway 30, then turn right onto Road West MN. Marks can be seen in the one-mile section just north of Highway 30, where the ruts angle from the east side to the west side of the road.

June 10

With the river crossing on June 9 leaving the travelers drained, they must have slept soundly that night. Perhaps too soundly, for they woke up on the morning of June 10 to another maddening development.

Bidwell:

> T. 10. This morning most of the Oxen were again at large, owing to the neglect of the Owners to the great danger of losing them by the Indians and by their mingling with Buffalo, or by their straying so far that it would be impossible to track them on account of the innumerable tracks of the Buffalo—making therefore, rather a late start, we continued to ascend the river on the N. side—We traveled about 14 miles and encamped on the river, Buffalo were seen in countless thousands on the opposite side of the river; from the time we began to journey this morning till we ceased to travel at night; the whole south side of the stream was completely clouded by these huge animals, grazing in the valley and on the hills— ruminating upon the margin of the river, or crowding down its banks for water. Through the remissness of the sentinels, the guard last night was nearly vacant; and as this was considered dangerous ground on account of the warlike Pawnees, Chiennes &c., a Court Martial was called to force those to their duty on guard, who were so negligent & remiss.

Something was terribly wrong here. While straying oxen had been problematic when the company first began their journey, we had not heard of animals straying during the last two weeks. Lightning, thunder, and hail were known to spook oxen and cause them to scatter in panic. The company had experienced some extreme weather recently, but no one reported that it had scattered their animals. The night guard problem seemed to have been solved. Yet, for some reason, the oxen had scattered again during the night of June 10. And it was not due to a storm. Even though Bidwell mentioned that thievish Indians were a risk, he also mentioned that oxen were inclined to run off and join their shaggy, brown-haired cousins when given a chance. Indeed, emigrants often wrote about finding their missing oxen grazing peacefully in the midst of a herd of buffalo.

Father Point explained at the beginning of the trip that everyone was expected to share in the duty of standing guard: "From the moment when the camp retired until the break of day, all the travelers, including the priests, stood watch according to roster in order to guard against surprise attack."[39] The Reverend Williams had recently suggested that they were still following this routine: "All this time, I had to stand guard every fourth night."[40] Bidwell assigned the blame in this incident to the dereliction of the night guards, which, strangely enough, he said were the oxen owners, the people with the most to lose. Of all people, this group should have been the most determined to keep a close eye on their animals, and they should have been the least likely to be neglectful.

Williams's account included his comment that Indians were being blamed: "This morning there was a great alarm given that the Indians had driven off some of the oxen, and our men went in pursuit of them, and brought them back. One man said he saw an Indian and shot at him, but some did not believe him."[41] This suggests that some doubted the Indian story, perhaps because it may have been concocted by the neglectful parties to exonerate themselves. But Indians could have been involved. After all, some of the Cheyenne had continued to travel with the company. Was it their plan to wait for an opportunity to steal oxen? Why would they steal oxen when there were so many buffalo to hunt in the region? One might argue that it impresses your peers far more if you make off with another's animals, whether from a rival tribe or from a party of white men, than if you simply charge into a buffalo herd and shoot a couple of arrows. Another possibility is that the oxen had wandered off under the neglectful noses of the night guards, after which Indians in the area came across them and invoked the time-honored principle of "finders keepers, losers weepers."

So how was Fitzpatrick reacting to this recurring problem of straying oxen? Dr. Wislizenus had described Fitzpatrick in 1839 as a man of "strong passions." Does this suggest that he would not have taken this recurring problem calmly? Was he fuming? Despite his skill and knowledge, he could not be everywhere, doing everyone else's job. He had to depend on others to be at their stations. He had issued stern warnings about not wandering off alone, and had stressed the necessity of dependable night guarding. Yet, it appeared that some were not good at taking orders.

The successful management of a wagon train required certain qualities in its leadership. There must be unquestioned confidence in the guide's knowledge and decisions, as well as a tangible fear of displeasing him. Of the former, there can be little doubt that they all had confidence in Fitzpatrick, but whether they feared him is unknown. After all, what could he do? We must remember that Fitzpatrick was employed by the missionaries as their guide and, to our knowledge, he was not employed by the Bartleson company. Even though the company had adopted rules during its organizational meeting on May 19, we do not know what those rules were. Fitzpatrick may not have had any disciplinary authority over the company's members. Bidwell reported earlier about a "court martial being called," but he did not identify the alleged slackers. We were not informed whether the proceeding was held and, if so, who conducted the proceedings and what its outcome was. If Fitzpatrick's hands were tied, that could explain why some of the more headstrong, independent, or contrary personalities felt free to ignore or defy him. Another possibility is that Fitzpatrick simply did not care, figuring that these people's oxen were not his problem: let them deal with it.

Jimmy John:

> *June 10th—This day was pleasant. We traveled about 25 miles today; killed but one buffalo, but was in sight of them all day. The river banks were lined with them. We can kill as many as we want. We encamped this evening on the banks of the south fork of the Platte. The plains here are sandy. The river has a level plain on each side; next to the plains there is on each side a ridge of sand hills.*

Oddly, Jimmy John's journal did not mention the straying oxen or anything about a court martial. The company evidently tracked down the missing animals and resumed their travel after a late start.

Although they proceeded up the north side of the South Fork, it is difficult to determine how many miles they traveled that day. Bidwell reported traveling fourteen, Jimmy John twenty-five, and Dawson twenty. That is quite a disparity. If we take their average—twenty miles—then the company would have camped along the north side of the South Fork, about ten miles west of today's Sutherland, Nebraska, and near Highway 30.

While these enormous buffalo herds were a wonder to gaze upon, they also represented a great danger. Crazed with thirst after grazing all day on the hot, waterless plains above the river, they would return to the river at the end of the day as a thundering mass, sometimes at stampede speed. If a wagon party had the misfortune of finding itself between them and the river, it had no choice but to try to stop or divert them. While Bidwell did not mention the following incident in his journal, he did in one of his memoirs:

> *One night when we were encamped on the south fork at the Platte they came in such droves that we had to sit up and fire guns and make what fires we could to keep them from running over us and trampling us into the dust. We were obliged to go out some distance from the camp to turn them; Captain Fitzpatrick told us that if we did not do this the buffaloes in front could not turn aside for the pressure of those behind . . . and if they had not been diverted, wagons, animals, and emigrants would have been trodden under their feet. One cannot nowadays describe the rush and wildness of the thing.*[42]

In the years to come, a number of wagon trains would be overrun by herds of buffalo on their way to the river because the emigrants did not have an experienced man like Thomas Fitzpatrick showing them how to avert disaster.

The expedition was also traveling through an area devoid of firewood. Because of the abundant buffalo, travelers usually resorted to using buffalo dung, or "buffalo chips," to do their cooking. As the wagons rolled along, it was commonly assigned to the children to collect the dry chips in sacks or to toss them into blankets slung beneath the rolling wagons. Repugnance was the initial reaction to the new fuel, but once they got used to the idea—they were merely undigested plant fiber—they appreciated their value. In 1846, Edwin Bryant endorsed buffalo chips as "burning with a lively blaze . . . an excellent substitute for wood."[43] Bidwell and Jimmy John did not mention it, but we will assume that the company was using buffalo chips by now.

Bidwell's and Jimmy John's journal entries did not comment on the merits of fresh buffalo meat. The naturally salty flesh had an excellent reputation. Bidwell later commented in one of his memoirs, "There is no better beef in the world than that of the buffalo."[44] Edwin Bryant in 1846 felt the same way, claiming it was "superior to our best beef."[45] The goal was to kill fat cows and heifers because their flesh was the juiciest and most tender. Bull meat, in contrast, was to be avoided. The males were too busy at this time of year breeding females and chasing off rivals to spend much time eating the spring grass, causing their meat to be lean, tough, and dry. A diet of buffalo meat must have been healthy, as many of the plains tribes lived almost exclusively on it during much of the year. Some observers wrote that judging by the appearance of the Sioux, buffalo flesh produced hardy, healthy people with no evidence of scurvy.

June 11

Bidwell:

F. 11. The Oxen had wandered about ½ mile from the camp this morning, when a man was sent to bring them in; he soon came running back in great haste, crying "the Indians are driving the Oxen off"!! In less than half an hour the oxen were at camp and not an Indian seen—all this is easily accounted for when we consider how timidity and fear will make every bush, stone, or stump an Indian, and 40 Indians, thousands—Vast herds of Buffalo continued to be seen on the opposite side of the river—Distance to day about 20 miles.

Jimmy John:

June 11th—this morning we were a little surprised. The oxen strayed away from camp. Two of the men went after them and saw four or five Indians driving them off. They came back running their horses and told the news. Twelve of the Company immediately set out to rescue the cattle. When the Indians seen us coming they left the cattle and fled, and we got them all safe to the camp again. We left the camp at 7 o'clock this morning. One of the men acted very imprudent. He was riding by the side of a clump of willows near the place where he seen the Indians driving away the oxen. He, being enraged at them, fired at the Indians, but they could not be found. Some of the company had a little sport today in killing a buffalo bull. They shot him 20 times or upwards before he fell. There are a great many prairie dogs here. They burrow in the ground and are about the size of a common house cat. This evening we encamped on the bank of the Platte. This day has been a warm day.

It is incomprehensible that the night guard problem had still not been rectified and the oxen had been allowed to wander off again. Bidwell and Jimmy John both mentioned Indians, although Bidwell did not sound convinced that they were responsible.

Bidwell estimated they traveled twenty miles on June 11, while Dawson's log only recorded twelve. Jimmy John did not record an estimate for that date. Their camp would have been near the river, perhaps a few miles west of the present-day town of Ogallala, Nebraska.

June 12

The wagons pulled out of camp on the morning of June 12 and left the South Platte River behind. They commenced a strenuous pull away from the South Platte Valley, heading northwest and ascending onto the elevated divide that separates the South Platte Fork from the North Platte Fork.

Bidwell:

> *S. 12th. Left the S. fork [of the Platte], and after a march of 12 miles found ourselves on the N. fork [of the Platte]—in the afternoon passed a small Ash grove of about 25 trees—timber is so scarce that such a grove is worthy of notice—we encamped on the N. fork having come about 18 miles—on leaving the S. fork we left the Buffalo also.*

Jimmy John:

> *June 12th—Left the south fork of the Platte this morning and arrived at the north fork of the Platte about noon. Took dinner here. Seen no buffaloes today except one. Encamped this night on the bank of the north fork of the Platte.*

When the company left the South Fork on the morning of June 12, they left the vast buffalo herds behind. Bidwell would look back years later and reminisce about these huge herds in one of his memoirs: "I think I can truthfully say," he fondly wrote, "that I saw in that region in one day more buffaloes than I have ever seen of cattle in all my life. I have seen the plains black with them for several days' journey as far as the eye could reach."[46]

The precise route of the company across the divide is uncertain because the trail changed in later years. Fitzpatrick probably led them along a route that he thought would be easy for wagons. We can guess at their route based on a few clues that our diarists left. After leaving their camp on the South Fork near today's Ogallala, they would have ascended the bluffs and traveled northwesterly, perhaps taking the route followed by today's Sunny Slope Road, which is three and a half miles west of Ogallala. Upon reaching the heights, the wagons would have lumbered across a waterless, rolling plateau carpeted with short buffalo grass and blue lupine, and occupied by numerous prairie-dog towns and immense numbers of rattlesnakes coiled along their path.

After crossing the divide, the company would have likely entered the head of Coyote Canyon and followed it down into the valley of the North Platte. It was an easy route for wagons, and a very direct way to reach grass and water beside the North Platte. Such a route would have followed today's Road West IN (no road sign) north, where it intersects Highway 26 about nine miles west of where Highway 26 joins Highway 61. The spot where the company likely struck the North Platte is on Road 44, about twelve miles east of where it leaves Highway 26 at Ash Hollow.

Upon reaching the North Platte, the company traveled west along the river's south bank for about three miles when, according to Bidwell, they passed "a small ash grove of about 25 trees." This description matches the ash grove located today at the mouth of Eagle Canyon. Upon traveling three more miles up the river, they stopped to set up camp, thereby completing a day of eighteen miles. Their campsite would have been near the mouth of Spring Canyon next to Road 44 and about four and a half miles east of where Road 44 leaves Highway 26 at Ash Hollow.

When the company encamped on the afternoon of June 12, they had been on the trail for over a month and had traveled about five hundred miles, or an average of sixteen miles per day. Josiah Belden had written in his memoirs that he had joined the expedition "to see something of a wild country, of buffalo hunting, and to have some adventure among the Indians."[47] By now, he had seen wild country, had perhaps hunted buffalo and had come face to face with a couple of Indian war parties. He had braved fierce storms and crossed some big rivers. Recent events had been anything but boring. Did Belden now feel that he had experienced the high adventure that had drawn him to the expedition? Had the hard-boiled reality of his adventures been better or worse than he had hoped for? He did not say. In any event, with these incidents behind them, the travelers may have been hoping to take a deep breath and enjoy a period of quietude and tranquility for a while.

June 13

The morning of June 13 began with anything but quietude and tranquility. A stunning incident occurred that would flip everyone's mood:

Bidwell:

> *S. 13th. A mournful accident occurred in the Camp this morning—a young man by the name of Shotwell while in the act of taking a gun out of the wagon, drew it, with the muzzle towards him in such a manner that it went off and shot him near the heart—he lived an hour and died in the full possession of his senses. His good behavior had secured him the respect and good will of all the company, he had resided some 8 or 9 months on or near the Nodaway river, Platte purchase Missouri prior to his starting on this expedition; but he said his mother lived in Laurel County, Kentucky, and was much opposed to his coming into the West—he was buried in the most decent manner our circumstances would admit of, after which a funeral sermon was preached by Mr. Williams. In the Afternoon we passed on about 5 miles, making an inland circuit over the hills which approached boldly to the river and compelled us to leave its banks—we however reached it again by descending the dry channel of Ash Creek on which was considerable timber—Ash, Cedar &c.*

Jimmy John:

> *June 13th—This morning had a bad accident happened to one of our men. I was out of the camp helping to keep the oxen from straying away (for we have to let them feed on grass and watch them to keep the Indians from driving them away), and while I was there I heard a gun fire in the camp and heard some man scream. I went to the camp, saw one of our men lay bleeding on the ground. He had shot himself with his gun. He was pulling*

his gun from his wagon by the muzzle and the lock caught something and fired and shot him through the left side. He lived about an hour and died. We buried him in the sand on a hill about a half mile from the camp. The company appointed a committee of five men to appoint an administrator for the estate of the deceased, which they did. The captain was appointed. We had a sermon delivered on the occasion by the Rev. Mr. Williams. We left there at 11 o'clock and went to Ash Creek. There we encamped and killed an elk.

The journey was no longer a pleasant amble. Tragedy had made its ugly appearance. Father Mengarini described the incident in his memoirs: "One morning [June 13] about an hour after sunrise, the discharge of a gun startled us. The report was followed by the prolonged moaning of one in pain. All hastened to the spot whence the cries proceeded, and, weltering in his blood, we found an American named Shotwell. The poor fellow had incautiously taken his gun by the muzzle to draw it from his wagon, the piece was accidentally discharged, the bullet pierced his liver, and in two hours he was dead. We could offer him no consolation for we found him insensible and he remained in that condition until death put an end to his agony."[48]

There was an irony in the accident, as Bidwell's memoirs explained: "No one in the party was seemingly more cautious and exemplary than he [Shotwell]. He was tall, young and of fine presence, and was uniformly liked by all. No one had so frequently cautioned others about handling guns carelessly. His loss produced a sadness which lasted many days."[49]

Because of recent encounters with the Pawnees and Cheyenne, Fitzpatrick had undoubtedly advised everyone to keep their rifles loaded and primed at all times. Whether on horseback, driving a wagon, or on foot, they must keep them handy. It was a cautious, prudent piece of advice, but it also created a hazardous situation in which tragic accidents such as this could happen. Shotwell would be one of the first emigrants to fall victim to his own loaded firearm. Evidence suggests that in the years before the Gold Rush far more people died along the trail from accidental, self-inflicted gunshots than from Indian attacks.[50]

Burying the dead along the trail would eventually become a common occurrence. As the number of emigrant wagon trains increased in the future, there would be more and more gravesites. When the

Gold Rush began, cholera made its appearance and claimed hundreds upon hundreds of victims. It has been estimated that between fifteen and thirty thousand people lost their lives along these trails, most of them caused by disease.[51] This translates to an average of one trailside grave about every five hundred to one thousand feet. Noticing that bodies were often exhumed by Indians to obtain the deceased's clothing, or by wolves for reasons we need not explain, the emigrants began to devise ingenious methods for disguising the deceased's last resting place. One of the more effective ways was to bury the dead at night under cover of darkness and within the trail itself. The next morning, as the wagons rolled out, each wagon would roll over the grave so that by the time the last wagon had passed there was no evidence of the grave. In the case of poor Shotwell, Jimmy John reported that the company carried his body a half-mile from camp and buried him on a high bluff overlooking the river valley. There is a good possibility that Shotwell's grave is on one of the bluffs on either side of the mouth of Spring Canyon. Because of its remote location and because emigrants soon adopted another route to reach the North Platte, there is no evidence that his gravesite has ever been discovered.

With sad hearts and shaken spirits the members of the company returned to their travels at eleven o'clock on the morning of June 13. Blocked by precipitous bluffs jutting out to the edge of the river, the company was forced inland and probably rolled up Spring Canyon. Two to three more miles took them over a ridge and then down a gentle slope into Ash Hollow. It is uncertain exactly where the expedition entered the hollow, but an examination of the topography suggests that they could have most easily descended a modest slope on its east side, about two and a half miles south of where today's Highway 26 bridge crosses the North Platte channel.

Ash Hollow was a small valley formed by tall bluffs rising up on either side. Ash Creek, fed by a number of springs, ran along the floor of the hollow. A grove of large and imposing ash trees grew on either side of the creek, together with grapevines, wild cherries, plums, gooseberries, and other wild currants. Abundant wild roses, wildflowers of all kinds, and cedar trees perfumed the air. The fragrant cedars would provide the camp with sweet-smelling firewood, a nice change from buffalo chips. They likely camped near the marshy area on either side of the creek to take advantage of the abundant grass. It was an oasis, a respite from the treeless regularity that had stabbed at their eyes for weeks. It was cool, shady, and refreshing, a place that could not help improving their spirits.

The route over which Fitzpatrick led them to Ash Hollow would eventually be abandoned, although it appears that Joel Palmer led his Oregon-bound wagon party over the same route in 1845. The most common route for wagon trains in the years to come, however, was to cross the South Platte near today's Brule, Nebraska, and then make a beeline across the divide to Ash Hollow. The problem with this route was that the travelers needed to lower their wagons with ropes down some very steep inclines in order to enter the head of the Hollow at its southern end.

June 14

Bidwell:

> *M.14th. The day was so cool and rainy we did not travel.*

Jimmy John:

> *June 14th—This being a rainy day we did not leave here until the 15th.*

After traveling over five hundred miles with very few pauses, both people and animals must have been weary and fatigued. So they remained in camp on June 14. There could not have been a better place to lick their wounds and restore their energies. Unfortunately, the weather had other ideas. Cold, dreary and uncomfortable, it ruined what otherwise could have been a perfect situation for resting up.

June 15

After spending a terribly cold night, the company woke up the next morning shivering.

Bidwell:

> *T. 15th. There was so sudden a change from cool to cold, that we were not comfortable in our best apparel. I do not remember, that I ever experienced weather so cold at this season of the year—traveled about 16 miles.*

Jimmy John:

> 15th—This morning we left here. The air has been cold for three days. The name of the creek we camped at last night is Ash Creek. Killed one deer there. The river [North Platte] here is wide, like the south fork, and has hills on each side consisting of sand and rock, and narrow plains next [to] the water. We encamped this night about 15 miles farther up the river.

It was well known by wagon train guides that once you left Ash Hollow there would be no wood for the next eighty miles. It seems likely, therefore, that Fitzpatrick urged the men to throw extra firewood into their wagons before leaving. This practice would be followed in the years to come in ever-increasing intensity, with inevitable results. By 1854, well into the Gold Rush era, a traveler sadly wrote that Ash Hollow's once-famous "forest of ash trees, like every other place near the road, has been stript of its wood to make light and chearfull the camp of the emigrants."[52] The completion of the transcontinental railroad in 1869 effectively ended wagon travel through Ash Hollow. From then on, Ash Hollow was essentially left alone and has slowly regained its former vegetative state. Today, it provides an enjoyable place to visit.

As the company left Ash Hollow, the trail tracked west, threading between the foot of flat-topped bluffs on the left and the North Platte River on the right. James Clyman estimated in 1844 that the North Platte was about one mile wide at this point. The landscape was also changing. Hundreds of miles of grassland had gradually transitioned to sparser and drier vegetation. The river bottom was well supplied with grass, but low hills, bluffs, and plains, drier and more arid than what the company had passed a week earlier, stretched out on either side. Sagebrush was making its appearance. The terrain was becoming more geologically provocative as well. The bluffs on the left rose about two hundred feet above the river plain, their nearly perpendicular faces exposing white clay marl. Stunted cedar grew at their base.

The company had also entered Sioux country. The Oglala branch of the Sioux began hunting buffalo and asserting their dominion over this area after migrating from the Black Hills of South Dakota in 1834 and 1835. The Oglala numbered a little over two thousand people, but were divided into a number of smaller bands. Each band lived in its own camp and was governed by its own chief. Camps were moved from place to place, often set up in grassy meadows along this section of the trail. Although not an especially large tribe, the Sioux were considered by many observers the most able and feared fighters of all the Plains tribes. They possessed an arrogant attitude of superiority, perhaps some of it justified. More than one white chronicler had described the Sioux as a tribe of superior physical specimens who saw themselves as the unchallenged rulers of whatever they coveted and as masters of all within it. Before the Sioux muscled their way into the area in 1834–35, it had been considered the land of the Cheyenne. But the Cheyenne eventually decided that it was more prudent to forge a friendly relationship with the Sioux and to peacefully coexist rather than be at war with them.

For ages, the buffalo-rich region of the South Fork had been the preferred hunting ground of the Pawnees. But when the Sioux discovered how rich the region was after they migrated south from the Black Hills, they wasted no time claiming this bounteous area as theirs. Almost immediately, the two tribes came to blows.[53] In 1835, shortly after the Sioux arrived, a war party of Sioux met a war party of Pawnees in Ash Hollow, and they locked horns in a ferocious battle to determine mastery over the region. The Pawnees were decisively outmatched and lost sixty braves, quickly learning that the new kid on the block was not to be trifled with.[54] Now in great fear of the Sioux, the Pawnees rarely traveled this far west again. In turn, the Sioux seemed to harbor a particularly intense hatred of the Pawnees, and sent uncommonly ruthless and unrelenting attacks against Pawnee villages on the lower Platte for many years thereafter.

About five miles west of Ash Hollow, the company passed a broad grassy meadow along the river. In coming years, wagon trains would often encounter a Sioux camp here, although there was no sign of them when Fitzpatrick led the company through on June 15. In fact, the company would not encounter any Sioux camps during the 140 miles between here and Fort Laramie. This is not surprising. As of 1841, no emigrant wagon trains had passed over the trail, and the Sioux would not have been expecting them. In later years, this would change. As the Sioux became accustomed to wagons trains passing through their country each June, they developed the habit of setting up their camps so as to straddle the trail, and would spread their blankets on the ground to receive "presents" from the emigrants. A "toll" or "tribute" was expected to be paid for the privilege of passing through their territory. Some emigrants chafed at the idea. George Curry, for example, an emigrant traveling to Oregon in 1846, expressed his indignation: "Their country, forsooth! Did they not steal it from the Cheyennes, and do they not hold possession of it because they are the more powerful?"[55]

The meadow mentioned above can be seen just north of Road 44, five miles west of its junction with Highway 26 at Ash Hollow. It is a dead-end road, so be prepared to turn around. West of here, future travelers would describe the trail as very sandy in places. It was hard going, with the narrow wagon wheels sinking six to ten inches into the sand and forcing the mules and oxen to strain at the extra resistance. Bidwell and Jimmy John did not mention the sand, but because the road had experienced virtually no wagon traffic as of 1841, perhaps the trail had not yet been disturbed sufficiently to be problematic.

About sixteen miles after leaving their Ash Hollow camp, the company stopped to camp beside the North Platte, near today's Road 54 and about three miles west of its junction with Highway 27 (south of Oshkosh, Nebraska).

Chapter 7

Fort Laramie and Beyond

JUNE 16 TO 30, 1841

June 16

On June 16, the wagon company continued to lumber along the south side of the North Platte. Recently, the days had been more tedious than difficult. No storms, no Indians, no buffalo, no deaths. By now, the tired travelers had been hardened by the discomforts and privations of trail life. But as they sluggishly plodded forward foot by foot, mile by mile, monotony may have been their greatest irritant, requiring uncommon patience.

Bidwell:

> W. 16th. Several wild horses were seen on the opposite side of the river—advanced about 20 miles—encamped on the river, opposite to the high and uneven Bluffs, bearing considerable forests of pine.

Jimmy John:

> June 16th—This morning we left camp at the usual hour. The day was pleasant. We made a good day's drive. Killed some rabbits and three antelopes, but have not seen buffalo for 4 days. We seen some wild horses on the opposite side of the river. The land here is almost entirely destitute of timber. There is some cedar along the creeks and on the islands, a few ash trees, some mountain cherries and currants of the largest size I have ever seen. We encamped on the banks of the Platte.

The estimated location of their June 16 camp can be reached by traveling southwest on Road 151 as it heads out of today's Lisco, Nebraska. After one mile, turn right onto Road 54, then turn right again onto Road 68 and go west about four miles. Their campsite would have been near the river. A dedicated trail hound, if so inclined, can travel in close proximity to the trail along the south bank of the river by continuing westward on this dirt road.

June 17

As the company continued forward at a snail's pace on June 17, a number of marvelous geological formations came into view.

Bidwell:

> T. 17th. Continued to coast along up the river—encamped on its banks nearly opposite to a huge isolated bluff, bearing some resemblance to an immense castle in ruins. Its distance from us no one supposed more than 1½ miles, and yet it was at least 7—this deception was owing to the pure atmosphere through which it was viewed, and the want of objects, by which only, accurate ideas of distance can be acquired without measure.

Jimmy John:

> June 17th—We left the camp this morning at 7 o'clock. Crossed a creek of excellent water [Cedar Creek] at 9 o'clock. Seen a considerable quantity of pine timber today, along the creeks and bluffs. Two of the hunters went out yesterday and did not return until 12 o'clock last night. They brought in some buffaloe meat with them, and had seen no Indians. We encamped on the bank of the river near the mouth of a large creek [Pumpkin Creek] in sight of a rock or clay peak called the Chimney [Chimney Rock], and in sight of a large clay mount which has the appearance of a large mansion house [Courthouse Rock].

About seven miles after leaving camp that morning, they crossed Cedar Creek, likely the first creek that Jimmy John mentioned. Cedar Creek crosses under Road 80 about three miles southeast of Broadwater, Nebraska. Another thirteen miles brought them to Pumpkin Creek, the second creek Jimmy John mentioned. It was a stream of clear running water that emptied into the North Platte and was a good place to camp after traveling about twenty miles that day. The "immense castle" and "large mansion house" mentioned by the diarists eventually became known by future travelers as Court-

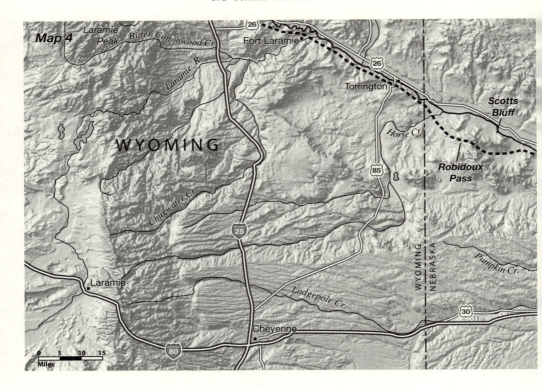

house Rock, while the smaller sister butte that stood nearby came to be called Jail Rock. At one time the area was a high plateau, but the persistent forces of rain, ice and wind had gradually eroded everything away except for these three-hundred-foot-high formations composed mostly of cemented clay.

While encamped five miles from Courthouse Rock and Jail Rock, Bidwell noted how the clear air and the deceiving size of the imposing buttes created the impression that they were much closer. This phenomenon would lure many emigrants of the future into leaving their wagons and venturing out for a closer look. After a number of miles of hard riding, and finding that they were still a great distance away, many would give up their merry jaunt.

The company's camp on June 17 was likely on the west side of Pumpkin Creek, where it crosses today's Highway 92, four miles southeast of Bridgeport, Nebraska.

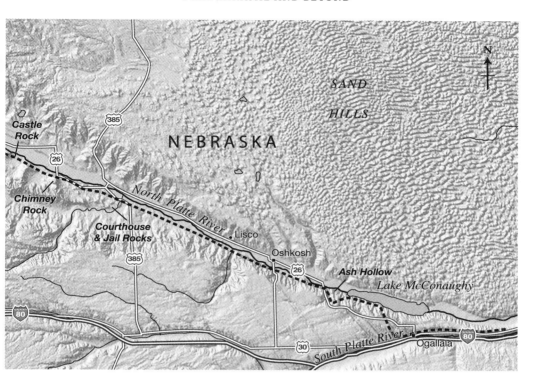

June 18

Bidwell:

> F. 18th. About 12 o'clock to day we passed another object, still more singular and interesting—it is called by the Mountaineers, the Chimney, from its resemblance to that object; and is composed of clay and sand so completely compact as to possess the hardness of rock. It stands near the high Bluffs that bound the Valley on the South, and has been formed from a high isolated mound which, being washed on every side by the rains and snows of ages, has been worn down till nothing is left but the centre which stands upon an obtuse cone, and is seen towering like a huge column at the distance of 30 miles. The column is 150 feet above the top of the cone and the whole, 250 feet above the level of the plain. Distance made today about 20 miles.

Approaching Chimney Rock, *by William Henry Jackson. Catalog No. SCBL-25. Courtesy of Scotts Bluff National Monument.*

Jimmy John:

> June 18th—*This morning we started at six o'clock. The weather is fine and the air pure. We traveled about 25 miles today and encamped about two miles from the Chimney or clay peak. It is a sharp peak of clay mingled with rock. We have killed no buffaloes today, but have [seen] 2 of them, and killed two antelopes and one deer.*

The trail they followed on June 16 through 18 generally followed the route of today's Highway 92/26 between Broadwater and Melbeta, Nebraska. Based on Jimmy John's account, they camped on the evening of June 18 near where present-day Highway 92 intersects with Highway 26 and about two miles directly south of the tiny community of Bayard, Nebraska (about two miles north of Chimney Rock). The Chimney Rock Visitor Center is on Chimney Rock Road, one mile south of its intersection with Highway 92.

As Bidwell explained, they caught their first glimpse of the funnel-shaped Chimney Rock while thirty miles away. One of Bidwell's later memoirs claimed that when they camped nearby he and a number of his companions approached the astonishing structure and painted their names on it with axle grease and tar.[1] If ever there was a symbol of the Oregon Trail, other than the covered wagon, it was Chimney Rock. No other feature on the trail was more frequently mentioned

Chimney Rock, *by William Henry Jackson. Catalog No. SCBL-24. Courtesy of Scotts Bluff National Monument.*

by diarists. The Reverend Williams described it as "a funnel, with the small end uppermost."[2] While it had nowhere near the bulk and massiveness as Courthouse Rock, travelers would still gape in disbelief at this unique spindle of hardened clay and rock. There seemed to be no way that anything so slender could have reached so impossibly high into the air, while defying the forces of gravity and strong winds. But it did. Rufus Sage, traveling through here later in the fall of 1841, estimated that its conical pedestal was three hundred feet tall, while its finger-like spire extended another two-hundred feet, for a total of five hundred feet.[3] Frémont's chief surveyor in 1842, Charles Preuss, a purportedly reputable authority, also estimated the structure to be five hundred feet tall. Bidwell claimed in a later memoir, "after we passed it [Chimney Rock] a portion of it fell off."[4] Indeed, the topmost thirty feet of the fragile finger was toppled by a bolt of lightning in 1849. Measurements taken in 1895 and in 1965 showed that the spire had lost another seventeen feet during that seventy-year period. After the top of the rock was officially measured at 325 feet above the surrounding plain in 1965, six more feet were blasted off by another disrespectful lightning strike.[5] Hence, it was almost a hundred feet taller in 1841 than it is now. It was undoubtedly much more spectacular in 1841. Yet, even in its more humbled state, the rocky spire is still such a striking creation that it cannot but impress the most indifferent modern-day tourist.

June 19

Resuming their travels early on the morning of June 19, the company left their camp beside the North Platte River. As the day progressed, they paraded by an avenue of towering bluffs to the south. Later called Castle Rock, Table Rock, and Coyote Rock, these bluffs, too, were remarkable monuments that rose from two hundred to four hundred feet above the surrounding plain. Bidwell did not mention them, but Williams did, reporting that the region abounded with many bluffs that had "many curious shapes and forms."[6] The company had previously spent a number of days lumbering through country that was otherwise painfully dull. These magnificent monoliths could not have come at a better time to stimulate their languid minds and provide them with something at which to marvel.

The attention of the company now shifted to what was ahead. Looming to the west was the eastern face of Scotts Bluff, a huge uplifted spine of sandstone and white chalky marl. Gleaming a resplendent creamy white in the morning sun, it resembled the remains of an ancient fortress rimmed with turrets, ramparts, and parapets. The bluff had been named after Hiram Scott, a clerk of the American Fur Company. Traveling east sometime in the 1820s, Scott had fallen seriously ill, and had been abandoned by his companions and left to die.[7]

The northern escarpment of Scotts Bluff squeezed hard against the edge of the North Platte River, making passage between the bluff and the river difficult. So the trail veered away from the river about nine miles from where the company left its camp (about two miles northwest of the tiny present-day community of Melbeta, Nebraska) and headed almost due west across a flat, waterless plain for another fifteen miles. The route closely followed today's Robidoux Road. Fitzpatrick was leading the expedition toward a low spot on the southern side of the bluff. Ascending a wide draw, the procession came to a deep ravine into which flowed the waters from a couple of springs. It had been a long day, so the company circled their wagons and set up camp beside the ravine.

Bidwell:

> *S. 19. We gradually receded from the river in order to pass through a gap in a range of hills, called Scot's Bluff, as we advanced towards these hills,*

the scenery of the sourrounding Country became beautifully grand and picturesque—they were worn in such a manner by the storms of unnumbered seasons, that they really counterfeited the lofty spires, towering edifices, spacious domes and in fine all beautiful mansions of Cities. We encamped among these envious objects having come about 20 miles. Here were found the mountain Sheep, two were killed and brought to camp— these animals are so often described in almost every little School Book that it is unnecessary for me to describe them here.

Jimmy John:

June 19th—This morning we left camp at the 30 minutes past six o'clock. The air is cool today and the wind blows hard. We have killed two mountain sheep and 3 elk today and one antelope. We encamped this evening near a deep ravine of water surrounded by high bluffs which have a splendid appearance.

Bidwell wrote that they had traveled twenty miles on June 19, but it was more like twenty-four miles. In 1846, J. Quinn Thornton described the same ravine where the company camped in detail: "At this place are two small springs of excellent water, one of them is under a high hill, where the emigrant road crosses the head of a small ravine. The other is better, more abundant, but one mile further on, and at the head of a very deep ravine."[8] James Clyman's 1844 diary described the same ravine, mentioning that it was filled with "wild currants & choke chirries of the finest kind."[9]

The company's camp was next to the ravine just north of today's Robidoux Road, about eight miles west of where the road joins Highway 71 (John McLellan Expressway) and south of the town of Gering, Nebraska. On a clear day, travelers could gaze eastward from their camp and see Castle Rock and Chimney Rock, twenty and twenty-five miles away.

As of June 19, the expedition had traveled six hundred miles since leaving Sapling Grove. As for the Bartleson group, they were only a third of the way to California, although they did not know it at the time.

June 20

Rolling out of camp on June 20, the company continued up the hill, crossed its summit, and then headed down its western slope. Later called Robidoux Pass, this route is presumed to have been named after a blacksmith who established a blacksmith shop and trading post here late in 1848. In 1846, Francis Parkman had mentioned a blacksmith by the name of Robidoux who was smithing at Fort Laramie at the time.[10] It is believed that he was the one who established the trading post here and that he was a nephew of both Antoine and Joseph Robidoux.[11]

Upon reaching the summit of Robidoux Pass on a clear day, travelers could see the Laramie Mountain Range, including Laramie Peak, about one hundred miles to the west. After coming over the pass, the trail headed northwest. The descent off the summit was gradual and over a gently undulating and arid plain. After rumbling about twelve miles, the wagon party came to Horse Creek and crossed it. They probably crossed it about two miles northeast of today's tiny community of Lyman, Nebraska.

The estimated location of the Horse Creek crossing can be seen by leaving Lyman and heading east on Highway 9 about a quarter-mile. Then turn north on Road 3 and travel one mile to Road F. The trail crossed the creek about one and a half miles east of that point. Horse Creek was a swift-running stream of cold, clear water, bordered on either side by broad and expansive meadows. Charles Preuss, one of Frémont's 1842 surveyors, described Horse Creek as "a shallow stream of clear water, about seventy yards wide. . . . It is lightly timbered, and great quantities of drift wood were piled upon the banks."[12] The meadows were notorious for their thick clouds of mean-biting mosquitoes. Bidwell and Jimmy John did not mention them, probably because the company passed through here on a day that was cold and windy. The mosquitoes were probably lying low.

Bidwell:

> *Sunday, 20th. Passed through the Gap—came into an extensive plain, the beautiful scenery gradually receded from view—came to a creek called Horse—passed it, reached the river [North Platte] again—cool and windy—having come about 23 miles.*

Jimmy John:

> *June 20th—We left here this morning at six o'clock. Took dinner on the banks of Horse creek. This is a cold, windy, disagreeable day for traveling. This night we encamped on the banks of the Platte about 30 miles from F. Laramy.*

Ten years later, the meadows around Horse Creek would become the scene of a great gathering. By 1851, incidents of Indians pestering the numerous wagon trains passing through had significantly increased. At the same time, the Plains tribes had been fighting with each other, usually over contested territory. These issues needed to be resolved and the Indians had to be pacified. Therefore, the Bureau of Indian Affairs called for a gathering of the tribes. Thomas Fitzpatrick had been appointed Indian Agent over the Plains tribes in 1846, and it fell to him to organize the event. To induce attendance, the government offered presents to all tribes who came. The gathering took place in September 1851 and was attended by large numbers of Crow, Snake, Cheyenne, Arapahoe, and Sioux. It was estimated that ten thousand Indians came and camped along the creek, while pasturing their thousands of horses on the extensive meadows. The obstreperous Pawnees did not attend, but it was because the government had not invited them.[13]

The tribes enjoyed two weeks of feasting, passing the pipe, and pledging peace. Negotiations with the chiefs led to territories being assigned to each tribe, together with a promise that each tribe signing the treaty would receive $50,000 in goods each year from the U.S. government for the next fifty years. Satisfied with the terms, the chiefs "touched the pen" to the treaty, took their presents, and headed for home. But the U.S. Senate refused to ratify the treaty, believing that fifty years of promised annuities was excessive and reduced the number to fifteen.[14] The Indians recalled what they had been promised and began to understand that the white man's promises were not to be trusted. This breach of trust would tragically lead to bloody repercussions in the decades to come. In addition, the "peace" that had been negotiated between the tribes lasted only three years.[15]

After "nooning" at Horse Creek, the Fitzpatrick-led expedition continued on. Bidwell reported that they traveled twenty-three miles that day. But Dawson seemed to have a better handle on the distances traveled through here, so we will adopt his estimate that they traveled twenty miles on June 20. This would mean that after crossing Horse Creek, they traveled another six miles before striking the North Platte. Here, they pitched camp.

Their camp would have been near the river's south bank, on today's N Road 61, near where it intersects with Road 58 (one and a half miles southwest of Henry, Nebraska).

June 21

On the morning of June 21, the company returned to the trail as it continued in close proximity to the North Platte River. The trail led the company west over a four-mile stretch of low hills, where a set of wagon ruts still mark portions of the old trail. The ruts head northwesterly from the intersection of present-day N Road 61 and Road 58. Ruts can also be seen by traveling two miles south of Torrington, Wyoming, on Highway 85, then going east on Highway 92 one and a half miles to Road 64. Take Road 64 east two miles. Ruts can be seen to the north.

Bidwell:

> *M. 21st. We had an uncommonly good road to day—an abundance of cotton wood timber—traveled late, having taken a stride of 27 miles.*

Jimmy John:

> *June 21—This morning we set out at the usual hour. The day pleasant except it is very windy, for one would judge from the shortness of the timber that it is always the case here. The hills are sandy and in some places rocky. Some have the appearance of chalk, consisting of a substance resembling plaster paris. We see but few buffaloes here, but have plenty of meat in the camp yet. There is plenty of small game. We enjoy good health, excepting two or three persons, who have been complaining for a few days, myself for one. We have killed no game today, but one antelope. We encamped this evening on the banks of the Platte.*

Large cottonwoods grew along this section of the North Platte. Our diarists did not mention it, but travelers in later years would often report seeing deceased Indians, usually Sioux, wrapped in blankets or buffalo skins and hoisted high into the limbs of the trees. The Sioux preferred this to digging graves as it would keep the bodies out of the reach of scavenger wolves. The emigrants began referring to these elevated coffins as the "nests of the dead."

After lumbering along the river, the company stopped to camp on the south side of the river about five miles west of the small present-day town of Lingle, Wyoming. Their estimated camp location can be reached by traveling about five and a half miles west from Lingle on Highway 26. Then take Road 157 south and travel about one and a half miles to the approximate location of their camp. The Grattan Massacre would occur in 1853 about a mile and a half east of this point. It began as a squabble between the U.S. Army and Sioux and then got out of hand. Many historians contend that the massacre was the watershed event that ignited a bloody twenty-year war between the whites and the Sioux.

June 22

On the morning of June 22, the company left their camp beside the North Platte. The travelers must have been exhilarated since they expected to arrive at Fort Laramie late that morning. They were undoubtedly looking forward to arriving at this first trace of civilization since leaving the settlements.

The company's final approach to the fort that morning was where Road 64 heads west from Road 157. After about a mile on Road 64, take the right fork (Road 63) and continue on it a short distance until you come to a private farm road. Unfortunately, there are no public roads beyond this point, but one can see where the wagon party traveled between the foot of the bluffs and the river.

When the company rounded the last bluff, a stockade made of wooden logs planted into the ground would have come into view on the north side of the Laramie River. This was the much-heralded Fort Laramie. Their first view may have been disappointing. The crude structure sat on the flat plain north of today's Laramie River Bridge on Road 15. Road 15 heads south from Road 160 just west of the North Platte River Bridge (west of the town of Fort Laramie).

One can see the company's final approach to the fort by continuing south on Road 15 and crossing the Laramie River Bridge. After continuing another mile, one reaches a fork in the road, where it is best to turn around and return to the site of the old fort.

To reach the fort, the company crossed the Laramie River. Schizophrenic and temperamental, the river was often low and only sixty feet wide. In such a state, it was a cinch to ford. But if the Laramie Mountain Range to the west had recently experienced heavy rains, the river would transform into a raging monster. At such times, it could be as much as two hundred feet wide, with a treacherous current running deep and swift and capable of claiming many a victim. It was best for travelers to patiently camp on the near bank and wait for its flow to subside. The 1841 company had apparently shown up during one of the river's placid phases, since Jimmy John would later record that "the river here is narrow and the water low."

Bidwell:

> *T. 22nd. Eight miles this morning took us to Ft. Larimie, which is on Larimie's fork of Platte about 800 miles from the frontiers of Missouri, it is owned by the American Fur Company. There is another fort, within a mile and a half of this Place, belonging to an individual by the name of Lupton, the Black Hills were now in view, a very noted Peak, called the Black Hill Mountain [Laramie Peak], was seen like a dark cloud in the Western horizon. The Country along Platte River is far from being fertile and is uncommonly destitute of timber, the Earth continues, as we ascend, to become more strongly impregnated with glauber Salts.*

Jimmy John:

> *June 22d—This day we arrived at Fort Laramy at 10 o'clock. The fort is on the north side of the river Laramy's fork, which we had to cross. It runs into the Platte half a mile from the fort. There is another fort building about half a mile from it. Its proprietor's name is Lupton. The new fort is on the banks of the Platte. We encamped this night in sight of both forts.*

When the wagon company finally arrived at the fort, it had traveled 650 miles instead of the eight hundred miles that Bidwell claimed. First established here by William Sublette and Robert Campbell in 1834, the log stockade sat on a narrow tongue of land wedged between the Laramie and North Platte rivers. The location was ideal; it was a strategic place along the trail, connecting the Rockies to the settlements along the Missouri River. Because of an abundance of water, grass, and wood, Indians, trappers, and traders had been stopping here for many years to congregate, communicate, recreate, and intoxicate.[16] It was a perfect place to establish a post to trade with the Indians and to temporarily store goods, furs, and buffalo skins pending further movement either east or west. They named it Fort William after Sublette, although people insisted on calling it Fort Laramie.

Campbell wanted to develop trade at their new stockade, and as soon as the post was completed in 1834, he sent two of his men to the Black Hills of South Dakota to invite the Oglala Sioux to visit. The men succeeded in persuading Bull Bear, a dominant Oglala chief, to bring his band. Another major Oglala band soon followed, and by 1835 it was estimated that two thousand Sioux had made the move.[17] Liking the area, the Sioux decided to stay and they staked their claim to the area, even though it infringed upon the Cheyenne and Arapahoe hunting grounds. Their move into this area also led to the Sioux violently driving the Pawnees from their longtime buffalo hunting grounds around the Forks of the Platte.

Once established, Fort Laramie became a major center where Indians (mostly Sioux) and trappers came to trade their furs and buffalo robes for guns, lead, powder, blankets, tobacco, and other goods. Dr. Wislizenus visited the stockade in 1839 and wrote this excellent description:

> It is on a slight elevation, and is built in a rectangle of about eighty by a hundred feet. The outside is made of cottonwood logs, about fifteen feet high, hewed off and wedged closely together. On three sides there are little towers on the walls that seem designed for watch and defense. In the middle a strong gate, built of blocks, constitutes the entrance. Within, little buildings with flat roofs are plastered all around against the wall, like swallows nests. One is a storehouse; another the smithy; the others are dwellings not unlike monks cells. A special portion of the courtyard is occupied by the so-called horsepen, in which horses are confined at night. The middle space is free, with a tall tree in it, on which the flag is raised on occasions of state.[18]

One of the more imposing features at the fort was the small cannon mounted in the blockhouse above the main entrance. A. J. Miller, a young artist capturing images in the West, remarked in 1837:

> The Indians have a mortal horror of the "big gun" which rests in the block house, as they have had experience of its prowess and witnessed the havoc produced by its loud "talk." They conceive it to be asleep and have a wholesome dread of its being waked up.[19]

When Fitzpatrick led his wagon company across the sixty-foot-wide Laramie Fork on June 22, he was returning to a familiar place. Before there was a fort, he had camped here many times while leading trapping parties or transporting supplies or furs. In 1835, Sublette and Campbell sold their new stockade to the Rocky Mountain Fur Company, a partnership that included Fitzpatrick.[20] Prior to 1834, the Oglala Sioux had been the trading partners of the American Fur Company, but the AFC lost them as customers when the Sioux moved south in 1834–35. In order to win back the Sioux, the AFC concluded that the best way was to purchase the fort. Because Fitzpatrick and his partners owed the AFC a substantial sum, the partnership soon transferred Fort Laramie to the AFC to satisfy the debt.[21] It is unknown whether Fitzpatrick announced to anyone in the Bartleson party that he had once been a part-owner of this outpost. If he had, Bidwell and Jimmy did not mention it.

When the wagon party arrived at the fort, a number of changes were in progress. After seven years of being sunk into the often-wet ground, the soft wood of the fort's cottonwood walls was rotting away. In response, the AFC had begun construction of a replacement fort, but this one was being made of sundried adobe bricks. Perched on an elevated bench beside a bend in the Laramie River, the new structure was about one mile west of the original stockade. The AFC would name it Fort John, but as with the original fort, everyone would persist in calling it Fort Laramie. Neither Bidwell nor Jimmy John mentioned the new construction in their journal entries for June 22, although they did mention another fort, the one being built by Lancaster P. Lupton. Work on this adobe brick structure, named Fort Platte, was begun in 1839 to serve as a competitor to Fort Laramie. While Bidwell said it was a mile and a half away, Jimmy John was more correct by reporting that it was a half-mile away, directly north of the original Fort Laramie. Fort Platte would struggle and then finally be abandoned in 1845.[22] Its location is just north of today's Road 160, about a thousand feet west of the North Platte River Bridge.[23]

June 23

Bidwell:

> W. 23d. Remained at the Fort, the things of Mr. Shotwell were sold at Auction.

Jimmy John:

> June 23d—We lay this day where camped last evening, in sight of both forts. Fort Laramee is situated on the north side of Laramy fork on the bank of the river. It has a pleasant site. It is built of a kind of brick made of clay not burned. They are 8 inches wide and 16 inches long. The fort is

not finished at this time. The wall is 16 inches wide on the top and at the bottom it is 3 feet, and 160 feet by 120 feet square. When finished it will be plastered with lime and white washed all around outside. The other fort is about one mile from it on the main fork of the Platte river. It is called Fort John, and will be built in the same way. We can see some of the Black Hills from these forts which are 50 miles distant. I visited these forts today, but cannot give a full description of them as they are not finished. The river here is narrow and the water low.

Jimmy John's entry for June 23 gives us a nice description of the new Fort Laramie under construction. More durable and commodious, the new fort would be completed the following year, and would become an imposing structure sitting in an otherwise barren landscape. When visiting it in 1842, Frémont complimented its "whitewashed walls" and its "clean appearance." He further described it:

I walked up to visit our friends at the fort, which is a quadrangular structure, built of clay, after the fashion of the Mexicans, who are generally employed in building them. The walls are about 15 feet high, surmounted by a wooden palisade, and form a portion of ranges of houses, which entirely surround a yard of about 130 feet square. Every apartment has its door and window, all of course opening on the inside. There are two entrances, opposite each other, and midway the wall, one of which is a large and public entrance; the other smaller and more private—a sort of postern gate. Over the great entrance is a square tower with loopholes, and, like the rest of the work, built of earth. At two of the angles, and diagonally opposite each other, are large square bastions, so arranged as to sweep the four faces of the walls.[24]

Once the new Fort Laramie was completed, the original wooden stockade was abandoned and its above-ground timbers cannibalized for use as firewood and in the construction of the new fort. There had once been glorious groves of cottonwoods growing along the banks of the North Platte and Laramie Fork near where the forts were built. But the construction of the forts, coupled with feeding countless campfires for large numbers of whites and Indians since 1834, especially during the winters, had decimated these groves. This is why Bidwell described the vicinity as "uncommonly destitute of timber." It would get progressively worse in the years to come. By the Gold Rush, there was not a tree in sight within miles of the fort. After the new fort was up and running, a new trail leading more directly to the

Fort Laramie, sketched by James F. Wilkins on his way to California in 1849. Image ID # 3935. Notice the absence of trees and vegetation on the banks of the Laramie River. Courtesy of Wisconsin Historical Society.

new fort was established, one that tracked a mile further west and traveled over the low bluffs before descending to the Laramie River.

When Francis Parkman visited the fort in 1846, he composed a masterful piece describing the arrival of an emigrant wagon train:

> *They gained the river, and, without turning or pausing, plunged in; they passed through, and slowly ascending the opposing bank, kept directly on their way by the fort and the Indian village until, gaining a spot a quarter of a mile distant, they wheeled into a circle. For some time our tranquility was undisturbed. The emigrants were preparing their encampment; but no sooner was this accomplished, than Fort Laramie was taken by storm. A crowd of broad-brimmed hats, thin visages, and staring eyes, appeared suddenly at the gate. Tall, awkward men in brown homespun; women with cadaverous faces and long lank figures, came thronging in together, and, as if inspired by the very demon of curiosity, ransacked every nook and corner of the fort. . . . The emigrants prosecuted their investigations with untiring*

> vigor. They penetrated the rooms, or rather dens, inhabited by the astonished squaws. Resolved to search every mystery to the bottom, they explored the apartments of the men . . . Having at length satisfied their curiosity, they next proceeded to business. The men occupied themselves in procuring supplies for their onward journey; either buying them, or giving in exchange superfluous articles of their own.[25]

The fort became known not only as a center of trade and commerce, but as a spot where occasions of drunken revelry and carousing took place whenever bands of trappers arrived.[26] Parkman remarked about the raucous "blow outs" that would take place—drunken sprees that were fueled by kegs of Taos Lightning brought by traders from New Mexico and sold for $4 a pint.[27]

The year-round residents of the forts were, for the most part, employees of the AFC, together with their Indian wives. John McPherson, bound for California in 1848, described them:

> Fort Laramie is occupied by the servants of the [American Fur] company, principally Canadian French. . . . [They are] happy with their squaws and yellow offspring. They appeared to take great pleasure guiding us through the fort, which appeared simply to consist of small square rooms, capable of affording scant accommodation for themselves and [their] squaws.[28]

While the new fort must have awed the Indians as another one of the white man's astonishing works, it did not remain dazzling for long. As soon as the last adobe brick was laid the corrosive forces of nature—rain, ice, and sun—began to eat away at the mud structure. When James Clyman departed the fort in 1844, he wrote that he "soon lost sight of the whitewashed mud walls."[29] By 1846, emigrants were no longer describing the walls as "whitewashed."[30] Father Lempfrit, a French priest heading to Oregon in 1848, was disappointed by its appearance, lamenting that "Fort Laramie has lost all its splendor. It is nothing but a pile of sun-baked bricks."[31] J. Goldsborough Bruff, a Gold Rusher of 1849, wrote in his 1849 journal that the fort, then eight years old, "has suffered much from time and neglect."[32] Eastbound William Kelly paused at the fort in 1849 and described it as nothing more than a "wretched reality—a miserable cracked, dilapidated, adobe."[33]

Congress enacted legislation in 1846 to establish "military stations on the route to Oregon," the same legislation under which Fort Kearny was established. By 1849, the War Department wanted a "second station . . . at or near Fort Laramie."[34] It was decided to try purchasing the fort from the AFC, "provided it can be done at a reasonable price."[35] The AFC must have been anxious to dispose of its falling-down outpost since it agreed to sell it for only $4,000. The Army moved in and immediately began constructing new buildings.[36] By 1858, the neglected old adobe had melted into the ground. Today, one can only see the outline of where old Fort Laramie once stood, but it is still thrilling to see where so many wagon companies stopped to refresh and restore themselves during their westward trek.

At this point in the journey, the company's wagons should have been showing the effects of thousands of jarring bumps in the trail. Future emigrants often mentioned their wagons being in terrible shape by the time they rattled into Fort Laramie. After hundreds of miles of hard-pulling over harsh gravel, abrasive sand, and irritating alkali, it was common for many of their oxen to arrive lame or sore-footed. The AFC owners of the fort began to recognize valuable business opportunities. They offered blacksmith services for a fee and traded desperate emigrants out of oxen unable to go on. The fort kept the worn-out animals and allowed them to recuperate and grow fat on the meadows surrounding the fort. The rehabilitated oxen were then available the following year to be sold or traded to a new crop of desperate emigrants who would pay dearly for them. In 1846, Francis Parkman described the men at the fort as "a set of mean swindlers."[37] Curiously, Bidwell and Jimmy John did not mention any problems with their wagons, carts, or animals, which seems surprising in light of the troubles experienced by future wagon parties.

ONLY A FEW INCIDENTS offer a glimpse into Thomas Fitzpatrick's personality, and not everything written about him was complimentary. One of these instances occurred here in 1831 near the mouth of the Laramie River, before there were any forts. Zenas Leonard was a member of a new trapping expedition that left St. Louis that spring. His company of about seventy men reached here and set up camp. It was then that Fitzpatrick appeared, leading his own small party of trappers. Leonard penned this recollection:

> [Fitzpatrick] was an old hand at the business and we expected to obtain some useful information from him, but we were disappointed. The selfishness of man is often disgraceful to human nature, and I never saw more striking evidence of this fact than was presented in the conduct of this man Fitzpatrick. Notwithstanding we had treated him with great friendship and hospitality, merely because we were to engage in the same business with him, which we knew we never could exhaust or even impair—he refused to give us any information whatever, and appeared to treat us as intruders.[38]

Leonard's description of Fitzpatrick was harsh and unflattering, but looking at it from Fitzpatrick's perspective, it is hard to condemn him. Trapping had become an overpopulated business. Beaver were in decline and intense competition was coming from all sides. It is quite understandable if Fitzpatrick was not overjoyed at stumbling across a party of new trappers who would be competing with him for a dwindling supply of beaver. It would have been difficult for anyone in Fitzpatrick's shoes to disguise his discomfiture or adopt an attitude of helpfulness.

Leonard was not the only one who had found fault with Fitzpatrick. In 1834, Fitzpatrick and his partner, Milton Sublette, entered into a contract with Nathaniel Wyeth to trade their furs to Wyeth for his supplies at the 1834 rendezvous. Wyeth intended to enter the field as a challenger to William Sublette's supply business. When Wyeth arrived at the rendezvous with his pack train of supplies, Fitzpatrick refused to trade their furs to him despite their binding contract. Left holding his supplies, Wyeth was livid, accusing Fitzpatrick of having been bribed by William Sublette to help ruin him.[39] In another example, two years later, Fitzpatrick's partner, Milton Sublette, wrote a letter to a business associate in which he excoriated Fitzpatrick for an unspecified offense, and vowed he would "naeve [never] have any thin[g] more to do with him."[40] One cannot challenge Fitzpatrick's credentials as a skilled and knowledgeable frontiersman, guide, and Indian interlocutor, but he managed to leave behind a wake of critics as well.

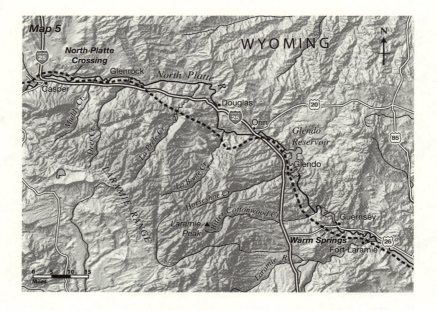

June 24

The company did not stay at Fort Laramie for long, departing on the morning of June 24. The travelers had been hearing about Fort Laramie as a wonderful outpost of civilization for some time. Having been on the trail six weeks, they had been impatiently anticipating their arrival. What they found, however, must have fallen short of their expectations. And now they were leaving it.

While it may seem surprising that the company did not linger here long, on careful reflection it is not surprising at all. In 1841, Fort Laramie did not have a great deal to offer other than the emotional salve of encountering a small dose of civilization. It was not yet the inviting place it would later become. The old stockade was small and decrepit, providing nothing in the way of comfort or luxury, and the new forts were in early stages of construction. Since this wagon train was the first emigrant party of significant size to pass through, the AFC had not yet set itself up to cater to the needs of wagon companies. It would take a few more years of increased wagon traffic to reveal the commercial opportunities that such traffic offered to the fort owners.

The members of the California-bound group knew they were eventually going to lose Fitzpatrick's services, so we wonder whether anyone had made inquiries at the fort whether there was someone in the area who would be competent to guide them to California. Had they asked about Joseph Walker? Because of Bidwell's and Jimmy John's youthfulness, it is unlikely that they ranked high in the expedition's leadership hierarchy. Bartleson and his closest confederates were unlikely to have made these youngsters privy to their plans, likely explaining why Bidwell's and Jimmy John's journals were silent on the issue.

As the fort slipped from view, one wonders what the mood and state of mind of the expedition might have been. Some may have experienced feelings of discouragement and hollow disappointment. What were they to look forward to now? They had surely been warned that the country ahead would be more difficult and daunting than what they had experienced so far.

Bidwell:

> *T. 24th. Left the Fort this morning and soon began to wind among the Black Hills, two of our men stopped at the Fort (Simpson and Mast) but, two other men with an Indian and his family joined us to travel to Green River—Encamped, having made about seventeen miles—hills here sandy—many wild Pears—likewise an abundance of Peas, wild—though the bush was dissimilar to ours, yet the pods bore an exact similarity, taste, the same.*

Jimmy John:

> *June 24—This day we left the forts and went about 16 miles by way of the road, but only 8 miles across the hills. We encamped in a deep valley and concluded to stay here until morning, for there is no water after we leave here for 20 miles. Near this encampment there is a large spring of clear water. It runs out of the side of a hill. The stream is large enough for an overshot mill. The valley is surrounded by high hills of limestone, with some scattering cedar and pine growing on them. We have seen no Indians lately except about 20 Soos [Sioux] at the fort. The men at the forts are nearly all French and Spanish. Some of them have squaws for their wives which they buy of the parents of the same.*

Bidwell mentioned that two members of the company—George Simpson and William Mast—were not proceeding further with the company. Since they were trappers, it is likely that they headed into the wilds to pursue their vocation. Bidwell also mentioned that two men and an Indian family joined the party at the forts. One of the men was named Richard Fillan (also referred to as R. Phelan, or Cocrum).[41] We will hear more about him later.

From Fort Laramie, the trail headed west, ascending an upland plain covered with sparse grass and scattered sage brush growing amidst weather-worn, chalky white limestone and clay outcroppings. In the crisp morning air, the distinctive aroma of sage would have filled their nostrils. Frémont described the smell as resembling "camphor and spirits of turpentine."[42] In front of them, about thirty miles further west, loomed the imposing Laramie Mountain Range. Laramie Peak, its highest point, commanded the horizon at an imposing height of almost ten thousand feet. From such distance, the timber growing on the upper elevations appeared black, the reason why the mountain range was usually called the Black Hills.

Upon leaving the forts, the company roughly followed the route of today's Road 92 for the first ten miles. Thereafter, Road 92 turns north on to S. Guernsey Road, although the trail would have continued west another four miles until it entered the head of a broad ravine that snaked about two miles before arriving at some springs. The springs, where they stopped to camp that afternoon, bled warm water from a steep limestone bank, the reason they were called Warm Springs. It would become a popular spot for emigrant trains to stop at the end of the day after leaving Fort Laramie. Because women took advantage of the warm water to do their laundry, in a few years the place would affectionately be called the "Emigrant's Laundry Tub."[43] The springs are in the canyon a mile southwest of the present-day town of Guernsey, Wyoming, but there are no public roads providing access to them.

The route the company took to reach Warm Springs on June 24 would not be a popular route in the future. It would largely be abandoned in favor of a slightly shorter route to Warm Springs, one that became known as the "river" route. This path would head northwest from the fort and over a ridge until it reached the North Platte River. Then it would head west, threading between the river on the north and some abrupt bluffs on the south. Emigrants would later carve their names on a bluff that came to be called Register Cliff. The trail would then continue west and across a hill of limestone outcroppings. By the end of the Gold Rush, so many thousands of wagons had rumbled over these outcroppings that their wheels had pulverized the limestone into spectacularly deep ruts, some as much as six feet deep. They are stunning evidence of the Oregon Trail era and can be seen today one-half mile south of Guernsey.

Almost as an afterthought, Jimmy John casually mentioned that they had seen twenty Sioux camping near the fort. There would be times when travelers reported seeing much larger numbers of this colorful tribe camping in the meadows around the fort. In 1835, for example, Samuel Parker, a missionary on his way to Oregon, reported that "a horde of Oglala Sioux come into the fort to trade."[44] Edwin Bryant estimated seeing three thousand Sioux camping around the fort when he passed through in 1846.[45] Francis Parkman made the same observation that year, reporting that thousands were camping in the vicinity. But 1846 was unusual. It was when Whirlwind, an Oglala Sioux chief, had sent out a war pipe, calling on Sioux bands from far and wide to assemble for a massive reprisal against one of their archenemies, the Snake tribe. Parkman wrote that once the bands had assembled near Fort Laramie, there was delay and indecisiveness among the chiefs. They were "like children that did not know their own minds," he wrote. "They were no better than a body without a head."[46] Such inaction caused their war fervor to cool to the point where the bored and disgruntled assembly soon broke up and headed for home without going to war. Two years later, in 1848, California-bound Richard May reported, "There was at this fort near 1000 Indians which annoyed us very much begging and stealing."[47]

It appeared very few Sioux were camping in the vicinity of the fort in 1841. Perhaps the reason for their scarcity at the fort was that they were camping about twenty miles upstream on the Laramie River, near the mouth of Chugwater Creek. One band was led by Chief Bull Bear, the chief who first moved his band here from the Black Hills of South Dakota in 1834. Since Bull Bear was friendly toward the whites, he was well liked by the traders. He had made quite an impression on the artist Alfred Jacob Miller, who traveled the West in 1837, painting images of landscapes and Indians. Miller's notes described Bull Bear as tall, statuesque, and well-muscled. "Nothing in Greek art," he wrote, "can surpass the reality here."[48] But Bull Bear was far more than physically impressive. His tribe regarded him as an arrogant, despotic bully. According to Francis Parkman, he had many wives and thirty sons. Size of family was important, as it was a great source of power. A large, menacing brood tended to instill fear and would protect a man from his adversaries. But Bull Bear was not invulnerable, and his bullying nature finally caught up with him. A few months after Fitzpatrick led his company through Fort Laramie, Bull Bear and his entourage were invited to visit the camp of one of his rivals, Chief Smoke. It may have been a trap. Bull Bear and his companions were treated to copious amounts of whiskey and became insensibly drunk. With Bull Bear and his protectors in a drunken stupor, an up-and-coming young warrior in the Smoke band by the name of Red Cloud shot and killed the tyrannical chief.[49] Bull Bear's death created a vacuum in Sioux leadership that had many ramifications, including the imperiling of a wagon party led by Fitzpatrick in the following year, 1842. There will be more about that later.

Travelers often mentioned how the Sioux women flashed and glittered in the sun. They were festooned with the jewelry of the frontier—the beads, bells, rings, and other baubles, bangles, and gewgaws that fur traders brought in by the ton to trade for skins and robes. As for the men, it was their physique. Edwin Bryant, for example, observed in 1846, "The men are powerfully made and possess a masculine beauty which I have never seen excelled."[50] Bryant also thought that "[c]onscious of their superior strength . . . they are arrogant and exacting towards their more feeble neighbors; and have thus, probably, acquired a reputation for cruelty and duplicity."[51] Parkman described them as "splendidly formed," noting that most were six feet tall or more. He went on to express the opinion that "[w]ar is the breath of their nostrils. Against most of the neighboring tribes they cherish a rancorous hatred, transmitted from father to son, and inflamed by constant aggression and retaliation."[52]

To say that alcohol was a problem among the Indians is an understatement. In the case of the Sioux, it was more than a problem; it was a scourge. They could go on drinking binges that would lead to drunken brawls and killings that turned families against families, and villages against villages.[53] Although the government had made it illegal to sell or give alcohol to Indians living in the Indian Territory, unscrupulous traders did it anyway because it undeniably helped establish and cement trading relationships. The traders could get away with it because the nearest government authorities were more than five hundred miles away, and the Indian agents sent by the government to enforce the law too often used their position to enrich themselves by accepting generous bribes to look the other way.[54]

June 25

When the company departed Warm Springs on the morning of June 25, the company emerged from the canyon and headed northwesterly across another hilly plain.

Bidwell:

> *F. 25th. Journeyed over hills and dales—encamped on a stream affording plenty of grass, bitter Cotton-wood timber. It resembles the sweet Cotton wood of Missouri, except the leaves are like those of the willow—distance 18 miles.*

Jimmy John:

> *June 25—We left the camp and warm spring this morning at 7 o'clock. We traveled about 20 miles today over high hills and through deep valleys, but there is plenty of game here and good water and a kind of mountain turnip. They are about as large as hen's eggs and are tender and good eating; also there is currants and mountain cherries. We were overtaken today by two men and a squaw from the fort. They are going to the mountains with us. Two of our men left us at the forts, but their place is filled by these men, and a squaw thrown in. We saw a number of buffaloes today, but have not killed any of them. We encamped in a valley. There is plenty of good water here and excellent grass for the cattle and horses and mules. The grass is equal to timothy grass, if not better. It is of different kinds in the valley. It resembles blue grass of the States. It grows tall here and thin on hills and plains and short [in the valleys].*

The trail they followed on the morning of June 25 crossed today's Highway 26 about four miles west of Guernsey. One can follow most of their route by taking a gravel road (it has no sign) north where it leaves Highway 26, about two and a quarter miles west of Guernsey. After traveling six miles, the company came to Bitter Cottonwood Creek, where Jimmy John said they stopped for a midday meal. Today, the creek is simply called Cottonwood Creek.

North of the creek, the land uplifted, resulting in the North Platte River carving a three-hundred-foot-deep canyon called the Black Hills Gap. Therefore, the river would be inaccessible for the next twelve miles. After the company crossed Bitter Cottonwood Creek, it followed the trail north, climbing a steep hill that caused them to gain about two hundred feet of elevation in one mile. Then weaving between dry, parched hills and through flats and canyons, the company finally emerged in the valley of Bear Creek. They stopped to camp beside the creek, completing a tiring day of eighteen miles. The location of their camp at the end of June 25 would have been just south of present-day Cassa Road, a mile east of its intersection with Highway 319 (Glendo Highway), and about eight miles south of Glendo, Wyoming. A dirt road can be seen angling south from this spot that follows the route of the old trail.

June 26

Bidwell:

> S. 26th. Travelled about 18 miles, and missing our road, encamped on the North fork, at noon we passed the best grass I had seen since I left the frontier of Missouri, it was like a meadow, kind of blue grass—found Buffalo, killed three.

Jimmy John:

> June 26—This morning we started at 3 minutes past six o'clock. Took dinner on the bank of a creek of good water and grass. In the afternoon myself and two others went out to hunt buffaloes. We killed one and wounded another. We packed our horses and set out for the place where [we] expected to find the wagons, but they had went a different way and encamped on the Platte on the main branch. We traveled until 12 o'clock at night before we reached the camp. There were some gray bears [grizzlies] there which are monsters. Large, but we have killed none of them yet. Some more hunters killed a buffalo today.

Upon leaving Bear Creek, the trail headed northwest, traveling closely to the route of today's Highway 319. About four miles after leaving camp, the company passed Red Springs, a place where many wagon trains would stop in the future because of its grass and excellent water. In 1848, Riley Root praised the spring for producing "the best water west of St. Josephs."[55] Seven miles after leaving camp they crossed Horseshoe Creek near where it passes beneath today's Interstate 25. This was probably the creek that Bidwell and Jimmy John both mentioned encountering around midday. They also both mentioned missing a road, probably referring to a trail that turned west just north of Horseshoe Creek and that ascended a bluff west of

Glendo. This trail led to La Bonte Creek. It sounded as if Fitzpatrick had overlooked it. But it was early in the wagon train era and the trail would have been so faint and indefinite that it could easily be missed if one was not paying close attention. Besides, much of this country looked the same. On the other hand, avoiding that route may have been intentional on Fitzpatrick's part. He may have continued to lead the company north because he knew that there was another trail ahead, perhaps a better one, that would also lead them to La Bonte Creek. In any event, they continued to travel north, their route closely following today's Highway 319. Bidwell explained that they traveled about eighteen miles on June 26, and ended the day beside the North Platte River. Their camp that evening was next to the river, probably about nine miles northwest of Glendo and just east of Highway 319.

The buffalo mentioned were probably grazing on the lush grass in the bottom of Horseshoe Creek. Since the creek bottoms of this region would support only limited numbers, there were no large herds of buffalo here, certainly not like those observed in the Forks region. Vulnerable to hunting by passing emigrant trains, these few buffalo would be hunted to extinction in just a few more years. It would be a matter of time when buffalo in this area would no longer be mentioned by future diarists.

Because of proximity to the mountains to the west, it is not surprising that Jimmy John mentioned large, gray bears. He was undoubtedly referring to grizzlies. Through the lessons of hard experience, frontiersmen had learned to stay out of their way. They were terribly dangerous and it was difficult to put one down even with a few well-placed shots. Hence, no one should go looking for a grizzly. If you stumbled across one, it was unwise to taunt or provoke him. Rather, it was advisable to turn around and leave as quickly as possible. Jimmy John did not sound as if he was aware of such advice.

June 27

Bidwell:

> S. 27th. Day was warm, road hilly, found no water for 20 miles, encamped on a stream affording grass and timber in abundance, cotton wood &c. found no hard timber.

Jimmy John:

> *June 27—We left the Platte early this morning. Traveled until 4 o'clock in the afternoon. Encamped on the bank of a creek of muddy water. There is but few springs in this country. The ground is so sandy that the water sinks. We killed one buffaloe today and some small game.*

Getting an early start, the company departed its encampment beside the North Platte River, and traveled northwest for a couple of miles between the bluffs and the river. The trail pretty much continued to follow the route of today's Highway 319. About one and a half miles south of the North Platte River Bridge on Interstate 25, the trail made a hard left turn away from the river. It then passed beneath the present path of the Interstate as it headed west. The wagons commenced a steady one-mile climb up the ridge, gaining about two hundred fifty feet in one mile (a 5 percent grade). After this arduous pull, the caravan continued traveling slightly south of west along the ridge dividing Spring Creek on the north and Indian Creek on the south. It was an arid region that was almost destitute of vegetation except for sparse grass and the ubiquitous sage.

Ever since the company had left the prairie behind, especially after leaving Fort Laramie, travel had become more difficult. It was not just the roughness of the country—the steeper inclines and rockier paths—it was the sagebrush. The aromatic plant was as tough as barbwire and could survive the most difficult environments in the West: cold winters, hot summers, arid conditions, and gravelly soils.

In imagining wagon trains rumbling along the trail, one is inclined to picture the trail as a narrow track, downtrodden and clear of sagebrush within its path. While that image would tend to be accurate in later years, it was not so true in 1841. The trail was still in its juvenile stage, with its traffic mostly being horses and pack mules traveling in single file. Very few wagons had traveled across it. The sage grew irregularly, not in straight lines or rows. Wagons, about five feet wide and pulled by mules or oxen two abreast, had to plow through and roll over it. Nicholas Dawson recalled the difficulty, describing this section as "covered with sage bushes two or three feet high, through which the wagons forced their way, raking and scraping. Horseback riders also had their clothes torn off."[56] One suspects that the abrasive and rough-stemmed sage scratched at the animals' legs, making them skinned and bleeding. Because previous wagon traffic had been so infrequent in those early years, Frémont registered the same complaint in 1842, saying that the road was rough and bumpy because of having to push over and through the sagebrush and its roots.[57]

After ten miles of travel along the ridge, the company veered to the northwest, marching northwesterly another six miles through more arid country. At last, the wagons descended into a pretty valley through which meandered La Bonte Creek, sometimes called Big Timber Creek. They had traveled about twenty miles that day, and should have been relieved that they could camp where there was good grass, water, and plenty of firewood.

It is difficult to see most of the route they traveled on June 27 because it crosses remote and privately owned land with no public roads. One can get close to their La Bonte Creek campsite, however, by traveling south on Highway 94 out of Douglas, Wyoming, for a distance of eleven miles. The creek crossing and their campsite are about one mile east of this point.

How can we be sure of the company's path when Bidwell's and Jimmy John's descriptions are so sketchy and lacking in detail? It is because their mileage estimates are consistent with this route and because it is a route that became a well-known, heavily traveled trail used by wagon trains for many years thereafter, including the Gold Rush years. Fitzpatrick was familiar with these trails, and may have played a role in pioneering them. He must have known that the route was suitable for wagons, and since wagon train guides tended to follow tracks laid down by previous wagon parties, these tracks would become more pronounced with each passing year. Indeed, the unmistakable marks that thousands of wagon wheels had left can still be seen in many stretches through there today.

June 28

When the company departed La Bonte Creek on the morning of June 28, they entered terrain that was more geologically complicated and fascinating.

Bidwell:

> M. 28th. Passed an immense quarry of beautiful white Alabaster, 3 buffalo killed, distance travelled 18 miles, encamped on a little rivulet affording as good water as ever run.

La Bonte Creek, *by William Henry Jackson. Catalog No. SCBL-30. Courtesy of Scotts Bluff National Monument.*

Jimmy John:

June 28—We started early this morning. Took dinner on the banks of a creek of good water, and as beautiful grass as I have ever seen. The grass is generally good in the valleys, but on the hills and plains it appears to be dried up. Near our dining place is a large cleft of rocks as white as snow. The rocks are a little harder than common chalk, and some of the earth is composed of this substance, which is the genuine plaster paris, or believed to be by most of the company. We left here and after a hard half day's drive camped on a creek near a spring of excellent water. We killed one buffaloe today. Seen some gray bears but did not kill them.

Pulling away from La Bonte Creek that morning, the expedition climbed a ridge and headed north. Evidence of that trail can be seen today. Within two miles, they entered what became known as Red Earth Country. This brick-red material—red rock, red sand, red dust—was high in iron oxide, causing some to call the area "Uncle Sam's brick-yard."[58]

Three miles after leaving their La Bonte camp, the group crossed the steep-banked Wagon Hound Creek about one mile west of where today's Highway 94 crosses the stream. Shortly, they trundled by a pyramidal mound of gray limestone to their immediate west that conspicuously and incongruously stood above its red surroundings. It has variously been called Knob Hill, Grindstone Butte, and Brigham's Peak, all names given to it years after Fitzpatrick led his party past.

The cavalcade continued north, following a route that ran close to Highway 94, passing through broken country that seemed to have no rhyme or reason to it. The trail weaved about, navigating through many draws, ravines, and flats. It was geological mayhem, with conical hills, rounded buttes, pushed-up ridges, and jumbled rockpiles. The features were made of many-colored rocks, sands, and clays, ranging from red to white and from black to gray. Some of it contained evidence of a volcanic past. Later emigrants could not resist describing these provocative geological features, but Bidwell and Jimmy John did not seem interested in wasting their valuable ink on them.

From Knob Hill, the trail headed northwest, almost in a straight line bearing 330 degrees. Sheep Mountain passed to their left, while the Chalk Buttes approached on their right. It was along here that they lost sight of Laramie Peak for good. It had been their lodestar ever since they had crossed Robidoux Pass nine days earlier. The company ambled past sagebrush and pink-blossomed prickly pear cactus. They crossed a small stream called Bed Tick Creek near where Highway 91 and some high-voltage transmission lines cross. To the northeast rose the Chalk Buttes. Bidwell and Jimmy John seemed impressed with some white material they encountered. Bidwell called it alabaster in his memoirs, describing it as "pure white translucent rock."[59] Father De Smet had the same opinion, writing in one of his letters: "We discovered an equally curious quarry, which, at first, we took for white marble. . . . It was alabaster."[60] For those who wish to see the location, take Highway 94 at Douglas and head south one mile, then turn right on Chalk Buttes Road (Road 91) and head west four miles to Road 8.

From here, the route of the trail tends to follow the course of the high-voltage lines until it reached the twenty-foot-wide La Prele Creek. After traveling eighteen miles that day, the company had marched far enough, and stopped to encamp. It was a fine place where their hungry livestock could enjoy an abundance of lush grass. Jimmy John again mentioned bears, probably grizzlies drawn from the mountains to feast on the currants and choke cherries growing along the creek.

Their La Prele Creek camp was one-half mile east of present-day Natural Bridge Road, two and three-quarters of a mile south of its intersection with Interstate 26 (eleven miles west of Douglas, Wyoming).

June 29

Bidwell:

> T. 29th. Arrived at the N. fork this evening, road good, distance travelled 15 miles.

Jimmy John:

> June 29—Did not start early this morning on account of some of the cattle straying away. We took dinner on a small creek. We are now traveling through the Black Hills, over high hills and through deep valleys. The hills are composed of different kinds of substances, some of granite, and some of fine sand, and some of a substance resembling chalk, and some of plaster paris and red stone and clay, also red sand in some places. They have a beautiful appearance. We encamped this evening on the bank of the north fork of the Platte river, about 200 miles from the main ridge of the Rocky Mountains. We are now in sight of some high mountains.

Upon leaving camp at La Prele Creek, the company followed the trail as it headed westerly, crossing today's Natural Bridge Road about two and a half miles south of Interstate 25. Shortly after crossing the road, the trail angled northwest, rolling over gentle hills until it came to the steep-sided, eight-foot-wide Box Elder Creek, the "small creek" where Jimmy John said they paused to eat their midday meal. This location is just east of Bixby Road, about two-thirds of a mile southwest of its intersection with the Interstate. From there the trail continued northwest. Three miles later the company splashed across the shallow Fourche Boise Creek just north of Interstate 25. A mile beyond the creek the company reached the North Platte River. But they did not stop there, and continued to travel a few more miles until they came to Deer Creek, near where it flowed into the North Platte River. It was a good place to end the day. While both diarists wrote about camping on the bank of the North Platte, neither mentioned Deer Creek. The actual distance between their morning camp at La Prele Creek and where Deer Creek flows into the North Platte is sixteen miles. Bidwell estimated they traveled fifteen miles that day, while Dawson estimated eighteen miles. Deer Creek became a popular camping site for future wagon trains owing to its cold, pristine waters and one of the finest grass meadows in the region. A few years later a Mormon diarist expressed delight at being able to pull a mess of silvery fish out of its clear waters. Since there are no other locations in the vicinity that would match the attributes of Deer Creek, it is inconceivable that the company did not camp there. It is just odd that our diarists did not mention it.

June 30

The company headed upstream along the south bank of the North Platte River on the morning of June 30, closely following the path of today's Highway 26. As they marched west, the Laramie Mountains remained on their left, rising to over seven thousand feet. It was an entirely different scene on their right, as sage-covered bluffs, not very tall, bordered the far side of the river. For the second consecutive day, Bidwell penned an uncommonly short entry in his journal, perhaps a sign of weariness.

Bidwell:

> *W. 30th. Assended the N. fork about 16 miles and encamped on it. Buffalo in abundance, killed six.*

Jimmy John:

> *June 30—Left the camp at six o'clock this morning. Took [dinner] on the bank of that river. The day was pleasant. We made a good day's travel. Encamped on the bank of the Platte. Killed five buffaloe cows today and two bulls. The river is about 200 yards wide here.*

Eleven miles after leaving their camp on the morning of June 30, and after crossing a number of steep-banked ravines, the company crossed Muddy Creek. After another five miles, they called it a day, stopping to camp on the south bank of the North Platte River. There were a number of deep gullies and ravines ahead that ran perpendicular to their path and into the river from the south. It might not have been so difficult for pack trains, but for wheeled vehicles the steep banks would be troublesome. Fitzpatrick must have decided to avoid them by crossing the company to the north side of the river first thing the next morning.

In the fall and winter, the North Platte tended to run low and was easy to ford. In the spring and summer, the copious runoff from upstream snowmelt, storms, and free-flowing springs changed the situation. At such times, wagon parties were faced with crossing a six-hundred-foot-wide river with swift and deep water. Crossing was not to be taken lightly. It would pose the most dangerous obstacle they had faced in quite some time, and it would not be surprising if many in the company slept fitfully that night, anticipating the next day with trepidation.

Their camp on the afternoon of June 30 would have been just north of present-day Highway 26, about two miles east of its intersection with Highway 256 and about five miles east of Casper, Wyoming.

Chapter 8

Crossing the North Platte and Up the Sweetwater

JULY 1 TO 15, 1841

July 1

July 1 would be a perilous day.

Bidwell:

> *July. T. 1st. Spent the day in passing over the river to the North side of it: the water ran very rapidly, and it was with considerable difficulty that we forded it. One Mule was drowned, and one waggon upset in the river, the water in the N. fork is not so muddy as the South fork.*

Bidwell was generally stingy with his words, but his succinct description of the river crossing is annoying since there was much more he could have reported about the day's experiences.

Jimmy John's entry was not much better:

> *July 1, 1841—This day we crossed the north fork of the Platte river about a mile from where we encamped last evening. We had some difficulty in crossing as the ford was deep and the water ran very swift. We got over safe, all excepting two teams—one drowned a mule, and the other turned over the wagon, but did not lose much. We encamped on the north side of the river this night, about two miles from where we stayed last night.*

Thankfully, Father Mengarini described the crossing in more detail and provided some dramatic images:

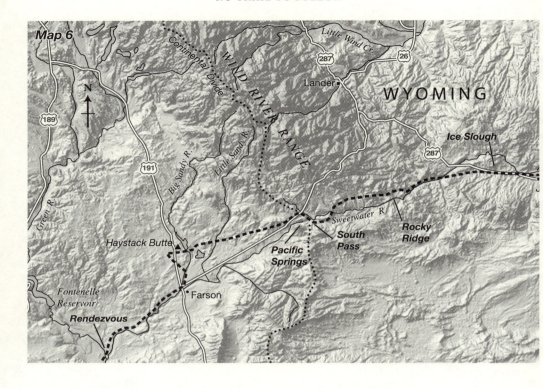

John Gray went in search of a ford and came back saying he had found one. He immediately started ahead, and the wagoners started to follow. But as people generally do, some thought that they could find a better way for themselves and so scattered after entering the river, thus leaving it uncertain, for those that came last, what way the guide had taken. A wagon had just entered the stream when I reached the bank, and I determined to follow it. All went well for some time, and we were nearing the other bank when suddenly I beheld the wagon upset, and at the same moment I felt the earth slipping from beneath my horse's feet. I clung to the neck of the animal, if not gracefully, at least firmly; for, as I could not swim, I held on to life the more vigorously. The current was strong but my horse was a good swimmer and in a few minutes both of us were landed on the bank. I turned to look at the wagon and saw it abandoned and floating down the stream. No lives were lost, but a man whom we called "the Major" had been in imminent danger.[1]

In future years, wagon trains usually traveled six miles farther upstream along the south bank of the North Platte before crossing.

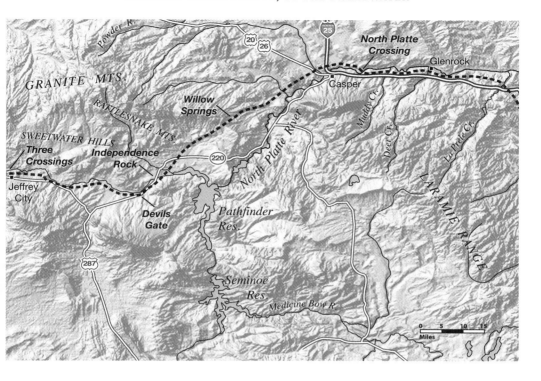

They usually forded about a half-mile west of where today's Bryan Stock Trail Bridge crosses the river, but it was dangerous wherever the river was crossed. It was not until 1847 that a significant improvement occurred. That was when a resourceful group of Mormons cut down some large cottonwood trees in the area, hollowed out their trunks, and lashed planks over the top of them to create platforms onto which wagons could be rolled. Their innovative ferry was so successful that they returned in June 1848 to provide crucial ferry services to a number of emigrant wagon parties, Mormon and non-Mormon alike.[2] Charging $1.50 a wagon, or goods of equivalent value, they did well financially, and the emigrants thought the cost was well worth it.

Since Jimmy John reported that the company camped on the evening of July 1 on the north side of the river, two miles beyond their previous camp, it appears that their camp was about one mile east of the Highway 256 Bridge across the North Platte (Yellowstone–Cole Creek Road).

July 2

Bidwell:

> *F, 2nd. Continued to coast up the N. fork, the bottoms of the river were in many places completely covered with Glauber Salts, so much so that even handfuls could be taken up perfectly white. A man (Mr. Belden) was hunting a short distance from the company, and left his horse tied while he crept in pursuit of a Buffalo but he was not able to find the same place again and consequently lost his horse. Though the country is perfectly free from timber, excepting near the river, yet there is so great a similarity in the hills that experienced hunters are frequently bewildered in a clear day, when attempting to find a certain place a second time.*

Jimmy John:

> *July 2d—Left the camp early this morning and traveled on the banks of the river. Killed 2 buffaloes. The country is sandy here and broken on the south side of the river. There is a range of high hills or mountains covered with pine trees, but on the north side there is barren sand hills and plains. We encamped on the bank of the river this evening.*

The company's route would have been along the north side of the river, north of present-day Casper. Since the river runs against some steep bluffs on its north side, there are places where it would have been difficult to squeeze wagons through. Did they climb the bluffs and travel above the river? Jimmy John suggested that they did not, writing that they "traveled on the banks of the river."

Dawson, the only one estimating distance for July 2, logged that they traveled twenty miles. This places their camp that evening near the north bank of the river, about one mile southeast of the intersection of today's Poison Spider Road and South Robertson Road (Road 305).

July 3

When the company departed camp on the morning of July 3, it left the North Platte River behind for good.

Bidwell:

> S. 3rd. Left the N. fork, a distance of 12 miles took us to a spring of cool, though unpleasantly tasted water. The day was intensely warm, and road mountainous, killed four Buffalo and two deer.

Jimmy John:

> July 3d—This day we traveled until about two o'clock and encamped for the night. Killed one buffaloe and two deer today. One of the men by the name of Belder [Belden] lost his horse yesterday when he was hunting buffaloe. He hitched his horse and could not find the place again. Himself and another man went back this morning, but the horse was gone. They found the place where the horse was hitched, but no horse.

Josiah Belden's experience seemed to capture the attention of both diarists, while it is not surprising that the embarrassed Belden did not mention it in his memoirs. It was not one of his proudest moments. Apparently, he had not been warned—or had ignored the warning—that it was not safe to hunt buffalo on foot since a wounded buffalo often charged and one stood a better chance of escaping if on horseback.

After the expedition left its North Platte camp that morning it followed the trail west, generally following the route of today's Poison Spider Road. The face of the country was changing and the company rumbled across some crumpled and dreadfully broken terrain. Over the ages, earthquakes and volcanoes had brought minerals to the surface, not all of them good. The trail snaked between ridges of jumbled rock formations and through crusty beds of salt, sulfur, and alkali. In some places there were patches of almost pure sodium bicarbonate, a raw form of baking powder. Called "saleratus" in those days, women would often gather it up for use in making bread.

The land had not seen rain for weeks. Rolling through this parched and forlorn land, the wagons and livestock would have kicked up clouds of caustic dust. Alkali had a bite to it, tasting bitter-sour, and possessing an acrid, chemical-like smell. It would burn the emigrants' eyes and nostrils and enflame their lungs. Of all the things emigrants complained about, dust ranked highest on their lists, with alkali being the worst. Thornton commented on it in 1846, writing "that among the most serious inconveniences the emigrant will have to encounter upon this journey will be the dust."[3]

After twelve miles, the company stopped to camp beside Poison Springs. One can follow the trail by taking Poison Spider Road as it continues southwest through Emigrant Gap. Upon descending from the Gap, turn south on Road 319 (Oregon Trail Road), and travel south one-half mile to Poison Springs.

Edwin Bryant described this section of trail and Poison Springs in 1846:

> The trail here finally leaves the Platte river. Ascending the bluffs on the right, we pursued our way over an arid plain, the only vegetation upon which is the wild sage, grease-wood, and a few perishing plants. We passed immense piles of rocks, red and black, sometimes in columnar and sometimes in conical and pyramidal shapes, thrown up by volcanic convulsions. These, with deep ravines, and chasms, and widespread sterility and desolation, are the distinguishing features of the landscape. We reached our camp at a spring impregnated with salt and sulfur, about ten o'clock at night.[4]

Bidwell had described Poison Springs water as tasting unpleasant. But it was worse than that. The brackish, alkali-contaminated water had a laxative effect, much like the salty fluids that are often used today to prepare a patient for a colonoscopy. In 1846, Edwin Bryant was probably experiencing the effects of drinking too much of this water when he wrote, "The soil and water of the country through which we are now traveling, are so impregnated with salt, alkali and sulphur; rendering the use of the water, in large quantities, deleterious to health, if not dangerous." After consuming the water, Bryant complained that he was seized that night "with a violent and exhausting sickness," such that he was scarcely able to mount his mule the next morning.[5]

It was rare for wagon parties to carry water forward with them, so the members of the company likely drank the alkali-tainted water to slake their thirst, with predictable and inescapable results, even though our diarists appeared loath to mention it.

There were springs and creeks in the immediate area whose waters were even more dangerous than those at Poison Springs. Highly alkaline water was a deadly trap for oxen. As ruminants, oxen are entirely dependent on the cellulose-digesting bacteria in their stomachs. Any dramatic increase in the pH can cause a catastrophic die-off of these beneficial bacteria, and can shut down their digestion. Cattlemen today would call the process as "going off feed." The cattle would bloat, or "burst," as the emigrants usually described it. In the years to come, seasoned trail guides knew where the most tainted springs and creeks were along this section of trail and would prevent their thirsty livestock from drinking from them. The lack of good grass in this area would create another problem in the years to come. Hungry livestock were inclined to wander off at night in search of something to eat. Such wanderings caused them to come across these troublesome waters, and their owners would often find them sick and dying.

Wagon parties led by inexperienced men often lost large numbers of animals at such places. Having traveled back and forth through here many times during his career, Fitzpatrick would have known where the problematic water was. He may have been busy riding up and down the line of wagons warning people what to avoid. That Bidwell and Jimmy John did not recount any livestock sickness or losses suggests that Fitzpatrick's knowledge and experience saved the expedition from potential disaster.

That there was no mention of sick or weakened oxen did not mean that all was well. At some point, the wagoneers must have looked at their teams with concern. It should have been evident to even the most unobservant that the poor beasts had lost a great deal of weight during the journey. It was not a simple matter of insufficiency of grass. The animals had sore feet and were tired at the end of each day's travels. This compelled them to spend much of the night lying down and resting. They simply could not graze all night. Because of the enormous effort needed to pull the heavy wagons, they were burning more energy each day than they replaced at night. Hence, the loss of flesh.

The arduous nature of the trip must have been wearing the people down as well. And they were not even halfway. The surroundings, bleak and perilous, could have been infecting some with a withering discouragement. Were they tiring of the squeaky complaint of saddle leather, the squeal of insufficiently greased wagon axles, and the effects of caustic dust? Were they sinking under prolonged exposure to solitude, empty space, blazing suns, and incessant winds? Were some now spending their nights in the throes of intestinal distress? Were dejected thoughts taking control of some? If so, wasn't it now too late to act upon a change of heart and turn back? The best place to have reversed course would have been at Fort Laramie, where the group could have eventually returned with an eastbound party of fur traders. Trying to venture back alone now was unthinkable. At this point, there were few practical choices other than to continue.

July 4

Anxious to get away from this inhospitable region, the company pulled out of camp early the next morning with their battered wagons and weakened animals. They slogged through the marsh surrounding Poison Springs and headed southwest.

Bidwell:

> S. 4th. Pursued our way over hills and dales, scorched with heat, came to a small copse of red willows, from which issued excellent springs of water, three buffalo killed, distance travelled 22 miles.

Jimmy John:

> July 4th—Started this morning at six o'clock. The day is warm and the road rough. We traveled about 15 miles and encamped at an excellent spring of water. We are about a day's travel from a stream called Sweetwater. The country here is hilly, abounding in sand hills and sand rocks and mountains. There is plenty of buffaloes and grizly bears and wolves. Killed 3 buffaloes today.

It was the 4th of July. Wagon trains often greeted the holiday by firing guns into the air and pulling out bottles of liquor that had been stashed away for such occasions. As can be seen, neither diarist mentioned the holiday or any form of celebration. In one of his letters, Father De Smet reported that indeed, they did not celebrate. He explained why: "We had in our company a young Englishman [Romaine], as jealous of the honor of his nation as the Americans; hence we had a double reason not to cry hurra for Independence."[6] This is a difficult pill to swallow. It is difficult to believe that this large group of Americans would have deferred to the sensitivities of a single Englishman by not celebrating the 4th.

The route the company followed on July 4 continued along Road 319. The path led them through stark and rocky country, at one point beside a narrow ridge of broken, ragged rock that became known as Rock Avenue or the Devil's Backbone.[7] The company then splashed across creeks containing more deadly water and had to snap their whips to keep the oxen and mules moving so they would not stop to

Modern day view of Willow Springs. Author's photograph.

drink. After sixteen difficult miles of trail, perhaps their worst so far, they finally arrived at Willow Springs. Here, the water was delightfully pure and the grass was good. The spring got its name from the willows growing there. The trees gradually disappeared in the years to come, however, falling victim to hordes of future travelers wanting wood for their campfires. It is not surprising that buffalo, grizzlies, and wolves were near, drawn by the good water and grass.

One can reach Willow Springs today by continuing along the gravel Road 319 about sixteen miles beyond Poison Springs. The spring is wedged between arid hills of stunted sage and is identified by clumps of young willows scattered throughout an elongated meadow.

July 5

When the party left their Willow Springs camp on the morning of July 5, they should have felt partially refreshed, their spirits buoyed by assurances that they would reach the Sweetwater River by the end of the day.

Bidwell:

> M. 5th. The hills continued to increase in height. After travelling 16 miles we encamped at a noted place called Independence Rock, this is a huge isolated rock covering an Area, perhaps of half a square mile, and rising in shape of an irregular obtuse mound, to the height of 100 feet. It took its name from the celebration of the 4th of July at this place by Capt. Wm. Sublette, and it now bears many names of the early travellers to these regions. Immediately at the base of these rocks flows a small stream called Sweet Water and is a branch of the N. fork, six Buffalo killed today.

Jimmy John:

> July 5th—This morning we left the camp at the usual hour, and after a hard day's drive came to a creek called Sweetwater. Here we encamped for the night. Killed some buffaloes today, and seen a good number of them. A band had liken to have run over some of the wagons, but we shot some of them and the others fled. We have seen no timber scarcely today, but a sandy plain nearly destitute of vegetation with now and then a cleft of rocks. Our encampment this night is near a rock called the independent [Independence] rock. It is a rock about 130 feet high of sollid granite.

The trail that the group followed on July 5 can be retraced by continuing southwest from Willow Springs on Road 319. They began their morning by climbing Prospect Hill, a daunting incline up a ridge that gained about four hundred feet of elevation in a mile (7 percent grade). There is a turnout at the summit where one can get a closeup view of old trail ruts. From here, the travelers were able to gaze southward across a huge sage-covered plain they would have to cross. Then the party began a gradual descent, rolling across Alkali Slough, which has since been dammed. The trail then crossed the narrow, steep-banked Horse Creek and continued to where the trail crossed today's Highway 220. As the long day neared its end, the wagon party veered westerly, passing west of Steamboat Rock, then passed a couple of small lakes fringed by crusty deposits of alkali and bicarbonate of soda. Just ahead was Independence Rock, an enormous hump of dark granite that looked like a huge whale surfacing from an earthen sea. Others thought it resembled a massive turtle. It was no small thing, about nineteen hundred feet long, seven hundred feet wide, and over a hundred feet high. The rock was so out of place, so incongruously rising out of the plain that no diarist would neglect mentioning it. It was a captivating curiosity, remarkable in

CROSSING NORTH PLATTE, UP THE SWEETWATER

Independence Rock, *by William Henry Jackson. Catalog No. SCBL-31. Courtesy of Scotts Bluff National Monument. Independence Rock is depicted in the foreground, Devil's Gate in the far distance.*

its size and shape. After so much monotony and dreariness, it was something to get excited about. Along with Chimney Rock, it was the most frequently mentioned geological formation along the trail. Even though the travelers must have been tired after traveling sixteen miles, there can be little doubt that many of them found it irresistible to clamber to the top of the rock that afternoon to enjoy captivating views in all directions.

The company camped between the rock and the Sweetwater River, a tributary of the North Platte River that flowed just to the south. Narrow and meandering, the Sweetwater was only about fifty feet wide, but it supported abundant grass on either side of its banks. The Sweetwater would now provide succor for the next hundred miles.

It is easy to imagine the camp that evening. While the livestock grazed beside the river, recuperating from straining at their yokes and harnesses all day, the campfires popped, sending sparks into the air like so many excited fireflies. It was around campfires like these that the folklore of the mountain men—their heroic deeds and narrow escapes, some true and some not—were told. We are not told whom Fitzpatrick generally associated with in the evenings, but he could have mesmerized whoever it was with his vast repertoire of stories. There was hardly a place along the trail where something interesting had not happened to him during his eighteen-year career. He could have related, for example, when and how Independence Rock acquired its name. One belief is that its name derived from Fitzpatrick and that his small party of trappers had cached furs at its base on July 4, 1824.[8] Other authorities, however, believe that the name was given because William Sublette and his party of trappers celebrated the national holiday there in 1830.[9] That Bidwell credited Sublette suggests that he and his fellow travelers were told the story by Fitzpatrick, who did not claim the honor for himself.

Fitzpatrick would be involved in a hair-raising incident here at Independence Rock the following year, in 1842. As mentioned earlier, Fitzpatrick returned east after delivering Father De Smet and his missionaries to the Flathead Indians at the end of this trip. He was at Fort Laramie in the summer of 1842 when Dr. Elijah White arrived with his Oregon-bound wagon party. White hired Fitzpatrick to escort his group as far as Fort Hall. Because the Sioux chief Bull Bear had been assassinated in the fall of 1841, restless, ambitious young warriors no longer felt constrained by Bull Bear's tight leash. As a result, a hostile war party of three hundred Sioux and Cheyenne was on the prowl in 1842 and looking for whites to kill. The war party stumbled across the Fitzpatrick-led wagon train as it encamped here at Independence Rock and were about to attack when Fitzpatrick rode out to parley. Somehow, almost miraculously, Fitzpatrick persuaded the Indians to let the wagon party go and resume its travels in safety, thereby further gilding his already illustrious reputation as an Indian mediator. As Bernard DeVoto, the distinguished western historian from Harvard, wrote, "No man in the West handled Indians better than Tom Fitzpatrick."[10]

July 6

Bidwell:

> T. 6th. This morning John Gray and Romaine were sent on to Green river to see if there were any Trappers at the rendezvous, and then return to the company with the intelligence, all hands were anxious to have their names inscribed on this memorable land mark, so that we did not start until near noon, went upstream about 8 miles and encamped on Sweet Water.

When the travelers rose on the morning of July 6, Bidwell reported that everyone was determined to add his name to the rock before leaving. It seemed to be a compulsion that afflicted just about everyone who passed by. Father Point recalled, "According to custom, each one of us wrote down his name."[11] Father De Smet wrote in his letter to his reverend provincial that they carved their names on the rock's south side. Owing to the host of names already chiseled, scratched, and painted on the massive monolith, De Smet labeled it the "Great Record of the Desert, while Father Point referred to it in his memoirs as the "The Great Register of the Wilderness."[12]

Passing through here the next year, Frémont recorded: "Everywhere within six to eight foot of the ground, where the surface is sufficiently smooth, and in some places sixty or eighty feet above, the rock is inscribed with the names of travelers." If the rock's surface seemed crowded in 1842, one can only imagine what it was like by the Gold Rush era. As early as 1849, when J. Goldsborough Bruff wanted to etch his name, he complained, "it was with difficulty I could find a place to inscribe on it."[13]

Historians universally contend that because of the precipitous decline in the trapping business, the last fur trade rendezvous was held in 1840. However, Bidwell was clearly reporting that Gray and Romaine were sent ahead to the Green River "rendezvous" being held there that year. Over the years, the trappers would agree before they left the rendezvous as to when and where to meet the following summer. It seems logical that when the 1840 rendezvous broke up, the trappers left with the understanding that they would meet at a designated place on the Green River late in July 1841. Belief that a rendezvous was planned that year along the Green River, even if it was not expected to be heavily attended, could have come from Fitzpatrick. But it also could have come from Father De Smet. After all, he had traveled with an American Fur Company supply caravan the previous year and was present at the 1840 rendezvous when the trappers would have decided where to assemble in 1841.

Jimmy John:

> *July 6th—We left the Independent Rock this morning at the usual hour of starting. We are now in a valley that will lead us over the mountains. Nothing happened today worthy of notice excepting we seen some curiosity in the rocks along each side of the creek. These are mountains of gran-*

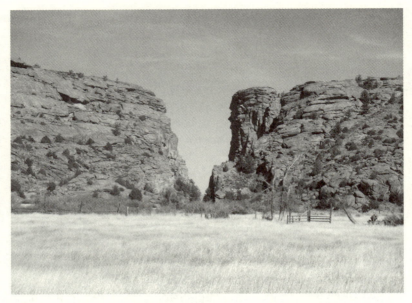

Modern view of Devil's Gate, looking east. Author's photograph.

> ite rocks. The creek runs through a gap in a sollid rock which is not less than 250 feet high on each side and about 50 feet wide at the narrowest place. It is nearly perpendicular on one side and on the other it is shelvey [shelving] over. We encamped this evening on the banks of the Sweetwater creek which extends the whole length of this valley.

While Bidwell claimed that the rock signing delayed the party's departure until "near noon," it is curious that Jimmy John wrote that they left camp "at the usual hour."

Upon leaving camp, the company splashed across the Sweetwater and headed west. With the morning's delay, the livestock had enjoyed a few extra hours of rest and grazing, perhaps pulling their wagons that morning with more alacrity. Three miles later, the company drew abreast of Devil's Gate, a rift in a towering granite ridge. The ridge was cleaved in two, allowing the Sweetwater to rush through a fifty-foot-wide "gap" between nearly perpendicular three-hundred-foot-high rock walls.

To get around the ridge, the trail detoured south through what was called Rattlesnake Pass. Once through the pass, the trail returned to the Sweetwater, the shallow stream indecisively meandering eastward along a flat river bottom. In one of his letters, Father

Modern view of Sweetwater River Valley, looking west. Author's photograph.

De Smet described the Sweetwater in glowing terms: "This stream is one of the most beautiful tributaries of the Platte. It owes its name, indeed, to the purity of its waters. It is distinguished from its fellow tributaries by the numerous wanderings of its current—proof that the fall of its bed is but slight."[14]

On Highway 220, just west of Devil's Gate, a lookout provides a breathtaking, unspoiled view. Devil's Gate can be seen to the east, while the Sweetwater Valley, averaging about five miles wide, stretches west to the horizon. The Sweetwater River sweeps back and forth through the valley's grassy bottom in lazy, snake-like loops, caused, as De Smet observed, by the flat gradient of the valley floor. Closely bordering the north side of the river is the Rattlesnake Range, a low wall of fractured granite virtually devoid of vegetation. To the south, farther off, are the taller Ferris Mountains, with timber visible on their higher elevations. This area is priceless, as it remains one of the least developed and unchanged sections of the Oregon Trail, looking much the same as when pioneers rumbled through here almost 180 years ago.

After traveling only eight miles on July 6, the party circled their wagons and encamped beside the Sweetwater. The marshy meadows beside the river spawned immense clouds of mosquitoes. Although Bidwell and Jimmy John never seemed to mention them, it would be surprising if they were not afflicted by them whenever they camped or traveled beside streams where the insects could breed. Father Point did not neglect them in his memoirs, however: "I will, therefore, mention them [rattlesnakes and mosquitoes] only to thank God publically for the protection he had gave us from the former [rattlesnakes] and for the patience he gave us to endure the latter [mosquitoes]."[15]

Bidwell and Jimmy John had not reported any broken wagons or loss of animals recently, other than the mule that had drowned while trying to cross the North Platte. But there was a great deal that our diarists neglected to record. Indeed, they rarely mentioned their fellow travelers, and it is often easy to forget that that there were over seventy people traveling in the company. Among the people not mentioned were the women and children. While there may not have been many of them, it would have been enjoyable hearing how they were faring, especially hearing about Nancy Kelsey and her infant daughter.

The trail was so rough and bumpy that it is difficult imagining anyone trying to ride in the wagons for any length of time. Outside of a few really young children, who had no choice but to endure a teeth-rattling ride, the others were more likely to have walked beside the wagons while inhaling copious quantities of dust.

Many dangers lurked along the trail, and the children were most at risk due to their incautious and impulsive tendencies. Rattlesnakes were prevalent and lay quietly coiled beside the trail, ready to strike the first inattentive person who came along. Ticks that carried rocky mountain spotted fever bacteria clung to the sagebrush. The ticks could attach to the clothing of those brushing against the plants and then infect them.

So far, there had been no accidents other than Shotwell's, and we have heard of no serious illnesses. While it had been hot at times, the journey had seen few violent summer storms and heavy rains. As trail experiences go, the company had been blessed. It had been the beneficiary of some extraordinarily good fortune up to this point. But would it last?

To see the location of their July 6 campsite, enter the Mormon Handcart Historic Site entrance on Highway 220, then go north about a half-mile and then about two miles west on Sun Ranch Road.

Modern view of meandering Sweetwater River in the Sweetwater River Valley. Author's photograph.

July 7

The company left camp on the morning of July 7 and returned to the trail. Heading west, the trail sometimes touched the Sweetwater, but it could also travel a mile or so away in order to cut off the stream's many bends. When the road strayed from the river, the wagons bumped across dry terrain where only sage, greasewood, and widely scattered grass grew.

Bidwell:

> W. 7th. As we journeyed, the mountains were high and naked, passed a pond that was nearly dried up, perfectly white with Glauber Salts, and in many places two or three inches deep, so that large lumps weighing several pounds were taken up.—Buffalo increased in number, 10 were killed, travelled to day about 14 miles.

Jimmy John:

> July 7th—This day was warm and the way rough. Nothing happened worth notice. We seen plenty of buffaloes and killed four. We encamped this night on the bank of the creek on a high cleft of rocks.

Bidwell mentioned passing Soda Lake, an almost dry alkali lake on their left about seven miles from their morning's camp. Plodding forward, the company continued to travel south of that low range of hills made of bald, naked granite, the same material from which Independence Rock and Devil's Gate were formed. As the day progressed, the travelers had nothing better to do than to watch the granite hills pass slowly on their right. The fractured rocks, indentations, coves, and other odd shapes produced many intriguing formations, some of which were eventually given names like Great Stone Face and Split Rock.

After fourteen miles of travel they circled the wagons and encamped. The present-day roads that most closely follow the day's trail are bumpy gravel roads. The most convenient way to reach their July 7 campsite is to take Highway 220 at the entrance of the Mormon Handcart Historical Site and travel west twelve miles to its junction with Highway 789. Then take 789 northwest about eight miles to Cranner Rock. The "high cleft of rocks" where Jimmy John reported that the party camped was probably Cranner Rock. From this point Great Stone Face can be seen to the northwest and Split Rock lies to the northeast.

July 8

Bidwell:

> T. 8th. This morning we came in sight of Wind River mountain, their snow enveloped summits were dimly seen through the misty clouds that obscured the Western horizon, made about 15 miles to day and encamped on Sweet Water, in full view of thousands of buffalo, 20 were killed, we now began to lay in meat to last us over the mountains to California.

Jimmy John:

> July 8th—The day was cool and the valley more level than it was yesterday. We made a good day's travel and seen a great number of buffaloes. Killed 3 and 2 antelopes. Encamped this evening on the bank of the Sweetwater Creek.

Leaving Cranner Rock, the travelers continued west, sometimes beside the Sweetwater and sometimes as much as a mile or so distant. During this stretch, the snowcapped Wind River Mountains came into view for the first time. To the northwest, they were an impressive, magnificent sight, with their snowcapped peaks rising to over twelve thousand feet.

About twelve miles after leaving camp the company came to a section of low hills. The trail would split into two alternative branches. The northern branch, called the Three Crossings Route, led through the hills by way of a narrow, mile-long canyon within which the Sweetwater squeezed through the narrow gap. In places, the walls of the defile pressed close to the stream, forcing wagon parties to cross to the opposite side three times before emerging onto a broad, half-mile-wide, grass-covered river bottom. The second branch, denominated the Deep Sand Route, angled south through a wide canyon covered in deep sand. It is unknown whether both branches of the trail were evident in 1841, and the diarists did not record any clues as to which route they took. Either way, they traveled fifteen miles that day and stopped to camp in the grassy river bottom. Their camp would have been on the north side of present-day Ore Road, about two miles northeast of where Ore Road intersects with Highway 789 at tiny Jeffrey City. The Deep Sand Route canyon is on the east side of Ore Road about two miles northeast of Jeffrey City. The Three Crossings Route is about three miles northeast of Jeffrey City, and can be seen looking east of where the Ore Road bridge crosses the Sweetwater.

Bidwell made it clear that the broad meadow where they camped that evening was home to "thousands" of buffalo, while Jimmy John described them as "a great number." With the Sweetwater meandering back and forth through a marshy river bottom that was about a half-mile wide and about ten miles long, there was enough grass to support a large buffalo population. Their numbers would significantly diminish in the years to come due to heavy hunting by the numerous wagon parties that would follow. Despite there being "thousands" of buffalo in 1841, they must have been gone by 1848 since none of the diarists from that year mentioned seeing any buffalo at all in that part of the Sweetwater River Valley.

Because of the abundance of buffalo there, and because Fitzpatrick would have known that there were few buffalo beyond the Sweetwater, he must have advised those going to California that this was the time for them to "make meat." Bidwell reported that they killed twenty, although Jimmy John oddly wrote that they only killed three.

Bidwell's comment about the need to lay in meat to last until California suggested that the California-bounds were beginning to realize that it would not be long before they would no longer have the services of Fitzpatrick. There had been talk of finding Joseph Walker, the traveler to California in 1833. But where was he? They had not found him yet. And if they found him, what if he declined to lead them? Had it crossed their mind that they might have to find their way to California without a guide? Bartleson may not have been concerned. After all, he had Dr. Marsh's directions, did he not?

July 9

Bidwell:

> F. 9th. Travelled about 18 miles, killed 10 Buffalo.

Jimmy John:

> July 9th—This day we started at the usual hour. The route is sandy and hard travelling. We are now in sight of some high mountains which are covered with snow. We seen thousands of buffaloes today and killed 16 of them. We encamped this evening on the bank of [the] creek.

Father Point's memoirs mentioned the abundant buffalo here in this area as well. Without identifying who it was, he mentioned a hunter who killed a number of them singlehandedly: "Buffalo were so plentiful in the area that a single member of the party killed eleven of them within a few hours, satisfying himself with bringing back only the tongues."[16]

Two miles west of their morning's camp, the Sweetwater made a wide, sweeping bend to the north. To avoid traveling unnecessary miles, the trail left the river and made a cutoff, heading almost due west. The path took the travelers across a dry, rolling plain that only grew wild sage and sparse grass. This stretch traveled north of and parallel to today's Highway 789 until it traveled down Ice Slough and then crossed to the south side of today's highway about miles ten west of Jeffrey City. Ice Slough was given its name because ice remained permanently frozen about a foot below its surface. It was formed from the area's long, cold winters and was kept from melting during the summer by the insulating sod covering it.

At the end of this cutoff, the trail struck the Sweetwater again, where it ran through a narrow river bottom. The company stopped there to camp, while men rode out to resume their buffalo hunting.

Once again, Bidwell and Jimmy John could not seem to agree on how many were killed.

The location of their July 9 camp can be reached by taking a gravel road that heads south just east of the present Mormon Handcart Historic Site and just east of the junction of Highway 135 with Highway 287. Proceed down the road about three and a half miles. The company's campsite should have been in the river bottom to the west of that point.

July 10

Bidwell:

> S. 10th. Travelled about 14 miles and stopped to kill and dry meat, Buffalo began to grow scarce.

Jimmy John:

> July 10th—This morning was cold and the wind blew hard, which made it disagreeable traveling. Nothing happened worthy of notice today. We encamped on the bank of the creek this afternoon. There are a great number of currants and gooseberries here.

Once they left their morning camp, the party continued to head up the Sweetwater. Because the surrounding terrain was beginning to rise, the Sweetwater was now winding through a narrow river bottom bordered by elevated bluffs on either side. Instead of the river bottom being a half-mile wide, as it had been in many places downstream, it now averaged about three hundred feet wide. With significantly less grass, it is no wonder that Bidwell noticed that the buffalo were growing scarce. To avoid getting bogged down in the marshy bottom, the trail crossed to the river's far side and traveled along higher ground. After about fourteen miles, the company came to a narrow canyon from which the river emerged. To proceed further, they would have to ascend the steep ridge to their right. But they were tired from the long day's march. Jimmy John reported that they set up camp beside the river and just below the canyon. They would make the strenuous climb up the ridge the next morning after a night of well-deserved rest.

The Reverend Williams complained about their miserable night: "July 10th. At night we were cold. I could not keep warm, although I had a buffalo robe to cover me."[17]

The location of the camp on July 10 is hard to access because it involves traveling across private land, through difficult country, and over many miles of rough gravel roads. This is a good place to again encourage the use of Google Earth to follow the company's path, especially along these remote, hard-to-get-to stretches. Google Earth is the next best thing to being there. In some ways, it is better. Its high-resolution imagery and ability to measure distances and determine elevations provide remarkable tools and perspectives that are of unparalleled value in studying the trail.

July 11

The wagons and carts did not move on July 11. They had not yet made enough meat, so the men rode out to hunt buffalo that morning.

Bidwell:

> *S. 11th. More than half the company sallied forth to kill meat, but the whole, killed but 6 or 7 Buffalo. Remained hunting and drying meat, killed to day but 4 or 5 buffalo.*

Jimmy John:

> *July 11th—We stopped at the place we encamped at yesterday for the purpose of laying in a supply of meat for the ballance of our journey for the old hunters say there is not buffaloes in the mountains and on the other side. We had poor success in killing buffaloes today. We have killed nothing but a cow and a steer, but their meet [meat] is of an excellent quality.*

This being Sunday, the Reverend Williams wanted to conduct services: "I proposed having prayers; several of the wicked class came up. . . . This night we have the sound of the violin, but not much dancing. 'Woe unto the wicked; for they shall have their reward.'" The reverend also complained, "Our company is mostly composed of Universalists and deists."[18]

July 12

In order to lay in a large quantity of meat, the wagons and carts remained in camp for the second day in a row, while the men continued to range out to find more buffalo.

Bidwell made no entry for July 12.

Jimmy John:

> July 12th—We stayed at the same place today that we encamped on the 10th until 13th and dried buffalo meat. Today we killed four buffaloe cows and some turkey and [caught] some fish.

Nicholas Dawson's memoirs made an alarming comment about these last couple of days: "On the Sweetwater river we began to lay by to kill and barbecue buffalo meat for future supply, but we had delayed too long and soon found them scarce. This resulted in our obtaining a scant supply and proved in the end our most fatal mistake."[19] His remark makes one wonder. On July 8, four days earlier, Bidwell and Jimmy John had both described large numbers—thousands of them. This was not unexpected since the meadow in that area was long, wide, and lush. At the time, Bidwell had acknowledged the need to lay in large quantities of dried meat to sustain the group in their long journey to California. That would have been the best place to do it, where the supply was plentiful. Fitzpatrick was likely aware that buffalo would be scarce beyond their July 8 camp. So why did they move on before laying in a sufficient quantity of meat? Had Fitzpatrick failed to give good advice? We must remember that he had been hired to deliver the missionaries. The stockpiling of large amounts of dried meat was more about the California party's needs than it was for the missionaries. Fitzpatrick owed no duty to those going to California.

Even so, did he have a moral duty to give the California people his best advice? We saw instances where he had given good advice, but it was ignored. We do not know what kind of relationship had brewed between Fitzpatrick and Bartleson. Had Fitzpatrick grown tired of Bartleson and his companions? Had he found them to be arrogant, argumentative, disobedient, or obnoxious? Had he reached the point where he was no longer extending them courtesies where it was not necessary? Unfortunately, neither diarist, not even the priests, shed any light on the question, and it remains a puzzle why the party was now in this predicament, despite an experienced resource like Fitzpatrick.

Not everyone in the company had gone buffalo hunting the last few days. The priests and the men who did not own horses probably remained in camp. The woman and children would have remained in camp as well. There was plenty to do. The meat that the hunters brought in needed to be cut into thin strips and hung beside fires to smoke and dry. One of Bidwell's memoirs had recalled, "There is no better beef in the world than that of the buffalo; it is also very good jerked—cut into strings and thoroughly dried."[20]

The women and some of the wagoneers may have taken the opportunity to do some housekeeping. They may have unloaded their wagons, taken inventory, and tossed aside anything deemed unnecessary. After cleaning their wagon boxes, they may have then reorganized everything and reloaded the wagons.

July 13

When the morning of July 13 arrived, it had been decided to move on. Because of the narrow river canyon ahead, the trail climbed a steep ridge on the right. It was called Rocky Ridge and was a steady climb of about three hundred feet in elevation in a little over a mile, about a 5 percent grade. The main problem was not so much its steepness. It was an ascending staircase of outcropping rocks, large and small. Riley Root, an 1848 emigrant, described it as a "very hilly road of coarse, sharp gravel stones" that put a "strain" on the wagons.[21] After the climb, the route leveled out and proceeded across a plateau. The company passed a couple of dry alkali beds, and then wound through some hilly country creased with deep draws and ravines, including Strawberry Creek. Then they turned southwest until they returned again to the Sweetwater River.

Bidwell:

> T. 13th. Left our hunting encampment and met John Gray and Romaine returning from Green river, they found no person at the rendezvous on Green river, nor any game ahead, it was therefore thought best to lay in more meat, while we were in the vicinity of the Buffalo. We therefore came to a halt, having travelled about 15 miles.

Jimmy John:

> July 13th—This morning we left the encampment and traveled over some rocky country. Killed one buffaloe. We met two of our men about

10 o'clock that had been sent by the company on the 6th of July to the rendezvous on Green river to make some arrangements for [the] company in exchanging the ox teams for mules, etc.; but they found no person there, not even an Indian on the whole route. We have not seen an Indian, except two, that are with us, since we left the Laramee fort. We encamped this evening on the banks of the same creek last mentioned.

John Gray and Lord Romaine had returned from the Green River. Bidwell explained in his memoirs that "John Gray had been sent some days previously [on July 5 from Independence Rock] to find if possible some party of trappers in order to leave letters with them to go east . . . . We also wished to dispose of to [the] trappers such extra goods and provisions as we felt obliged to part with in order to lighten our wagons. We also wanted to trade for some fresh animals."[22] The two men had brought the disappointing news that they had been unable to locate any traders or trappers.

Jimmy John's journal added that the men had been sent to find traders with whom their oxen could be exchanged for mules. What was the problem with the oxen? Were they lame, weak, sick, or deemed too slow? Did it suggest that the mules were holding up better? It took a few more years for people to eventually learn that oxen were ordinarily a better choice when taking wagons across the arid Far West. They tended to do better on the poor-quality forage, had more endurance, and were a darn sight better eating if all other food ran out. This pioneer company would eventually learn the value of their oxen, and their experiences would provide valuable lessons from which future wagon parties would benefit.

Since Gray reported that there was no game ahead, the company would have to remain in the area if it was to lay in more buffalo meat. Since the surrounding hills and plains were bleak, with little vegetation, the buffalo would only be found in the narrow bottoms of the Sweetwater River and its small tributaries, the only places with enough water and grass to attract and sustain the group.

To see where the company encamped on the evening of July 13, head south out of the tiny community of Atlantic City. Then travel one mile until encountering Riverview Cutoff Road. Follow the road south about eleven miles to a bridge that crosses the Sweetwater. The company probably camped in the grassy bottom southeast of the bridge.

July 14

The company remained in camp on July 14 and continued to hunt.

Bidwell:

> W. 14th. Company engaged in hunting and curing meat.

Jimmy John:

> July 14th—This day we lay here for the purpose of killing and laying in more meat. We had a hard frost here this morning. We have killed a fine chance of buffalo today. I do not know the number: perhaps about 8 or 9.

July 15

Probably because they had killed all of the buffalo in the vicinity, they moved further up the Sweetwater on July 15.

Bidwell:

> T. 15th. As many of the company had articles of traffic which they wished to dispose of at Green river, a subscription was raised to recompense any who would go and find the trappers. John Gray started in pursuit of them, while the company marched on slowly waiting his return, travelled about 6 miles to day.

Jimmy John:

> July 15th—This day we moved about 8 miles and camped until next day on Sweetwater creek. The nights are cool here and there is frost nearly every morning. There is no timber here except a few willows along the creek. We are at this time about 8 miles from what is called Wind river mountains. They are in sight of us and are covered with snow. We have seen them for the last 10 days. We leave them to the right hand.

The Reverend Williams also described the day's events:

> The next day [July 15] we came in sight of the Sweet River [Wind River] Mountains. Its peaks were tolerably well whitened with snow. There are some white bears in these mountains, but we have not killed any yet. There are also some white wolves, about as white as sheep. They are a dull, sleepy looking animal, and very surly; not very mindful of any thing, nor much afraid. They are about the size of a common wolf.[23]

Leaving camp on the morning of July 15, the company pushed further upstream, stopping to camp along another section of the Sweetwater River. The diarists agreed that they did not move far, although there was a difference in their perception. Bidwell estimated six miles, Jimmy John eight miles, and Dawson five. To see their likely campsite, based on Bidwell's estimate, travel on Highway 28 three-quarters of a mile southwest of where the highway crosses the Sweetwater River. Take Oregon Buttes Road where it heads southeast from its intersection with the highway. After traveling almost three miles, turn left onto Emigrant Trail Road and travel east about eight miles. Their camp should have been in the river bottom just north of this point.

To the northwest, the lofty Wind River Mountains stood tall and majestic, their jagged peaks topping out at over twelve thousand feet. Just eight miles south of the mountains, their camp was at seven thousand feet. These high elevations explained why, even though it was in the middle of summer, Jimmy John complained of a cold night.

Chapter 9

Over South Pass and On to the Green River

JULY 16 TO 31, 1841

July 16

The next morning, the company pulled out of the grassy bottom of the Sweetwater and headed west across a sage-covered bluff bordering the south side of the river. Their probable route would have tried to avoid moving across the stream's marshy, boggy bottom. After ten miles, they returned to the river bottom again and set up camp. We assume they found no buffalo in the vicinity since neither diarist mentioned that any were killed.

Bidwell:
F. 16th. Travelled about 10 miles and encamped opposite the wind river Mountains where we were in full view of many lofty peaks glittering with eternal snow and frost under the blaze of a July sun.

Jimmy John:

> July 16th—This day we moved about ten miles farther up the creek and encamped about noon for the purpose of drying meat and getting good range for our cattle and horses. We killed a good number of fowl which they call sage cocks. They are larger than a common domestic chicken.

The Reverend Williams also mentioned drying meat that day: "16th July. We are engaged in drying our meat for crossing the mountains. This morning, we had a very great frost and some ice."[1]

The estimated location of the camp on July 16 is about a half-mile north of Emigrant Trail Road, a mile and a half east of its intersection with Oregon Buttes Road.

July 17

The company moved only a few miles upriver on July 17.

Bidwell:

> Saturday, 17th. Travelled about 5 miles—still on Sweet Water.

Jimmy John:

> July 17th—This morning I caught some good fish at the camp. We left the camp at 8 o'clock and moved three miles farther up the creek. We have killed 3 buffaloe bulls today and a number of sage chickens. Buffaloes are getting scarce here. Nothing but bulls. There is no cows here.

The Reverend Williams reported on July 17 that the company sent John Gray to look for Snake Indians with whom the company could trade:

> Today [July 17], we lay by for the arrival of the Snake Indians to come and trade for our articles, and a man was sent [John Gray] to tell them to come. Today, Col. Bartleson gave some of our deists a down-setting, which pleased me very well. We moved about three miles up the river, to get better grazing for our animals. This river is very beautiful; clear running water, fine springs all along; no timber, soil poor & barren.[2]

In his memoirs, Bidwell also reported sending John Gray ahead: "John Gray was sent ahead to see if he could find a trapping party and he was instructed, if successful, to have them come to a certain place on Green River."[3] It is interesting that Williams thought Gray was to look for Snake Indians and bring them to the Sweetwater, while Bidwell believed that he was sent to find trappers and that the company would proceed to meet them at the Green River. Bidwell's understanding, and not Williams's, will be shown to have been the correct one.

In moving further upstream, the company may have again marched across higher ground on the west side of the river to avoid bogging down in its spongy bottom. After going only a few miles, they encamped. They must not have found many buffalo since Jimmy John complained that they only killed three tough-fleshed bulls.

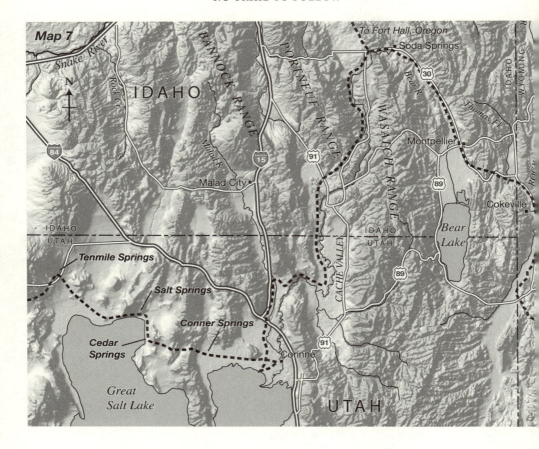

Using Bidwell's estimate of traveling five miles on July 17, the company likely camped beside the Sweetwater, in the flatland near where the Highway 28 Bridge crosses the river. Based on the estimated location of their camp, Fitzpatrick had led the company about two miles north of what would eventually become the heavily traveled Oregon Trail over South Pass. If the company had followed that route, they would have left the Sweetwater about ten miles earlier and, shortly after crossing the Divide, they would have encountered Pacific Springs. It was a spring-fed, elongated basin of boggy meadows. While virtually all diarists traveling in the future would describe Pacific Springs, Bidwell and Jimmy John had not. It was further evidence that the company had not followed what would become the standard trail.

It seems clear that Fitzpatrick had led the company further north,

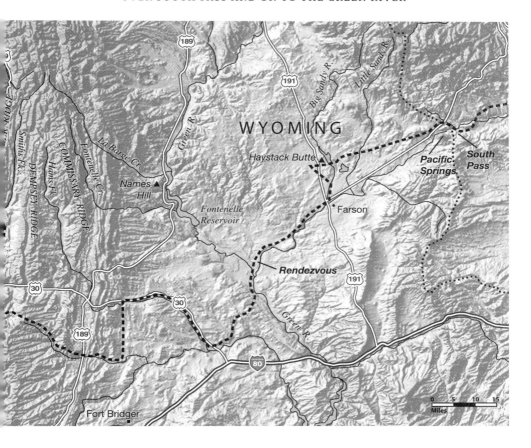

despite its being slightly longer and less direct, to pursue their foremost objective of finding and hunting buffalo. In just a few years, however, these buffalo would be hunted out. Once they were gone, there was no longer any reason for future wagon parties to follow this path.

July 18

When the sun rose on the morning of July 18, the company began to stir. Placidly grazing on the lush grass beside the river, the animals should have been easy to catch. There was little likelihood of them wandering far as there was virtually nothing but sagebrush and sparse, dry grass growing on the adjacent hills.

Bidwell:

> S. 18th. Left Sweet Water this morning, course S.W. Crossed the divide which separates the water of the Atlantic and Pacific oceans, and after a travel of 20 miles reached Little Sandy, a branch of the Green river—1 Buffalo was killed.

Jimmy John:

> July 18th—We left Sweetwater creek this morning at 6 o'clock and traveled about 17 miles and encamped on one of the head branches of the Coloradoe of the west. We have killed 2 buffaloe today and one antelope. The day was pleasant and we have had no rain since we left the north fork of the Platte river.

The company loaded their wagons on the morning of July 18 and left the Sweetwater for good. Their buffalo hunting had come to an end. It is interesting to speculate how much jerked meat they ended up with. Beginning with when they began killing buffalo in earnest on July 8 for the purpose of laying in meat, Bidwell's journal had recorded the killing of approximately fifty-five head. Modern-day authorities claim that a mature buffalo cow weighs nearly one thousand pounds and yields about 250 pounds of quality meat cuts (leaving out that which is normally processed into ground meat). Drying or "jerking" the meat would cause it to lose about two-thirds of its weight. Thus, it appears that the company may have produced about forty-five hundred pounds of dried meat. Divided among fifteen wagons, each wagon would have been loaded with an average of about three hundred pounds. Was this why Bidwell had mentioned in his memoirs that they wanted to find trappers along the Green River with whom they could trade away some of their "extra goods and provisions" in order to "lighten" their wagons?[4]

The dried buffalo meat would prove to not be enough and the shortage would eventually rear its ugly head. As Dawson lamented in his memoirs years later, their failure to kill more buffalo "resulted in a scant supply, and proved in the end our most fatal mistake."[5]

On this day, July 18, the company entered a new phase in their journey. After ascending a slope west of the Sweetwater for about a mile, they passed over the Continental Divide. The place where they departed the Sweetwater is about where today's Highway 28 crosses the Sweetwater River. For most emigrants the Divide was a memorable milestone. They would often remark how waters east of here eventually made it into the Gulf of Mexico, while waters west of here flowed into the Green River, then into the Colorado River, and from there to the Gulf of California and the Pacific. This unique area of the Divide was called South Pass. It was a remarkable anomaly in the Rocky Mountain Range, where the tall and rugged Wind River Mountains petered out and the great hand of Nature pressed its heavy thumb down to create a low spot in the mountain chain. It was as if Providence had intentionally created this section of gentle gradients to create an easy portal through which thousands of emigrants and their covered wagons would be able to easily pour across into the Far West.

Those interested in seeing a clearly marked section of the heavily used Oregon Trail where it proceeds over South Pass should take Oregon Buttes Road south from Highway 28 about one mile west of the highway bridge over the Sweetwater. Travel about three miles to its intersection with an east-west dirt road called Emigrant Trail. Turn right and follow Emigrant Trail west, and it will proceed over South Pass and toward Pacific Springs. This is the path that would be so heavily used in future years. One cannot help being struck by how the ascent to the summit of the Divide and its transition to a descent are so gradual that it is virtually impossible to fix its highest point.

After the company crossed the divide and began a gradual descent, they could see a great rolling plain ahead, a huge, undulating expanse of emptiness. It was called the Green River Valley or the Little Colorado Desert, an awful solitude about 60 miles wide and 150 miles long. It had been at the heart of fur trade activity during its heyday, a crossroads where wide-ranging brigades of trappers were drawn to attend the various rendezvous held at various places along the Green River.

There were few distinguishing features to the west by which one could set one's course. A couple of small buttes could be made out far to the west and southwest, sticking up like small islands in a sea of nothing. People like Fitzpatrick, who had traversed this region countless times, could use them as valuable signposts in this otherwise featureless country. It let them know where they were and in what direction to head.

Upon leaving South Pass, the company was leaving behind not only buffalo, but also the domain of the fierce Sioux. They were now entering the territory of the Snake Indians, also called Shoshones. The Snakes and Sioux were implacable enemies, and the Snakes would make a slashing motion across the throat to indicate by sign language that their name for the hated Sioux was "cutthroats."[6] Although the Snakes were generally friendly toward the whites, they were also regarded by some as helping themselves to anything not closely watched.[7]

The company marched southwesterly at first, their path closely following the route of today's Highway 28. Then they began heading almost due west, angling north of and away from today's highway because of their need to reach the closest source of good water and grass by the end of the day. This would be Little Sandy Creek. Since the creek meandered southwesterly, they would have eventually struck it if they had continued in that direction, but they would have had to travel too far without water before striking it. By heading northwest, however, they could reach it in twenty-three miles.

As the company's wagons and carts rattled forward, they were crossing a desert. It was a stern land that had few features of softness and gentleness. The mark of man was painfully absent. An extreme lack of precipitation produced little but the ubiquitous sagebrush. The ground was sandy and each sage plant was surrounded by a wind-blown hillock of sand. The wagons creaked and groaned as they lurched through sage and over hillocks, and rumbled into and out of washes and draws.

Fitzpatrick was probably leading the company along a faint horse and mule trail that fur trappers and fur trade suppliers had used in the past. In fact, the trail was probably not well defined or clearly marked, meaning that Fitzpatrick may have had to rely on the sun and one or more of the distant buttes as reference points.

As the day advanced and the hot sun climbed higher into the sky, the distance would have shimmered in the heat waves. Standing tall and grandiose over their right shoulders, the Wind River Mountains loomed high with their jagged, snow-clad peaks. About midday, after traveling about fourteen miles, they crossed Dry Sandy Creek. There was no water in it because it was a dry wash that conveyed a rush of water only when heavy rains or snowmelt drained off the western slopes of the Wind River Range. Eight miles later they came to Little Sandy Creek. Twenty feet wide, three feet deep, and bordered by grass, willows, dense undergrowth, and blue lupines, it was described by the Reverend Williams as a "beautiful stream."[8] But there were also legions of mosquitoes that seemed to get excited whenever a fresh supply of blood arrived. Nevertheless, the company would camp there. Bidwell estimated that they had traveled twenty miles that day, while Jimmy John estimated seventeen and Dawson estimated twenty-five.

The camp along the Little Sandy is one of their most uncertain camp locations. Our best estimate is that it was approximately eighteen miles northeast of the tiny present-day community of Farson, Wyoming. To approach this location, proceed east four and a half miles on Highway 28 from its intersection with Highway 191 at Farson. Then take Farson 4th East Road (Road 108) north about fifteen miles. The estimated campsite would have been about a mile and a half east of this point.

July 19

The next morning, the company left the Little Sandy and headed southwest across bleak country, heading toward Big Sandy Creek.

Bidwell:

> M. 19th. 15 miles took us on to Big Sandy, which is likewise a branch of Green river—2 Buffalo killed.

Jimmy John:

> July 19th—This day we traveled about 15 miles and encamped on the bank of a creek called Big Sandy. There is good grass and wild unions grow nearly 3 ft. high. We are still in sight of some mountains [Wind River Mountains to the northeast] that we seen on the ninth day of this month and others that are covered with snow.

The two buffalo killed would be the last the company would bag. The diarists failed to specify whether they traveled fifteen miles before striking and camping on the Big Sandy or struck the stream and then followed it south for a few miles before stopping to camp. Therefore, it is difficult to know precisely where they camped. Our best estimate is that it was beside the stream about nine miles north of Farson. Proceed north on Highway 191 nine miles from its intersection with Highway 28. At Haystack Butte Road, turn right and travel east on the road two miles to where they likely camped that evening.

July 20

Bidwell:

> T. 20th. Traveled about 18 miles in a circuitous direction, first west and then South, Country was extremely dry and dusty—no game seen but a few antelope—encamped on Big Sandy, having come about 18 miles.

Jimmy John:

> July 20th—Today we traveled hard all day, and did not get more than 7 or 8 miles on a straight line. Killed no game today except one antelope. We encamped on the bank of the Big Sandy this evening. The valley is still destitute of timber and almost everything else but sage. The valley is wider in some places than others, varying from one to 60 miles in width.

Bidwell did not explain why their route that day was "circuitous." De Smet gave the impression that Fitzpatrick had missed a turn, writing in one of his letters: "In the vicinity of the latter [Big Sandy], as the captain had mistaken one road for another, the caravan wandered for three days at random." When they finally encamped that evening, De Smet claimed that the company was "still ignorant of its position."[9]

This is the first time that Fitzpatrick has left us flummoxed. It is uncertain what he did on July 20 and why. We can only speculate. In prior years, men on horseback and pack mule trains had traveled north and south, east and west, marching to and from beaver trapping areas and to and from their annual rendezvous. In 1832, Captain Benjamin Bonneville took wagons across South Pass and then traveled almost due west to the Green River before moving upstream to where he established Fort Bonneville. During the ten years before 1841, five of the annual rendezvous had been held on Horse Creek, near Fort Bonneville. In fact, Fitzpatrick had led supply pack trains to two of them. In 1844, the eighty-year-old Caleb Greenwood would pilot an emigrant wagon party from Big Sandy due west on a forty-five-mile, waterless tramp to the Green River.[10] It is likely that Greenwood did not pioneer this trail, but rather led his party along the same path that earlier pack mule trains had followed on their way to a rendezvous. Although this route was a difficult ordeal for man and animal, it was also a shortcut to the Bear River that would knock fifty miles and three days off the trip. It became known as "Greenwood's Cutoff."

It is only speculation, but we suspect that the company camped on the afternoon of July 19 near where the Greenwood's Cutoff would strike the Big Sandy. De Smet claimed the company had "missed a turn," but Fitzpatrick may have crossed the company to the west side of Big Sandy on the morning of July 20 and continued west. He may have been looking for an infrequently traveled trail somewhere to the west of Big Sandy that headed south. But the south-headed trail may have been obliterated by recent winds or rains. Indeed, Bidwell mentioned in one of his memoirs that prior to their trip in 1841, William Sublette had hauled supplies in wagons to a rendezvous along the Green River, but that they were the only wagons to have gone this far before the Bartleson expedition. This was probably the reason why Greenwood's Cutoff was also called Sublette's Cutoff by others. Bidwell also recalled that sometimes they "came across the tracks, but generally they were obliterated, and thus were of no service."[11] After traveling a distance Fitzpatrick must have realized that he had somehow missed the south-heading trail, and then turned the company southward until he again made contact with the Big Sandy.

De Smet commented that they "wandered for three days at random," and Father Point recalled, "for three days our column floundered through the sand."[12] But Fitzpatrick knew the country, having traveled through it for many years. It seems reasonably certain that he was not wandering aimlessly, as De Smet and Point suggested. During the next few days, Fitzpatrick would lead his company in close proximity to the Big Sandy until they came to where it flowed into the Green River. Because the terrain was rolling and rugged, with a number of deep ravines draining into the Big Sandy, the company was forced to travel a distance from it. Because it flowed through a deep, meandering channel, it was, for the most part, hidden from view even to those traveling nearby. This could have been why the priests incorrectly thought that the skilled and experienced mountain man was lost. He was probably not "lost" in the conventional sense of the word. Although Fitzpatrick was De Smet's employee, and it was understood that the two men respected each other and got along well, perhaps he had failed to explain to De Smet and the others where they were, what he was doing, and why.

Bidwell's entry reported that they traveled eighteen miles on July 20, although Jimmy John estimated that had they traveled south "on a straight line" only eight miles that day. This suggests that they stopped to camp beside the Big Sandy about four miles northeast of Farson. To reach that point, take Highway 191 and travel two and a quarter miles north from its intersection with Highway 28 at Farson. Then turn right onto Haystack Butte Road and proceed north one mile. Their camp was probably along the Big Sandy to the east of this point.

July 21

On the morning of July 21, the company continued on a southwesterly track, traveling near the Big Sandy all day.

Bidwell:

> W. 21st. Descended Big Sandy about 15 miles and again encamped upon it—no grass, had a little rain this Evening but not enough to lay the dust.

Jimmy John:

> July 21st—This morning was pleasant and we traveled all day on the banks of Big Sandy, the same creek that we camped on last evening and encamped on it this evening.

It was not much, but they got a little rain. The last time the company had experienced a rainstorm was just west of Ash Hollow on June 14, about five weeks earlier. The expedition probably set up camp along the creek at the end of Simpson's Gulch on the east side of today's Highway 28 and about ten miles southwest of its intersection with Highway 191.

July 22

With a little moisture in the morning air, it would have been heavy with the penetrating scent of sage. Gathering themselves, the travelers resumed their determined march toward the Green River. Their path on July 22 continued southwest, closely following the route of today's Highway 28. The character of the country remained the same; exceedingly dry, sandy, and desolate. They continued to travel a mile or more away from the Big Sandy because of its looping back and forth as it ran through its deep, narrow channel. When they were able to get next to it, the water and grass at the bottom of the deep, steep-banked channel were difficult to reach.

OVER SOUTH PASS AND ON TO THE GREEN RIVER

Bidwell:

> T. 22nd. Descended Big Sandy about 12 miles and stopped where we found plenty of grass—this was very acceptable as our teams were already much jaded for want of grass. The oxen, however, stood travel, &c. as well as the horses and mules. Gray returned this evening having found Trapp's [Fraeb's] company, which consisted of about 20 men. They had returned to meet our Company though on their way to hunt Buffalo, and were now encamped on Green river about 8 miles distant. Gray had suffered much in overtaking the Trappers, his mule gave out, there being no water for a great distance, and he, himself was so much reduced by hunger and thirst that he was unable to walk, he was therefore compelled to crawl upon his hands and feet, and at last came up with the Company in the most forlorn situation imaginable—if they had been another half mile farther, he never could have reached them.

Jimmy John:

> July 22d—Today we traveled about 12 miles and encamped at noon on the bank of Big Sandy. Here we stayed until the 23d. Today a man [John Gray] has returned to camp who was sent out on the 14th to try to find some trader on Coloradoe [Green] river in order to get information respecting the route to California and get a pilot. He brought about 60 men with him who came to trade with us. They informed us that it was impossible for wagons to get to California, but they could get down on the Columbia without much trouble.

At the end of the day, the company camped at the northeast corner of a bend in the Big Sandy, about eight miles northeast of its mouth on the Green River. This location is just south of today's Highway 28, and about eight miles northeast of the highway's bridge across the Green River. The location became known as Big Timbers, owing to a grove of large cottonwoods that once grew there. The trees would eventually be consumed by thousands of emigrant campfires in the years to come. Bidwell described the abundant grass in the bottom of the channel, but one will be hard pressed to find much grass on the banks of this section of the Big Sandy today. During the last century a great deal of land has been developed for farming around Farson. Much of the water that once flowed down the Big Sandy is now diverted to irrigation. Hence, the river is but a vestige of its former self. It is also important to note that Bidwell remarked how the oxen were holding up as well as the horses and mules.

It is significant that Jimmy John recorded that they were looking to find someone on the Green River who knew how to get to California, and better yet, who would pilot them there.

John Gray had found Henry Fraeb (some spelled it Trapp or Frapp) and his band of trappers. Fraeb and his companions had been on their way to the Sweetwater to hunt buffalo when John Gray found them and coaxed them into turning around and following him back to where on the Green River he expected Fitzpatrick to bring the company.[13]

Fitzpatrick would have been well acquainted with Fraeb, a longtime trapper and trader. The two had worked together for many years in the mountains and had been partners in the Rocky Mountain Fur Company for five years, from 1830 to 1834. It is unknown whether the two were on good terms, keeping in mind that Fitzpatrick had managed to alienate some of his former business associates.

Fraeb had led fall trapping parties for the RMFC along the Snake River in 1830 and 1832 as far as the Malheur River in today's Oregon. During those years, he periodically left the Snake and crossed the arid country to the south to trap along the Humboldt River.[14] In 1840, Fraeb, Joseph Walker, and their men had traveled to California. They traded the pelts they had taken along the way to a Los Angeles merchant by the name of Abel Stearns. In exchange, they received about a hundred horses and some supplies. It is uncertain what route the party took in returning in the spring of 1841, but since the horses were purchased in the Los Angeles area, it is believed that they left Southern California and returned east by way of the Old Spanish Trail.[15]

July 23

On the morning of July 23, the company marched the final eight miles along the west side of the Big Sandy to where it flowed into the Green River. Although the California-bounds did not know it, they were now about halfway to their destination.

Bidwell:

> *F. 23d. Went to Green river—distance 8 miles—spent the remainder of the day trading with the hunters.*

OVER SOUTH PASS AND ON TO THE GREEN RIVER

Jimmy John:

> July 23d—This day we traveled about 10 miles and arrived at Green or Coloradoe river, attended by the men that came to us yesterday, and a number of Snake Indians. The river here is about 100 yards wide and has a little timber on its banks, such as cottonwood and willow. Here we stayed until the 25th and traded with the Indians and trappers for packhorses, robes, etc. There is frost here nearly every night, but the days are warm and pleasant. The plains around here are barren and destitute of timber.

Their camp on the evening of July 23 was about a mile and a half south of the Highway 28 Bridge across the Green.

It is difficult to get a clear picture of what happened on the Green River. To begin with, Bidwell and Jimmy John could not come close to agreeing on how many men were in Fraeb's party. Bidwell said twenty while Jimmy John said sixty. It is unclear whether the Fraeb party was the only group of trappers and traders they met there. The Reverend Williams's memoirs described the trappers as "mostly composed of half-breeds, French and Dutch, and all sorts of people collected together in the mountains," and he complained that they were a "wicked, swearing company of men."[16] Dawson described the trappers as "a rough looking set, dressed in their home-made leather clothes, and at a distance resembled Indians."[17] Jimmy John also mentioned the presence of Snake Indians, writing that members of the company traded goods to both the trappers and Indians in exchange for packhorses and buffalo robes. However, no one made it clear when the Snakes showed up or how many there were. De Smet and Point both mentioned that a couple of Flathead Indians were there awaiting the missionaries' arrival at the Green River, mentioning that they were advance envoys sent by the Flathead tribe to greet the priests and to escort them the rest of the way to their villages.[18]

Dawson recalled that the company members exchanged some of their "store clothes and ammunition for dressed skins, buckskin clothing, moccasins and ropes." In one of his memoirs, Bidwell mentioned that some of the trappers "had tasted nothing but meat for ten years." He was astonished that after all their years of eating meat in the wilderness, they had no interest in trading for flour or bread. But it turned out that they craved bacon.[19]

Williams reported that sugar was selling for "$1.50 per pound;

powder and lead from $1.50 to $2.50 per pound."[20] Bidwell's entry for July 25 described the trade value of a number of items:

> *I will not omit to state the prices of several kinds of mountain goods. Powder which is sold by the cupful (pint) is worth $1 per cup, Lead 1.50 per lb. good Mackanaw Blankets 8 to 15 dollars, sugar $1 per cupful. Pepper $1 also Cotton and Calico shirts from 3 to 5$, Rifles from 30 to 60; in return, you will receive dressed deerskins at $3, Pants made of deer skins $10, Beaver skins $10, Moccasins $1; flour sold in the Mts. at 50 cents per cupful, Tobacco at $2 per lb., Butcher knives from 1 to 3$, a good gun is worth as much as a horse; a cap lock is preferred, caps worth $1 per box.*

Bidwell mentioned in his memoirs that he was surprised to discover that some of his fellow travelers sold alcohol to the trappers:

> *Approaching Green River in the Rocky Mountains, it was found that some of the wagons, including Captain Bartleson's, had alcohol on board, and that the owners wanted to find trappers in the Rocky Mountains to whom they might sell it. This was a surprise to many of us, as there had been no drinking on the way. . . . [The trappers bought the] greater part, if not all, of the alcohol, it first having been diluted so as to make what they called whisky—three or four gallons of water to a gallon of alcohol."*[21]

Trappers had a reputation for getting stupidly drunk when alcohol came their way. One wonders if Bartleson and his colleagues had hoped to trade with the trappers after reducing them to an impaired state. But if they had, it could have produced some unwanted consequences. If you hoped to learn how to get to the Humboldt River, getting that information from a heavily intoxicated informant might not have been a wise idea.

Dawson related an incident in his memoirs that may have involved the Snake Indians who were present. He explained how he had traded his horse for a mule before the journey began, although he did not explain why. He went on to amusingly describe why the trade was a mistake and how he was able to rectify the error:

> *Before we passed beyond the range of friendly Indians, I made a trade, which, as it brought in what proved to be a very important member of our company, I will tell of. The old mule I traded my horse for proved very unsatisfactory. When I wanted him to go to water he wanted to go to grass; when I wanted him to go to grass, he wanted water—perhaps enough is*

told when I say that it was he who taught me to swear. One day we met a gang of Indians. The leader was riding a spirited white pony, which I at once coveted. Riding up alongside the Indian, I drew my forefingers across each other and halloed "swap!" "Swap," grunted the Indian. He jumped from his horse, I from my mule. He took off his saddle, I took off mine. He fastened his saddle upon my old mule, and I girthed mine around the white pony. Then we each sprang into our saddles and rode off. Thus came into my possession, "Monte." This was the only trade I remember ever in which I did not get the worst of the bargain.[22]

Dawson did not identify where the trade for the white pony occurred, but it is almost certain it did not happen during their earlier encounters with the Kansa or Pawnees because he was still riding a mule when he encountered the Cheyenne. It also seems unlikely that he would have conducted any business with the Cheyenne considering how badly they had abused and humiliated him. This only leaves a few Sioux who were camping near Fort Laramie, or the Snake Indians they met on the Green River. Since Jimmy John reported that they "traded with the Indians and trappers for packhorses, robes, etc," it suggests that his "swap" for the white pony took place with a Snake Indian at the Green River.

July 24

As of July 24, they had been on the trail for over ten weeks and had traveled about one thousand miles. Father Point wrote that the reason they remained on the Green for two days was that they "were in need of rest."[23] They remained in camp all day on July 24 and continued trading.

Bidwell:

> S. 24th. Remained at this encampment and continued our traffic with the hunters. Chiles sold his oxen, 2 yoke, and wagon, another also was left.

Jimmy John made no entry on July 24.

It is disappointing that Bidwell failed to provide more details about Joseph Chiles selling two yoke of oxen and his wagon. Since Chiles had started the journey with one wagon, the other wagon that "was left" must have belonged to someone else. Sadly, Bidwell failed to identify its owner and the reason it was left.

July 25

It was time for Fitzpatrick to get his company moving again. He led them across the Green River on the morning of July 25, fording to its west side about a mile and a half south of where the Highway 28 Bridge crosses the river. They then headed south, bumping along beside the river's west side. Depending on whether Bidwell or Jimmy John was correct, the company stopped to camp beside the river between six and eight miles south of the present intersection of Highway 28 and Highway 372.

Bidwell:

> S. 25th. Left the rendezvous this morning, 6 of the company, viz., John Gray, Payton, Frye, Rogers, Jones and Romaine, started to return to the United States. Baker stopped in the Mountains to trap, crossed Greene river and descended it about 8 miles. Trapp [Frapp] and his company likewise left in pursuit of Buffalo. . . . We crossed Green river, went about 8 miles downstream and encamped.

Jimmy John:

> July 25th—Today we crossed the river and traveled about six miles down it and camped on its bank. The Snake Indians and trappers camped with us. There is no buffaloe here nor any other kind of game that we can kill except fish. We caught some good fish called chubs. The river is clear at this place and the water is very pure.

The Bartleson party was acutely aware that they would soon be separating from Fitzpatrick. To travel across a vast uncharted solitude without someone who knew the way should have been a terrifying thought. Imagine the initial delight of those headed to California when they learned that the Fraeb party had recently returned from that far-off land. It was a great opportunity to learn about the country where they were going. Better yet, it was an opportunity to hire one of them to be their pilot. But when Fraeb and his men were asked if one was willing to lead them there, Father Point's memoir said that all of the trappers declined: "As for the travelers returning from California," the priest wrote, "many acknowledged that they had more than one duty to fulfill, and all promised to fulfill them—*but next year.*"[24] One would think that at least one of the trappers could have been hired if the price was right. Perhaps we can understand why there were no takers. A trip to California was no small thing, and it is hard to imagine anyone wanting to repeat the ordeal so soon.

Bartleson still had Dr. Marsh's letter of directions, and we wonder if he showed it to someone in Fraeb's party. If he had, it would have likely been laughed at as worthless trash. And the "map" Bidwell had? It, too, should have been denounced as inaccurate rubbish.

As Jimmy John's journal entry for July 22 reported, the Fraeb party made no bones about warning that it was impossible to get wagons through to California, while getting wagons to Oregon would not be difficult. Such disheartening news had the same effect as a grenade being tossed into their midst. It would fragment their company, and the effect was felt immediately. Father De Smet wrote: "What they [Fraeb party] told us concerning that distant country [California] dissipated many illusions, and caused some of our companions, who had traveled for amusement, to return."[25] Father Point echoed the notion, recalling that the trappers "painted a picture so little encouraging that many of our party thought only of the opportunity to turn back."[26]

The men who decided they had gone far enough included the English sportsman Lord Romaine; his Iroquois hunter, John Gray; Amos Frye; Henry Payton; J. M. Jones; and the man named Rogers. Two months later, in late September, an article appeared in a Missouri newspaper announcing that a group of "nine or ten of the California company returned a few days since. . . . [They] were attacked six or eight times, but not seriously injured. They seemed satisfied completely with their Quixotic adventure."[27]

James Baker, whose aim had been to engage in trapping in the Rocky Mountains and who had probably traveled west with the company for protection, left the expedition, thinking this was probably a good place to head into the mountains to begin trapping.

As the parties bade their adieus, those intending to go to California had failed to recruit a guide. Worse, there was no mention of the company getting any useful information about how to get to there. For whatever the reason, it appears that the California-bounds had gained very little from this important opportunity.

There was also no mention of Joseph Walker. Since Walker was more widely known than Fraeb, one of our narrators surely would have mentioned him if he had been present. Walker had a Snake wife, whom he had not seen for a while. Some historians believe that when he and Fraeb returned from California, Walker was somewhere in the region, spending time with her and their children. Others add that Walker was at Brown's Hole in northern Utah, allowing the horses they purchased in California to recruit from the strenuous trip before driving them further east.[28] But Dawson's memoirs recalled that they expected to find Walker at Fort Hall. It does make one wonder, however, whether Fraeb or his men had planted this idea to take pressure away from providing a guide.[29]

Even if the company had found Walker, it is doubtful he would have agreed to serve as their pilot. He was intending to return to Missouri for the first time in ten years.[30] After Joseph Chiles made it to California, he returned to Missouri in 1842 by way of the southern route through Santa Fe. He then organized a wagon party heading for California in 1843. He found Walker at Fort Laramie this time and promptly hired him. Nevertheless, this Walker-led party would abandon its wagons during a very difficult and stressful journey.[31] So even if the Bartleson party had succeeded in finding Walker in 1841 and had persuaded him to be their guide, it appears that their trip would have been difficult anyway.

Bidwell understood that Fraeb and his men departed the Green River with the intent of heading over South Pass to the meadows of the Sweetwater in order to lay in buffalo meat. On August 21, almost a month later, Fraeb and his group were traveling along Battle Creek, a tributary of the Little Snake River and about two hundred miles southwest of here. While looking for beaver, they encountered a large war party of Sioux, Arapahoe, and Cheyenne and a fight ensued. Fraeb and four of his men were killed and scalped.[32] After describing Fraeb as "the greatest blasphemer of the party," Father Point's memoirs related that he had heard that Fraeb "had been one of the first to fall, struck by a stray bullet."[33] Bidwell wrote in his memoirs that "they [Fraeb party] were attacked by Indians the very first night after they left us."[34] This was incorrect. It was almost a month after the two parties separated. Bidwell also expressed the opinion that the alcohol acquired by Fraeb and his men from Bartleson and his friends may have played a role in their being killed by the Indians.[35]

Because a few Sioux were killed in the skirmish with Fraeb, the Sioux vowed retribution. This is why in 1842, the following year, a large war party of Sioux set out determined to kill whites. It was this vengeance-seeking party that Fitzpatrick encountered at Independence Rock when he was leading Dr. White's Oregon-bound emigrant party to Fort Hall.

As the parties separated and each went its own way on July 25, one wonders about the state of mind of those in the Bartleson party. If anything, their conversations with the Fraeb party should have driven home the reality that California was still very far away, separated by harsh deserts and dauntingly high mountain ranges. One wonders if the Fraeb people reminded everyone that California was a foreign country, a part of Mexico, and that the Mexican authorities were squeamish, even paranoid, about foreigners. It was Americans, primarily ship deserters and former fur trappers who had recently threatened a Texas-like insurrection in California. Any group of Americans arriving in California, especially young men without families, would be viewed with suspicion and could be greeted with hostility.[36]

About four miles south of where the company crossed the Green River, they passed a spot on its west bank where a trading post would be built of cottonwood logs in the coming weeks. It was supposedly built in August, shortly after the Fitzpatrick company had passed this way. Some historians claim that the post was built by a partnership composed of Jim Bridger and Henry Fraeb shortly before Fraeb and his companions left on their fateful journey.[37] But that is probably incorrect since Bidwell's journal said that Fraeb left the Green River on the same day that his own company pulled out, which would have been on July 25.

After Fraeb was killed, Bridger took on Louis Vasquez as his new partner. The trading post on the Green was short-lived. The two men abandoned it the following year and built a new post on Black's Fork, forty-five miles southwest. Named Fort Bridger, it would become a popular stop for future wagon parties.[38]

July 26

Bidwell:

> M. 26th. Left Green river—moved off in a W. direction—distance 12 miles—encamped on a branch of green river called Ham's fork— land high, dry and barren, except upon the streams, which afford grass in abundance; also black currants, which though not delicious are acceptable.

Jimmy John:

> *July 26th—This morning we left the [Green] river and went about 12 miles and encamped on the bank of a stream called Ham's Fork. It em[p]ties into Green River or Coloradoe. The Indians and some of the trappers camped with us this evening.*

Upon leaving the Green River on the morning of July 26, the company followed Fitzpatrick southwesterly across a barren plain. Eight and a half miles south of Highway 372's intersection with Highway 28, one can see a faint, rarely used dirt track that crosses Highway 372 diagonally from the northeast and then heads southwesterly into the sage-covered hills. This path is designated "Emigrant Trail" on some maps and is likely the route across which Fitzpatrick led his company away from the Green River and toward Blacks Fork. The trail was probably very faint then, but it would eventually become a heavily traveled, easy-to-follow trail as numerous wagon parties aimed for Fort Bridger on their way west. Modern-day explorers are discouraged from trying to follow this track, as it is in poor shape and leads across rough, difficult country where one could become lost or disabled far away from water or help.

After lumbering twelve dry miles, the company finally struck Blacks Fork. Here, they set up camp and turned their livestock loose to graze on the grass growing beside the stream. Their camp was on the north bank about four miles northeast of the present-day town of Granger, Wyoming. Both diarists incorrectly called it Hams Fork, a stream that flowed into Blacks Fork about five miles upstream. Dawson had it right, however, as he correctly reported in his log that they camped on Blacks Fork that evening. Both Blacks Fork and Hams Fork are about of equal width where the two streams join. Below the confluence, the stream is called Blacks Fork, but it could have just as easily been confused as Hams Fork.

July 27

Bidwell:

> *T. 27th. Advanced upstream about 12 miles.*

Jimmy John:

> *July 27th—Today we traveled about twelve miles up Ham's Fork and encamped on its banks for the night. Killed two antelope and caught some*

fish today. *The nights are cool and sometime frosty, the valley being surrounded by mountains that are covered with perpetual snow which has a tendency to cool the air at night.*

After leaving camp on the morning of July 27, they moved up the river bottom of Blacks Fork about five miles and came to where Hams Fork joined it from the north. Beginning in 1843, after Jim Bridger had established his Fort Bridger on Blacks Fork, wagon parties would head southwesterly from this point and aim toward the new trading post.

Fitzpatrick had spent almost sixteen years crisscrossing this region and would have been familiar with trails that navigated through the mountains to the west, having traveled to such places as Bear River, Bear Lake, Cache Valley, and beyond. He had never taken wagons west of here, but must have known of a route that he believed would accommodate wheeled vehicles.

When they reached the mouth of Hams Fork, Fitzpatrick directed his company to the right, and they began their march up it. It was a nice stream, about fifty feet wide, not very deep and full of fish. The stream meandered wildly back and forth through a grass-covered river bottom that averaged about a quarter of a mile wide. After traveling about five miles, they stopped to camp. Their camp would have been just to the west of today's Highway 30, and about four miles north of the Highway 30 Bridge over Blacks Fork.

July 28

The next day the company continued marching northwesterly up the Hams Fork river bottom.

Bidwell:

> *W. 28th. do [ditto, advanced upstream about 12 miles.]*

Jimmy John:

> *July 28th—Today we traveled up Ham's Fork about 15 miles and encamped in the afternoon on its banks, for we frequently travel until the afternoon and lay by until the next day. We caught some good fish here this afternoon. I caught 23 silver myself and one trout.*

The company continued to travel through country that was stark and grew little besides sagebrush. However, the stream bottom provided plenty of cold, pure water, firewood, and abundant grass. So long as they traveled along the outside edge of the bottoms, avoiding marshy and boggy ground, the going should have been easy. But their route had a downside as well. They and their animals must have been pestered unremittingly by hordes of mosquitoes. Our diarists failed to mention them, but since virtually every diarist in later years complained about mosquitoes wherever there was water, it seems certain that they were a problem.

Even though neither Bidwell nor Jimmy John mentioned it, the Reverend Williams claimed that one of the wagons broke down on Hams Fork on July 28, although he gave no details.[39]

Their camp at the end of the day would have been about a mile west of today's Highway 30, about twelve miles north of the Highway 30 Bridge over Blacks Fork.

July 29

Bidwell:

> T. 29th. do [advanced up stream another 12 miles].

Jimmy John:

> July 29th—Nothing happened today worthy of notice. We traveled about 10 or twelve miles farther up the creek and encamped on its banks in the afternoon.

The day brought more of the same, although the course of Hams Fork slowly changed and began coming in from the west. There were a few places where steep banks left no room to squeeze between the stream and the bank. Since the stream was not deep, it would not have been difficult to cross to the opposite side.

The camp that afternoon would have been in the river bottom south of Highway 30, approximately five miles east of where Highway 240 intersects with Highway 30.

July 30

Bidwell:

> F. 30th. Traveled about 5 miles and encamped. Guess what took place; another family was created! Widow Gray, who was a sister to Mrs. Kelsey, was married to a man who joined our Company at Ft. Larimie, his right name I forget; but his every where name, in the Mountains, was Cocrum. He had but one eye—marriage ceremony performed by Father De Smet.

Jimmy John:

> July 30th—Today we traveled about 10 miles farther up the creek and encamped for the ballence of the day, for the pilot thought, as we had to leave the creek, we could probably could not get to any more water this afternoon, therefore we encamped on its banks. The water is very good here and the grass is excellent in the creek bottom but the planes [plains] and mountains are barren and destitute of timber as far as we can see.

The Reverend Williams also mentioned the wedding: "While here, a wedding took place in our company between Mr. Richard Fillan and a Mrs. Gray, who had left her husband in Missouri. They were married by Mr. de Smidt, the Catholic priest."[40] Bidwell believed that the bride, Mrs. Gray, was a widow and a sister to Samuel Kelsey's wife, while Williams said she "left her husband."[41] Recall that Mr. Fillan, also known as Phelan, had joined the company at Fort Laramie.

Although Bidwell estimated that the company traveled only five miles on July 30, Dawson and Jimmy John claimed that they traveled ten before stopping to camp. Based upon the estimates of the latter two, their camp would have been along the river, approximately four miles west of where today's Highway 240 intersects with Highway 30.

July 31

Bidwell:

> S. 31st. Left Ham's fork this morning. A distance of 14 miles, over uncommonly hilly road, took us to Black's fork of Green river, on which we encamped. Here we found little grass and no wood. The hills, which were every where rose to view, were thinly clad with shrubby cedars. The fruit found in this lonesome part of creation—Serviceberries on the Mts and currants on the Streams. In the afternoon we descried a large smoke ris-

ing from beyond the intervening chain of hills, from this and other signs, we were assured, that there were plenty of Indians in the country. It was necessary therefore to keep a vigilant look-out, lest the Black Feet should leave us minus a few horses.

Jimmy John:

July 31st—We left Ham's Fork this morning and traveled about 15 miles and encamped on the bank of a small stream called Black's Fork of Green River. The way we traveled today was hilly, rough and rocky, and we were in sight of a large range of high mountains on our left which are covered with perpetual snow. There is a large smoke in sight and west of the encampment resembling that of a volcano, which we suppose to be grass set on fire by the Indians.

On the morning of July 31, Fitzpatrick led them out of the river bottom. They traveled south fourteen miles across dry, rough country before finally coming to Little Muddy Creek. Bidwell and Jimmy John were mistaken in calling it Blacks Fork, although it was a small tributary of Muddy Creek, which is a tributary of Blacks Fork. The Little Muddy was a small stream, only about ten feet wide, and it looped back and forth in its bed like a snake.

The location of their camp on the evening of July 31 is difficult to reach, being about eleven miles east of the intersection of present-day Highway 189 and Highway 225/412. The snow-covered mountains mentioned by Jimmy John to their left were likely the Uinta Mountains. They are about forty-five miles south and its tallest peaks top out at over thirteen thousand feet.

Chapter 10

Along the Bear River

AUGUST 1 TO 15, 1841

August 1

Bidwell:

> S. August 1st. Ascended Black's fork [Little Muddy Creek] about 12 miles.

Jimmy John:

> 1841, August 1—Today we traveled about 12 miles through a rough mountainous country and encamped on the bank of a small creek [Little Muddy Creek] that enters into Black Fork.

The month of August began with the company heading west. They proceeded slowly up the Little Muddy, making good progress because there was very little vegetation in the flat creek bottom. To the immediate west was a series of north-south ridges or escarpments running parallel to each other. As they rolled forward, they gazed in wonderment at the escarpments rising on either side. They were tilted, bald, and barren, their eastern sides steep and their western sides gradually sloping. The formation, now known as Oyster Ridge, would have been a daunting barrier to westward travel had it not been for the gap that the Little Muddy Creek had chewed through over tens of thousands of years, if not longer. Cumberland Gap, as it is known today, was the gateway through which Fitzpatrick would lead them.

Nine miles after leaving their morning's camp, they had made it through the gap, which can be seen east of the junction of today's Highway 189 and Highway 225/412. After rumbling a few more miles up the creek, they arrived at the eastern foot of the Bear River Divide. They had reached a small hollow where two tributaries joined the Little Muddy, one from the north and one from the south. The hollow was flat and marshy with abundant grass. Having completed twelve miles, they stopped to camp.

It was Sunday and the ever-righteous Reverend Williams again expressed displeasure with his fellow travelers: "At night [August 1st] I tried to preach to the deists and swearers. Some of them seemed angry, but I thought I cleared my conscience."[1]

Their camp that night was west of Highway 189, about two miles south of its junction with Highway 225/412.

August 2

Bidwell:

> M. 2nd. Retraced about 2 miles of yesterday's travel, and went up another defile, in order to find a practicable route across, the divide between the waters of Green and Bear rivers, plenty of grass, good spring water, distance 11 miles.

Jimmy John:

> August 2d—This day we went about 12 miles up one fork of the same branch that we encamped on last night, Here one of the wagons broke down and we were obliged to camp until morning and mend it. We are in a small valley this evening, surrounded by high hills and mountains, and in sight of mountains on the right and left or north and south that are covered with snow, some of which are, perhaps, more than one hundred miles off.

When the sun rose on the morning of August 2, the company made ready to head into the mountains to their west. But the Little Muddy emerged from a narrow canyon west of camp. Bidwell had reported that Fitzpatrick retraced their previous day's trail for two miles, while Father Point wrote that they had ended up "in a blind alley," and "had to retrace" their steps.[2] Had Fitzpatrick made a mistake? Probably not. It is more likely that Father Point had misunderstood the situation, and that this was another instance where Fitzpatrick had not bothered to explain what he was doing or why. Fitzpatrick had probably led them first to this grass-filled hollow because it was an excellent place to camp. Since the canyon ahead was narrow and its walls were cut by a number of deep gullies, Fitzpatrick retraced their steps and then led them up and across a ridge instead. Descending to the Little Muddy canyon a short distance above its troublesome section, it was easy from there on.

    The creek bottom was relatively smooth and free of brush and obstacles. The ascent was gentle, not more than a 1 percent grade. The company marched steadily up the canyon, as tall hills towered above them on either side. A couple of ravines opened on their left, each heading west toward the summit, but each ravine looked alike. As mentioned before, trappers in the past (including Fitzpatrick) had used these canyons and ravines as routes to and from the Bear River region. The trappers may have initially followed an earlier Indian trail. Fitzpatrick was undoubtedly leading the company along such a trail. But with fur trade traffic falling off in recent years, runoff from heavy rains and snowmelt may have erased most of the marks that horse and mule hooves had left in the past. Fitzpatrick may have needed to trust his memory as to which was the right ravine to enter.

    It appears that he led the company up the second ravine, the one that now appears on maps as Road Hollow. James Clyman may have been describing this route in his 1844 journal: "[T]he road up the East side follows a ravine whose sides are finely clothed in many places with aspin groves and the assent not verry Steep or difficult."[3] After ascending two miles up the ravine, the company had still not reached the summit of the Divide. But they had come to a small basin where the ravine widened. This may have been where Jimmy John said one of their wagons broke down. Despite this breakdown, it is remarkable that their wagons had not experienced more of them, a testament to their being stoutly built.

    Fed by a small spring, the basin had plenty of grass. The group had traveled eleven or twelve miles that day, and it was a good place to repair the wagon and camp. It was a pretty place as well, graced with a few small groves of quaking aspens nestled in the hollows above them. The night must have been cold since they were camping at almost eight thousand feet.

    Their campsite is difficult to reach. One can follow part of the day's journey by heading west on Haul Road where it leaves Highway 189 about two miles south of its junction with Highway 225/412. When Haul Road forks about one mile west of 189, take the right fork as it heads up the Little Muddy Creek Canyon. Significantly, this gravel road is named Emigrant Trail. It is not advisable to go too far, as it is a primitive road leading into a rugged and complex region where it would be easy to get lost or stranded.

August 3

The company would put in an arduous day on August 3, when they would reach the summit of the Bear River Divide and then descend to the Bear River.

Bidwell:

> T. 3rd. Ascended a high divide and passed down by a most difficult route into the valley of Bear River, the course of this stream was marked out as it wound its way through the vale by the willows that skirted its banks. Reached the river, where we found an abundance of grass, having come about 20 miles.

Jimmy John:

> August 3d—We traveled about 20 miles today over high hills and rough places and arrived at Bear river and encamped on its bank. The river is about 50 yards wide here and has a sandy bottom and no timber on its banks excepting small willows. Killed one antelope here.

When the group set out in the morning, they needed to climb out of the basin where they had encamped. Panting heavily in the thin, high-altitude air, the oxen and mules must have struggled hauling their loads up a steep incline of about 7 percent. After a few more miles they reached the summit, a flat and grassy place, almost meadow-like. From the top, they could look west and see the great valley of the Bear River below them.

They marched northerly along the relatively flat summit for a few miles, and then began their descent. It would be one of the more wicked sections of their trip. They steered downhill, zigzagging as they looked for the friendliest path. In some places they had to plunge down steep drop-offs. In other places they had to travel precariously along the sides of ridges. The wagons creaked and groaned from the awkward strains being put on them. The men did not dare let a wagon slip out of their grasp, otherwise it could career down the mountain side and smash into a pile of useless splinters. Father De Smet described their descent in one of his letters: "[A]ll hands would be called upon to support the wagons on the inclined edge of an abyss or hold them back in some too rapid descent, to prevent what after all was not always prevented, for how many overturnings did we not behold?"[4]

Dawson's memoirs described a similar scene: "At times we could pass along the mountain sides only by having fastened to the top of our loads ropes to which men clung to keep the load from tipping the wagon over, and we descended steeps by having behind the wagons men clinging to ropes."[5] His reference to the use of ropes brings to mind his earlier recollection that on the Green River they had traded some of their "store clothes and ammunition for dressed skins, buckskin clothing, moccasins and *ropes*." Fitzpatrick must have foreseen the need for extra ropes through this section and may have encouraged members of the party to trade for them when they had a chance to do so.

Continuing down the mountain, the company probably followed Bridger Creek the rest of the way to the Bear River. By the time they finally reached it, they had traveled twenty grueling miles. Much fatigued, they set up camp. Bridger Creek crosses Highway 89 about four miles southwest of its intersection with Highway 30. Their campsite would have been near the river, about two miles northwest of where the creek crosses Highway 89.

According to Jimmy John, the river was about one hundred fifty feet wide and meandered through a flat, marshy river plain. Secondary channels or sloughs braided through the grassy flats, while schools of mountain trout drifted gracefully in the sluggish water. Colorful patches of blue flax grew within the river plain, while lofty mountains, rising two to three thousand feet above them, overlooked the valley on both sides. And there must have been hordes of mosquitoes.

There was a different feel to this wide river valley. It was a refreshing change after two months of plodding through parched desert. There was no longer that feeling of dryness. Even the usually gloomy Reverend Williams thought it was a grand place, declaring, "A fine settlement might be formed along this river."[6]

Bidwell's and Jimmy John's sketchy journal entries did not provide enough detail to confirm the precise route the company took over the Bear River Divide that day. But Gregory Franzwa's 1990 edition of his *Maps of the Oregon Trail* provides the key. Bidwell's and Jimmy John's descriptions of the geography and their estimates of distance perfectly fit the trail route between the Cumberland Gap and the Bear River shown on pages 67 and 68 of Franzwa's book.

Dawson's memoirs claimed that they "were the first wagons to pass over this route."[7] The tracks they left would be followed by wagon parties in coming years. Each time a wagon train passed through, the tracks became more pronounced and easier to follow. It eventually became one of the more commonly traveled Oregon Trail routes. Other routes, shortcuts that passed to the north, would be pioneered later, but the one over which Fitzpatrick led his wagons in 1841 remained a good road for any wagon party that, commencing with 1843, traveled south in order to pass through Fort Bridger.

August 4

Bidwell:

> W. 4th. Did not travel.

Jimmy John:

> *August 4th—Today we did not move from the camp, but lay by and caught a good number of trout, some of which were 18 inches in length. There is a great number of wild geese here and other fowls, and antelopes.*

The company decided to stay in camp on August 4. Wagon owners could attend to their stressed wagons. Men on horseback could range out to hunt game, although they no longer had the services of their skilled hunters, John Gray and Lord Romain. But they would not be hunting buffalo. Small numbers had once roamed through here, but no longer, having been hunted out by earlier fur trappers. Passing through there in 1844, James Clyman wrote in his journal that he had hunted buffalo there in 1827, but lamented that they were now entirely gone.[8]

As the company paused to catch its breath, one wonders how everyone was getting along. Were members of the California expedition fraternizing much with members of the missionary party? Although an intriguing question, Bidwell and Jimmy John were not gossipers and did not shed much light on the issue. While our diarists had described some disgruntlement early in the trip, they have not mentioned anything significant during the last two months. If there was any friction or conflict, it must not have risen to a level where they were willing to use any of their precious ink on it.

August 5

Bidwell:

> T. 5th. Proceeded down stream about 18 miles.

Jimmy John:

> August 5th—We traveled about 18 miles today down the bank of Bear River. We caught some trout, and killed an antelope and some wild geese. They are very plenty here.

The scenery did not change much as the company rolled north along the east side of the meandering Bear River. Their route closely matched today's Highway 30/89. After eighteen miles of travel on August 5, they stopped to camp. The location is about five miles south of today's Cokeville, Wyoming, and just west of the highway.

August 6

Bidwell:

> F. 5th [6th]. Had a fine road down the valley of Bear river and made about 25 miles during the day. Found many kinds of wild Currants, red, black, yellow, &c., some of which were of an excellent quality.

Jimmy John:

> August 6th—We traveled 21 miles today on the bank of Bear River. There is high hills and mountains on each side of the river. We caught a good number of fine trout, and other fish and killed one Porquepine and some antelope.

The diarists did not mention it, but about five miles after leaving camp on August 6 they would have crossed Smith's Fork. It was a significant stream that came down from the mountains on their right before emptying into the Bear River. Another ten miles brought them to Thomas Fork, another significant stream, where it entered the Bear River from the northeast. Owing to its steep and muddy banks, the Thomas Fork crossing would have been difficult. They probably camped just northwest of where Highway 30/89 crosses Thomas Fork (about twelve miles north of Cokeville).

August 7

To the immediate west of their camp, a spur of tall hills ran down to the river, forcing the river to change course. The river had to run around the spur's southern tip. The spur ran close to the river, so there was no room for the company's wagons to pass and forced it to climb the daunting hills just to the west.

Bidwell:

> S. 7th. This morning we were obliged to make an inland circuit from the river, the Bluffs approaching so near the river as to render it impossible to continue along its banks. We however reached it again by a most beautiful defile, and beautifully watered by a small rivulet proceeding from a spring. In the afternoon we again left the river on account of the hills, and did not reach it until dark. The bluffs were exceedingly high, and no person could ever believe that wagons ever passed these huge eminences of nature, did he not witness it with his own eyes. But the pleasing view we had from their top, just as the sun was going to sleep behind the western mountains, paid us for all our trouble. A most beautiful landscape presented itself to view, the rugged summits of almost every shape were fantastically pictured upon the sky bounding the western horizon, a beautiful little lake [Bear Lake] was seen to the South, whose surface was fancifully mottled with numerous islands, while the river meandered proudly through the valley among willows and scattering cotton-woods, till it disappeared among the hills in the shades of the evening. Distance traveled to day 16 miles.

Jimmy John:

> August 7th—This morning we left the river and came to it again at twelve o'clock. Nooned at it and left it again on account of being closed in by high hills on each side. We came to it at night and encamped on its bank.

As Bidwell explained, they ascended ravines, snaked through gaps, and marched across basins. Finally, late in the day, they had to make a final steep descent off of these hills in order to return to the valley floor and the Bear River. As Bidwell mentioned, they could see Bear Lake from the heights of the summit. Dropping down eight hundred feet in a mile, it was one of their steepest descents so far. They undoubtedly had to use their ropes again to hold the wagons back. The route they took over the hills hewed closely to today's Highway 30/89. The final hill down which they descended looms directly east of Highway 30/89, about seven miles south of where it intersects with Highway 89 in Montpelier, Idaho. As Bidwell emphasized, the challenges of the day were so great that he thought no one would have believed what they had done without seeing it with their own eyes. One can detect a sense of pride in what they had accomplished.

It is likely that the company camped on the evening of August 7 about a half-mile west of present-day Highway 30/89, five miles south of where it intersects with Highway 89 in Montpelier.

August 8

Crossing the mountain spur the previous day had left everyone much fatigued. It was the probable reason why they delayed returning to the trail until noon on August 8.

Bidwell:

> S. 8th. Started about noon and went ten miles, scenery of the country was grand.

Jimmy John:

> August 8th—We did not leave the camp today until twelve o'clock. We traveled about 10 miles and encamped on the bank of a small branch of pure spring water about a mile from the river. We have caught a great number of fish today, trout and chubs.

As the travelers continued their march northward along the east side of the river plain, the scenery remained beautiful, with tall mountains continuing to border the valley on both sides. The mosquitoes, spawned in the marshes along the river, must have pestered the travelers miserably, especially in the evenings. Yet, there was not a whisper of complaint from our diarists.

August 8 was Sunday, and the Reverend Williams complained of feeling weak from the lack of bread and having to subsist on dried buffalo meat. Initially traveling by himself and on horseback, he had probably not brought much in the way of his own provisions. Had he expected to find some good Methodists in the company who would provide for him? Neither he nor anyone else explained his situation in their journals or memoirs. Once again, Williams expressed revulsion at the men's irreverent speech: "The employment is still fishing and hunting, and such swearing as I never heard in my life before. God will surely punish these swearers."9

The company probably camped on the evening of August 8 just west of the present-day community of Bennington, Idaho.

August 9

The company continued advancing through the Bear River Valley on August 9. Between today's Montpelier and Soda Springs, their path substantially followed the route of Highway 30.

Bidwell:

> M. 9th. Distance 18 miles.

Jimmy John:

> August 9th—Today we traveled about 15 miles on the bank of the river except in the afternoon and returned to it again in the evening and encamped on its bank. Killed two antelope today and caught a number of fine fish.

The company continued their trek along the east side of the river, closely following the route of Highway 30. Just north of the present-day community of Georgetown, Idaho, another set of hills pressed hard against the river, forcing the company to bear right. The wagons would have generally followed the route of Highway 30's gradual ascent over what is today called the Georgetown Summit. At this point they were about a mile east of the river. After traveling over some high country about two miles east of the river, the company rejoined the river and camped beside its bank. Their camp would have been about nine miles south of today's Soda Springs, Idaho, and a half-mile west of Highway 30.

August 10

Bidwell:

> T. 10th. The day was fine and pleasant; a soft and cheerful breeze and the sky bedimmed by smoke brought to mind the tranquil season of Au-

> tumn. A distance of 10 miles took us to the Soda Fountain, where we stopped the remainder of the day. This is a noted place in the mountains and is considered a great curiosity—within the circumference of 3 or 4 miles there are included no less than 100 springs, some bursting out on top of the ground, others along the banks of the river which are very low at this place, and some, even in the bottom of the river. The water is strongly impregnated with Soda, and wherever it gushes out of the ground, a sediment is deposited, of a redish color, which petrifies and forms around the springs large mounds of porus rock; some of which are no less than 50 feet high—Some of these fountains have become entirely dry, in consequence of the column of water which they contained becoming so high as to create sufficient power by its pressure, to force the water to the surface in another place, in several of the springs the water was lukewarm—but none were very cold. The ground was very dry at this time, and made a noise as we passed over it with horses, as though it was hollow underneath. Cedar grows here in abundance, and the scenery of the country is romantic. Father De Smet, with 2 or 3 Flathead Indians, started about dark this evening to go to Fort Hall, which is about 50 miles distant.

Jimmy John:

> August 10th—We traveled about 10 miles today and arrived at the Soda springs on the banks of Bear river. There is a great number of these springs which are constantly bubling and throwing off gass. Some spout water to a considerable distance and roar like a steamboat. Others form mounds which are round. The water boils out of the middle and forms them by the sediment running down the side. There are high mountains here on each side of the river.

One of Bidwell's observations is easy to overlook. He called attention to smoke in the air. These arid regions were frequently afflicted by wildfires, sometimes ignited by lightning strikes and sometimes by Indians. As a result, smoky air was frequently mentioned by future emigrants crossing the West.

Soda Springs was an intriguing place, with novel sights and sounds. This was volcanic country, evidenced not only by hot springs and steam vents, but also by high banks and ledges of hardened black lava flows. Bidwell made up for his previous day's weak entry by producing one of his more detailed efforts. The waters of the springs had produced cones of colorful mineral deposits, ranging in color from red to white and from cream to flesh-colored. The more noteworthy were Soda Springs, Beer Springs, and Steamboat Springs. Soda Springs was about a half-mile west of Soda Creek, and was given its name because its water tasted like soda. Beer Springs, a few hundred feet farther west, produced waters possessing an acidic, beer-like taste. Another half-mile west was Steamboat Springs, which was noted for spewing gas and hot mineral water into the air every fifteen seconds and for producing a hissing noise, much like that of a steamboat boiler releasing excess steam. Regrettably, most of the springs have since disappeared beneath the waters of Anderson Reservoir after the Bear River was dammed. Yet, a couple of hot springs remain at the west end of the present-day Cedar View Golf Course. Bidwell also mentioned the cedars, which future diarists would often mention as being near Steamboat Springs. Wagon companies would camp there and enjoy the fragrant smoke produced by burning the cedar wood.

That evening, members of the company sat with their mess. Pulled close to the warmth of their campfires, they would have listened to the strange sound of Steamboat Springs in the background. It must have been a somber time and a time of intense emotions. It would be the last night the entire company would spend together. It must have been a time of anxiety for the California-bounds because they knew the time had arrived when they would be losing the services of Fitzpatrick. Their failure to secure the services of someone who knew the way to California, coupled with warnings of the impossibility of getting wagons through, had undoubtedly spurred heated debates and arguments ever since leaving the Green River. The moment of decision was at hand: Should they abandon their original goal of going to California and go to Oregon instead? According to Josiah Belden's memoirs, Fitzpatrick offered his advice:

> *Fitzpatrick advised us to give up our expedition and go to Ft. Hall, one of the Hudson Bay Stations, as there was no road for us to follow, nothing was known of the country, and we had nothing to guide us, and so he advised us to give up the California project. He thought it was doubtful if we ever got there; we might get caught in the snow of the mountains and perish there, and he considered it very hazardous to attempt it.*[10]

Consider the husbands and fathers sitting beside their campfires that night, looking across at the delicate faces of their wives and children. They had heard more than enough. Their primary responsibility was to their loved ones, and they must choose the safer option.

August 11

The next morning, the company caught up their oxen and mules and assembled together for the last time.

Bidwell:

> W. 11th. Having traveled about 6 miles this morning the Company came to a halt—the Oregon Company were now going to leave Bear river for Ft. Hall, which is situated on Lewis [Snake] river, a branch of the Columbia—many, who purposed in setting out, to go immediately through to California, here, concluded to go on into Oregon so that the California company now consisted of only 32 men and one woman and child, there being but one family. The two companies, after bidding each other a parting farewell, started and were soon out of sight, several of our company however went to Ft. Hall to procure provisions, and to hire if possible a pilot to conduct us to the Gap in the California Mountains, or at least, to the head of Mary's river, we were therefore to move on slowly 'till their return. Encamped on Bear river, having come about 12 miles.

Jimmy John:

> August 11th—Today we traveled about 4 miles and the company became divided; 4 carts and 4 waggons for Oregon, and 9 waggons for California, myself for one. We traveled about 14 miles farther and encamped on the bank of the river. The river here runs through a deep channel of black rock having the appearance of being melted at some future [previous] time.

Not counting the missionaries' wagons, the company had left Missouri with fifteen wagons. The above reveals that just before the company divided they were down to thirteen. Joseph Chiles had sold one and another was left at the Green River. It is quite remarkable that the company had not lost more of them after traveling such a great distance over such rough country.

Except for Benjamin Kelsey, all of the other men with wives and children had declared for Oregon. They had reached the conclusion that trying for California was too insanely reckless and uncertain. Their families were too precious to take the risk. In later years, Bidwell reflected on this in one of his memoirs:

> Thirty-two of our party, becoming discouraged, decided not to venture without path or guide into the unknown and trackless regions toward California, but concluded to go with the missionary party to Fort Hall and thence find their way down Snake and Columbia rivers into Oregon. The rest of us—also thirty-two in number—including Benjamin Kelsey, his wife and little daughter—remained firm, refusing to be diverted from our original purpose of going direct to California. After getting all the information we could from Captain Fitzpatrick, we regretfully bade good-by to our fellow emigrants and to Father De Smet and his party.[11]

As Bidwell noted, thirty-two had not been swayed. Setting their jaws, they declared for California, regardless. Wise advice, prudence, and overwhelming odds against success be damned. Josiah Belden explained their thinking: "[W]e determined we would not give it up but continue the attempt, and do the best we could to get through," he wrote in his memoirs.[12] While some might call it courage, others might describe it as hard-headed foolishness.

Father Point recalled that some had debated remaining at Soda Springs through the winter. The priest wrote that Soda Springs was "the most beautiful campsite that we had seen. Limpid springs, refreshing fruits, game in great abundance, the most varied and picturesque views, all seemed to invite travelers to make this their winter quarters. There were some who thought seriously of doing this, but not all deemed it advisable. Since the small size of the group would not make a safe stay here possible, the march was resumed."[13]

Four miles after leaving camp, the parties divided, each going their own way, for bad or good. Their paths split at the intersection of today's Highway 39 and Highway 34, four miles west of the Cedar Grove Golf Course. As the missionary party and the Oregon-bound group headed northwest, rolling out of sight, the California party, now significantly diminished, turned south and followed the Bear River as it headed toward the Great Salt Lake. With Fitzpatrick gone, Bidwell mentioned in one of his memoirs how rudderless they were:

> We were now thrown entirely upon our resources. All the country was to us a veritable terra incognita, and we only knew that California lay to the west. Captain Fitzpatrick was not much better informed, but he had heard that parties had penetrated the country to the southwest and west of Salt Lake to trap for beaver; and by his advice four of our men went with the parties to Fort Hall to consult

> Captain Grant, who was in charge there, and to gain information.
> Meanwhile our depleted party slowly made it down the west side of
> Bear River.[14]

Nicholas Dawson's memoirs described how they had decided to proceed upon leaving Soda Springs:

> At Soda Springs we parted company with the crowd that was going to Oregon, which crowd included Fitzpatrick and the priests. Thirty-one of us, including one woman (Mrs. Benjamin Kelsey) and her child, decided to strike for California. We knew nothing positive of the route, except that it went west. True, we had some old maps picturing a river Buenaventura, or St. Mary's river, which, flowing out of Great Salt Lake and pursuing a westerly course emptied into the Pacific; and from this map we had thought that all we should have to do was to find our river and follow it. However, we had been told by trappers that there was no river flowing from the lake, but that there was a river (which they called Ogden's) that had its source west of the lake and flowed west, and that it might take us to California. There was but one man in the mountains that had ever been to California—Joel [Joseph] Walker by name—and he was supposed to be at Fort Hall, on Snake river. So we sent two men to the fort for Walker, and the rest of us were to travel leisurely down Bear river until we reached a beautiful valley which the trappers called Cache, and there await their return.[15]

Dawson explained that trappers, probably those in the Fraeb party, had discredited their maps, insisting that they were wrong. The trappers had encouraged them to find Ogden's River (the Humboldt) somewhere west of the Great Salt Lake. Someone must have told them to follow the Bear River south to the Great Salt Lake and then head west in search of the headwaters of Ogden's River. Peter Skene Ogden, an employee of the Hudson Bay Company, had discovered the river in 1829 during one of his trapping excursions. Although he referred to it as the Unknown River in his reports, it was later called Ogden's River by some, and Mary's River by others. It was not until John C. Frémont's Third Expedition in 1845 that he gave the river the new name of the Humboldt, naming it after the famed European explorer and naturalist Baron Alexander von Humboldt.[16]

In 1832, a brigade of trappers from Fitzpatrick's Rocky Mountain Fur Company had traveled west along the north side of the Great

Salt Lake and struck the headwaters of the Humboldt. A number of old maps showed a river called the Buenaventura draining from the western shore of the Salt Lake and flowing all the way to the Pacific Ocean. In 1833, Bonneville sent Joseph Walker with a party of trappers to explore the western side of the Great Salt Lake in search of the fabled Buenaventura. Walker discovered that these maps were wrong; no river flowed out of the Lake, let alone from its west side. Upon completing his exploration, Walker led his band of trappers away from Salt Lake and headed west until they struck the headwaters of the Humboldt, and then followed it all the way to the Sierra Nevada Mountains.[17] After making it into California in 1833, Walker again traveled to California in 1840, but we do not know what route he took that year.

Even if they had found Joseph Walker, it is likely he would have declined to act as their guide. As mentioned earlier, he had other plans. If he was available to give advice, his prior experiences suggest that he would have advised them to do what he done earlier, namely, travel along the north side of the Great Salt Lake and continue west until striking the Humboldt. The problem was that it would have been difficult for Walker or any old trapper to adequately describe the route with precision. All of the jumbled mountain ranges separated by waterless deserts would have made it difficult to draw an accurate and sufficiently detailed map.

In a few more years, a superb, wagon-easy route to California with ample grass and water would be found. This route would proceed to Fort Hall, and then follow the Snake River to the Raft River in today's Idaho. It would proceed up the Raft and over a divide to Goose Creek. Traveling up Goose Creek, it would then cross another divide and lead into Thousand Springs Valley. The path then traveled up the valley and over a final divide to the headwaters of the Humboldt River just north of today's Wells, Nevada. Unfortunately, this route was not known as of 1841. Or if it was known, it was known by very few. Fitzpatrick and Grant did not know about it. Historians claim that Joseph Walker pioneered this route in 1843, when he escorted Joseph Chiles's wagon party of emigrants to California. Walker may have been following directions he obtained from trappers, or from those who learned of it from Indians, or from Indians directly. It was amazing what one could learn from Indians. After all, they had been crisscrossing this country for thousands of years and usually knew the best way to get from here to there.

When the Bartleson group divided into those heading to Oregon and those going to California, it is hoped that some in the California party approached Fitzpatrick and thanked him. Maybe they had. They had greatly benefitted from his knowledge and experience during the three months that they had traveled under his guidance.

From this point on, the California group—thirty-two adult men, one woman, and one child—would begin the truly challenging part. They would no longer be following someone who knew the way. They would have no trail and no map that was worth anything. Joseph Chiles recalled in his memoirs that at this point they had "[n]o guide, no compass, nothing but the sun to direct them."[18] There was so much ahead that they knew nothing about, and for which they would be unprepared. Indeed, they would have to be explorers, navigating across some of the most meanspirited country imaginable. Did they have the skills to pull it off? More importantly, did they have the right leadership?

Their leader would be John Bartleson. By virtue of his age and assertiveness, he had been elected their captain at their organizational meeting on May 18. During the time Fitzpatrick acted as the company's pilot, it appeared that Bartleson had tried to play a leadership role at times. Father Point, for example, wrote that when the Cheyenne war party first appeared, it was "colonel [Bartleson] who had ordered this maneuver [saddling, mounting and ranging their horses in battle line]." De Smet and Point made other comments indicating that they regarded Bartleson as the California venture's leader. One cannot help wondering, however, whether some of those electing to go to Oregon had changed their minds because they were uncomfortable with the prospect of Bartleson leading them. For those determined to go on to California, one wonders to what extent they respected Bartleson or felt comfortable with his competency. Nevertheless, for better or for worse, he would be the man on whom their fate would largely depend.

There is some uncertainty regarding whom the California party sent to Fort Hall and what they were sent to accomplish. Bidwell's journal said they sent "several" to "procure provisions" and "hire if possible a pilot." Later, his memoirs recorded that Fitzpatrick advised them to send men to Fort Hall "to gain information in regard to the country to the west. It was thought that Captain Grant, then in charge of the fort, or trappers who might be there, would give knowledge of the almost unknown region."[19] Richard Grant was the

Hudson Bay Company's man in charge at Fort Hall. De Smet's letter from Fort Hall said that the Bartleson group sent a "few men" to "revictual," including "the leader of the Colony [Bartleson]," but De Smet was the only one reporting that Bartleson traveled to Fort Hall. Later accounts will show that De Smet was mistaken. Bartleson continued to travel with the California-bound wagon party, and was not one of the men who went to Fort Hall. Dawson was the only one recalling that they sent men to Fort Hall to recruit Joseph Walker. But Walker was not there.

Both priests, De Smet and Point, commented on their relationship with the non-Catholics. Prejudice is common among men, and bias against Catholics was prevalent in Protestant America at the time. It was not surprising that awkward barriers existed between the two groups. Yet, everything indicated that the two groups had maintained a harmonious relationship and had cooperated remarkably well. Bidwell expressed respect for De Smet, and others may have felt similarly. The priests acknowledged these prejudices, but felt they had made some inroads. Father De Smet expressed these feelings in his letter from Fort Hall:

> *I had daily conversations with some of the caravan, and frequently with several. And although Americans are slow to change their creed, we had the consolation to relieve our traveling companions of a heavy load of prejudice against our holy religion. They parted from us, exhibiting signs of respect and veneration; nay, even of preference for Catholicity.*[20]

Charles Weber was likely one of those with whom De Smet engaged in frequent "conversations." At some point, the priest gave Weber a set of rosary beads, which are currently displayed in the San Joaquin County Historical Society Museum in Stockton, California. Weber had been educated in Germany, where he had studied Latin, Greek, French, and political science.[21] That is the kind of education that would have enticed De Smet to converse with Weber around the campfires at night. De Smet likely offered the beads to Weber as a token of his friendship. Since Weber was not a Catholic, but rather the son of a dedicated Reformed Protestant Church minister in Germany, it is interesting that Weber accepted the gift and kept it.

Father Point had his own comments on the relationships that had evolved during the trip: "Many prejudices had disappeared during the journey. But since most of them seemed firmly attached to error, there seemed little hope that we should see each other in the true fatherland."[22] Specifically relating to Bartleson, Father Point wrote in his memoirs years later that "through the maintenance of mutual respect, the most perfect concord reigned between him [Bartleson] and us right up to the end."[23] De Smet wrote in his letter sent from Fort Hall that both the Reverend Williams and Bartleson "were of a peaceable disposition, and manifested for us the highest regard."[24] Whether the feelings were mutual is impossible to say since neither Williams nor Bartleson left behind any words commenting on the relationship.

From where the parties separated, Bidwell reported that the California group traveled south twelve miles on August 11 and then stopped to camp beside the Bear River. During most of the day's travels, they could not access the river since it flowed through a narrow, deep channel.

One can view their campsite by entering the present-day town of Grace, Idaho, on Highway 34. In town, turn west on Center Street and head west out of town. Just out of town, Center Street becomes Turner Road. One will notice when crossing the Bear River Bridge how the river cuts through the black volcanic rock in a narrow channel that runs between fifty and seventy feet below the surface of the surrounding terrain. One will come to Hegstrom Road four miles west of town on Turner Road. Travel south on Hegstrom Road about one and a half miles to the bend. Proceed around the bend another half-mile and turn south on to Gentile Valley Road. Follow the curving Gentile Valley Road south to Ralph Hansen Lane. Turn left and follow it east and then south about one mile. There, on the west bank of the river, is where the Bartleson party stopped to camp on the afternoon of August 11. It was a good place, where the river was easily accessible.

It was early afternoon when the company stopped. Many in the party must have experienced a sensation of naked vulnerability, because Fitzpatrick's stabilizing presence was suddenly missing. It was a smaller group now, with fewer arms to defend them. They were uncertain how to get to California, were without a guide, and had no skills of exploration beyond whatever they had assimilated from Fitzpatrick during the three months of traveling with him.

In the meantime, our two diarists, Bidwell and Jimmy John, had decided to go fishing along the river earlier in the afternoon. But when darkness arrived, they had not returned to camp. Unsuccessful with their fishing, Bidwell and Jimmy John had decided on an ambitious jaunt, which Bidwell described in his journal entry of August 11:

> [August 11] I, in company with another man (J. John) went some distance below the camp to fish in the river; fished sometime without success—concluded we could spend the afternoon more agreeably, the day was uncomfortably warm, could find no place to shelter us from the burning sun, except the thick copses of willows—these we did not like to enter on account of the danger of falling in with bears, we concluded to ascend the mountain, where, were two spots of snow in full view, in order to enjoy the contrast between a scorching valley and a snowy mountain. Supposed the snow not more than 4 miles distant, set out without our guns knowing they would be a hindrance in ascending the mountain. Our march was unremitted for at least 4 miles, had only gained the side of a hill which we at first supposed not more than a mile off; here, we lingered to observe several kinds of trees which we had not before observed, among which were a kind of Rock maple, choke cherry &c. But conscious of being defeated in our object, if we lost much time, we ran up the eminence with renewed vigor, till at last gained the summit. But being determined not to be outdone, we continued on under all the strength we could command; Crossed a valley ¾ of a mile wide, ascended craggy steeps and passed through thickets of the densest kind, night obscured the valley below us, lost sight of the snow above us, afraid to return lest we fall in with bears, as their signs were plenty and fresh, continued to ascend the mountain till midnight, could not find the snow—we were cold, not having our coats. Clouds drifted against the mountain and made us wet—slept under a pine tree which afforded us a good shelter—Morning came [August 12], it found us about a half a mile below the snow, took as much as we could conveniently carry; took another route down the mountain, running and jumping as fast as our strength would permit, arrived at camp about noon. They supposed, without doubt, that the blackfeet had got us, had been up all night on guard, every fire had been put out, they had been out twice in search of us and were about to start again, when we arrived. We were received with a mixture of joy and reprehension, the company was soon under way and traveled about 4 miles.

Years later, Bidwell's memoirs added additional facts. He admitted that he and Jimmy John had not advised the camp in advance of their intentions. He said they thought they could reach the snow and be back by sundown. But their decision was foolish. Their objective, Sedgwick Peak, is seven miles west of where the company had camped. In the clear air, it deceptively looked much closer. Rising to nine thousand feet, the peak often still has snow on its summit in mid-August. Bidwell mentioned that he was wearing buckskin clothing and moccasins, which he had possibly acquired from the Snake Indians or the Fraeb trappers while camping on the Green River. He had worn out the bottoms of his moccasins in his trek up the mountain and it left his feet bloody.

Bidwell related that Fitzpatrick, when separating from the California company, had warned them that Blackfeet Indians, a dangerous and hostile tribe, lurked in the area and that the company should be cautious. While crossing the small valley (known as Beaver Basin today) he and Jimmy John saw "Indian fires" and "Indian signs." Upon their descent the next morning, he related crossing the small valley again, noticing that "numerous Indians had left that very morning."[25]

Because members of the company feared the young men had been killed, they corralled their wagons, barricaded their camp, and sat up the rest of the night on guard. When daylight arrived, Bidwell said that "half of the company mounted animals and went in search of us. They saw our tracks but mistook them for Indian tracks and returned and reported that we must certainly be dead . . . . Under the impression that we were beyond doubt killed by Indians, our company started on."[26] Nearing the company's campsite at one o'clock that afternoon, Bidwell recounted that they saw that their company was already on the move. When they caught up, they were sternly asked where they had gone. Bidwell said he "triumphantly" told them, "to the snow."[27] He admitted that while some "rejoiced to see us," others were angry, one going so far as to suggest that they ought to be horsewhipped.[28] The company had been up half the night with worry and alarm, and had spent most of the next morning searching for them.

It is noticeable that Jimmy John did not mention this exploit in his journal. He was clearly embarrassed and chagrined, his silence indicating that he knew he and Bidwell had misbehaved in circumstances where such shenanigans were unacceptable.

A number in the company long remembered the incident. Nicholas "Cheyenne" Dawson was one of them, using his memoirs as an opportunity to show that he had not been the only irresponsible knucklehead during the trip:

> *Bidwell and Jimmy John had gone off fishing. They did not return, and much anxiety was felt. At midnight the guard reported that they had not come in. Then the camp was aroused, the wagons were corraled, and everything ready, we awaited til day-break—for that was the Indians' time. We were sure that Bidwell and Johns had been killed, and we expected to have to fight for our lives. Daybreak at last came, but no Indians. Later in the day, we decided to send out parties to search for the bodies of our comrades. I was riding along, looking for Indian signs and gory corpses, when I saw two men running down a mountain. When they came nearer I saw that it was the supposed dead. As soon as Bidwell was within hearing, he triumphantly held up a handkerchief full of something and shouted "Snow!" Then I spoke forcibly, "Snow! ___! ___! We thought you were dead."*[29]

Charles Hopper, the hunter from Independence and John Bartleson's right-hand man, also made a point of describing the incident in his short memoir of 1871:

> *While encamped near Soda Springs, Mr. Bidwell became excited on beholding snow upon the mountains apparently close to camp and asked, "Can't I go to it and get back this evening?" He was assured he could not and that the mountains were a long distance. He pretended that he was going fishing but started for the mountains to see the snow. He was gone all night and the company was sure he was killed by the Indians. I took his track for the mountains and at last found him. Bidwell came laughing into camp, but he got soundly rebuked by the Captain [Bartleson] for being so venturesome and giving trouble to the company when there was no need of it.*[30]

Hopper's account is valuable in that it confirmed that Bartleson was with the company at the time, and had not traveled to Fort Hall despite De Smet's having written that he had. It is odd that Hopper only mentioned Bidwell and not Jimmy John as being one of the misadventurers. It is curious that Hopper claimed he was the one who "found" Bidwell because it conflicts with Dawson's claim. Hopper was a close friend and perhaps employee of Bartleson, and for reasons that will come out later, Hopper may have had a motive for making Bidwell look bad.

But Bidwell's own accounts were sufficiently damaging. Hopper did not need to show the young man's fall from grace. Bidwell had engaged in an inexcusably reckless and irresponsible act, yet he seemed so pride-blinded that he did not express a shred of remorse or regret—not when he recorded his journal entry on August 11, and not when he composed his memoirs fifty years later.

Common sense tells us that members of the company would have been justifiably peeved. They must have been nervous to begin with and would not have appreciated needless alarms. They must have been agitated by the delay and inconvenience of having to search for these two "strays." Whatever Bidwell's reputation was before, this venture must have irremediably branded him as a foolish, impulsive youngster with flawed judgment. It would be an unwanted reputation from which he could not easily recover. As the old adage goes: Once you have a reputation for getting up late, it does not do any good to get up early.

We have also learned from this incident that the company had not circled their wagons when they rolled into camp. It was only after the guards became alarmed late at night because the two young men had not returned that they "corralled" them. We do not know whether Fitzpatrick had recently allowed the company to become slack about circling their wagons, but this incident showed that on the very first night under Bartleson's leadership, they had failed to take that precaution. This is especially concerning in light of Fitzpatrick's warning about Blackfeet being in the area. It was a tribe whose reputation suggested that you should not let your guard down.

Before leaving this incident, one wonders if Bidwell's and Jimmy John's foolishness had ironically saved the company. Fitzpatrick's warnings, coupled with the Indian signs seen by the young men, suggest that Blackfeet may have indeed been in the area. Did going on alert and corralling the wagons discourage a raiding party from attempting a surprise attack on the wagon company that night?

August 12

Bidwell's report for August 12 was included in his entry for August 11. As mentioned, the company did not get underway until about noon on August 12.

Jimmy John:

> August 12th—Today we traveled but 4 miles and encamped on the bank of the river. The Indians that were with us are gone with the Oregon company. The most of them are missionaries.

The company rolled along a flat, sage-covered river plain with few obstacles on August 12. The company called it a day after advancing just four miles and stopped to camp beside the west bank of the river.

To visit their estimated campsite of August 12, return to Gentile Valley Road and travel south three miles to its intersection with River Road. Follow the curvy River Road south one and a half miles. The campsite would have been along the river just east of there.

August 13

Bidwell:

> F. 13th. Traveled about 10 miles in a southerly direction. It was the intention of the company to stop and hunt in cash [Cache] valley, which is on the bear river 3 or 4 day's travel from its mouth.

Jimmy John:

> August 13th—Today we traveled about 10 miles and encamped for the balance of the day on the bank of the river.

The company traveled ten miles on August 13, continuing to follow the Bear River southward along the flat river bottom. The terrain barely changed, with tall mountains continuing to stare down on them from both sides. The approximate location of their camp can be seen east of today's Highway 34, about two and a half miles east of the highway's junction with Cleveland Road, and four and a half miles south of Thatcher, Idaho.

August 14

Just south and west of their camp the terrain was elevated, forcing the river to flow through a twelve-mile-long narrow canyon called the Oneida Narrows. The company had to leave the river and head west over the uplands.

Bidwell:

> S. 14th. Left the river on account of the hills which obstructed our way on it, found an abundance of choke cherries, many of which were ripe, road uncommonly broken, did not reach the river, distance about 14 miles.

Jimmy John:

> August 14th—This morning we passed by a hot spring near the encampment. It is constantly boiling and smoking and is strongly impregnated with soda. We traveled about 15 miles today over hills and mountains and encamped on a small brook about 4 miles from the river.

Just a half-mile west of their camp the company passed by the hot spring mentioned by Jimmy John. The spring can be seen as a couple of adjacent ponds just south of Highway 34. The path the company took that day follows Highway 34 southwest for about ten miles. The company then departed from the course followed by the highway and headed almost due west for another four miles. They were now traversing country that was far more challenging than the flat river bottom they had been following. Reconnaissance parties needed to be sent forward to examine the terrain to make sure the company was not heading into dead-end canyons or toward terrain too difficult to traverse.

After traveling fourteen miles, they stopped on the north bank of Battle Creek and set up camp. The approximate location of their camp is on the north side of Battle Creek, just west of where it crosses Highway 91, and about nine miles northwest of the small town of Preston, Idaho.

August 15

Bidwell:

> S. 15th. Continued our journey over hills and ravines, going to almost every point of the compass, in order to pass them. The day was very warm—the grass had been very good, but it was now very much parched up; having come about 15 miles, we encamped on a small stream proceeding out of the Mountains at no great distance from us. But we were surprised to see it become perfectly dry in the course of an hour, some of the guards said there was plenty of water in it about mid night.

Jimmy John:

> *August 15th—Today we did not travel far, perhaps not more than 8 miles on a straight line, but the way was rough and winding and hilly. We encamped on a small branch about three miles from the river, that is, from Bear river. We killed very little game for a few days, except for a few antelope and fishing. The mountain cherries and kerrants [currants] are ripe at this time and other fruits of various kinds of good flavor.*

When the company left camp that morning, it traveled along the west side of Battle Creek. The creek flowed through a channel that turned southward toward the Bear River, about four miles away. The company was forced to travel along high ground to the west of the ravine because it continued to grow in width and depth. After rounding the south end of a mountain spur called Little Mountain, the company encountered Deep Creek ravine, another deep and impassable obstacle that forced the company to turn north for about three miles before they were able to cross to the west side of the ravine. The company had now entered an upper arm of Cache Valley near today's town of Clifton, Idaho. The company then marched across the sage-covered west side of the valley near the foot of the hills until they came to Weston Creek. Here, the party stopped to camp.

Bidwell's memoirs later complained that the numerous ravines and gullies and the dense sagebrush slowed them down and made progress very arduous. But he also explained that their slow progress was intentional:

> *Part of the time we had purposely traveled slowly to enable the men from Fort Hall the sooner to overtake us. But unavoidable delays were frequent: daily, often hourly, the road had to be made passable for our wagons by digging down steep banks, filling gulches, etc. Indian fires obscured mountains and valleys in a dense, smoky atmosphere, so that we could not see any considerable distance in order to avoid obstacles. The principal growth, on plain and hill alike, was the interminable sagebrush, and often it was difficult, for miles at a time, to break a road through it, and sometimes a lightly laden wagon would be overturned.*[31]

After a hard day, the company came to rest on the north bank of the creek just south of the town of Weston. The last ten miles of their travels on August 15 can be followed by heading south on today's

West Side Highway (Road D 1) between Clifton, Idaho, and Weston, Idaho.

When the company entered what would become the future State of Utah on August 15, it had scored a number of firsts in Western History. It was the first party to bring wagons into Utah, and Nancy Kelsey and her infant daughter were the first white woman and child to enter the state.

Chapter 11

Across the Great Salt Lake Country

AUGUST 16 TO 31, 1841

August 16

After leaving their Weston Creek camp on the morning of August 16, the company headed south, following a route that generally corresponded to that of today's Highway 23 as it proceeds south through the tiny communities of Cornish and Trenton, Utah. Continuing to follow the Bear River at a slight distance, the company veered southeasterly, crossing a flat plain covered with coarse marsh grasses until it came to the edge of the river.

Bidwell:

> M. 16th. This morning there was abundance of water in the little stream [Weston Creek] and it was running briskly when we left it. If the water was not supplied by the melting of the snow in the mountains, it was really an interesting spring, found an abundance of choke cherries, very large and exquisitely delicious, better than any I ever eat before. Distance traveled, 12 miles.

Jimmy John:

> August 16th—Traveled about ten miles and camped on Bear River near a place called Cash [Cache] Valley.

After traveling twelve miles by Bidwell's estimate, the company stopped to camp beside the Bear River just east of the small present-day community of Amalga, Utah. They had been traveling through Cache Valley for two days. Bidwell's entries revealed no awareness of that fact, although Jimmy John reported that they were "near" Cache Valley.

August 17

The company arose on the morning of August 17 and prepared to move out. They would leave Cache Valley that day.

Bidwell:

> T. 17th. Traveled about 16 miles; saw a large smoke rising out of the mountains before us. It had probably been raised by the Indians, as a telegraph, to warn the tribe, that their land was visited by strangers. We were unable to procure any fuel this evening, we therefore slept without fire. The Indians found in this region are Shoshonees, they are friendly.

Jimmy John:

> August 16th [17th]. Today we traveled about 20 miles and encamped in Cash Valley on the banks of Bear River, two miles below the falls of that river. Here the river runs through a cut in the mountain which is narrow and nearly perpendicular and about 300 feet high.

After leaving their camp on the banks of the Bear River near today's Amalga, the diarists' mileage estimates for August 17 indicate that they continued to travel close to the river, even though it meandered south for about five miles before turning around and doubling back. The river then headed northwest about five miles, after which it turned west and poured through a narrow cut in a long ridge that bounded the western side of Cache Valley. It is clear that the route the company took that day caused them to travel approximately ten unnecessary miles in following the river along its great bend. Bidwell had mentioned in his memoirs how the dense smoke in the air had limited visibility and why it resulted in them not avoiding obstacles in their path. It sounded as if Bartleson was failing to send out horse-mounted scouts to reconnoiter and then guide the wagons along helpful shortcuts.

As the company neared the end of the day on August 17, they came to where the small town of Newton is now located. Then they proceeded over the ridge just to the north of the narrow canyon through which the Bear River roared.

To follow the company's path over the ridge, head one mile north-

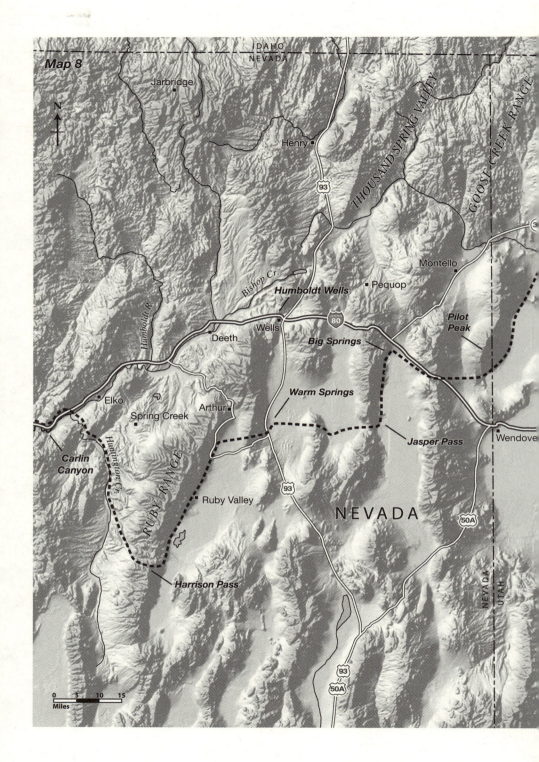

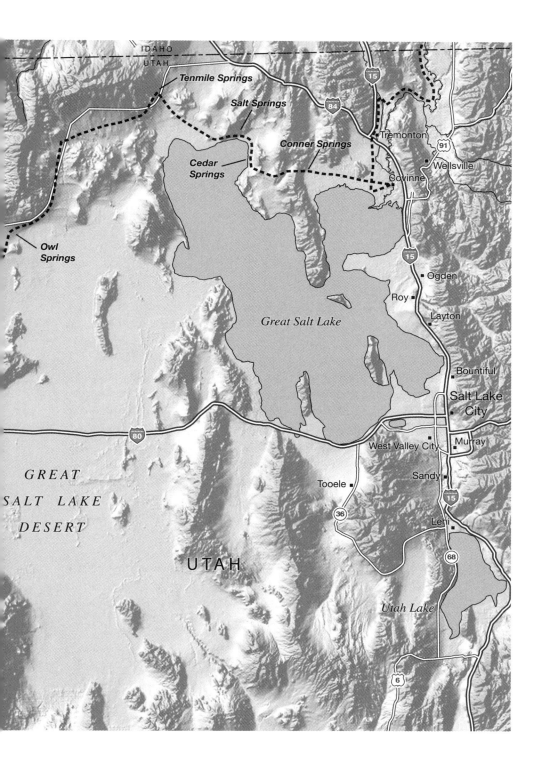

west on Highway 142 and turn west on Road W 7800 N. Turn left on Fielding Road and follow it five and a half miles over the ridge. After descending from the ridge, Fielding Road will turn into 2000 W Road. Their camp on the evening of August 17 was about one mile south of that point, beside the river bank.

In passing over the ridge, they had left Cache Valley. They had entered the Malade River Valley, which Jimmy John incorrectly thought was Cache Valley. Dawson's memoirs had recalled that the company was "to travel leisurely down Bear river until we reached a beautiful valley which the trappers called Cache, and there await their return [the men sent to Fort Hall]."[1] He also wrote that "we intended to await at Cache valley the return of the messengers we had sent for Walker, but we passed Cache Valley without recognizing it."[2] Bidwell recalled in his memoirs that they had passed through Cache Valley without knowing it. It was a large valley, about fifty miles long and ten miles wide, and they had traveled through it for three days. It should have been unmistakable. How could a basin that large been difficult to identify? Thomas Fitzpatrick had been to Cache Valley a number of times during his trapping career, so Bartleson could have obtained a hand-drawn map from him. Maybe he had. But if he knew, he had not shared the knowledge with the entire company since Bidwell and Jimmy John did not know. And why would Bartleson lead the company out of the valley without waiting for the men sent to Fort Hall to catch up? Was he impatient and wanted to keep moving? After all, the men returning from Fort Hall were on horseback and could travel fast enough to catch up to a company hampered by the slow-moving ox-drawn wagons.

August 18

August 18 would be the beginning of unprecedented difficulties. Even in their wildest imaginations, the company likely did not understand the difficulty of the bleak, tough country they were about to cross from here on.

Bidwell:

> W. 18th. Traveled but a short distance when we discovered that a deep salt creek prevented our continuing near the river. In ascending this stream in search of a place to cross it, we found on its margin a hot

spring, very deep and clear. The day was very warm and we were unable to reach the river; encamped on this salt creek and suffered much for water, the water being so salt we could not drink it, distance 15 miles.

Jimmy John:

> August 18th—This forenoon we came to a muddy, deep creek which we could not cross without going nearly a half day's journey up it, and consequently we traveled about 5 miles today and came down on opposite bank and camped. There is a large number of hot salt springs on the bank of this creek. Some of them are nearly as hot as boiling water.

In this area, the Malade River meandered about two miles west of and parallel to the Bear River. The "salt creek" that Jimmy John described may have been a branch of the Malade. There were no other watercourses in the area. The fact that they encountered it "a short distance" from their camp rules out the Malade's main channel because the river did not flow into the Bear River until fifteen miles further south. If the company encountered such a branch, it does not exist today. The region has been developed for many years, during which many old sloughs and other small channels were filled in and reclaimed. There is aerial evidence of an old channel in that area that may have existed in 1841.

Since the company's southern progress was impeded by the "salt creek," they turned northwest and marched along its eastern side looking for a place to cross. A few miles from where they turned north, the branch may have connected to the Malade's main channel. The Malade was notoriously difficult to cross because of its steep, high banks and its muddy bottom. However, six miles from where they began ascending the branch, they came to where the Malade had a firm, rock-covered bottom, a place that had been a popular crossing place in the past for Indians and trappers. Known as Rocky Crossing today, it would remain a popular crossing in the years to come. The spot is on the Malade, just west of Interstate 15 and about six miles north of its intersection with Highway 30. After crossing the river, the company headed south along the Malade's west bank, passing the hot springs that both diarists mentioned. These springs still exist and are about a half-mile east of Interstate 15, and five miles north of its intersection with Highway 30. About seven miles south of where the company crossed the river, it stopped to set up camp on the Malade's west bank.

The estimated location of the party's camp on the evening of August 18 is just east of Highway 13, and about one mile south of its intersection with Highway 30 (south of the community of Riverside, Utah).

August 19

Bidwell:

> T. 19th. Started early, hoping to soon find fresh water, when we could refresh ourselves and animals, but alas! The sun beamed heavy on our heads as the day advanced, and we could see nothing before us but extensive arid plains, glimmering with heat and salt, at length the plains became so impregnated with salt, that vegetation entirely ceased; the ground was in many places white as snow with salt & perfectly smooth— the mid-day sun, beaming with uncommon splendor upon these shining plains, made us fancy we could see timber upon the plains, and wherever timber is found there is water always. We marched forward with unremitted pace till we discovered it was an illusion, and lest our teams should give out we returned from S. to E, and hastened to the river [Bear River] which we reached in about 5 miles. A high mountain overlooked us on the East and the river was thickly bordered with willows—grass plenty but so salty, our animals could scarcely eat it; salt glitters upon its blades like frost. Distance 20 miles.

Jimmy John:

> August 19th—We traveled about 16 miles today in a roundabout direction. We left the river and had to return to it again in case of having no water. Traveled through a dry, salt plain and could find no water until we returned to the river.

Bidwell elaborated even more in his memoirs about their travel south on August 19 in search of their next source of water:

> [W]e traveled all day without water, and at midnight found ourselves in a plain, level as a floor, incrusted with salt, and as white as snow. Crusts of salt broken up by our wagons, and driven by the chilly night wind like ice on the surface of a frozen pond, was to me a most striking counterfeit of a winter scene. This plain became softer and softer until our poor, almost famished, animals could not pull our wagons. In fact, we were going direct to Salt Lake and did not know it. So, in search of water, we turned

from a southerly to an eastern course, and went about ten miles, and soon after daylight arrived at Bear River. So near to Salt Lake were we that the water in the river was too salt for us or our animals to use, but we had to use it; it would not quench thirst, but it did save life. The grass looked most luxuriant, and sparkled as if covered with frost. But it was salt; our hungry, jaded animals refused to eat it, and we had to lie by a whole day to rest them before we could travel.[3]

They were truly in salt country. It was everywhere—on the ground, on the grass, and in the water. However, the Malade River Valley does not look like that today. Canal systems have been built that divert fresh water from the Bear River for irrigation. Over the years, farmers have reclaimed the land by using this fresh water to flush and drain away much of the salt. They have transformed it into a region of fertile farms.

Bidwell's journal entry estimated they traveled twenty miles on August 19, the first fifteen of which were southward and the last five eastward. The reason that Bidwell reported the ground was becoming soft was that the travelers were beginning to encounter the salt-marshes along the northern edge of Salt Lake. Note that Bidwell's memoirs recalled that the latter part of the day's journey was in the dark and they did not reach the Bear River until daylight the next morning. In contrast to Bidwell, Dawson recalled that the group encountered the marshy area while it was still daylight and turned east to aim toward the timber they saw bordering the Bear River:

> *[We] were astonished one day to find our teams and wagons sinking in a mire, while there lay in front of us, apparently, a wide plain. What could it mean? We halted, and holding a consultation, concluded we must be near the Salt Lake. Seeing the timber of Bear river to the left, we set out in that direction, intending to lay by there until the two men should return. We could use the river water, although we found it quite brackish, proving that we were near to the Salt Lake.*[4]

Upon arriving at the Bear River after five miles of travel, they set up camp. They did not encounter the Malade because it had already flowed into the Bear about two miles upstream. The salty waters of the Malade were now a part of those of the Bear, and was probably why Bidwell and Dawson described the Bear River water as salty.

Ignorance of what was ahead suggests that Bartleson was still not sending scouts ahead to explore. The company had just passed two miles east of Little Mountain. Why had Bartleson not sent a couple of riders up the mountain to gain the elevation from which to reconnoiter? The mountain stands about eight hundred feet above the plain and would have provided a great panoramic view of the lake and the surrounding countryside.

To follow the company's southbound leg on August 19, head south on Highway 82 into the town of Tremonton. Then in the middle of Tremonton take Highway 102 west a short distance to Road N 6800 W; turn left and follow it south about ten miles to Highway 83. Just south of this point, the company turned east to return to the Bear River. Head east on Highway 83 about four and a half miles to the town of Corrine. Their camp was beside the Bear River on the east side of Corrine. The "high mountain" to the east that was mentioned by Bidwell was Black Peak. It is six miles away and rises to seventy-five hundred feet.

August 20

Bidwell:

> F. 20th. Company remained here while two men went to explore the country, they returned bringing the intelligence that we were within ten miles of where the river disembogued itself into the Great Salt Lake, this was the fruit of having no pilot—we had passed through cash valley, where we intended to have stopped and we did not know it.

Jimmy John:

> August 20th—Today we did not travel, but lay by at camp for the purpose of sending seven men on ahead to search for the Salt Lake as we have no pilot, for he went the Oregon route.

For the first time, we find Bidwell complaining about traveling without a person familiar with the country. He must have been dissatisfied with their erratic wanderings the last few days. It did not bode well for the future. It was also the first time the diarists mentioned men being sent forward to scout, suggesting that this may have been the first time Bartleson took steps to explore ahead. If it was, the uncomfortable question is why Bartleson had not ordered it earlier. How many obstacles could have been avoided and how many miles saved if there had been sufficient forward scouting?

August 21

Bartleson got the company moving again on the morning of August 21. Despite Dawson's recollection that the company intended to wait at the Bear River until the Fort Hall men caught up, the impatient Bartleson was still not waiting. Because of their experience and what the scouting party observed, the company knew that there was boggy ground due west. So, they veered northwest.

Bidwell:

> S. 21st. Marched off in a N.W. direction, and intersected our trail of Thursday last, having made a complete triangle in the plain. At this intersection of the trails, we left a paper elevated by a pole, that the men, returning from Fort Hall might shun the tedious rounds we had taken. Found grass and water which answered our purposes very well, though both were salt. Distance ten miles.

Jimmy John:

> [August] 21st. Travelled about 12 miles and came to a large Salt Spring where we camped. There was no timber here except a few willows. Salt bushes and Stormwood and Pine on the tops of the mountains. Game is scarce. We have killed nothing for days except a few antelope and some fishes.

Five miles after leaving camp, they had crossed their southbound leg on August 19. They had not forgotten about their Fort Hall men and left a message posted on a tall pole at the intersection of their tracks, advising them to not follow their tracks east, but rather to follow those going west.

That we know of, the company was continuing to travel where there was no trail, path, or track. As Dawson had said in his memoirs, they would have to navigate from here on by the simplest of means—head westward, ever westward, using the sun as their guide.[5]

The problem was that they had to avoid the northern shores of Salt Lake, which was reaching further northward. They could not go directly west. They were forced to skirt the barren southern base of Little Mountain. They then marched toward the naked Blue Spring Hills to the northwest. They had likely spotted some green color in the distance at the foot of those hills, indicating water. It drew them forward, and they crossed the narrow and brackish Salt Creek. After traveling twelve miles that day, they reached a spring at the base of the hills. There they found grass and salty water. It is called Conner Springs today.

The route the company took on August 21 is easy to trace. Follow Highway 83 out of Corrine. They planted their message pole about four and a half miles west of Corrine, probably near the intersection of Highway 83 and Road N 7600 W. From there, continue west on Highway 83 about ten miles, and then turn right onto Road 102. Travel one and three-quarter miles on Road 102 to Conner Springs, which is on the right-hand side of the road.

Unknown to the company, August 21 was also the day when Henry Fraeb and his band of trappers were being attacked by hundreds of Sioux and Cheyenne Indians three hundred miles east on Battle Creek, near its mouth with the Little Snake River in northern Colorado.

August 22

Bidwell:

> S. 22nd. This morning a man (Bralaski) returned from the Fort, and said the reason, why he came alone, was, the other men had left him, because he was unable to keep up with them; he having a pack horse laden with provision. He had seen the paper at the intersection of the trails, and was guided by it to the camp, the others were undoubtedly going the rounds of the triangle, sure enough, they came up in the afternoon, having gone to the river and back, no pilot could be got at the Fort. The families, that went into Oregon, had disposed of their oxen at the fort and were going to descend the Columbia River with pack horses—they in exchange, received one horse for every ox. Their wagons they could not sell. They procured flour at 50 cents a pint, sugar same price and other things in proportion, near where we were encamped here, were a few Hackberry trees.

Jimmy John:

> 22nd. Stayed in camp on account of Oxen straying. We found them towards evening. The men who went to Fort Hall, 4 in number, returned today. They obtained some provisions but could get no Pilot. The governor of the fort informed them that it was about 7 hundred miles to Fort Van Couver [Vancouver] on the Columbia river.

Jimmy John and Dawson continued to claim that four men had been sent to Fort Hall. None had been identified until Bidwell reported in his journal that Henry Brolaski was one of them. The returning men made it official: there would be no pilot to lead them to California. That hope had finally been dashed upon the rocks.

Neither diarist reported in his journal entries whether the Fort Hall men brought back any directions. A few years later, however, Bidwell recounted in his memoirs:

> They [the men] brought the information that we must strike out west of Salt Lake—as it was even then called by the trappers—being careful not to go too far south, lest we should get into waterless country without grass. They also said we must be careful not to go too far north, lest we should get into broken country and steep cañons, and wander about, as trapping parties had been known to do, and become bewildered and perish.[6]

Bidwell's memoirs had said that Fitzpatrick had urged the company to send men to Fort Hall in order to consult with Richard Grant, the Hudson Bay Company's chief trader in charge at Fort Hall.[7] Fitzpatrick must have thought that Grant possessed knowledge about the best way to get to the Humboldt River from the Salt Lake. But this does not make sense. Grant had been an employee of the HBC for over twenty years, but had spent all of it at HBC trading outposts in northern Canada. He was not assigned to Fort Hall until 1841.[8] Thus, Grant would not have been there long. Any directions from him would not have been firsthand knowledge. It seems more likely that these directions came from one or more trappers at the fort.

Nicholas Dawson's memoirs lamented that the returning men had not brought Joseph Walker with them. He added that they "brought word that we must be careful in searching for Ogden river to avoid falling over into feeders of Snake river, lest we should get into the cañons without grass or water."[9] These instructions to head west and not go "too far south" or "too far north" were simple, much too simple. They were essentially worthless, providing no details regarding what would be "too far south" and what would be "too far north." In short, the men from Fort Hall had returned virtually emptyhanded. They had brought no guide, the directions were too vague, and the provisions they brought were so meager that it sounds as if they were carried on one pack horse.

August 23

From the hillside just north of Conner Springs, the elevation was high enough that the travelers could see the salt flats and the Salt Lake to the south. The Promontory Mountains rose up in the west, blocking their view of what was beyond them. Their directive was to go west, so that was the direction they took when they rolled away from camp on the morning of August 23.

Bidwell:

> M. 23rd. Started, bearing our course west, in order to pass the Salt Lake—passed many salt plains and springs in the forenoon, the day was hot—the hills, and land bordering on the plains were covered with wild sage. In passing the declivity of a hill, we observed this sage had been plucked up and arranged in long minows [windrows?], extending near a mile in length. It had been done by the Indians, but for what purpose we could not imagine, unless it was to decoy game. At evening we arrived in full view of the Salt Lake, water was very scarce. Cedar grows here both on the hills and valleys, distance 20 miles.

Jimmy John:

> 23rd. Traveled about 20 miles. Passed a number of Salt Springs. Some difficulty in finding fresh water. Camped at night at a small spring where we did not get half enough for the animals. We were near the Salt Lake and frequently travelled over plains covered with salts which is good for use.

The path they followed on August 23 was west along the base of the Blue Spring Hills, then across some salt flats so dazzling white that they were uncomfortable to the eye. They then crossed a low spot in the Promontory Mountains. Upon reaching the summit, they were about a thousand feet higher in elevation than the Salt Lake, and were presented a stunning view of its northwestern arm about eight miles west. Resuming their march, they arrived a few miles later at a small spring, one that produced very little water and grass. They would camp there. Because of the cedars growing in the vicinity it became known as Cedar Springs.

To follow the company's path during August 23, return to Highway 83 from Conner Springs and take it northwest three and a half miles to 7200 N Road. Turn left and proceed west about two miles to a fork. Take the right fork—West Golden Spike Drive N (18400

W Road). After four and a half miles, a road (2200 W Road) turns south to the Golden Spike National Historic Site. Do not turn south. Rather, continue west on Cedar Springs Road (7480 W Road) another four and three-quarter miles to Cedar Springs where the company camped on the evening of August 23. The spring is on the west side of the road.

The circumstances were becoming much more difficult. It was a stern and unfriendly land, having few features of softness and gentleness. It cannot be emphasized enough what a perilous venture it was going to be traveling north and west of the Great Salt Lake.

Josiah Belden recalled those miserable days in his memoirs:

> We had some knowledge of the Lake from some of the trappers who had been there. We turned off more to the west and went round the northerly end of Salt Lake. There we found a great difficulty in getting water for several days, all the water near the lake being brackish. We had to make it into strong coffee to drink it. We went on, hunting our way along the best we could, amongst the rocks and gullies, and through the sage brush, working along slowly for a number of days, aiming to travel westward as fast as we could, having no other guide than an intention to get west.[10]

Even when the company traveled where grass was lush and abundant, such as on the prairie or in the river bottoms of the Sweetwater, Hams Fork, and Bear River, it should be remembered that their oxen were still losing weight. It was because the calories they burned each day pulling those heavy wagons exceeded the calories they consumed while grazing at night. Because the animals were tired and had sore feet, their desire to lie down and get off their feet at the end of the day was at least as strong as their desire to eat. Out here on the salty plains, with quality forage virtually nonexistent, the rate at which the animals were now losing weight had become alarming.

August 24

Bidwell:

> T. 24th. Cattle strayed this morning to seek water—late start—day was warm—traveled about 10 miles in a W. direction, encamped where we found numerous springs, deep, clear and somewhat impregnated with salt. The plains were snowy white with salt. Here we procured salt of the

best quality. The grass that grew in small spots on the plains was laden with salt which had formed itself on the stalks and blades in lumps, from the size of a pea to that of a hen's egg. This was the kind we procured, it being very white, strong and pure.

Jimmy John:

24th. This morning we were detained by the Oxen straying. Did not find them till about 10 o'clock. Traveled about 10 miles and camped near a number of Salt Springs not far from the Lake. These springs are deep. One of our horses would have drowned had we not saved them in time. There are also extensive plains here which border on the Lake.

Salt! Salt! Salt! It was no wonder that the poor oxen, thirsty and hungry, had wandered away from camp during the night of August 23 to look for better grass and water. How were the men's morale? Was there a lack discipline among the night guards? Or were there no night guards at all? Regrettably, our diarists failed to tell us.

Because of the delay caused by tracking down the errant oxen, the company did not roll out of camp until late in the morning. To the west was what appeared to be a vast salt plain, about as poisonous and barren as one could imagine. With their beaten-up wagons and their thirsty, gaunt animals, they turned north and lumbered along the western front of the Promontory Mountains. Not knowing what was ahead and whether they would find a satisfactory water supply before they and their animals perished must have been frightening. After ten miles, they came across another brackish spring, a place now called Salt Wells. With nothing better in sight, they stopped and camped.

Their camp on August 24 was about ten miles directly north of their previous camp at Cedar Springs. However, the route is circuitous, with the last section crossing private property for which permission would be required. To get to the springs, one would have to travel up Cedar Springs Road about ten miles, and then turn right on to Salt Wells Road. The springs are about seven miles east on the right fork of Salt Wells Road.

August 25

Bidwell:

W. 25th. Remained here all day.

Jimmy John:

25th. Did not travel.

Our diarists did not explain why they stayed in camp on August 25, but their livestock must have been failing and needed more rest before going on.

August 26

Leaving camp on the morning of August 26, they headed west, venturing into an empty vastness. They were marching deeper and deeper into the unknown.

Bidwell:

T. 26th. Traveled all day over dry, barren plains, producing nothing but sage, or rather it ought to be called, wormwood, and which I believe will grow without water or soil. Two men were sent a head in search of water, but returned a little while before dark, unsuccessful. Our course intersected an Indian trail, which we followed directly towards the mountains, knowing that in these dry countries, the Indian trails always lead to the nearest water. Having traveled till about 10 o'clock P.M. made a halt, and waited till morning—distance about 30 miles.

Jimmy John:

26th. Traveled until ten at night and found no water and camped without it or grass west about 35 miles.

Nicholas Dawson's memoirs set forth his own recollection of their travels on August 26:

We now skirted the north end of the lake, sometimes traveling in a valley and again along the shore of the lake when the mountains jutted down nearing to its shores. In places our wagons would break a crust of salt, like ice in a northern clime. We found water in holes, like wells, but it was all brackish. Finally a wide valley opened out before us, and we struck across it toward the mountains on our right, hoping to find water fit for use. After pushing on until late in the night, our animals fagging from thirst, we halted and went into camp, still without fresh water.[11]

August 26 was a terribly long and difficult day. Upon leaving their camp at Salt Wells, their dust-covered column rumbled beside the north shore of the lake, across a snowy white salt plain. Based on Dawson's recollections, it sounded as if they passed just south of Monument Point, where the "mountains" jutted down to the lake's edge. They must have been racked by uncertainty, heading across this endless and forbidding expanse. Sometime near midday, they altered their course and headed northwest. In doing so they missed Locomotive Springs, which would have been a source of fresh water. They would have encountered the springs if they had continued west, or if scouts had climbed Indian Knolls to their north. From that elevated location they could have spotted the green vegetation that marked the springs. But they had done neither.

The company continued forward through the blistering heat, tormented by the salt parching their lips, burning their eyes, and inflaming their lungs. Behavior is altered when people are terribly thirsty. Their eyes constantly probe the distance for any sign of water. A dark color, a sign of vegetation, becomes an object of intense interest. Two men were finally sent forward to find water but returned before dark with the disheartening news that they had found none. The party kept trudging onward until they came across a narrow path that headed north. Bidwell called it an Indian trail, while Dawson recalled that it was an "antelope trail." In either case, in a desert like this, they prayed that it headed toward water

The people and the animals had been inhaling salt and alkali dust all day. Suffering from fatigue and thirst, worried that their jaded animals would give out, and surrounded on all sides by disheartening prospects, the party must have been at a low point. Yet, they crawled on. It is regrettable that our diarists were not more gossipy, as it would have been interesting to learn who, if any, were strong and encouraging, and who, if any, were complainers and defeatists. Eventually, darkness enveloped them. But they continued until late at night, when their fatigue and weakness finally forced them to stop in the middle of nowhere to snatch a few hours of much-needed sleep.

Since they had stopped at no known landmark, one can only approximate where they spent the night. It is unknown where they encountered the Indian or antelope trail they followed, but we are told it angled toward the Raft River Mountains to their northwest, and we know that they traveled between thirty and thirty-five miles that day. Their estimated camp location that night is about three miles east of the junction of today's Kelton Road with Highway 30, and about twenty-five miles west of where Highway 30 leaves Interstate 84. It is out in the middle of nowhere.

August 27

The sun rose the next morning on what must have been a terribly beat-down camp. With the arrival of dawn, the curtain of darkness pulled back and the sun's rays began to shine upon the eastern base of the Raft River Mountains, about five miles ahead. The mountains were tall, rising to over nine thousand feet in elevation, and they offered the promise of a creek or spring. The men spotted something that they had been unable to see in the dark the previous night. It was an intriguing area of color at the base of the mountains. So they gathered themselves and began a determined march. The nostrils of the animals twitched as they picked up the scent of water and, despite their weakness and fatigue, they must have quickened their pace.

Bidwell:

> F. 27th. Daylight discovered to us a spot of green grass on the declivity of the mountain towards which we were advancing. 5 miles took us to this place, where we found to our great joy, an excellent spring of water and an abundance of grass—here we determined to continue 'till the route was explored to the head of Mary's River and run no more risks of perishing for want of water in this desolated region.

Jimmy John:

> 27th. Started early and travelled about 6 miles. Came to plenty [of] water and grass. Here we remained for several days.

The company had finally found a spring of good water. Dawson recalled it as "a beautiful spring of fresh, cold water and abundant grass."[12] Known today as Tenmile Springs, it sits in a ravine on the eastern flank of the Raft River Mountains. The hills on either side were barren, but the bottom of the ravine accommodated a meadow on which the livestock could feast and recuperate. The hillside afforded a sweeping view of the Great Salt Lake and the bleak desert across which they had crawled the day before. Tired, emotionally and physically, they breathed a sigh of relief and collapsed at this oasis for a much-needed period of rest and recuperation.

Bidwell recalled in his memoirs, "The condition of our animals compelled us to rest here for nearly a week."[13] His journal entry declared that the company decided to stay there until a route to the Humboldt was found that would avoid "more risks of perishing for want of water." It sounded as if the party had moved beyond being mildly irritated with Bartleson's insufficient scouting. After their near-disaster, they did not want to repeat the experience. They would refuse to budge until a suitable path to the Humboldt was found. They had tempted fate too often.

August 28

Bidwell:

> S. 28th. Company remained here. A Shoshonee Indian came to our camp, from him we learned, that there were more Indians not far off, who had horses. Several men and myself went in search of them: having gone about 5 miles, up hills and down hills covered with thick groves of Cedar (red), we unexpectedly came to an Indian, who was in the act of taking care of some meat—venison—which he had just killed; about half of which we readily purchased for 12 Cartridges of Powder & ball. With him, as pilot we went in pursuit of other Indians; he led us far up in the Mountains by a difficult path, where we found two or three families, hid as it were from all the world, by the roughness of nature. The only provision which they seemed to have was a few elder berries and a few seeds; under a temporary covert of bushes, I observed the aged Patriarch, whose head looked as it had been whitened by the frosts of at least 90 Winters. The Scars on his arms and legs were almost countless—a higher forehead I never saw on a man's head. But here in the solitude of the mountains and with the utmost contentment, he was willing to spend the last days of his life among the hoary rocks and craggy cliffs, where perhaps he, in his youthful gayety, used to sport along crystal streams which run purling from the mountains—not succeeding in finding horses, we returned to the Camp.

Jimmy John:

> [28th] Some Snake Indians camped near us and came out and traded some berries for Powder & bullets.

A good spring attracts life, particularly in a desert, so it comes as no surprise that there were Indians near. Bidwell's description of his encounter with the Indians is superb, revealing how talented a writer he could be when he had the time and energy. These were Shoshone, or Snake Indians. More precisely, they would have been Western Shoshone, a branch of the Snakes related to those the company encountered at the Green River. These were their lowly cousins, the ones consigned to scrape out a meager subsistence from the hardscrabble Great Basin region that other Indian tribes shunned. The desire of these Shoshones to trade for ball and powder is understandable. Antelope appeared to be the only significant large game in the area, and it would take firearms, not bows and arrows, to bring them down from a distance.

August 29

Bidwell:

> S. 29th. Capt. Bartleson with C. Hopper started to explore the route to the head of Mary's river, expecting to be absent about 8 or 9 days—the Company to await here his return.

Jimmy John:
No journal entry for August 29.

August 30

Bidwell:

> M. 30th. Nothing of importance occurred.

Jimmy John:

> [30th] The Captain and another man named Charles Hopers [Hopper] left camp on the 30th for the purpose of finding Marys River. There is neither rain nor dew this season of the year. We have had no rain since we left the Platte river.

Bidwell reported that Bartleson and Hopper left to explore on August 29 while Jimmy reported that they left on August 30. And why was Bartleson going? Was the atmosphere in camp tense and uncomfortable? Did he want to get away from a grumbling and disenchanted company? Charles Hopper, Bartleson's right-hand man, was also going with him. It is unfortunate that Bidwell and Jimmy John did not provide more detail.

Jimmy John reminded us that the party had not seen rain since they had been on the Platte River. This is unusual and remarkable, as most wagon parties in the years to come would experience a number of storms during an equivalent period. The company had been extraordinarily lucky in avoiding the headaches that wet and stormy weather brought.

August 31

Bidwell:

T. 31st. No success hunting.

Jimmy John made no journal entries for August 31 through September 4.

Chapter 12

Languishing North and West of the Salt Lake

SEPTEMBER 1 TO 15, 1841

September 1

The party was still at Tenmile Springs on September 1, recuperating and waiting for Bartleson and Hopper to return from their explorations.

Bidwell:

> Sept. W. 1st. An ox killed for beef.

This is the first we have read about the company killing an ox to eat. Dawson recalled, "Though we had been eating very sparingly for several weeks, our last provisions had been consumed just before we reached Salt Lake, and since we had been subsisting on what game we could kill, and when no game was to be had, [we killed] an ox out of our train."[1] These comments suggest that the travelers had already eaten their way through all of the buffalo meat they had put up before leaving the Sweetwater River on July 18.

All of the company's animals must have lost a great deal of weight by now. The oxen must have been extremely thin. The oxen belonged to individuals and not to the company at large, but no one explained how they determined which ox to slaughter and how, if at all, its owner was compensated by the others to share the meat.

September 2

Bidwell:

> T. 2d. Idle in camp.

September 3

Bidwell:

> F. 3d. 4 or 5 Indians came to camp—bought three horses of them.

September 4

Bidwell:

> S. 4th. Bought a few service berries of the Indians.

September 5

Bidwell:

> S. 5th. Grass having become scarce, we concluded to move on a little every day to meet Capt. B. & H. Traveled about 6 miles and encamped by a beautiful Cedar grove.

Jimmy John:

> September 5th. Left the camp that we came to on the 27th of August and went about 6 miles and camped in a Cedar grove near a Spring of water and in sight of the Plain which borders on the Salt Lake. Captain Bartleson and Mr. Hopper has not yet returned.

The group had vowed to stay put until they heard from Bartleson. Jimmy John said they expected the scouting party to be gone eight to nine days. Although only seven days had passed, the company had become restless. Were they refreshed to the point where they were unwilling to lie around any longer? Bidwell said they were eager to move on because they were running short of grass in the small meadow. So they moved, although only a short distance. They moved south, then west to a spring six miles away that was concealed within a grove of large cedar trees. It seems likely that the spring had been discovered by someone from the company exploring ahead. They must have concluded that they could move forward safely.

Cedar Springs, where they encamped on September 5, is six miles southwest of their encampment at Tenmile Springs. From where Tenmile Springs Road enters Highway 30, travel four and a half miles southwest on the highway. The springs are on private ranch property and are hidden in the cedar grove about a half-mile south of that point.

September 6

Bidwell:

> M. 6th. Traveled about 7 miles.

Jimmy John:

> 6th. We traveled about 10 miles today in a south west direction and we killed a rabbit and an antelope, game being scarce. Here we were compelled to kill Oxen.

The company moved again, this time to another small spring. It is again assumed that riders had ridden forward and found the spring before the company made their move. Perhaps they had ridden along the base of the mountains, high enough that they could look across the countryside and spot any colors that indicated vegetation different from the surrounding drab sagebrush. Jimmy John did not specify how many oxen were killed or why, although it seems likely they were slaughtered for food.

The spring where they camped on September 6 is about three miles south of Highway 30 and southwest of the tiny community of Park Valley, Utah. Since the location is on private ranch property, it is inaccessible but can be identified on Google Earth as a small, green oasis in the midst of a landscape of light browns and grays.

September 7

The company ventured forward again on the morning of September 7. They headed southwest, but did not travel far.

Bidwell:

> T. 7th. Traveled about 7 miles, antelope appeared to be plenty.

Jimmy John:

> On the 7th we traveled 6 miles and encamped at the foot of a mountain near a small brook. Killed one antelope today. This night was cold and windy. There were some Shoshanen [Shoshone] Indians camped near us. One of them agreed to pilot us [to] Marys river for 6 lbs. of powder and 100 balls.

Traveling only six or seven miles, the company came to a "small brook," as Jimmy John described it. Only a few feet wide, the narrow brook flowed out of the western end of the Raft River Mountains. A cold front moved in that night. They spent a miserable night taking refuge beneath their blankets, while their wagon covers flapped loudly in the frigid wind.

At the brook, they encountered another camp of Western Shoshones. Since this tribe ranged through country as far west as the Humboldt River, the Indian agreeing to act as their guide probably knew of an Indian trail that would take them to the Humboldt. Whether it would be passable for wagons is uncertain, but it seems a smart decision to have engaged his services.

To reach the location of their September 7 camp, take Highway 30 about one-half mile west of the tiny settlement of Rosette, Utah, and then travel south on Cedar Hill Road about five miles. Their campsite was beside the stream in the green meadow below.

September 8

Both diarists complained about the bitterly cold weather on September 8, but the wind should have blown the smoky air away and improved visibility. Because of the bad weather, many wanted to remain in camp that day. But not all felt that way.

Bidwell:

> W. 8th. Exceedingly cold; ice in our water buckets. Part of the Company remained on account of the cold—2 wagons with owners being contrary, went on.

Jimmy John:

> 8th. This morning was cold and windy. Part of the company were in favor of remaining at camp and six wagons stayed at camp and two went on and expected to meet the next day.

The company was fracturing. Bartleson was still gone on his scouting trip. He and Hopper had been gone for ten days, and their absence may have left a void in leadership. Discord appeared to be rising to the surface and some had decided to act on their own, even if contrary to the decision of others. A barrier had been breached, and it was a dangerous precedent.

Bidwell and Jimmy John were part of the company that remained in camp on September 8. Jimmy John reported that two wagons went on, while six remained in camp. This amounts to eight wagons. When he reported about the company dividing near Soda Springs on August 11, he noted that four wagons were going to Oregon and nine to California. Something had apparently happened to one of the wagons after they left Soda Springs, but neither Bidwell nor Jimmy John had mentioned it.

September 9

Leaving the brook, the group with six wagons moved forward, following the tracks of the two wagons that had left the previous day. After twelve miles of pushing through abrasive sagebrush, they came to an elevated area at the base of the Grouse Creek Mountain Range. They caught up to the two wagons at a small stream that derived its water from Rosebud Springs.

After being gone for twelve days, Captain Barltelson and Charles Hopper had finally shown up and rejoined the company at their Rosebud stream camp.

Bidwell:

> *T. 9th. The part of the Company that remained yesterday went on and overtook the 2 wagons. Capt. Bartleson & Hopper returned, bringing Intelligence that they had found the head of Mary's river—distant about 5 days' travel, distance traveled to day about 12 miles S.W. direction. The Indians stole a horse—day cool.*

Jimmy John:

> *9th. We traveled perhaps 12 miles today and met with the two wagons that left us yesterday and also the two men that left us to search for Marys river. They discovered a small branch which they thought to be some of the headwaters of Marys river. We camped all together this evening with our two Indian guides.*

Dawson's memoirs recalled: "They [Bartleson and Hopper] soon returned, having found the river, but reported the route impracticable for wagons. They thought, however, that a wagon route could be found further to the south."[2] Josiah Belden's memoirs recalled that "these men came back, and reported that they had found a small stream of water that seemed to be running westward, and they thought that might perhaps be the headwaters or some branch of the Mary's River that we wished to find."[3]

Even though Bidwell's entry for September 9 reported that Bartleson had found the headwaters of the Humboldt, he recorded in his memoirs years later that "The party was gone eight days, but obtained no definite idea regarding the country."[4] We will see over the next two weeks why Bidwell would make such a statement in retrospect.

To reach the location of their September 9 camp, travel seventeen miles southwest of Rosette on Highway 30, then turn right (west) onto Immigrant Trail Road and proceed two miles west to Rosebud Creek. The company probably camped in the grassy meadow to the south.

September 10

The company resumed their southward march on September 10 along the eastern foot of the Grouse Creek Mountains.

Bidwell:

> F. 10th. Traveled about 15 miles and encamped without water.

Jimmy John:

> 10th. This morning the Indians were dismissed and we gave them some powder and leads and balls which appeared to satisfy them for their service. We traveled about 14 miles today and encamped near the foot of a mountain with neither water nor grass for our animals.

When Bartleson rode into camp, claiming he had found the way to the headwaters of the Humboldt, he would have discovered that the company had employed two Indians to lead them there. Why were these guides dismissed? Had Bartleson decided that there was no need for them? In any event, their dismissal was probably a big mistake.

Their camp on September 10 was at the southern tip of the Grouse Creek Mountains, a grassless, waterless place. Their camp was near Highway 30 about twenty miles east of the Utah-Nevada border.

September 11

As people climbed from under their blankets on the morning of September 11, they had managed to keep their animals from straying despite there being no water in camp. But water had to be found soon. Shortly, the early morning quiet was disturbed by the sounds of catching up and hitching the animals, then by the annoying squeaks as their beat-up wagons began to roll.

Their route that morning was across elevated terrain, and the company soon spotted a grove of tall cottonwood trees in the distance rising from the desert floor. It signaled a source of water and they headed toward it.

Bidwell:

S. 11th. Traveled about 15 miles and came to water, course W.

Jimmy John:

11th. This morning we started early. Traveled about 14 miles to the south west and found water and grass. Here we camped for the night.

By the end of the day, they had arrived at either Owl Springs or Rabbit Springs. It is easy to reach both. Eight and a half miles east of the Utah-Nevada border, turn southeast off of Highway 30 on to Rabbit Springs Loop (do not go down Grouse Creek Road). Owl Springs is one mile south of the highway, on the left side of the road, while Rabbit Springs is on the same road, but one mile further south.

September 12

Bidwell:

S. 12th. Mr. Kelsey left his wagons and took his family and goods on pack horses, his oxen not being able to keep up: distance to day about 12 miles.

Jimmy John:

12th. This morning left 2 waggons belonging to B [Benjamin] Kelsey, their oxen being worn down with fatigue. They were compelled to leave their

Crossing the Plains, 1856, *by Charles Christian Nahl. Oil on canvas, 132 in. × 204 in. Courtesy of Crocker Art Museum, Sacramento, Calif., on a transfer from the Iris and B. Gerald Cantor Center for Visual Arts at Stanford University.*

waggons and pack their baggage on horses and mules. We traveled about 10 miles today south west and camped at an excellent spring near a large plain covered with salt, partly surrounded by high mountains.

The two Kelsey wagons were left at the spring. A rusty piece of iron from an ancient wagon was found at Owl Springs a few years ago, causing some to claim it was evidence that this was the spring where the two Kelsey wagons were left. Others dispute the claim, pointing out that Dawson called their stopping place "Rabbit Spring" in his log. But this does not necessarily settle the issue since most geographical features in this forsaken land had not yet been given names by white men.

Our diarists explained that the Kelsey oxen were worn down and unable to keep up. Lack of good grass and prolonged periods of no water had been taking a severe toll. But were the Kelsey animals in worse condition than those of the others? If so, why? Some people are less skilled at caring for their oxen. Or the animals' condition may have been due to the Kelsey wagons, or what was in them. Since Benjamin Kelsey was taking a family, it is possible that his wagons were more weighted with heavy items like furniture. It was common in later years for wagons to be overloaded, and emigrants were eventually forced to abandon anything unnecessary along the trail.

Nancy Kelsey explained in her brief memoirs that when the travelers left their wagons behind "I carried my baby in front of me on the horse."[5] The seventeen-year-old was an inspiration to many in the party. Joseph Chiles recalled Nancy with admiration and affection in the memoirs he wrote years later: "It was considered almost rash for a woman to venture on so perilous a journey, but [Mrs. Kelsey] said, 'Where my husband goes, I can go. I can better endure the hardship of the journey than the anxieties for an absent husband.'"[6] He also recalled that "her cheerful nature and kind heart brought many a ray of sunshine through the clouds that gathered round a company [of] so many weary travelers. She bore the fatigues of the journey with so much heroism, patience and kindness that there still exists a warmth in every heart for the mother and child that were always forming silver linings for every dark cloud that assailed them."[7]

Upon leaving the springs, the company continued southwest. They were traveling across brutal, heat-blistered country, and were aiming toward the Pilot Mountains ahead. The base of high mountains should be a good place to find springs. This range of mountains included Pilot Peak, the highest peak in the area at over ten thousand feet. Since the peak can be seen from great distances, it often served as a guiding landmark for early travelers.

The pace, set by the struggling oxen, would have been maddeningly slow. After traveling between ten and twelve miles, the group finally made it to the foot of the mountains and were delighted to find a small spring nestled in a ravine. Dawson's log described it as "Mountain Spring," but in later years it became known as Tunnel Springs. The spring is usually dry now because much of its water was piped underground to Lucin, a former railroad community.

It is a challenge getting to this spring because one must travel a great distance over rough gravel roads that are a long way from anywhere. If the reader is determined, it is best to take Grouse Creek Road where it intersects with Highway 30 (at the same location where Rabbit Springs Loop intersects with Highway 30) and travel south five and a half miles to the railroad tracks. Cross the tracks to their southern side. This is the site of the abandoned railroad town of Lucin. From Lucin, continue south on Grouse Creek Road a quarter mile, then take the left fork, which is Pilot Mountain Road. Travel south on Pilot Mountain Road five miles to another fork. Take the right fork, which is Loop Road. After two miles on Loop Road, continue forward on what is called Tunnel Springs Road. The company likely camped on the left, about three-quarters of a mile up the road.

Just south of Lucin, the road crosses Thousand Springs Creek. This creek was probably dry when the company crossed its bed that day, as our diarists failed to mention it in their entries. If Bartleson had bothered to send a scouting party twelve miles up the creek bed, they would have encountered the first of a number of springs and sections of grass within its channel. If they had followed the creek even further upstream, they would have soon come to a dependable flow of water in the creek. About seventy miles upstream of where the company crossed the dry creek bed was a gentle divide. On the other side of the divide, they would have encountered the headwaters of the sought-after Humboldt River. It was a missed opportunity. It is possible that it was this route over which the dismissed Indian guides had planned to take them.

September 13

Bidwell:

> M. 13th. Traveled about 15 miles south, between salt plains on the E. and high mts. on the W.

Jimmy John:

> 13th. Today we traveled about 15 miles on a south course, leaving large salt plains to our left and high mountains to the right and camped at a spring of good water this evening.

On the morning of September 13, the company left camp and continued south along the eastern base of the Pilot Mountain Range. They were soon traveling between a broad salt plain on their left and the steep Pilot Mountains on their right. The famous Bonneville Salt Flats are only fifteen miles east of their path. The modern tourist would find these vistas spectacular, almost surreal. The various mountain ranges—isolated, rocky, and barren—rise up from the plains here and there, like stark islands. The salt plains are a dazzling white, almost painful to the eyes. Water was hard to find and grass was almost nonexistent. It was a deadly geography in which the

Bartleson company was just trying to survive. They probably viewed these sights as menacing rather than beautiful.

All along the eastern base of the Pilot Mountains were a series of springs seeping good water, but because the company had been struggling across a dismal, waterless plain all day with jaded animals and tired wagons, it seems logical that they stopped to camp at the first spring they came to. This would have been Shibley Springs, about fifteen miles from the Tunnel Springs camp they left that morning.

Anyone who also wants to visit Shibley Springs after seeing Tunnel Springs should return to Pilot Mountain Road and travel south fourteen miles. If the plan is to reach Shibley Springs from the south, take Leppy Pass Road north where it leaves Interstate 80 just east of Wendover. Continue north on Pilot Mountain Road. The spring is a twenty-eight-mile trip north of Interstate 80. However, one should be warned that these roads are rough, unpaved, and very far from help or services.

September 14

Bidwell:

> T. 14th. Traveled about 25 miles and stopped about 9 o'clock at night, in the middle of a dry plain, destitute of water.

Jimmy John:

> 14th. We started early this morning. Passed a number of good springs. Took dinner at one of them. We traveled on the border of the salt plain until night. The same plain that we traveled on yesterday, leaving it to the left and the mountains to the right. These plains border on the salt lake. In the evening we left the salt plain, turned our course to the west, crossed the mountain through a gap and could find no water. We traveled until ten o'clock at night and could find no water and was obliged to camp without water or grass.

September 14 would be a long and trying day. After leaving Shibley Springs, the party passed other springs seeping from the eastern base of the Pilot Mountains. According to Jimmy John, they stopped near midday to eat at one of them, likely watering their livestock there as well. Some historians think they stopped at what would later be called Donner Springs, named after the Donner party that refreshed themselves there in 1846. However, Donner Springs is only four miles south of Shibley Springs, so it seems unlikely the company stopped there for "dinner." It is more likely that they stopped to have their meal at Hall Springs, which is just east of Pilot Mountain Road, four and a half miles south of Donner Springs and ten miles south of Shibley Springs.

Somewhere in this vicinity, Edwin Bryant reported in 1846 that he and his westbound companions came across the Bartleson party's wheel marks somewhere in this vicinity.[8]

About fifteen miles southwest of Shibley Springs is a rough, little-used gravel road that heads southwest from Pilot Mountain Road. It winds over a low gap in the mountains. As the sun was about to set, the company turned west to cross what is called Bidwell Pass today. Later in 1846, Edwin Bryant and his mule-riding companions were traveling west through this pass on their way to California. He reported that they "struck a wagon trail, which evidently had been made several years [earlier]." He attributed those wagon tracks to the Bartleson party by writing that "some five or six years ago an emigrating expedition to California was fitted out by Colonel Bartleson, Mr. J. Chiles and others of Missouri."[9]

From the summit of Bidwell Pass, the Bartleson company could look west across a wide valley in the failing light and see a low spot in the Toano Range on the other side. Today, Interstate 80 winds through this gap, presently called Silver Zone Pass. The company descended and began crossing the desolate, sage-covered plain as darkness enveloped them. By nine or ten o'clock that night they had reached the mouth of a ravine that led into the pass. They had not found water but were too fatigued to continue. They stopped and set up camp for the night, probably in the ravine just east of where Interstate 80 emerges from Silver Zone Pass and begins to turn southeast.

There is something unsettling about the day's travels. The group traveled late into the night on September 14, after a long day of twenty-five miles, and yet had not come to water. If scouts had been sent forward, they would have found water further on. With such knowledge, Bartleson should have halted the company at Hall Springs, the southernmost spring along the Pilot Mountains. The next day would have been a long one, but they could have made it to water.

Had Bartleson been making too many poor decisions? In the years to come, wagon parties would frequently vote unsatisfactory leaders out of office. But we have seen little evidence of either diarist criticizing him so far. Perhaps his decisions were regarded as satisfactory for reasons that are not readily apparent.

September 15

The party raised camp early the next morning, their hoarse and throaty voices spurring their animals to get moving. They needed to find water. Having traveled a grueling twenty-five miles the previous day, and coming to rest late at night at a place devoid of water, they must have been in a bad mood.

Bidwell:

> W. 15th. Started very early, day was exceedingly warm, passed through a gap in a ridge of mountains, came into a high dry plain, traveled some distance into it, saw the form of a high mountain through the smoky atmosphere—reached it, having come about 15 miles—found plenty of water—our animals were nearly given out. We were obliged to go so much further, in order to get along with the wagons. We concluded to leave them, and pack as many things as we could.

Jimmy John:

> 15th. This morning we left the camp at daylight. Traveled 4 miles in the gap of another mountain and found a little water but not half enough to water the animals. Pased the mountain [and] traveled through a plain about 8 miles and came to water and grass at the foot of a large mountain. Here we encamped.

After leaving camp on the morning of September 15, the company continued to ascend Silver Zone Pass. Dawson recalled, "[We] found a pass where, by roping them, we took the wagons through. This led to a valley which offered good grass and water."[10]

Ascending the pass was not easy. The climb was almost a thousand feet within a three-mile distance. The animals, already suffering from thirst, must have been on the verge of collapse. When they reached the summit, Bidwell complained that they were unable to see what was beyond because of smoky air. On the far side of the "high dry plain," as Bidwell described it, was the Pequop Mountains. Because of the smoke, his memoirs explained, "we did not become aware of our approach to them [the mountains] till we saw the crags looming up ahead of us in the smoky sky almost over our heads."[11]

According to Jimmy John, they had found a limited source of water just on the other side of the pass. It was not nearly enough water, but probably helped them get across the plain ahead. When they finally crossed the plain and reached the foot of the Pequop Mountains, eight miles away, they found plenty of grass and water. After traveling a total of fifteen miles that day, they had reached what is now called Big Springs. Animals are exceptionally sensitive to the smell of water and are able to detect it from afar. One can imagine their trying to hold their horses back. Even the fatigued, wagon-pulling oxen and mules may have picked up their pace.

Bidwell's memoirs recalled that when they reached Big Springs, they had become alarmed at their situation. They were concerned that their wagons were holding them back and were forcing them to travel greater distances to find routes that would accommodate them. Winter was fast approaching, and they had no idea how much further they had to go. Bidwell wrote in one of his memoirs: "It was painfully evident that we must make greater progress or winter would set in long before we could reach the Pacific Coast," They feared that "the snows will overtake us before we get to California."[12]

Moreover, Bidwell expressed concern that the animals pulling these heavy cumbersome vehicles had been reduced to "skeletons."[13] Indeed, it had been a mighty struggle getting them over that pass earlier in the day. "That night," he recalled, "we determined to leave our wagons."[14] Dawson's memoirs expressed the same assessment: "We had been delayed so much by our wagons and had to toil so hard to get them this far—we held a consultation that night and decided to abandon our wagons here, make pack saddles, and pack through."[15] Both Bidwell and Dawson suggest that the decision was reached during a meeting of the members. Since there were only four wagons left, their owners were few in number and would have been easily outvoted.

Unfortunately, Big Springs cannot be reached. It lies four and a half miles southwest of the Highway 233 off-ramp on Interstate 80, but the gravel road to it is a private one and access is not possible.

Chapter 13

Ignorant Wanderings

SEPTEMBER 16 TO 30, 1841

September 16

The company remained in their Big Springs camp on September 16. With the travelers having decided to abandon the wagons, the camp buzzed with activity as they spent the day making pack saddles.

Bidwell:

> *T. 16th. All hands were busy making Pack saddles and getting ready to pack. While thus engaged, an Indian, well advanced in years, came down out of the Mountains to our camp. He told us by signs that the Great Spirit had spoken to him, to go down upon the plains in the morning, and on the E. side of the mts. he would find some strange people, who would give him a great many things, accordingly he had come. We gave him all such things as we had intended to throw away; whenever he received anything which he thought useful to him, he paused and looking steadfastly at the sun, addressed him in a loud voice, marking out his course in the sky, as he advanced in his invocation, which took him about 2 minutes to perform—as he received quite a number of articles, it took him a considerable part of the day to repeat his blessings. No Persian, in appearance, could be more sincere.*

Bidwell also recalled the day in his memoirs:

> *[E]arly the next morning [September 16] we set to work making pack-saddles for our animals. We had to pack mules, horses, and oxen. . . . No one of us had seen horses packed or helped to pack any, and our first day's*

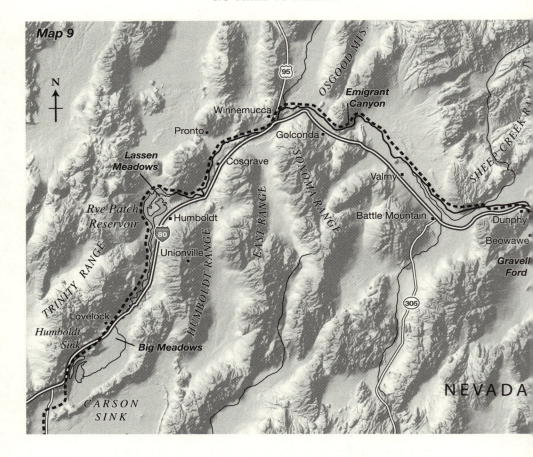

experience is almost painful to recall to mind.... On Green River, we had seen the style of pack-saddles used by the trapping party, and had learned a little about how to make them.[1]

Bidwell was not the only one mentioning the old Indian appearing at the springs on September 16. The event also made an impression on Nicholas Dawson. He related the incident years later in his memoirs, writing that an "old Indian" came to meet them, "laughing and making gestures of extravagant joy." He told them that "he had dreamed of our coming." Members of the company gave him presents of "old clothing, pieces of iron, etc. His joy was childish. As each gift was made, he would point a bony finger to the east and slowly revolve his hand to the west, apparently mumbling as he did so a prayer."[2]

Undoubtedly, the old Indian was Western Shoshone. This branch of the Shoshone tribe, unable to hold on to the more bounteous re-

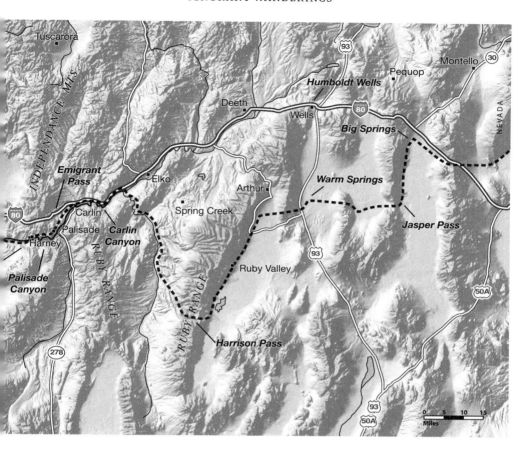

gions, survived by the thinnest of threads, scratching a precarious living out of this hardscrabble land. They dug up roots, insects, and worms. They caught reptiles, small rodents, and other unappealing foods when larger game, like antelope, could not be had. Because they were often seen digging in the ground for their food, emigrants began calling them Digger Indians, or Diggers for short. It seems unimaginable that this desolation could be inhabited by humans. Yet, it was. Like iron to magnets, the Indians and their game were drawn to springs such as these, usually found at the base of mountains.

Jimmy John:

> 16th. Today we lay at camp and made pack saddles and packed up our goods [and] chattles for we left the ballance of the wagons here, 4 in number, for we cannot get them through to California.

On September 8, the company still had eight wagons. Then Benjamin Kelsey abandoned his two wagons at Owl Springs on September 12. Jimmy John's surprising report that they only had four wagons on September 16 raises the question of what happened to the other two. And whom had they belonged to?

September 17

Bidwell:

> F. 17th. About 11 A.M. all were ready to start; horses, mules and 4 oxen, packed, proceeded south along the mts. seeking a place to pass through. At length an Indian trail took us across into a dry plain, perfectly destitute of grass and water. Traveled 'till about midnight, having come about 17 [27?] miles. This plain was white in many places with salt, and the cool evening contrasting with the color of the salt on the ground gave a striking similarity to winter—two of the oxen that were carrying Packs, got lost from the Company in the night, about 8 miles from where we encamped, but it was supposed they would follow on.

Jimmy John:

> 17th By morning we left the ballance of the wagons and some packed their goods on oxen. The oxen being not used to such sport run away and strewed the goods over the plain which caused some sport and a little trouble. Here we gave a great many things to the Indians not being able to take them along. One old Indian in particular appeared to be very thankful for every thing he received if any one gave him a present. He would hold it up between him and the sun and say over [it] a long preamble. This evening we traveled over a mountain and traveled until 10 oclock at night. Found no water or grass. Traveled perhaps about 30 miles today.

Dawson's memoirs reported that they used boards from the wagons to make pack saddles and tore up their canvas tents to make into ropes.[3] Bidwell's memoirs focused on the maddening ordeal of converting many of their horses, mules, and oxen into pack animals:

> Packing is an art, and something that only an experienced mountaineer can do well so as to save his animal and keep his pack from falling off. We were unaccustomed to it, and the difficulties we had at first were simply indescribable. It is much more difficult to fasten a pack on an ox than on a mule or a horse. The trouble began the very first day. But we started—most of us on foot, for nearly all of the animals, including several of the

oxen, had to carry packs. It was but a few minutes before the packs began to turn; horses became scared, mules kicked, oxen jumped and bellowed, and articles were scattered in all directions. We took pains, fixed things, made a new start, and did better, though packs continued occasionally to fall off and delay us. Those that had better pack-saddles and had tied their loads securely were ahead, while the others were obliged to lag behind.[4]

Because of their difficulties in getting their animals packed and settled down, they did not leave their Big Springs camp until late that morning. When they finally departed, Dawson recalled that they bequeathed everything they left behind to the old Indian, making him "the happiest, richest and most religious man I ever saw."[5]

As the four wagons were left behind, their owners may have experienced a somber sense of loss, like leaving a close friend or companion behind. The rest of the party, on the other hand, probably breathed a deep sigh of relief, delighted to finally rid themselves of those clumsy, slow-moving anchors. They were now liberated. When Bartleson and Hopper returned from their scouting trip on September 9, they claimed they had found the Humboldt, but the route was "impracticable for wagons."[6] Now that wagons no longer restricted them, the company was free to use the path that Bartleson boasted he had found. Once they got past the awkward phase of learning how to securely tie their packs and getting their animals used to their new role, the company should be able to travel faster and farther each day. There would be no more digging down of ravines and stream banks to help the wagons cross. There would be no more double-teaming to get wagons up steep inclines, and no more holding on to ropes to hold them back or keep them from tipping over. There would be no more bumping over sagebrush. They could now choose routes that were impossible for wheeled vehicles. Nicholas Dawson's memoirs mentioned one other benefit of abandoning the wagons: "Now some of us were inwardly rejoicing over leaving the wagons behind, for it meant more beef—poor beef, but a long way better than nothing to eat."[7]

However, leaving the wagons behind was not all beneficial. The party would now be more vulnerable to attack. They could no longer fort up behind circled wagons. Indeed, the ability to fort up was a powerful deterrent, discouraging hostiles from attacking in the first place.

Bidwell reported that when they left Big Springs they traveled south across the plain on the east side of the Pequop Mountains. Bartleson had claimed that he and Hopper had found a path to the Humboldt that was not suitable for wagons. But their wagons no longer encumbered them. As the crow flies, the headwaters of the Humboldt were only twenty-five miles away to the northwest. So why were they heading south? Was Bartleson lost? Or had he lied about finding the Humboldt? His reasoning is unknown as neither diarist explained this move.

Continuing south, the company kept an eye on the mountains to their right, looking for any gap through which they could turn west. Late in the afternoon, after traveling about sixteen miles, they saw a low spot. According to Bidwell, they turned west, following an Indian trail. As the sun dipped toward the western horizon, it appears that they entered a narrow ravine that leads into what is now called Jasper Pass. The Pequop Range was narrow, so they made it through the pass quickly and descended into Independence Valley on the other side. By now it was dark. Because they had not encountered any water, they continued, trudging west another eight miles across a barren salt plain. About midnight, they had still not found a source of water. Unable to continue, they stopped to camp at the eastern base of some cedar-covered hills now called Spruce Mountain Ridge. Dawson's log labeled their camp "Dry Cedar," while Jimmy John confirmed that the camp was without grass and water. Dawson's log estimated the company had traveled an exhausting twenty-five miles that day, while Jimmy John estimated thirty. Bidwell's entry said that it was seventeen miles, but that was probably an error in transcription from his original entry.

There were two springs within two miles of where they camped. It seems that Bartleson had not sent scouts ahead to search for water during daylight. Rather, he pushed forward through the dark without knowing what was ahead.

Bidwell's memoirs further described what happened that night:

> *The first night I happened to be among those that kept pretty well back, because the horses out-traveled the oxen. The foremost came to a place and stopped where there was no water or grass, and built a fire so that we could see it and come up to them. We got there about midnight, but some of our oxen that had packs on had not come up, and among them were my two.*[8]

Bidwell reveals that Bartleson had not kept the company together and allowed everyone to travel at his or her own pace. With the horses and mules traveling faster than the slow-gaited oxen, coupled with a few having to stop and repack their oxen, the caravan became dangerously spread out. The area was occupied by Indians, some perhaps hostile, so not keeping everyone together was exposing people to being ambushed or picked off. The fire the advance party built as a beacon to the stragglers behind might sound like a good idea, but it was dangerous as well. It could help unfriendly Indians locate them. Since it was the company's first night without their wagons to take cover behind, one wonders if anyone felt exposed and vulnerable.

Bidwell's journal reported that his two oxen had disappeared in the dark somewhere in the valley, about eight miles short of where the company finally stopped to camp. As their owner and because they were carrying his possessions, he was probably at fault for not keeping a closer eye on them. He did not yet appear concerned, thinking that his oxen would follow and soon catch up.

The location of their camp on September 17 is remote and difficult to reach. It is on a very rough road far from help, and is not recommended. Those determined to see generally where their camp was should head south on Highway 93 where it leaves Interstate 80, near Wells, Nevada, and continue for twenty-five miles. Their camp was on the eastern side of the hills seen to the east, about ten miles distant.

September 18

Bidwell's derelict oxen did not show up during the night. He and a companion retraced their tracks in the morning, hoping to find them. The two animals had been a team since the journey began in Missouri, so it is not surprising that they did things together, including this.

Bidwell:

> S. 18th. Morning found us on the east side of the Mountain not far from its base but there were no signs of water; the lost oxen not having come up, I, in company with another young man went in search of them, while the company went on, promising to stop as soon as they found water. I went back about 10 miles, but found nothing of their trail—the sun was

in a melting mood—the young man became discouraged and in spite of all my entreaties returned to the company. About an hour after I found the trail of the oxen which bore directly north (the Com. were traveling S.W.) after pursuing it some distance, I discovered fresh mocasin tracks upon the trail. And there began to be high grass which made me mistrust the Indians had got the oxen. But my horse was good and my Rifle ready, and I knew the Indians in these parts to be very timid, for they were generally seen in the attitude of flight. But what made me most anxious to find the oxen was the prospect of our wanting them for beef. We had already killed 4 oxen and there were but 13 remaining, including the lost ones, and the Co. was now killing an ox every two or three days. Having followed the trail about 10 miles directly north, to my great delight I found the oxen. I was soon in motion for the company, but not able to overtake them, was obliged to stop about dark. I passed the night rather uncomfortably, having neither fire nor blanket. I knew Indians to be plenty from numerous signs, and even where I slept, the ground had been dug up that very day for roots. The plains here were almost barren, and the hills were covered with cedar.

Bidwell again recounted the incident in his memoirs, and added some new details:

So I had to return the next morning and find them, Cheyenne Dawson alone volunteering to go with me. . . . It was a burning hot day. We could not find the trail of the oxen for a long time, and Dawson refused to go further, saying there were plenty of cattle in California, but I had to do it, for the oxen were carrying our provisions and other things. Afterwards I struck the trail, and found that the oxen instead of going west had gone north, and I followed them until nearly sundown. They had got into a grassy country, which showed that they were nearing water. Seeing Indian tracks on their trail following them, I felt there was imminent danger, and at once examined my gun and pistols to see that they were primed and ready. But soon I found my oxen lying down in tall grass by the side of the trail. Seeing no Indians, I hastened to fasten the packs and make my way to overtake the company. They had promised to stop when they came to water and wait for me. I traveled all night, and at early dawn came to where there was plenty of water and where the company had taken dinner the day before, but they had failed to stop for me according to promise. I was much perplexed, because I had seen many fires in the night, which I took to be Indian fires.[9]

Bidwell's memoirs disclosed that it was Nicholas Dawson who set out with him. Wanting to pick up the trail of the wayward animals, the two men retraced the previous night's path. They headed east, but apparently not so far east that they passed through Jasper Pass again. Otherwise, Bidwell would have likely mentioned it. After Dawson left, Bidwell stubbornly marched on. He finally located the oxen's tracks heading north, probably just to the west of Jasper Pass. He estimated that he had followed their tracks north about ten miles, and found them lying down in tall grass. There is a grassy marsh about ten miles north of where Bidwell turned to follow them. Animals, such as oxen, have a keen sense of smell and are able to detect water at great distances. He found them just as the sun was setting and had to drive them back in the dark.

The company had left their dry camp that morning, needing to move on to find water. It seems inconceivable that Bidwell could have followed their tracks in the dark, but he probably knew that they were heading west, and must have aimed in that direction. In one of his memoirs, he wrote that he saw fires to the west. They were likely those of his company camping at Warm Springs. Not knowing it at the time, he feared that they were Indian fires. Exhausted, he suspended further travel that night somewhere in the middle of the valley, probably close to where the company camped at Warm Springs. He waited until daylight to continue.

When Bidwell finally stopped that night, he had traveled an astonishing fifty or so miles during a period of almost twenty-four hours. It was an impressive feat of determination, grit, and endurance. Bidwell has generally not been given enough praise by historians for what he had just done. A lesser man would have become quickly discouraged and abandoned the search. But Bidwell had not. If he had given up easily, as Dawson had, the company would have surely lost the two oxen, the meat they could provide, and the provisions they carried. Such a loss would have been tough on the company, as will be seen.

Jimmy John's journal entry for September 18 revealed what he and the rest of the company did after Bidwell and Dawson left that morning on their search for the errant oxen. The thirsty company raised camp and headed west.

Jimmy John:

> 18th. Left camp early this morning and came to water and grass about 10 o'clock, Here we encamped. The Indians saw us and ran in every direction but when they saw that we were friendly with them, they came back and some of them made signs that a company had been here and killed some of them. We supposed it to have been Walker with a company of trapers about 6 years ago.

When the company left camp it traveled northwest through a low pass in the hills and descended into the large Clover Valley. They aimed toward a green area near the far side of the valley. After about twelve miles, they came to a marsh of tall grass and short willows created by the waters of Warm Springs, which was at the eastern foot of the East Humboldt Range. The waters from the springs are carried toward the valley floor by a number of narrow channels, collectively called Warm Creek. After skirting the marsh and creek channels, the company arrived at the springs, where they stopped to camp.

It is interesting what Jimmy John seemed to know about Joseph Walker's prior travels, but he was probably mistaken about these Indians' having been involved in an incident with Walker. Although Walker had led a brigade of trappers about twenty miles north of here in 1833 on his way to California, the only recorded deadly confrontation between Indians and the Walker brigade occurred near the Humboldt Sink, about two hundred miles west of here. The incident involved Paiutes, not Western Shoshones. It is possible that these Indians were describing an incident involving a trapping party not led by Walker.

Warm Springs and the site of the company's camp are on the east side of Highway 93, twenty-five miles south of where it intersects with Interstate 80 at Wells, Nevada.

September 19

The company spent September 19 resting and allowing their animals to recruit on the grass around Warm Springs.

Jimmy John:

> 19th. This day we did not travel in consequence of Bidwell losing his oxen on the night of the 17th. He left the camp alone and on the 19th inst. re-

turned and brought his cattle with him. We killed a wolf and antelope today and an ox for beef.

Bidwell had mentioned in his entry the day before that the company had already killed four oxen and that they had thirteen left. Since Jimmy John recorded the killing of an ox on September 19, the company was now down to twelve.

Bidwell:

> S. 19th. This morning, I met 3 men who were coming to bring me water &c. arrived at camp, they journeyed yesterday about 12 miles, did not travel today.

Bidwell's entry for September 19 was short, and after what he had just gone through, who can blame him? He would have been exhausted. He was also probably fuming at the indifference and lack of help he received from Bartleson and the rest of the company. His memoirs substantially expanded upon what happened on the morning of September 19. While the company was eating breakfast at its Warm Springs encampment, Bidwell was somewhere east of them, probably not far. It sounded as if he was near one of the channels of Warm Creek. When dawn broke, he could not see the company and tried to pick up its trail. But he was having difficulty:

> I fastened my oxen to a scraggy willow and began to make circles around to see which way the company had gone. The ground was so hard that the animals had made no impressions, which bewildered me. Finally, while making a circle of about three miles away off to the south, I saw two men coming on horseback. In the glare of the mirage, which distorted everything, I could not tell whether they were Indians or white men, but I supposed them to be Indians, feeling sure our party would go west and not south. In a mirage a man on horseback looks as tall as a tree, and I could only tell by the motion that they were mounted. I made a beeline to my oxen, to make breastworks of them. In doing this, I came to a small stream resembling running water, into which I urged my horse, he went down into a quagmire, over head and ears, out of sight. My gun also went under the mire. I got hold of something on the bank, threw out my gun, which was full of mud and water, and holding to the rope attached to my horse, by dint of hard pulling I succeeded in getting him out— a sorry sight, his ears and eyes full of mud, and his body covered

with it. At last, just in time, I was able to move and get behind the oxen. My gun was in no condition to shoot. However, putting dry powder in the pan I determined to do my best in case the supposed Indians came up; but lo! They were two of our party coming to meet me, bringing water and provisions. It was a great relief. I felt indignant that the party had not stopped for me—not the less so when I learned that Captain Bartleson had said, when they started back to find me, that they "would be in better business to go ahead and look for a road."[10]

In another memoir, Bidwell identified Robert Thomes and Grove Cook as the two men who came looking for him.[11] Thomes was Bidwell's friend from Weston, Missouri, while Cook had joined Bartleson's group at Independence. Bidwell would have been justified had he been seething with contempt for Bartleson. If Bidwell had confronted the man, he would probably have mentioned it. But because he did not, it appears that he pocketed his bruised feelings . . . for now.

It was bad enough that Bartleson had allowed the company to spread out and become vulnerable to Indian attack. It was even more disturbing that he had not sent a team of men to help Bidwell or to look for him and the lost oxen. The two men who went looking for Bidwell the following morning had done so on their own initiative, not because Bartleson sent them. Instead, Bartleson had discouraged them.

Had Bartleson been acting like a stern father, feeling that because Bidwell had failed to keep a closer eye on his animals, it was his responsibility to find and recover them? But such an attitude put Bidwell's life at great risk. What kind of moral code was that? Even if he believed Bidwell was not worthy of help, the company was short of critical provisions. Recovering the two oxen, the meat they represented and the provisions they carried, should have been a priority. It could eventually be the difference between the company starving or surviving. Bartleson's role in this affair is not only sordid and distasteful, it also flagged a disturbing mentality that would portend his behavior in the future. Aside from Bartleson's contemptible attitude, it is also troubling that there had not been more support from Bidwell's trail-mates.

September 20

Feeling much revived from their two days at Warm Springs, the company resumed their march on the morning of September 20. Bartleson directed the company to head southwest, skirting the east side of the East Humboldt Range. His recent wanderings—heading south when the Humboldt was north—did not seem consistent with someone who knew where he was or where the Humboldt River was.

Bidwell:

> M. 20th. Passed along one of the highest mountains we had seen in our whole journey, seeking a place to scale it, as we wished to travel W. instead of S. being convinced, that we were already far enough South. At length passed through and descended into a beautiful valley, inclining towards the W. All now felt confident that we were close on the headwaters of Mary's river—distance 25 miles. Two hunters slept out last night, the Company taking a different direction from that which they expected.

Jimmy John:

> 20th. We crosed a high mountain today to our right and traveled about 20 miles. Crosed a handsome valley today and camped at the foot of a high mountain near the foot of a mountain near a small brook of water. Camped by an intermiting spring.

The directions the company received from Fort Hall were to not go too far north nor too far south. Aside from the company's movements west, all of its other movements since leaving Tenmile Springs on September 5 had been south. The company had never significantly traveled north. Perhaps the time to head north was long overdue. While resting at Warm Springs, Bartleson had an opportunity to dispatch scouts to explore north. If he had, they would have found the headwaters of the Humboldt near today's Wells, Nevada, only twenty-six miles away, and across easy terrain.

Bidwell's entry expressed feelings that they were as far south as they ought to go. In using the term "we," he was suggesting that others beside himself felt that way. Did anyone question or challenge Bartleson? Likely not. It would take a brave man to draw the ire of a captain who had just shown a willingness to leave Bidwell to his own fate.

Modern view of east side of Ruby Mountains. It is the view the party had shortly after leaving Warm Springs. Author's photograph.

About two miles after leaving Warm Springs, but before reaching the southernmost tip of the East Humboldt Range, the company turned west and ascended a canyon leading into the narrow range. At the summit of the range, the spectacular Ruby Mountains were visible on the other side of the Ruby Valley ahead of them. After marching across the northern end of the valley, they encountered a number of springs seeping from the foot of the Rubys. Although the company wanted to continue west, the exceedingly tall and steep Rubys blocked their way. They would have to go either north or south to find a way around or through them. If Bartleson had sent riders north to scout the terrain, they would have discovered Secret Pass only ten miles away. It was a pass that John C. Frémont and Lansford Hastings would use in the near future. On the other side of the pass, they would have immediately struck Secret Creek, one of the headwaters of the Humboldt.

But the company turned left and continued south along the eastern base of the Rubys, suggesting that Bartleson had not sent scouts north. It was the second time that day that he made a bad navigating decision. He was again leading the company further from the Humboldt, adding to the suspicion that Bartleson and Hopper had lied to the company when they claimed on September 9 that they had found its headwaters.

After traveling a few miles south along the base of the mountains, the diarists reported that the company stopped at a "small brook" and camped at an intermittent spring. A number of brooks tumble down from the steep eastern slopes of the Ruby Mountains, which makes it difficult to know where the company camped. Our diarists were not particularly helpful because of the wide variation in their mileage estimates. Bidwell estimated that they traveled twenty-five miles that day, while Jimmy John estimated twenty, and Dawson estimated fifteen. A possible brook is one that crosses Highway 229 about one and a half miles north of its junction with Highway 767.

The route between Secret Pass and Jasper Pass would be traveled in future years. When Frémont led an expedition to California in 1845, he led them north of the Great Salt Lake, following a similar route to that taken by the Bartleson party. Once Frémont's party reached the southern tip of the Pilot Mountains, they traveled south, then turned west through a break in the Toano Mountain Range. Then they crossed the Goshute Valley and threaded through Jasper Pass, where they should have seen the four-year-old tracks of the Bartleson company between Jasper Pass and Warm Springs. After reaching Warm Springs, Frémont, who was smarter than Bartleson, headed north through Secret Pass to easily reach the Humboldt River.

The following year, in the spring of 1846, Lansford Hastings, James Clyman, and a number of others were returning to Missouri from California. They had talked to Frémont before leaving California and learned about his route from the Great Salt Lake. When their party came to where the Humboldt branched near today's Halleck, Nevada, Hastings wanted to try Frémont's route. They located Frémont's wagon tracks and followed them through Secret Pass to Warm Springs, then continued through Jasper Pass and beyond. This route would become known as Hastings Cutoff.

September 21

On the morning of September 21, the company continued to proceed southwest along the eastern base of the Ruby Mountains. During the day's travel, they could overlook the broad, level plain of the Ruby Valley on their left.

Bidwell:

> T. 21st. Hunters returned: many antelope were seen and 2 or 3 killed. About 10 o'clock A.M. as we were coasting along the mountain in a W. direction, we came to some hot Springs, which were to me a great curiosity. Within the circumference of a mile there were perhaps 20 Springs: the most of which were extremely beautiful, the water being so transparent we could see the smallest 20 or 30 feet deep. The rocks which walled the Springs, and the beautifully white sediment lodged among them, reflected the sun's rays in such a manner, as to exhibit the most splendid combination of colors, blue, green, red &c., I ever witnessed. The water in most of them was boiling hot. There was one, however, more beautiful than the rest; it really appeared more like the work of art than of nature. It was about 4 feet in diameter, round as a circle, and deeper than we could see—the cavity looked like a well cut in a solid rock, its walls being smooth and perpendicular. Just as I was viewing this curiosity, some hunters came up with some meat, we all partook, putting it into the spring, where it cooked perfectly done in 10 minutes—this is no fish story! The earth around the Springs was white with a substance which tasted strongly of Potash, and the water in the springs was of this quality. Traveled about 15 miles,—several Indians came to our camp, several of whom had guns. From signs, the valley contained thousands.

Jimmy John:

> 21st. We traveled on a south course today, having a rugged mountain on our right hand and some hot springs at the foot of the mountain. The water in them is boiling hot. It is strongly [ink smeared, illegible] substance [ink smeared, illegible] taste and appearance. This is found where the water came up from the edge of the streams and small lakes and is white like potash. Where the water dries up the ground is covered with it. We traveled about 12 miles today. Killed an antelope and camped at a small brook near the foot of the mountains.

The Ruby Mountains are quite spectacular, one of the most picturesque mountain ranges in all of Nevada. Many of its peaks rise to almost ten thousand feet, fully five thousand feet above the broad Ruby Valley bordering its east side. The upper elevations of the mountains are snow-covered much of the year and support large timber. Their eastern slopes are steep. Late in the summer, after the snowmelt has diminished, their eastern streams often go dry. A good deal of the runoff seeps through fissures in the rocky slopes and resurfaces at the base of the mountains as springs and wet marshes. It is why so much of the east side is green. Of course, where there is water there is life, which is likely why Bidwell believed that the Ruby Valley contained thousands of Indians.

Jimmy John described the group's travel as "south" along the base of the mountains, while Bidwell thought they were traveling "west." But the year was getting late, and the sun was setting further south on the horizon. Together with the slight southwestern alignment of the Ruby Range, Bidwell's sense of direction must have been slightly distorted.

The pavement on Highway 767 ends two miles south of its intersection with Highway 229. Travel beyond this point is on a rough gravel road that should be taken only by the most determined drivers willing to subject their vehicles to a great deal of abuse.

The captivating hot springs mentioned by the diarists are about four and a half miles south of where they left camp that morning. They can be seen on the east side of Highway 767, three miles south of its junction with Highway 229. After marveling at them, the company resumed their march south, looking for a way to turn west. They stopped to camp at another "small brook" tumbling out of the mountains. A small brook that crosses Highway 767 about eight and a half miles south of its junction with Highway 229 was the company's most likely campsite on September 21.

September 22

As the members of the company climbed from under their blankets on the morning on September 22 and began packing their animals, they soon had cause for alarm.

Bidwell:

> *W. 22d. This morning 80 or 90 Indians were seen coming full speed from the W, many had horses—one was sent about a half a mile in advance of the rest—so we also ought to have done, but Capt. B. was perfectly ignorant of Indian customs, and the whole band of savages were suffered to come directly up to us, and almost surround our Camp, when Mr. B. Kelsey showed by forcible gestures, they would be allowed to proceed no farther. The Indians were well armed with guns and bows and arrows. The only words, I recollect of hearing Capt. Bartleson say, were "let them*

gratify their curiosity!!" The Indians were Sheshonees, but like other savages always take the advantage where they can. Besides, they were not a little acquainted with warfare, for they undoubtedly visited the Buffalo Country (having many robes) which requires much bravery to contend with the Blackfeet and Chiennes, who continually guard the Buffalo in the region of the Rocky mountains, they traveled as near us as they were allowed, till about noon, when they began to drop off, one by one, and at night there were but 8 or 10 remaining—distance about 12 miles.

Jimmy John:

22nd. This morning we were a little surprised by a band of the natives about the time that we were ready for starting. About 100 of them surrounded us. They were well armed with bows and arrows, guns and lances and knives. They tried to get into our corell [corral] and mix in with us under pretense of trading with us, but we beckned [beckoned] them to shove off which made them look very angry. They stood all in a line close along side of our camp with their weapons in their hands ready for battle while part of the men kept them off and the ballance loaded the pack animals. The Indians followed us nearly all day and some of them camped near us all night. We traveled near 15 miles today keeping the same mountain [on] our right hand that we traveled along side of yesterday and camped at the foot of it on a stream that ran from the mountain.

Jimmy John described the situation as more tense and dangerous than Bidwell had. There seemed no doubt in Jimmy John's mind that the Indians would have attacked if allowed into camp.

Bidwell retold the story in his memoirs:

One morning, just as we were packing up, a party of about ninety Indians, on horseback, a regular war party, were descried coming up. Some of us begged the captain to send men out to prevent them from coming to us while we were in the confusion of packing. But he said "Boys, you must not show any signs of hostility, if you go out there with guns the Indians will think us hostile, and may get mad and hurt us." However, five or six of us took our guns and went out, and by signs made them halt. They did not prove to be hostile, but they had carbines, and if we had been careless and had let them come near they might, and probably would, have killed us. At last we packed up and started, and the Indians traveled along three or four hundred yards one side or the other of us or behind all day. They ap-

peared anxious to trade, and offered a buckskin, well dressed, worth two or three dollars, for three or four charges of powder and three or four balls. This showed that they were in want of ammunition. The carbines indicated that they had communication with some trading post belonging to the Hudson's Bay Company. They had buffalo-robes also, which showed that they were a roving hunting party, as there were no buffalo within three or four hundred miles. At this time I had spoken my mind freely concerning Captain Bartleson's lack of judgment, as one could scarcely help doing under the circumstances.[12]

In another memoir, Bidwell revealed that he had condemned Bartleson's judgment to one of Bartleson's friends: "During that day I said to one of the men who messed with Captain Bartleson 'Our captain don't appear to understand Indian character. If we don't make those fellows afraid of us, they will certainly attack us. Captain Bartleson is too timid and cautious with them.' This must have been repeated to Captain Bartleson."[13]

There were a few, including Bidwell, who may have been influenced by Fitzpatrick's belief in being cautious and not leading Indians into thinking they had an advantage. It had been two days since Bartleson had abandoned Bidwell when he went in search of his oxen. Bidwell must have still been fuming over the captain's indifference. His scorn for the man must have been intense, and rightfully so. Openly criticizing Bartleson was a brave act. But criticizing his judgment to a person likely to betray his words was probably as injudicious as it was brave. Bidwell's brashness was setting himself up for greater difficulties later.

Was anyone besides Bidwell troubled by Bartleson's judgment or leadership? We have no evidence that anyone else had openly expressed disenchantment. These people were in the middle of a remote and dangerous solitude, far from any help. It likely discouraged open expressions of discord. If they were to make it to their destination alive, it was probably best to suppress any disgruntlement. There was no telling how Bartleson would react. He appeared to be the kind who could be vindictive, and he had his supporters to back him. It was not worth a showdown.

This encounter with the Indians had been frightening. Bidwell must have shuddered at the thought that he could have easily run into the party while recovering his oxen. Alone and vulnerable, he may have been treated kindly, and then again, he may not have.

Bidwell was probably correct that the Indians were Shoshones, more precisely, Western Shoshones. Noticing their carbines, he deduced that they had acquired them at a Hudson's Bay Company post, the closest one of which would have been Fort Hall. He noted how they were intent on trading for a few rounds of ammunition, something that was scarce in these remote parts. It makes one think that they would not have attacked the company. If they had been unsuccessful, they not only would have suffered some casualties, they would have likely used up what little ammunition they had, leaving them with none with which to hunt game or defend themselves from their enemies.

Bidwell's journal mentioned that it was Benjamin Kelsey who led a small group out to intercept the Indians. Kelsey's wife, Nancy, produced a short recollection many years later. One of the few things she mentioned showed how proud she was of her husband's role in this incident: "At one place the Indians surrounded us, armed with bows and arrows, but my husband leveled his gun at the chief and made him order his Indians out of arrow range."[14]

While keeping the Indians at a distance, the party packed their animals and hastened out of camp, continuing to head southwest. After twelve miles of trudging along the base of the Ruby Mountains, they stopped and camped beside a small stream. Their camp was probably near where a stream crosses Highway 767, about four miles north of where a rough gravel road heads west up a twisty canyon and over Harrison Pass.

September 23

According to both diarists, a few Indians camped not far from the company during the night of September 22. It is likely the camp's guards were exceptionally vigilant that night.

The following day would be momentous; it was when the company would make its first contact with waters flowing to the Humboldt River.

Bidwell:

> T. 23d. We could see no termination of the valley, nor any signs of Mary's river, we therefore concluded that we were too far South—and passed over the mountains to the North, where we struck a small stream running

towards the N.W. on this we encamped and found plenty of grass,—a few fish were caught, some of which were trout, which led us to the conclusion that this was a branch of Mary's river. Distance 18 miles.

Jimmy John:

23rd. This morning the Indians all left us. We traveled westward [and] crossed the mountain on our right. Traveled about 20 miles today and camped on the bank of a small creek, the head of the south branch of Marys river. Here we caught a few small trout.

Leaving camp that morning, the company continued southwest. After traveling only two miles, the company noticed a narrow canyon leading west toward a low spot in the Ruby Range, later named Harrison Pass. They threaded their way up the canyon. Peaks rose on either side, some as high as ten thousand feet. The summit of the pass was seven thousand feet, about twelve hundred feet above where they had left the valley floor. Crossing the summit, they began a gentle descent and encountered Toyn Creek, a small, west-flowing stream that would have been dry this time of year. After a few more miles, the creek merged with Corral Creek, another dry stream, although abundant grass grew in its bottom. About thirteen miles beyond the summit, Corral Creek merged with Smith Creek in the middle of a large, grassy meadow. After traveling between eighteen and twenty miles, the company called it a day. Smith Creek had sufficient water to support fish, so they took out their fishing lines and began to haul in trout.

It must have been a jubilant camp that night. Both diarists expressed their belief that they were now on a branch of the Humboldt. They were correct. Since they understood that the Humboldt was supposed to lead them the rest of the way to California, it is easy to imagine them sitting beside their fires that night, engaged in exuberant conversation while enjoying a meal of freshly caught fish.

Since the road ascending Harrison Pass from the Ruby Valley is over a narrow, rough, and winding gravel road, the easiest way to see the company's route over Harrison Pass is to come up Highway 228 where it heads south of Elko, Nevada. This route is paved all the way to the top of Harrison Pass. The company's camp that evening should have been about a third of a mile south of the tiny community of Jiggs, Nevada, and in the meadow near where the Highway 228 Bridge crosses Smith Creek.

September 24

Bidwell:

> F. 24th. As we descended the stream, it rapidly increased in size, and proved to be a branch of a larger stream. The country was desolate and barren, excepting immediately on the streams, where grew a few willows and cotton woods, the hills in some places produced a few shrubby cedars. Traveled today about 20 miles.

Jimmy John:

> 24th. We traveled down the stream today about 24 miles and camped on its bank. We killed an ox this evening for beef.

Leaving their camp on Smith Creek on the morning of September 24, the group moved downstream along the creek bottom. After four miles, they came to where it flowed into Huntington Creek. They followed the Huntington for twelve miles until it flowed into the South Fork of the Humboldt River. After making about two miles along the South Fork, the company stopped to camp, likely in the grassy meadow bordering the stream. Bidwell's memoirs recalled that they often followed Indian and antelope trails along these creeks.[15] While abundant grass grew along the creek bottoms, they were bordered by bleak, arid hills covered with sparse vegetation, mostly sage. To their right, the Ruby Mountains rose high above them, providing a grand view. Jimmy John recorded that they killed another ox, leaving them with eleven.

Highway 228 travels a number of miles east of the creeks the company followed on September 24. If interested in following the company's path that day, take the Hamilton Stage Road where it leaves Highway 228 about two miles north of Jiggs. The road heads northwest, tracking close to the creeks. After about seventeen miles, the road comes to a bridge crossing the South Fork of the Humboldt. Cross the bridge and travel two miles further north to Gasway Road. The company's camp on the evening of September 24 was probably in the meadow near the Gasway Road Bridge over the South Fork.

September 25

Thinking that California could not be far, the party probably left camp that morning in an upbeat mood. About four miles north of where they left camp, the South Fork approached some hills and then entered a canyon that cut through them.

Bidwell:

S. 25th. The creek became perfectly dry and its banks rose to high perpendicular precipices, so that there was no other road than the dry bed of the stream. Having come about 15 miles, we encamped in a place, affording a little grass and water—where we could see nothing but the sky. But the men who ascended the precipice to see what was the prospect ahead, said that in about a mile, we would come to a valley,—this was delightful news.

Jimmy John:

25th. Today we traveled about 16 miles down the creek through a deep valley with high cliffs on each side. We found the banks dry today for about 8 miles and camped on its bank this evening.

The diarists mentioned how the riverbed went dry somewhere after entering the canyon. It was late in the year, so losses in the river channel from seepage and evaporation in this long, meandering canyon finally exceeded the upstream inflows. As the travelers progressed into the canyon, it became extremely narrow, with high, steep walls rising above them hundreds of feet above the streambed. The canyon twisted and turned, back and forth, and must have been very disorienting.

The diarists' accounts for September 25 did not describe their difficulties in the canyon to the degree that Bidwell did in one of his memoirs:

In the afternoon we entered a cañon the walls of which were precipitous and several hundred feet high. Finally the pleasant bermy banks gave out entirely, and we could travel only in the dry bed of what in the wet season was a raging river. It became a solid mass of stones and huge boulders, and the animals became tender-footed and sore so that they could hardly stand up, and as we continued the way became worse and worse. There was no place to lie down and sleep, nor could our animals lie down; the water had given out, and the prospect was indeed gloomy—the cañon had been leading us directly north. All agreed that the animals were too jaded and worn to go back. Then we called the men: "What did they tell you at Fort Hall about the north-

ern region?" They repeated, "You must not go too far north; if you do you will get into difficult cañons that lead towards the Columbia River, where you may become bewildered and wander about and perish." This cañon was going nearly north; in fact it seemed a little east of north.[16]

Two days earlier, Bidwell had described the company's joy when they believed they had finally fallen upon one of the headwaters of the long-sought Humboldt. But his memoirs above showed that stumbling through this convoluted, boulder-strewn canyon had shaken their earlier belief. Because of the warning they had received from Fort Hall about the danger of falling into canyons in which they could perish, canyons made them nervous. Alarmed about how far this canyon went and where it led, their fickle emotions abruptly shifted from elation to fear.

At a distance, the company evokes pity. Up close, not so much. They had brought much of their misery upon themselves. Bartleson's inauspicious leadership and poor decisions were largely responsible. If only he had sent men to scout just east of the canyon, they would have discovered an easy path over the hills. Indeed, in just a few miles, the scouts would have arrived at a summit from which they could have seen the Humboldt River and its broad valley ahead. Such a route would have circumvented the rocky bottom of the canyon and would have allayed their fears about where they were heading. Equally important, it would have shortened the distance to the Humboldt by at least ten miles. Would Bartleson ever learn the basic fundamentals of exploration?

When the company paused to camp at the bottom of the canyon on the afternoon of September 25, Bidwell's journal reported that a couple of resourceful men clambered to the top of the cliffs. Their eyes were gladdened by the sight of the Humboldt River valley just a few miles beyond. That night the company was able to retire with rejuvenated spirits, knowing that they were not traveling in a canyon of doom after all and that they would be out of it the next morning.

The location of their canyon camp on September 25 is not accessible by public or private roads. It is about one mile inside of the northern mouth of the canyon.

September 26

On the morning of September 26, the company traveled the last winding miles of canyon and emerged into a valley through which the main channel of the Humboldt River coursed.

Bidwell:

> S. 26th. The valley, seen yesterday evening, was but 4 or 5 miles in length and led into another difficult defile, though not so long as the one yesterday, for we passed it into another valley. Distance 18 miles—the stream continued to increase in size.

Jimmy John:

> 26th. This morning we came to the east branch of the river and traveled down the river about 18 miles and camped near its bank on the north side. No timber here except willows.

When the travelers emerged from the South Fork Canyon, they came to a new river, hoping and praying that it was the long-sought Humboldt. They reached its banks about eight miles west of present-day Elko, Nevada. It must have struck them that this was a significant river, one that had to be taken seriously. It headed west. It must be the Humboldt. Surely, California could not be far.

The river was shallow and averaged about fifty to sixty feet wide. It occasionally split into separate channels that formed small islands in between. They tasted the water. It was slightly alkaline, but not bad. It would do. It would be a dependable source of water and grass for the next two hundred miles. In many ways it resembled the Sweetwater River, although its water was not nearly as good. The Humboldt would be much like the Sweetwater in another way. Due to its flat declination, the channel looped back and forth, snakelike, while grass and thickets of small willows grew within its bottom.

The company understood that this river was their path to California. Perhaps they thought their destination was not far, even though they really had no idea how much further. Certainly the worst must be behind them. So they turned west, and began to follow the river downstream. They were now traveling a route that an estimated 250,000 California-bound emigrants and Gold Rushers would eventually travel, with few variations, in the years to come. The next time a party of emigrants would tread beside this river would be two years later, when Joseph Walker led Joseph Chiles's wagon party on their way to California.

Just north of this spot, on the north side of today's Interstate 80, stands the beautiful California Trail Interpretive Center, a recently built facility operated by the Bureau of Land Management in partnership with the Southern Nevada Conservancy and other sponsors. How fitting is it that the Trail Center was built where the first emigrant party to California first came into contact with this important lifeline to the West.

If Bartleson had led his company northwest from Warm Springs and through Secret Pass, instead of their roundabout southern route, they would have reached this point on the Humboldt about two days earlier and shortened the trip by about forty miles In future years, the popular emigrant route through Fort Hall to the Raft River, then up Goose Creek and through the Thousand Springs Valley, would be about eight days of travel and 130 miles shorter than the ill-guided route taken by the Bartleson-led company.

Outside the river bottom, there was not much to delight the eye. The hills on both sides of the bottom were quite drab, so barren that even the hardy sagebrush was rarely seen. In his memoirs, Bidwell described the country bordering the river:

> *The country is almost destitute of game. We saw scarcely any deer or antelope. The whole region had been burned over. Almost our only dependence therefore was on our oxen, which we were still driving to meet any emergency, although they had become so poor that they could carry no loads.*[17]

Nicholas Dawson's memoirs echoed Bidwell's recollection. He complained that "there was no more game to be had."[18] There were thirty-two people to feed and they only had eleven oxen left. Bidwell mentioned the poor condition of the oxen, but they were all they had to keep from starving. They had been killing an ox about every three days, so they had a thirty-three-day supply. Would it be enough?

Five miles after the company struck the Humboldt, the river valley narrowed and the river entered Carlin Canyon, a crooked defile about three miles long. The land rose steeply on either side and bordered the canyon with high cliffs towering close together. The high cliffs forced the company to travel close to the banks of the meandering river, sometimes forcing them to cross to the other side. Emerging from the rocky gorge, the company stopped to camp on the north bank of the river where the river bottom widened.

Because Carlin Canyon was so narrow and difficult for wagons, a trail would later be established that skirted the gorge by crossing the hills to the north. It became known as Greenhorn's Cutoff. Interstate 80 travels through much of Carlin Canyon today, and the location of the company's campsite on September 26 can be seen just south of the Interstate about a mile east of the present town of Carlin, Nevada.

September 27

The company made good progress along the river on September 27.

Bidwell:

> M. 27th. Road was very difficult all day, course of the stream W. Traveled about 20 miles.

Jimmy John:

> 27th. Today we traveled about 25 miles down Marys river through a deep valley with clifts of rock on each side some times perpendicular for some hundred feet through which the river runs in a southwest course. We camped on the bank of the river this evening where the valley widens a little. We killed an ox this evening for beef.

The company continued to travel west on September 27, then turned southwest through a handsome river bottom with plenty of grass and the occasional thicket of willows growing along the margins of the river. They still could not see much beyond the river bottom as it was bordered on both sides with barren hills. About eight miles after leaving camp, the company entered another canyon, known today as Palisades Canyon. It was their third canyon in three days. Once again, high cliffs closed in on both sides of the river, forcing the party to cross to its opposite side from time to time. After snaking about fifteen miles through this wandering canyon, the company came to where the river bottom widened again. They stopped to camp here after a long day of about twenty miles. Jimmy John recorded the killing of another ox, leaving them with ten.

It is going to be difficult to pinpoint the precise location of some of the company's camps along the Humboldt, there being few distinctive landmarks aside from the river itself, which can be used to make the determination. We will continue to consider the diarists' mileage estimates, although they rarely agree, and when they do, they can still be slightly inaccurate. As a result, we will suggest camp locations that could be off by as much as a few miles.

The estimated location of their camp on September 27 can be seen by turning south off of Interstate 80 onto Hwy 306. Travel south on 306 about six miles, crossing first the Humboldt River and then the Union Pacific Railroad tracks to the tiny settlement of Beowawe, Nevada. About a third of a mile south of the settlement, turn east on Pioneer Pass Road and travel on it southeast approximately eight miles. The campsite would have been along the river bottom about a half-mile north of this point. The diarists did not report whether they camped on the north or south side of the river.

Future emigrants, wanting to avoid the extra miles caused by the circuitous canyon, established a trail that left the river a few miles west of Carlin. It was a significant mile-saving cutoff that traveled over the hills before returning to the river about four miles west of where the company is estimated to have camped on September 27. The route of this cutoff mostly follows the route of today's Interstate 80.

September 28

Bidwell:

> T. 28th. Traveled about 20 miles,—several Indians came to our Camp this evening—no timber excepting willows, grass plenty.

Jimmy John:

> 28th. We followed the river about 26 miles today in a northwest course and encamped on its banks. The valley is wide here and the mountain not high. We see plenty of Indian signs today and where they have made fish traps along the river and fresh signs at their camps but have not seen any since we came to this river until this evening. A few of the Root digers [diggers] came to us this evening. They are poor and nearly naked and barefooted.

Upon getting underway on the morning of September 28, the company continued west, following the river. Neither diarist mentioned on which side of the river they traveled. About a mile after leaving camp, they passed Gravely Ford, where future emigrant trains would cross the river to its south bank after descending from the cutoff across the hills to the north. Four miles beyond Gravely Ford, the river turned and headed north for ten miles, and then turned west again. After a day of traveling about twenty-five miles, they stopped to camp beside the river.

Both diarists reported being visited that evening by a few Indians, but neither provided any details. Since arriving on the Humboldt, neither diarist had mentioned seeing Indians or signs of Indians until now. It was not that they were lacking. There were plenty of them. Emigrants in later years recorded countless encounters with Indians along this section of the river. But until these natives showed up in camp on September 28, they had probably been keeping out of sight. Before 1841, few white men had traveled along the Humboldt. The ones who had were with trapping expeditions, such as the brigade led by Joseph Walker that traveled to California in 1833.

Some of these natives would have never seen a white man before. Some would have never seen a horse or a mule. It is certain that none of them had ever seen those strange beasts called oxen. There is a good chance they had heard about white men, but not in a good way. As mentioned earlier, the Joseph Walker party had an encounter with a large group of armed Paiute warriors near the Humboldt Sink. The Indians emerged from a dense thicket of willows and surrounded the brigade in a threatening manner. One of the party's members, George Nidever, reported that there were between four hundred and five hundred, although another member, Zenas Leonard, said that it was between eighty and a hundred.[19] Using sign language, Walker urged the Indians to step aside and let them pass, but the Indians refused to give way. Fearing for their lives and not willing to take any chances, Walker ordered his men to open fire. Nidever said they killed thirty-three, while Leonard said it was thirty-nine. The rest of the warriors turned and fled, disappearing into thick brush. Even though the incident occurred eight years earlier and about two hundred miles further west, it seems likely that the story of the massacre would have slowly made its way through the native population living along the river. It would be understandable, therefore, if these Indians lived in fear of the white man, and would explain why most stayed out of sight and watched this strange procession from a distance.

The company's campsite on the evening of September 28 was about a half-mile north of Interstate 80, and approximately eighteen miles east of the community of Battle Mountain.

September 29

Breaking camp on the morning of September 29, the expedition continued to follow the twisting river west. Battle Mountain, just west of the present-day town bearing that name, loomed fifteen miles ahead of them.

Bidwell:

> W. 29th. Traveled about 20 miles, course of the stream was W.N.W. According to the map Mary's river ran W.S.W. Strong doubts were entertained about this being Mary's river. The men who got directions at Fort Hall were cautioned, that if we got too far South, we would get into the Great Sandy Desert—if too far North, we would wander and starve to death on the waters of the Columbia, there being no possibility of getting through that way. We had now been 6 days on this stream, and our course had changed considerably North of West.

Jimmy John:

> 29th. Traveled about 20 miles today in a west course and camped on the bank of the river.

About ten miles west of their company's camp, the river turned and headed northwest. The company trudged near the river another ten miles before calling it a day. Bidwell's journal entry that evening expressed alarm. The warning from Fort Hall about going too far north continued to haunt them. Their alarm was not about canyons this time; it was about the direction of the river. Why was this confounding river so determined to head north? Doubts were creeping into their minds about whether it was even the Humboldt. Bidwell sounded as if they continued to put stock in a map that showed that the Humboldt flowed more to the southwest. But hadn't their maps been discredited by the trappers at Green River as virtually worthless? Why were they still consulting them?

Their concern about the direction of the Humboldt, and whether it was the Humboldt, was an example of what fundamentally distinguished the Bartleson party from the many thousands of emigrants and Gold Rushers who followed. The travelers of the future would know where they were, where they were going, and what to expect. Even if their journey was long and difficult, they knew that others had successfully made the trip in the past, a comforting thought that would have bolstered their confidence. They did not have to worry about what path to take since a reassuring, well-marked trail, often through deep dust, always lay in front of them. All they had to do was follow it. They also had the consolation of knowing that there were wagon parties ahead and behind that could support them.

The Bartleson party had none of this. Their maps were all but useless. Their directions were uncertain. They had no idea of distances. They had no established trail, although they often marched along Indian trails. Joseph Walker had led his trappers through here eight years earlier, but neither of our diarists ever mentioned seeing evidence of their tracks. This is not unexpected since eight years of rain and wind would have surely erased them from the landscape. They knew they were supposed to travel west, but continually suffered from anxieties because this perplexing river was always changing directions. Hence, their doubts and uncertainties would torment them every bit as much as cold, heat, hunger, and fatigue. But they forged ahead anyway. If they had lacked optimistic personalities they probably would not have joined this venture in the first place.

Their campsite on September 29 is about four miles east of Interstate 80, and about nine twelve miles north of the present-town of Battle Mountain.

September 30

Bidwell:

> T. 30th. Our course today was about due North, 18 miles.

Jimmy John:

> 30th. We traveled about 14 miles today in a northwest course and camped on the bank of the river.

The diarists' alarm about the river's general direction probably intensified during the day since the river continued winding back and forth in a northwesterly direction through this long, flat, sage-covered valley. The river's serpentine meandering through this thirty-five-mile section were so extreme through here that it sometimes provoked comments from future diarists. One Gold Rusher complained that it was "the crookedest stream that I ever saw. . . . It sometimes runs 2 or 3 miles and gets not over 30 rods from where it started from."[20] The windings of the Humboldt were so radical that the company probably traveled a mile or so distant from it, approaching it only when the animals needed a drink or at the end of the day to camp.

By now, the company was probably weary of the routine of unloading their pack mules and oxen each evening, and then repacking them each morning. They must have been tiring of the Humboldt as well. It had been another day of dreary, mind-numbing sameness. They had been crawling like snails for a week, moving past an endless panorama of drab-colored, lookalike hills and mountains, inhabited only by sagebrush and greasewood.

One of the bigger complaints expressed by future emigrants and Gold Rushers through this stretch was the salty incrustations covering part of the plain. Light and powdery, they had the appearance of lime and ash. With at least thirty head of animals—horses, mules, and oxen—their many hooves likely stirred up clouds of choking dust.

Would this soul-sapping journey ever end? The travelers had no idea how much further they had to go. They understood they still had to cross the California mountains. The tragedy of the Donner party would not occur for another five years, but the Bartleson party knew it was getting late and some must have been worrying about getting trapped in snowstorms and becoming snowbound in the mountains.

They were no longer held back by their wagons, but their oxen were slow-moving, and a good number of men in the party were walking. According to Bidwell's memoirs, some of the men were on foot because their horses or mules had given out and had been abandoned: "From the time we left our wagons many had to walk, and more and more as we advanced," Bidwell recalled. "Going down the Humboldt at least half were on foot. . . . [W]alking was very fatiguing."[21]

Even though there were areas along the river that produced good grass, the animals spent much of each day walking and each night resting, leaving little time and energy for grazing. As each day ticked by, their daily exertions continued to consume them. The men's nutritional needs were not being met either. Their provisions were depleted. Their supply of flour, beans, cornmeal, and sugar—carbohydrate energy—was exhausted, or nearly so. There would have been very little fat on the rail-thin oxen they were slaughtering. A future emigrant complained that he could not even get a bubble of fat to rise to the top of the pot in which he boiled the meat of his emaciated ox. The Bartleson company was trying to subsist on an unbalanced diet that was almost exclusively meat protein. Poor nutrition can adversely affect energy, health, and mood. All things considered, the party members appeared to be reasonably healthy, since our diarists have not mentioned anyone being ill. But we are not sure how the party was handling things emotionally at this point. Aside from Bidwell's complaints about Bartleson's judgment and leadership, neither he nor Jimmy John has remarked about anyone else's behavior, suggesting that the party members were still behaving within acceptable norms.

Important nutritional stocks were not the only provisions that were depleted. By the time the venturers were coasting down the Humboldt, they no longer had salt to season their meat and may have also been out of coffee. Bidwell's memoirs mentioned that tobacco was in short supply as well:

> *Some of our men had used up their tobacco and would do most anything to obtain more of it. I remember that some men cut out their pockets and chewed them. One man by the name of William Belty had a riding mule that kept in pretty good condition. He offered to let one of them ride the mule each day for a small piece of tobacco enough for him to chew during the day. One morning Belty lost his daily allowance of the weed, and though he looked closely, he could not find it. During the afternoon an Indian overtook us. He struck himself and said, "Shoshonie! Shoshonie!" We knew these Indians to be friendly. He at the same time held out in his hand the piece of tobacco, which he must have found after we left camp, for no Indians were around at that time. Belty was so unreasonable that he said the Indian was a thief and ought to be shot. I have no doubt he would have shot the Indian if I had not been with him.*[22]

The understandably shy Indians would wait until the company pulled away from camp in the morning before scurrying in to grab whatever was left behind. They were scavengers, an important trait for people trying to survive in a tight-fisted land. Bidwell did not specify where along the Humboldt the above incident occurred, but if the Indian was Shoshone, it was probably near one of their camps between today's Battle Mountain and Winnemucca. William Belty's attitude proved that the Indians' fear of the white man was well founded. The Indian might have lost his life if it had not been for Bidwell's intervention. Belty was depicted as a hard man. Others in the company may have been hard men to begin with, but the difficulties and privations over the last few months had likely hardened them even more.

As the Bartleson party advanced along the Humboldt, they were marching along an unlittered path. Years later, especially during the Gold Rush era, after an immense mass of humanity had struggled through here, the road had changed. About every few feet, according to diarists, one would pass abandoned wagons, iron stoves, heavy tools, and the bleached skeletons of horses, mules, and oxen that had not made it. Some described the trail as an endless outdoor emporium of discarded items. If a man stumbled across a shirt or jacket lying on the ground that appeared to be better than what he was wearing, he would put it on. If it fit, he would take it and leave his old one behind.[23]

After about eighteen miles of monotonous progress on September 30, the company stopped to camp by the river again. Their camp would be about seven miles east of Interstate 80 and thirty miles northwest of Battle Mountain.

Chapter 14

Will the Humboldt Ever End?

OCTOBER 1 TO 15, 1841

October 1

October 1 was an uneventful day.

Bidwell:

> Oct. 1st. The stream had already attained the size of which we supposed Mary's river to be, and yet its course was due N W—distance 20 miles.

Jimmy John:

> Oct. 1st. Today we traveled about 22 miles to the northwest and camped on the bank of the river in the evening.

After endless days of crawling snail-like past a monotonously dreary landscape, the company must have been tiring of it. It was October 1 and they had not yet reached the great California Mountains. In fact, they were not even close.

After six miles of travel that day, the river suddenly turned and began heading southwest, passing through a quarter-mile-wide canyon created by the southern spur of the Osgood Mountains on the north and the point of the tall Sonoma Mountains on the south. It would be named Emigrant Canyon in the future. Then the river changed course again, returning to a northwesterly direction. After traveling nine more miles, the company set up camp beside the river.

Their October 1 camp was next to the river, just north of Interstate 80 and about eight miles northeast of the present town of Winnemucca, Nevada.

October 2

October 2 should have brought optimism and renewed spirits due to an encouraging change in the direction of the river.

Bidwell:

> S. 2d. Having traveled about 5 miles, we all beheld with delight the course of the river change to S W—here was excellent grass—it was 3 or 4 feet high, and stood thick like a meadow, it was a kind of Bluegrass. The whole valley seemed to be swarming with Indians, but they were very timid. Their sable heads were seen in groups of 15 or 20, just above the tops of the grass to catch a view of us passing by. Whenever we approached their huts, they beckoned us to go on –they are extremely filthy in their habits. Game was scarce, 'tho the Indians looked fat and fine. They were Shashonees.

Jimmy John:

> 2nd. This day we traveled about 20 miles westward and camped on the bank of the river in the evening. We saw a good many natives today, perhaps 200. They were friendly and some of them came and traded with us at night. They told us that two days travel would take us to the mouth of this river where it forms lakes which have no outlet.

Indeed, the river had turned southwest, much to their delight. For most of the day, the company traveled through a river plain that stretched both west and east of today's Winnemucca. The river plain was rich, green, and marshy. The grass grew tall and abundant. The flow of the river today is substantially diminished compared to what it was in 1841. Modern upstream diversions for municipal and agricultural uses have markedly reduced its flows. Because of the larger flows back then, the river snaked through multiple channels, forming islands in between. Unusually heavy rains could cause the river to overflow its banks and flood large areas of the river plain, something that can still occasionally happen today. The periodic floodings produced boggy meadows. Our diarists did not mention it, but they had to be careful to ensure that their animals did not sink up to their bellies in the soft, mushy ground next to the river when they approached it to get a drink. In the years to come, wagon trains would often pause here long enough to take out their scythes to cut the tall grass and dry it for hay. They would load it into their wagons and use it during the grassless stretches that were ahead.

Where there was abundant water, there was abundant vegetation. Where there was vegetation and water, there were fish, berries, roots, and some game. Where there was food, there were Indians, swarms of them according to our diarists. Bidwell thought that the Indians, whom he described as Shoshones, appeared well fed. He may have been mistaken about the tribe since they were now in what was considered Paiute territory. In fact, the town of Winnemucca was named after a Paiute chief.

The Indians were timid. But 1841 represented an early stage of contact between white men and Indians along the Humboldt. Each group looked upon the other with wariness and caution. Their relationship would slowly evolve in the years to come as increased numbers of white travelers led to incidents of misunderstanding and ill will. It would not be long before it would become perilous for both groups. The Indians became more bold and aggressive, often trying to kill, wound, or steal the travelers' livestock. Angry or mean whites occasionally shot any Indian coming within gunshot range. In retaliation, some Indians would ambush and kill any white man who made the mistake of wandering too far from his companions.

The location of the company's camp on October 2 is near the river about a mile north of Interstate 80 and about thirteen miles southwest of Winnemucca. It is not known on which side of the river the company was on at this point, although Bidwell explained in one of his memoirs, "In going down the [Humboldt] river, we went sometimes on one side and sometimes on the other, but mostly on the north side, till we were nearing what are now known as the Humboldt Mountains."[1]

October 3

Bidwell:

> S. 3d. Traveled about 12 miles today West.

Jimmy John:

> 3rd. We traveled about 12 miles today, a southwest course over sandhills and plains of loose sand which made hard traveling. We camped on the bank of the river this evening and killed a beef and a few ducks.

Although Bidwell said in his memoirs that they saw antelope, they were unable to kill any.[2] The company had been killing an ox about every three days for meat. The last journal entry reporting the killing of an ox was on September 27, six days earlier. Therefore, it is reasonable to assume that an ox was also killed on or about September 30, even though neither diarist mentioned it. Under that assumption, the killing of an ox on October 3 left the company with eight.

Their October 3 camp is estimated to have been about one and a half miles west of Interstate 80 and twenty miles southwest of Winnemucca.

October 4

Bidwell:

> *M. 4th. Distance 25 miles S W Country, dry, barren, sandy except on the river.*

Jimmy John:

> *4th. To[day] we traveled about 23 miles in a southwest course and camped on the bank of the river. The valley is wide here with mountains on each side of the river and a high range of mountains west of us running north and south.*

East of them was the East Range, tall and forbidding. To the west were the Eugene Mountains, farther away. Our diarists mentioned crossing sandy country on October 3 and 4. Beginning five miles southwest of Winnemucca, a stretch of sandhills lay along both sides of the river.

The company was continuing to travel through arid country with meager rainfall and snow, meaning that there were no significant streams adding to the river's flow. With no new water to offset the river's losses from seepage and evaporation, the quality of the water was growing worse, becoming more muddy and alkaline and degrading the oxen's digestion. The high pH of the alkaline water was killing off billions of rumen bacteria upon which the oxen depended to digest the cellulose in the grass they consumed. Even with adequate grass to eat, the impaired digestion would have caused the condition of the oxen to decline in any event.

By the end of the day, the company had probably reached Lassen

Meadows. The place is a wide valley surrounded by high bluffs. This is where the Humboldt makes a wide turn to the west, followed by a pronounced turn to the south. The Meadows acquired its name a few years later, after Peter Lassen left the main trail here in 1848 to lead his company of ten wagons across a parched desert in an attempt to take a more northerly, and what he thought would be a more direct, route into California.

The company's camp on October 4 would have been about six miles west of Interstate 80 and about thirty-seven miles southwest of Winnemucca.

October 5

The company made an early start on the morning of October 5. Bartleson was pushing them hard, leading them toward another one of his bizarre and troublesome incidents.

Bidwell:

> T. 5th. To day was very warm, and the oxen were not able to keep up with the horses. Traveled about 30 miles and stopped on the river about dark—grass plenty, willows—this going so fast was the fault of Capt. B., nothing kept him from going as fast as his mules could possibly travel. But his dependence was on the oxen for Beef,—for it was all we had to live upon.

Jimmy John:

> 5th. Today we only came about 3 miles and camped on the bank of the river. Our animals are growing poorer and even the grass is growing scarce here. There is no grass in these mountain valleys except on the lowest banks of the stream and this river has high banks in general.

Since Bidwell's journal and Dawson's log both recorded that they traveled thirty miles on October 5, Jimmy's John's estimate of three miles was an obvious transcription error. As the company left Lassen Meadows and proceeded south, the river snaked through a narrow channel that ran between twenty and one hundred feet below the surrounding terrain. It was virtually impossible to find a place where they could get their livestock down to graze or drink. The company likely followed Indian trails through the sage-covered desert, tracking a mile or so west of the deep-cut river in order to avoid the deep ravines and gullies that drained into it. It was tough going, as the sagebrush was large and abrasive, scratching and clawing at them as they hurried along.

The day's travel was drawing them ever closer to the Humboldt Sink. By now, the river's waters were heavily impregnated with alkali and other salts. Jimmy John's journal entry spotlighted how the long trip, inadequate feed, and poor-quality water were taking a tremendous toll on their animals.

Barren plains and hills bordered them on either side. Further out, the Humboldt Range stretched along their east, while a long, low longitudinal range called the Trinity Range stood out to their west. A rough gravel road named Old Emigrant Road parallels much of their route that day.

Even though the group would have passed a few widely spaced springs through this stretch, they had to distinguish between those with good and bad water. A Gold Rusher in the future explained how one determined the difference: "[I]f it is full of snakes frogs and other reptiles, it is alright. We drive them out and take a drink ourselves; but if the water looks black and we can't find no water varmint, not even a snake, we let it alone."[3]

After an exhausting thirty miles of travel, this hungry and dust-covered company finally stopped to camp just north of where the river made its way through an area that would later be called Big Meadows. Much like the broad, grassy areas near Winnemucca and at Lassen Meadows, this was another area where the river flooded occasionally and spread out, creating an area of tule marshes and tall grasses that future travelers would cut for hay. Today, the area has developed into rich farming country around the present-day town of Lovelock, Nevada.

The location of the company's camp on the evening of October 5 was on the west side of the river, about three miles northeast of Lovelock.

Although Bidwell's journal entry for October 5 did not reveal it, one of his later memoirs made it clear that he was the unfortunate person whose turn had come to drive the slow-gaited oxen:

> We were getting tired, and some were in favor of leaving the oxen, of which we then had only about seven or eight, and rushing on

> into California. They said there was plenty of beef in California. But some of us said: "No, our oxen are now our only supply of food. We are doing well, making eighteen or twenty miles per day." One morning [October 5th], when it was my turn at driving the oxen, the captain traveled so fast that I could not keep up, and was left far behind. When night came I had to leave the trail and go over a rocky declivity for a mile and a half into a gloomy, damp bottom, and unpack the oxen and turn them out to eat, sleeping myself without blankets.[4]

As October 5 drew to a close, Bidwell and the oxen plodded far behind the company. Alone and unsupported by help, Bidwell had plenty of time to think and his thoughts probably smoldered. Once again, he must have been experiencing a keen sense of abandonment. Unable to continue and fearful of Indians, he needed to stop and spend the night where he could conceal himself and his animals. He left the trail and proceeded east down a mile-and-a-half-long peninsula formed by a pronounced loop in the river. The tip of the loop was secluded and there was grass for the oxen and a thicket of willows in which to hide.[5] He later recorded that the spot was nine miles north of where the company had encamped. A river loop and peninsula fitting Bidwell's descriptions—a mile-and-a-half-long peninsula with a grassy bottom and willows at its tip—exists today about nine miles north of the company's estimated camp location. It can be seen just west of Interstate 80, nine miles northeast of Lovelock.

Bidwell's memoirs show that Bartleson had made another one of his stultifying decisions. He was letting Bidwell lag behind without support and protection. Why would he want to rush forward at such a rapid pace if it resulted in their major, if not exclusive, food source becoming unprotected and vulnerable to Indian depredation? As a critical resource that stood between survival and starvation, why would he put the company at such risk? Bidwell's memoirs contained an explanation: Bartleson and others were thinking that California must not be far away. If they could get to their destination rapidly, they would no longer need to depend on the oxen for food. But Bidwell said that there were others who did not agree, recognizing it was a dangerous idea. And why had no one else in the company insisted on accompanying Bidwell to help him? It is disturbing.

October 6

Because Bidwell had hunkered down with the oxen nine miles north of the company on the night of October 5, the company deservedly spent the night and the next morning without any meat.

Bidwell:

> *W. 6th. Company was out of meat and remained till the oxen came up: several Indians came to Camp, one of whom we hired to Pilot us on.*

Jimmy John:

> *6th. This day we did not travel but stayed at camp and killed an ox for beef.*

Strangely, Bidwell's journal entry for October 6, like his entry for October 5, failed to point out that he was the one driving the oxen. Jimmy John also ignored the issue. But Bidwell's memoirs explained how, after spending the night alone, he set out the next morning to catch up to the company:

> *I got up the next morning [October 6th], hunted the oxen out of the willow thicket and re-packed them. Not having had supper or breakfast, and having to travel nine miles before I overtook the party, perhaps I was not in the best humor. They were waiting, and for very good reason that they could have nothing to eat till I came up with the oxen and one could be killed. I felt badly treated, and let the captain know it plainly; but, much to my surprise, he made no reply, and none of his men said a word. We killed an ox, ate our breakfast.*[6]

Famished, the company killed an ox to satisfy their hunger as soon as Bidwell stumbled into camp. There were now seven oxen left. Bidwell's fuse had been burning for a long time and it had finally reached the gunpowder. Prudence and circumspection be damned. He unflinchingly gave Bartleson a piece of his mind. But there was something quietly cold about Bartleson, and the callous, rock-headed man would not give Bidwell the satisfaction of engaging in a word-scuffle.

Instead of resuming their march that day, the company remained in camp and spent another night there. Dawson's memoirs mentioned that they hired an Indian to act as their pilot and revealed how the appearance of this native would change things:

> *One day [October 6] while we were toiling on, but forebodingly, an Indian wearing a ragged calico shirt came into camp. Thinking that the shirt meant California was close to us, we by signs made him understand that we wished him to pilot us. This he agreed to do.*[7]

It is evident that the wheels were turning in their minds, racing forward with thoughts that the land of milk and honey was not far away. Surely, the calico shirt came from California. It was likely true since Paiutes from the region engaged in trade with California Indians by way of established trails across the Sierra Nevada Mountains.

October 7

The idea that California was close at hand had clearly taken root and it erupted the next morning in a sudden and alarming development.

Bidwell:

> *T. 7th. Capt. Bartleson, having got enough meat to last him a day or two, and supposing he would be able to reach the mountains of California in 2 or 3 days, rushed forward with his own mess, consisting of 8 persons at a rate entirely too fast for the oxen,—leaving the rest to keep up if they could, and if they could not, it was all the same to him. The day was very warm. The Indian Pilot remained with us—the river spread into a high, wide swamp, covered with high cane grass—Indians were numerous—Encamped by the swamp about dark, having come about 25 miles—water bad—no fuel, excepting weeds and dry cane grass which the Indians had cut in large heaps, to procure sugar from the honey dew with which it was covered.*

Jimmy John:

> *7th. Traveled about 22 miles today through deep dust which was both disagreeable and fatiguing. Captain Bartleson and nine others went ahead and left the Company today for California for having the tough animals, being all mules, they thought they could leave us behind and have the first site [sight] of the beautiful plains of California. Our animals are giving out. Left one horse and mule today and threw away some havy [heavy] bagage. We camped tonight at a small Lake near the first Lake that the river emties [empties] into.*

One of Bidwell's memoirs described when Bartleson and his group left the company:

> When nearly ready to go, the Captain and one or two of his mess came to us and said: "Boys, our animals are better than yours, and we always get out of meat before any of the rest of you. Let us have the most of the meat this time, and we will pay you back the next ox we kill." We gladly let them have all they wished. But as soon as they had taken it, and were mounted and ready to start, the captain in a loud voice exclaimed: "Now we have been found fault with long enough, and we are going to California. If you can keep up with us, all right; if you cannot, you may go to H[ell]," and away they started, the captain and eight men. One of the men would not go with the captain; he said, "The captain is wrong, and I will stay with you, boys."[8]

It is unfortunate that the person refusing to go with Bartleson was not identified. Until now, Bidwell had been the only one expressing criticism of Bartleson. But Jimmy John's journal entry corroborated Bidwell's account. Josiah Belden's memoirs confirmed the same: "At the sink of the Humboldt River, a portion of the company who had the best animals, about nine of them, parted from the others, and said they were going to travel faster, and get in [to California] before they became exhausted."[9]

It was no longer Bidwell being left high and dry; it was now everyone who could not keep up. It was a stomach-turning, "every-man-for-himself," disgraceful act that stamped an irrefutable stigma on Bartleson and his friends. There was not much left to admire in them. It is fortunate that no one in the party had become terribly ill, as it is frightening to contemplate how Bartleson would have dealt with anyone he thought was holding things up.

The company's strength was not in the wolf, but in the pack. Bartleson was not astute enough to understand this. Dimwitted self-interest was as far as his brain would think. As we will see, it would get him and his friends into trouble. Deluding themselves that California and its bounteous food supply was only a couple of days away, and confident that the small quantity of meat they took would be enough, they failed to consider what would happen if California was farther than they thought.

Nicholas Dawson was a member of Bartleson's departing group, and through his memoirs, he was the only one in the group to provide a narrative from their point of view. Elias Barnett and Charles

Hopper, Bartleson's friend, hunter, and right-hand man, were part of the group because they were identified by Bidwell and Dawson. The others are speculation, but it seems almost certain that Talbot Green, Robert Rickman, Gwinn Patton, and Grove Cook were part of the departing group because they were in Bartleson's mess. Joseph Chiles and William Overton could also have been in the group as well. If so, this would be ten men.

When the Bartleson party left camp that morning, they continued along the western side of the Humboldt River until they came to where its sluggish waters spread out at the Humboldt Sink. The Sink was where the river finally came to die. With no outlet, the waters simply ponded and evaporated. As a result, it was a hellish, putrid place: sloughs, swamps, marshes, and shallow ponds covered with reeds, bulrushes, and tules growing in a brackish brew of stinking, polluted water that contained a high concentration of dissolved alkali and other salts. In short, it was one of the most damnable places imaginable. The Sink has changed a great deal since 1841 because the volume of water flowing down the Humboldt is profoundly less than it was a hundred and seventy years ago. Due to upstream diversions, the Sink is now mostly a wide, dry alkali bed.

The Bartleson group circled around the southern end of the Sink that day until they came to a channel where excess waters from the Sink overflowed into another lake to the south. Dawson's log recorded that Bartleson and his group traveled thirty miles on October 7. They finally stopped to camp at what Dawson's log described as a "Slough." He was undoubtedly referring to this narrow overflow channel, which is today called the Lower Humboldt Drain.

Bidwell's memoirs recalled that once Bartleson and his friends departed, a group of slightly more than twenty persons was left behind. The cards they had suddenly been dealt were not what they had anticipated. How would they play their hand now? Bidwell wrote that they turned to Benjamin Kelsey. He would be their leader.[10]

When the Kelsey-led group pulled out of camp on the morning of October 7, they must have been in shock. They must have been a pitiable-looking group—dirty, ragged, long hair and beards, with faces weathered like tough leather. Some were mounted on horses, perhaps a few on mules, but most would have been walking. And they were driving seven oxen. Bartleson's sudden abandonment must have stunned them. It could have demoralized them at first. But maybe not. Upon sober reflection, many may have viewed Bartleson's irksome departure as fortuitous—addition by subtraction. After all, they now had nine or ten fewer mouths to feed. It seems unlikely that Bidwell would have shed any tears. Indeed, he may have rejoiced. There were probably others as well who breathed a sigh of relief at being liberated from that hard-boiled old man. He would no longer be around to bedevil them.

Even if they had wanted to, the Kelsey-led group, with their slow-moving oxen, could not catch up to Bartleson's. In one of his memoirs, Bidwell explained that they intended to follow the Bartleson tracks because they respected Charles Hopper as a skilled mountaineer: "All had confidence in his [Hopper's] ability to find the best route through the mountains. As long as we could—about one day—we followed their [Bartleson party's] tracks."[11]

After making only twenty-two to twenty-five miles, they stopped to camp along the western fringe of the swampy Sink and about five miles northeast of the "Slough" where Bartleson's group had stopped to camp the night before.

The Bartleson camp on October 7 at the overflow slough was about three miles south of a point on Interstate 80 that is two and a half miles northeast of its intersection with Highway 95. The Kelsey camp, on the other hand, was just east of the Interstate, and five miles northeast of its intersection with Highway 95.

In the future, many emigrants and Gold Rushers would leave the Sink near where the Kelsey group camped on October 7, and head west across a waterless forty-mile stretch that became known as the Forty-Mile Desert. This route pretty much matches the path of Interstate 80 between the Sink and Fernley, Nevada. It was a punishing, animal-killing expanse that had to be crossed to reach the Truckee River. From there, the parties would ascend the Truckee River until they eventually reached Donner Pass. This route was first pioneered in 1844 by Caleb Greenwood leading the Stephens-Murphy party to California.

October 8

Dawson's memoirs explained that he and his Bartleson party left the slough and continued south on the morning of October 8:

> Under his guidance we left the river [Humboldt/overflow slough] the next morning [October 8], and traveled all day in a southeast direction,

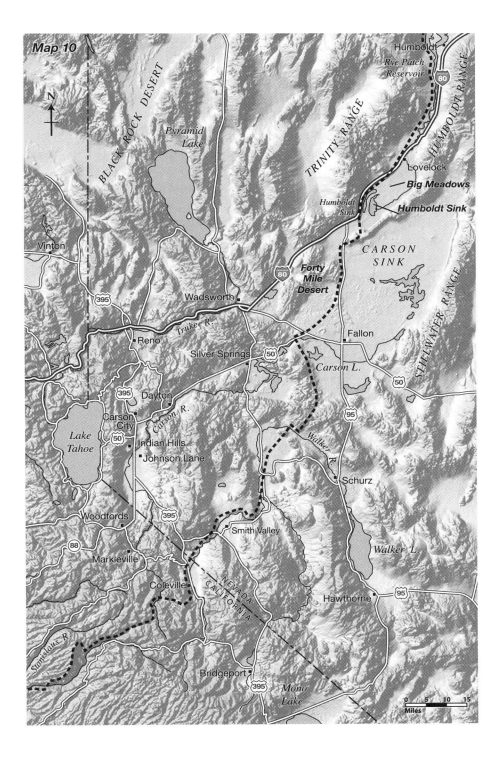

> over a sandy desert. At night we struck a lake on the bank of which was an Indian village. The Indians supplied us with fish, roasted whole, which we gladly ate without criticizing the method of cooking.[12]

Dawson was referring to an Indian guiding them, but it may not have been the calico-shirted one, because Bidwell seemed to be referring to him when he reported in his journal on October 7 that "the Indian Pilot remained with us." Following their Indian guide, the Bartleson group moved west along the northerly side of a long, barren ridge, and then turned south and continued across a flat plain of alkali and salts. About eight miles from where they left camp, they crossed another overflow channel that drained excess water from the overflow lake on the west to a much larger lake of about twenty miles in diameter to the east. They then trudged across a stretch of deep, stifling sand, including sand dunes and sand hills. By evening they came in contact with a western arm of this larger lake. The lake was fed not only by overflows from the Humboldt River, but also by the overflows from the Carson River coming down from the Sierra Nevada Range. After traveling twenty-five arduous miles, according to Dawson, his Bartleson group finally stopped to camp near an Indian village on the shores of this large lake. The Indians would have been Paiutes.

One can retrace much of Bartleson's path on October 8 by following Highway 95 where it heads south from Interstate 80. The precise location of the Bartleson camp is difficult to establish since the lake has largely disappeared due to heavy diversions of Carson River water for farming and municipal uses. The camp would have been close to the lake's former shore, about a mile east of Highway 95, and about eight miles north of its intersection with Highway 50 in Fallon, Nevada.

IN THE MEANTIME, the Kelsey group, consisting of about twenty-three men, one woman, and one child, traveled only a short distance on October 8.

Bidwell:

> F. 8th. The Swamp was clouded with wild Geese, ducks &c., which rose from its surface at the report of our guns. We traveled about 6 miles and stopped to kill a couple of oxen that were unable to travel.

Jimmy John:

> 8th. We traveled but about 4 miles today for we hired an Indian to guide who told us that we would have to camp here or get to no other watering place today.

According to Bidwell, they killed "a couple of oxen that were unable to travel." If his term "a couple" meant two, then the group would now have been down to five.

They only traveled between four and six miles that day along the shores of the Sink because of their Indian guide advising them of a long, waterless stretch ahead. Therefore, their camp was probably at the same overflow slough where the Bartleson party had camped the night before. This left them about twenty-five miles behind Bartleson.

October 9

Dawson's memoirs continued to describe the progress of his Bartleson party:

> The next day [October 9] we passed another lake having a considerable stream [Carson River] emptying into it. There was a plain trail, which we were following, and we hoped it would lead to a pass in the mountains that still confronted us on the west. After fording the stream [Carson River] that flowed into this lake some ten or twelve of us who had no pack animals to look after went ahead on the trail, expecting the others, with the pilot, to follow. Crossing a ridge we came in sight of another lake [Carson Lake] and went onto it, intending to await there the rest of the crowd. They never came. We concluded they must have gone up the river.[13]

Leaving the Indian village on the edge of the lake and continuing south, Bartleson and his companions appeared to have reached the Carson River, a robust river carrying cold, pure water from the Sierra Nevada Range. After fording the river and ascending a ridge, they could see another lake to the southeast, which was undoubtedly Carson Lake. In those days, the Carson River split, with some of its waters flowing northeast into the large lake they had camped beside the night before, and with the rest flowing into Carson Lake. It sounded as if the Bartleson group camped somewhere beside the western shore of Carson Lake on the evening of October 9.

By October 9, Bartleson and his companions had been traveling on their own for three days. Yet, they had not yet made it to the land of milk and honey. They had probably run out of their two- to three-day supply of meat and were hungry. Bartleson had misjudged matters again. They must have decided they needed to find their former travel mates—the ones with the oxen. Dawson makes it sound as if they expected their recently abandoned trail mates to greet them with warm smiles and "all-is-forgiven" embraces.

Dawson's memoirs were written in 1901, sixty years later, and he appeared to be trying to create the impression that they were simply traveling ahead of the Kelsey group, which they expected would catch up to them. That is a tough pill to swallow. Not only does it conflict with the narratives of Bidwell, Jimmy John, and Josiah Belden, but Dawson's log betrays his spurious claim. From October 7 through October 9, he recorded that his Bartleson party traveled between fifteen and thirty miles each day, hardly a pace that would allow the slow Kelsey party to catch up. What Bartleson and his friends did was morally indefensible, and it explains why Dawson was loath to admit it. Years later, he still lacked the character to own up to what really happened.

ON THE MORNING of October 9, the Kelsey party broke camp early in the morning near the overflow slough on the south end of the Sink, and headed south.

Bidwell:

> S. 9th. Crossed Mary's river [the overflow slough] where it led from the Swamp into a Lake beyond—our Pilot led us South on the trail of Capt. B—crossed a plain which is covered with water the greater part of the year—then came into sand hills, among which traveling was very laborious. Saw to the W. of us a Lake, presenting a sheet of water 20 or 30 miles in extent. Encamped by another swamp, in which the water was very nauseous. Distance 28 miles. Large numbers of Indians lived about this place, but few (50 or 60 visited our camp).

Jimmy John:

> 9th. Our guide made signs that we must start early or we could not get to water so we made an early start. Crosed the outlet of the first Lake and traveled about 30 miles in a south course and came to another small Lake.

Here we camped. There are a great many Indians at these lakes. They appear to be friendly. One of the Company lost a mule yesterday and the Indian found it and brought him to us today. We hired an Indian to guide us across the California mountains. We understood by his signs that we could [get] over 3 days from the time we should get to the foot of it.

When the Kelsey party left their camp that morning, they left the Humboldt Sink behind. Jimmy John recorded how they had just hired an Indian to guide them across the "California mountains." This appears to have been a second guide, one to help the calico-shirted one. Considering how clumsy and ambiguous sign language was, one cannot help wondering how well they could understand each other. With so many smaller mountain ranges intervening between them and the Sierra Nevada Range, how could they be sure the Indians understood what they meant by the term "California mountains," or how far they were expected to lead them?

The country south of the Sink across which both parties had trudged was abject desolation, no trees, no grass, just a plain of powdery alkali and widely scattered sage. The only water was the occasional toxic pool. In their weakened condition, it was a wonder the Kelsey party's animals survived the day.

The lake to the west that Bidwell mentioned was probably the overflow lake south of the Sink. Into this region the Humboldt, Truckee, Carson, and Walker rivers all flowed into a large, low area from which there was no outlet. The landscape has changed a great deal since then. A number of these lakes and marshlands are now dry, flat plains of white salt and alkali due to modern-day dams, reservoirs, and upstream water diversions.

According to Bidwell's memoirs, the Kelsey group eventually lost Bartleson's tracks: "We followed their trail for two or three days, but after they crossed over to the south side of the Humboldt and turned south we came into a sandy waste where the wind had entirely obliterated their tracks. We were then thrown entirely on our own resources."[14]

Judging by the diarists' descriptions and distances, the Kelsey-led party appeared to have camped on October 9 on the swampy shore of the same large lake and near the same Indian village where Bartleson had camped the night before, namely about one mile east of Highway 95 and eight miles north of its intersection with Highway 50 in Fallon.

Bidwell described the Indians as friendly. This was different from what many emigrants and Gold Rushers would experience in the years to come. They commonly complained that the Indians, whom they called "Diggers," killed, wounded, or stole their livestock.

In one of his memoirs, Bidwell described a scene when his group camped near the large lake: "In the edges of the water the tule was covered with honeydew to an extent that enabled the Indians to gather it in large quantities. They made it into balls about the size of ones fist and we bought and ate considerable of it. When we afterwards saw them gathering it, we saw that the Indians collected the insects that covered the honeydew as well and formed the whole into the ball."[15] The route that the Bartleson and Kelsey groups both took south from the Sink to reach the Carson River closely matched the one taken by emigrants and Gold Rushers who would someday follow the Carson River into the Sierra Nevada Mountains and over what would become known as Carson Pass. It proved to be a popular, and some said easier, alternative to the Truckee River–Donner Pass route. The Carson Pass route went south of the Humboldt Sink, closely following the route of present-day Highway 95 between its intersection with Interstate 80 and its intersection with Highway 50 in Fallon, Nevada.

October 10

Bidwell:

> [Sunday, 10th] Crossed Mary's river—it was here running E leading from the Lake which we saw to the W of us yesterday, into the swamp by which we staid last night. Our course to day was S W. Distance 15 miles—encamped upon the Lake.

Jimmy John:

> 10th. We traveled about 17 miles today and camped on the bank of the middle Lake for there are three Lakes which drain Mary's river. There are a great many kind of fowls here.

The Kelsey party left their camp on the shores of the large lake on the morning of October 10 and headed southwest. Bidwell and Jimmy John were clearly ignorant of the geography of the area, both making the mistake of thinking that the river they crossed that day was the Mary's (Humboldt) River. Given the distance and direction they traveled, it is clear that they had crossed the east-flowing Carson River a few miles west of today's Fallon, then proceeded south until they came to Carson Lake, one of the lakes created by the Carson River. Indeed, Bidwell's memoirs later confirmed that they had crossed the Carson River and camped at Carson Lake.[16] Due to upstream usage of Carson River water, Carson Lake is dramatically smaller today. They probably camped near the lake's western shore, which, in those days, would have been about eight miles further west of where it is today. It would have been close to where Bartleson and his companions had camped the night before.

The probable vicinity of the Bidwell party's camp on the evening of October 10 is about seven miles west of Hwy 95 and about seven miles south of Highways 95's intersection with Highway 50 in Fallon. The area where they camped is part of the Fallon Naval Air Station and is off-limits to the public.

WHEN THE BARTLESON GROUP stirred on the morning of October 10 at their Carson Lake camp, they were approximately fifteen miles south of where the Kelsey party had camped the night before. To the west was a range of low mountains now called the Dead Camel Mountains. Dawson's memoirs continued:

> [10th] In front the mountains jutted up against the lake. We thought we would explore a little, to see if we could find a road leading to the said-to-be pass. Finding no road and no signs of a pass, we decided to bear towards the river, hoping to strike the trail of the rest of the company. In the meantime, Hopper had seen some deer signs; so we camped, and sure enough, Hopper soon killed and brought in a black-tailed deer. We made short work of eating him all up. We also found some baskets of grass seed hidden away by Indians. We confiscated them, poured the seed into the water we had boiled the deer in, and made a delicious soup. While we were devouring the deer, I noticed [Elias] Barnett cramming bones into his pocket.[17]

The Bartleson party was hungry. They were surely regretting their decision to leave the oxen behind. Dawson said they explored the mountains to their west, suggesting that they no longer had an Indian guide. It would not have been out of character for Bartleson to dismiss the Indian, foolishly thinking that he no longer needed one.

Because Dawson expressed his belief that the Kelsey group had "gone up the river," he explained that they headed toward "the river, hoping to strike the trail of the rest of the company." His log recorded that they traveled twenty-five miles on October 10, and while the two parties may have been in close proximity at some point that day, they obviously missed each other.

October 11

Dawson's memoirs continued to describe the difficulties of his desperately hungry party:

> *Traveling on the next day [October 11] we finally struck the [Carson] river. On the opposite side was a bunch of Indians preparing to leave in haste. By shaking a white rag, we induced them to remain until we approached, for we had nothing left to eat, and thought they might have something we could barter out of them. Although they were frightened at first, we soon gained their good will, and having smoked the pipe of peace with them, let them know by signs our wishes. They produced their stock of trade—a gallon or two of pinion nuts. After tasting these we agreed to take them all, swapping butcher knives for them. We and the Indians then parted, very good friends, each thinking he had the best of the bargain. We now divided the nuts by measure; and I remember that I cogitated for some time—should I make one bait of mine, or dribble them out? I decided on the latter course, and dropped them into my pocket; but they were delicious.*[18]

Dawson's log reported that they struck the river on October 11. Besides trading with the local Indians for food, they waited for the Kelsey party to appear. His log reported that they camped that night on "Unknown R," which undoubtedly was the Carson River. They were probably just west of Fallon, near where they had crossed the river on October 9.

Bidwell:

> *M. 11th. Left the Lake this morning, going into the mountains on a S W course: to day, we left the trail of Capt. B and having traveled 19 miles, arrived on a stream which flowed rapidly, and afforded more water than Mary's river. We thought now, without doubt, that we were safe on the waters of the St. Joaquin (pronounced St. Wawkeen) according to*

> Marsh's letter. Here grew willows, balm gilead, and a few cotton woods. The course of the stream as far as we could see was S,—but knew not how soon it might take a turn here in the Mountains.

Jimmy John:

> 11th. We traveled about 20 miles today, a south course in the mountains, and came to a stream which some supposed to be the head waters of the Sacrimenta [Sacramento] but it seemed to run the [w]rong course. Here we encamped for the night and killed a beef. This stream is about 40 yds wide here and affords good clear water and some timber known by the name of Balm of Gilead, and a pine here and there.

Bidwell's memoirs explained that upon leaving their camp on the western shore of Carson Lake on October 11, "we endeavored to make our course more westerly, for we knew the Pacific Ocean lay to the west."[19] According to his journal, they headed southwest that morning and "left the trail of Capt. B." They had lost Bartleson's tracks after leaving the Humboldt Sink on October 9. They must have picked their tracks up again. Yet, they were willing to leave the Bartleson tracks at Carson Lake, suggesting that they had no desire to rejoin their former trail mates. Instead, they would follow their Indian guides, who seemed to know where they were going. Jimmy John reported that they killed another ox, meaning that they were down to only four.

Heading southwest from the shores of Carson Lake, they crossed some low mountains. After about ten miles they descended onto a sagebrush-covered plain and moved across it until they struck a hundred-foot-wide river with a swift current of fresh, clear water. Thinking it was the San Joaquin or Sacramento River, some must have believed they were now in California. Because the river ran south, Jimmy John expressed skepticism. Frémont would later name it the Walker River, after Joseph Walker.

To think that the Walker River was the San Joaquin or Sacramento in California shows an ignorance of the geography. Inaccurate maps continued to fill the travelers' minds with false ideas, and they were trying to reconcile these false ideas with what they were experiencing. Years later, Bidwell's memoirs confirmed what they had encountered: "Leaving the Sink of the Humboldt, we crossed a considerable stream which must have been Carson River, and came to another stream which must have been the Walker River."[20]

They did not know it, but the Sierra Nevada Mountains were still sixty miles to the west. A number of smaller mountain ranges lay in between, so the distant Sierras were still blocked from view. Even if they could have seen them through the haze, they were so far away that these mountains would not have appeared measurably different from other mountain ranges they had seen from a distance in recent months. The group would have to get much closer before their scale and magnitude would become evident.

The location of the Kelsey camp on October 11 is remote. In order to visit, one should take Highway 95A north from Yerrington, Nevada, and go twelve miles to a challenging gravel road called Julian Lane. Take Julian Lane, which follows the Walker River, and head east and then south about sixteen miles to the approximate location of their camp along the river.

October 12

The only information about the starving Bartleson party on October 12 came from Dawson's log, in which he recorded that they had traveled fifteen miles that day and spent the night at a "Mountain" camp. Discussion of the Bartleson group's travels will be deferred until a few days later, when more information about them is disclosed.

Bidwell:

> T. 12th. Traveled about 4 miles up stream, and encamped,— understanding our Indian (having hired another Pilot) that it would be a long day's travel to water, after leaving the Creek.

Jimmy John:

> 12th. Today we only traveled 4 miles for our Indian guide told us that we could not get water without a hard day[s] travel and we camped on the bank of the creek. We lay on last night 4 miles above this river [It] runs eastward.

The diarists reported that on October 12 they moved north up the Walker River only four miles. Because the river made a great bend upstream to the north, they would take a shortcut across the bend. The cutoff would be waterless for many miles, until they struck the river again to the west. This is why their guide advised that it was best to spend the night on the river. Besides, their jaded animals could use some extra rest and grazing time.

The location of their camp would have been next to the river, west of Julian Lane and about twelve miles southeast of where it leaves Highway 95A.

October 13

Bidwell:

> W. 13th. Traveled about 13 miles and only crossed a bend of the river, at this place it run due North, day was hot, the creek had dwindled to half its first size.

Jimmy John:

> 13th. Today we traveled about 25 miles in a southwest course. Crosed the creek that we camped on the last two nights at the foot of a high mountain where we encamped this evening.

The journal entries of the two diarists had been very brief the last couple of days, perhaps indicating fatigue. Breaking camp the next morning, the Kelsey party crossed and left the river. They followed their guide west through an opening in the hills and into the Mason Valley. The Indian trail they followed probably traveled southwest and along the eastern fringe of the valley to avoid the marshes and sloughs created by the various branches of the Walker River winding through the valley. According to Jimmy John's estimate, they struck the Walker River again on the far side of the valley after twenty-five miles of travel. Bidwell estimated the distance at thirteen miles, but that was likely a transcription error. Crossing the north-flowing river there, they ended the day by camping at the base of a "high mountain." This was undoubtedly Mount Wilson, since it is almost seven thousand feet high and towers about two thousand feet above the valley floor.

Their camp on the night of October 13 was about one and a half miles northeast of where Highways 339 and 208 merge, and about nine miles south of Yerington, Nevada.

October 14

Bidwell:

> T. 14th. This morning we saw at a distance Capt. B. with his 7 men, coming in a direction towards us, but we made no halt, ascended the stream about 20 miles, the Mountains, continued to increase in height.

Jimmy John:

> 14th. This day we traveled about 20 miles in a southwest course. Crosed two high ridges and camped near the California mountains.

A few miles southwest of their camp, the Walker River cut through a ridge of high hills and emerged from Wilson Canyon. The bottom of the gorge was narrow and hemmed in by steep walls. It was also congested with large rocks and dense vegetation, making traveling through it virtually impossible. Since the party had crossed to the west side of the river the day before, it seems likely that they followed an Indian footpath that scaled the high ridge just north of the canyon. Bidwell's report of seeing the Bartleson party in the distance supports the notion that they saw them from the top of the ridge. They must have seen their dust to the northeast, the direction from which they had come. Assuming the air was clear, they may have been able to see as much as fifteen miles distant, perhaps more. Bidwell's entry did not suggest any uncertainty; he was certain it was Bartleson. It would not have been local Indians, who traveled on foot and had no horses. Indians would not have stirred up clouds of dust as mules would. The Bartleson party was evidently following the tracks laid down by the Kelsey group. What a shock it must have been. The "fast-moving" Bartleson troop was supposed to be ahead of them, not behind. Surely, the Kelsey party would wait. But Bidwell reported that they "made no halt." Why wait for those who would not wait for you?

Looking west from the ridge, the Kelsey party should have had their first meaningful view of the eastern front of the Sierra Nevada Range about thirty miles west. But at that distance, the size of those mountains would not be fully appreciated. First, however, they had to cross Smith Valley ahead of them and then move beyond the Wellington Hills on the far side of the valley.

Descending off the ridge, the Kelsey party continued following their Indian guide, marching west across Smith Valley. Parched and arid, it was vegetated only by sparse sagebrush. On the west side of the valley, the Walker River cut through the Wellington Hills by way of another gorge. Called Hoye Canyon today, it was much like Wilson Canyon, narrow and choked with rocks and vegetation. As Jimmy John reported, they crossed over the hills, likely to the north of the canyon. Trudging single file on horse, mule, and foot, they descended off the hills to the river floor west of the canyon and where the bottom widened out into a wide meadow. After traveling twenty miles that day they pitched camp in the meadow along the river. The Sierra Nevada Range was now only five miles ahead. For the first time, there were no intervening mountains to conceal or diminish this massive wall that rose up ahead.

The Kelsey camp on October 14 was in the river bottom about two miles south of today's Highway 208, and about four miles east of its intersection with Highway 395.

October 15

October 15 must have been a sobering day. As the party continued to creep up the Walker River through what is now called Antelope Valley, the size and steepness of the Sierra Nevada Mountain Range became alarmingly more evident. The party had heard about the "California mountains," probably understanding that they would be higher and larger than any they had previously encountered. What towered in front of them must have been terribly different from what they had imagined. They were monstrous, unlike anything they had seen before. Stretching north and south as far as the eye could see, and with no low spot evident, they appeared to be a solid, unbreachable wall, impervious to penetration. How could the party not have been overwhelmed by a profound feeling of despair?

Bidwell:

> F. 15th. Advanced up stream about 12 miles, and arrived at the base of very high mountains, the creek had become a small spring branch, and it took its rise at no great distance in the mountains. But we saw plainly, that it was impossible to progress farther without scaling the Mtns., and our Indian Guides said, they knew no further.

Jimmy John:

> 15th. Traveled about 10 miles in a south course today up the creek and encamped at the foot of the California mountains. The mountains here are partly covered with fine timber.

For many years, the path the expedition took across the Sierra Nevada Mountains was a mystery because of the complexity of the terrain and the diarists' inability to name the various creeks, rivers, canyons, flats, ridges, and other features they encountered. In recent years, three significant trail historians wrestled with the subject: William Paden in 1940, David H. Johnson in 1998, and Michael J. Gillis also in 1998. They studied the journal entries, read the memoirs, looked at maps, and walked the landscape. The expedition's way forward from here is based on the collective assessments and conclusions of these historians. While they do not agree in every particular, they do agree for the most part on a route that is consistent with the diarists' descriptions and the geographic features.[21]

One of the historians thought that the party left the Walker River near here and traveled up Slinkard Creek on October 15, stopping to camp at the upper end of the Slinkard Valley at the end of the day. After traveling three miles west on Highway 89, after it leaves Highway 395 four and a half miles north of the tiny community of Coleville, California, one can see Slinkard Valley stretch out to the south. The other two historians more persuasively think that the party continued further south along the Walker River. The party would then begin their trans-Sierra crossing by ascending onto an elevated bench called the Little Antelope Valley just above the river. The comments of the two diarists suggest that they camped beside the river, just below the Little Antelope Valley. Their camp would be just to the east of Highway 395, about two miles south of Coleville and two miles north of the tiny community of Walker, California.

Chapter 15

Struggling over the Sierra Nevada Mountains

OCTOBER 16 TO 31, 1841

October 16

October 16 would be a day of misgivings and discouragement. A crucial decision would need to be made. While most of the Kelsey party stayed in camp that morning, a few men were sent forward to scale the heights to see if they could discover a pass.

Bidwell:

> S. 16th. This morning 4 or 5 men started to ascend several of the high peaks, to ascertain if it was possible to pass the mountains. Just as they were going to start Capt. B. [Bartleson] came up, he was in rather a hungry condition, and had been travelling several days without provision, excepting a few nuts which they had purchased from the Indians and which they had eaten on a very small allowance. We killed yesterday the best ox we had. This we shared freely with them. There were now but 3 oxen left and they were very poor. But there was no time to loose. The explorers returned & reported that they thought it almost an impracticability to scale the mountains, which continued to increase in height as far as they could see. This evening the Company was convened for the purpose of deciding by vote whether we would go back to the Lake and take a path which we saw leading to the N.W., or, to undertake to climb the mountains. We had no more provision than would last us to the Lake,—nearly all were unanimous against turning back. I should have mentioned that our Indian Pilots last night absconded. This stream I shall call Balm river: there being many Balm Gilead trees upon it. (It is not laid down on any map.)

Jimmy John:

> 16th. Today we did not travel but lay by to rest our animals. The men that left us on the 7th of this month came to us this morning following our trail. They followed the stream that we thought to be the Sacrimenta [Sacramento] to its mouth where it empties into a Lake having no outlet. They said that they suffered much for want of food, allowing themselves on[ly] one meal a day. Our Indian pilot left us last night and left us in a bad condition here. We are nearly surrounded by high mountains on all sides. We see no prospect of getting over the mountains. They are very high and the top covered [with] snow and we have but 3 more cattle to live on and they are poor and consequently we have to live on small allowance or starve.

The diarists agreed that they only had three oxen left on October 16. In a later journal entry, Bidwell will report that when they had arrived at the foot of the Sierra mountains they had used up their scant flour supply. Therefore, it would be meat only from here on.

Josiah Belden's memoirs described the arrival of Bartleson and his colleagues:

> In looking back we saw the dust rising on the trail we had followed the day before, and we waited to see what it was, and presently we saw the nine men who left us several days before with the idea of going ahead, coming up on our trail, very hungry and forlorn looking. We had a quarter of beef from the last animal we had killed, and gave them something to eat. They had made a kind of circle, and reached our camp, having struck our trail.[1]

Years later, Bidwell's memoirs provided a surprising twist:

> [L]ooking to the east, something was discovered moving in the distance. At first we supposed it to be Indians but our curiosity grew as we noticed their slow advance. Finally we discovered horses, but still we could not account for the continued halting of the party when it was seen plainly that they were men with animals, and every now and then one of the men would sit down as if to rest. To cut the story short, they proved to be the party who had left us nine days before in such haste to get to California. We learned from them that they had continued further south after passing the sink of the Humboldt River and came to a considerable lake, probably what is now known

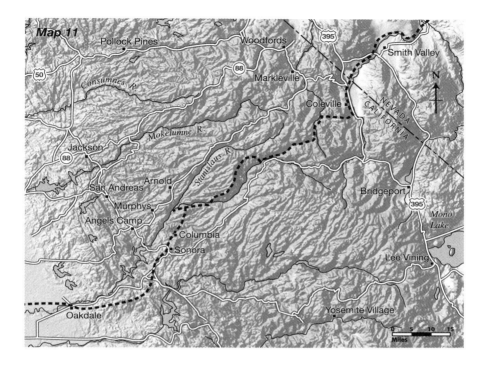

as Walker Lake. Having obtained from the Indians quantities of pine nuts and fresh fish, they had started west for the mountains. Fresh fish had given them all the dysentery, and they were so weak they could hardly stand. I well remember Captain Bartleson's exclamation as he sat eating what we had cooked for him. "Boys! If I ever get back to Missouri, I will never leave there again. Why I would be glad to eat from the same trough with my dogs there."[2]

Bidwell's journal reported that from atop the ridge on October 14 they had seen Bartleson's party at a distance advancing toward them. His journal entry for October 16 reported that "Capt. B. came up." There was no hint of surprise; Bidwell knew they were coming. Why, therefore, did his memoir years later fail to mention seeing them on October 14? And why did he express uncertainty as to who was approaching on October 16? His memory had either dimmed a great deal, or he was too embarrassed to confess that they had decided to not wait for the Bartleson party despite knowing that they were coming.

Bidwell's memoirs continued:

> *We were glad to see them although they had deserted us. We ran out to meet them and shook hands, and put our frying-pans on and gave them the best supper we could. Captain Bartleson, who when we started from Missouri was a portly man, was reduced to half his former girth. . . . He seemed to be heartily sick of his late experience, but that did not prevent him from leaving us twice after that.*[3]

Bidwell's account that Bartleson and his friends were welcomed in a spirit of hospitality and forgiveness is difficult to imagine. If they did, the Kelsey group was uncommonly magnanimous. Besides, the return of the Bartleson party meant that there would be nine more mouths with whom to share their few remaining oxen. If Bidwell could be dishonest about being surprised at their approach, was he also dishonest about the Kelsey group welcoming them like prodigal sons? It seems that a cool and tense reunion would have been more likely. In any event, the beaten-down and humiliated Bartleson had to swallow his pride, because he desperately needed the succor of the Kelsey party.

The foregoing sources reveal that after leaving the Carson River, Bartleson and his companions traveled south until they came to where the Walker River flowed into Walker Lake. Seeing no outlet in the lake, they realized they were not following California's Sacramento River. Turning around, they must have retraced their steps up the Walker River until they eventually came across the Kelsey tracks near the river. Following them, the starving group had finally managed to catch up.

Both diarists mentioned the Indian guides having left them the night before. Bidwell used the word "absconded," while Jimmy John complained that they "left us in a bad condition." Their comments suggest that the Indians had reneged on their agreement to lead them over the mountains although Bidwell's entry for the previous day had reported that the guides claimed "they knew no further." But this may have been untrue. It is possible that the Indians did know of a way, but feared the risk of getting trapped by an alpine snowstorm this late in the year. They may have been unwilling to become victims of such foolishness.

It was prudent for the Kelsey group to send men into the mountains to look for a pass. Leaving their camp beside the Walker River, the scouts likely entered the Little Antelope Valley just to the east of their camp, generally following the path of Mill Canyon Road, where it heads west from Highway 395 about two miles south of Coleville. They would have navigated up Mill Canyon at the valley's western end until they reached Rodriquez Flat. The scouts were now five miles from camp and about three thousand feet higher in elevation. They probably ascended a ridge at the northwest end of the Flat. Now at over eighty-six hundred feet, they would have faced a jaw-dropping view. The sight must have hit them like a ton of bricks. It was terrifying. They were looking at a mountain range unlike any they had encountered before. Range upon range, peak after peak, and ridge after ridge stretched as far as the eye could see. They could see peaks ten miles west of them that were over ten thousand feet high. It was time to return and report their disheartening news. One of the scouts was Josiah Belden. His memoirs recalled what they told the company when they returned:

> [On October 16] two others and myself left the party, and went up to some of the higher peaks of the mountains to explore and see if we could find any place where we could cross. We returned and reported that we could see no opening in the mountains, that so far as we could see, the mountains seemed to be rather higher beyond than lower, and there was no appearance of any end or termination of them, and very little chance to get through. There was a vote taken in the company to determine whether we should go on and try to get across the mountains, or turn back and try to reach Ft. Hall. I think we had only one majority for going ahead. Although it looked discouraging on the mountains, my idea was that we should perish in trying to get back to Fort Hall, and we had better take our chances of getting across the mountains. So we decided to travel on.[4]

Belden and his fellow scouts had not sugarcoated what they saw. It is understandable that many in the company were instantly demoralized. Some lobbied for turning around and retreating to Fort Hall. Bidwell's entry suggests that they considered a more moderate option—that of returning to Carson Lake and then heading northwest. The party debated these options but, upon sober reflection, they understood that neither was a good one. They had no choice but to press on. Belden recalled that their vote to proceed won by a slim majority, while Bidwell's journal entry claimed that it was nearly unanimous.

When the sun set on the company on October 16, they sat around their fires and commiserated over what seemed like a dismal future. Perhaps some in the Kelsey party ambled over to the Bartleson mess and sat down, asked questions, swapped stories, and mended fences. But it seems likely that others would have still harbored bitter grudges about what the Bartleson group had done. It was not the sort of thing that could easily be forgotten or forgiven.

October 17

On the morning of October 17, the reunited company would now begin the last leg of their momentous journey. Their food supply was all but exhausted and their last oxen were little more than walking skeletons. With the scouting reports echoing in their minds, they must have quailed at what lay ahead. Although they had no information about how high or wide the mountains were or how long it would take to cross them, it was obvious that they had to get across quickly before they starved to death or a deadly snowstorm rolled in. If there was one desire that bound the group, it was the desire to survive. Surely, most must have understood the need to pull together as a team. Bartleson's stupid, selfish gambit should have demonstrated what recklessness and selfishness could lead to.

Bidwell:

> S. 17th. This morning we set forth into the rolling mountains, in many places it was so steep that all were obliged to take it on foot. Part of the day we travelled through vallies between Peaks, where the way was quite level—passed down and up thro' forests of pine, fir, cedar &c.; many of the pines were 12 ft. in diameter and no less than 200 ft. high,—encamped on the side of the mountain, so elevated that ice remained all day in the streams—but we had not yet arrived at the summit. Killed another ox this evening—made 12 miles.

Jimmy John:

> 17th. This morning we set out to try to get over the mountains. We traveled up a deep valley on a southwest course and through thick forests of timber, over high ridges and small streams of pure water rushing down the mountain, roaring and foaming over the rocks. These forests and fine streams of water have to us a beautiful appearance after traveling so long through an allmost entire Desert. We seen some Indians today and

Modern view of October 15 camp on Walker River, with the Sierras to the west of camp. Line shows route that the party took from camp into Little Antelope Valley and then up Mill Canyon to Rodriguez Flat. Author's photograph.

traded with them for some venison. We traveled about 16 miles today and camped in the mountain on a small brook that ran from the snow peaks. There are thick forests of pines near our camp of which has a bark resembling beach which is smoothe and white. The wood is very heavy and full of pitch. The air is getting cool as we ascend the mountain.

West of camp, they soon encountered slopes too steep to ride, forcing them to climb on foot while leading their horses and mules. The effort was exhausting, and their animals were in a weakened state. They had to periodically stop to catch their breath and rest. By the time they reached Rodriguez Flat, they had ascended three thousand feet in a distance of only four miles. To the east, they could see thirty, perhaps fifty, miles through the clean air. To the west, they saw what their scouts had seen the day before—a horrifying panorama of what seemed to be endless mountains. They did indeed seem impossible to cross.

At the western end of the Flat they found a ravine heading downward. They followed it down to tiny Snodgrass Creek and then followed the creek in a northwardly direction, carefully picking their way between and around boulders and fallen trees until they came to where Snodgrass Creek joined Silver King Creek. They continued north along Silver King Creek for about four miles, threading between two high ridges on either side until they came to where the creek flowed into the Silver King Valley. Here, they entered a beautiful meadow. From the west, the East Fork of the Carson River rushed out of a canyon opening on their left and merged with Silver King Creek. The company then made a critical call. If they had followed the East Fork downstream far enough, it would have eventually led them right back to where they had crossed the Carson River on October 9.

Fortunately, the company made a left turn instead and followed the East Fork upstream. Those with intelligence and common sense realized that they had seen higher peaks and ridges west of Rodriguez Flat. They needed to ascend, not descend. If they were to surmount those heights to the west, they had to gain a great deal of elevation. Since the East Fork Canyon led west and ascended, this was the way to go.

When they started up the East Fork Canyon, they had already traveled ten miles that day. The canyon floor was a little over six thousand feet in elevation, so they had descended about two thousand feet since leaving Rodriguez Flat. The bottom of the canyon was fairly flat and traveling was easy. A determined procession of those on horseback and mules, followed by men on foot and three oxen, moved up the canyon as it turned south and then west. Somewhere in the procession, we must not forget, was the young wife, Nancy Kelsey, riding her horse and holding her infant daughter in her arms.

They had entered an entirely new world. Gone were the barren deserts and scrubby sagebrush through which they had pushed the last three months. The drab, colorless hues of the desert had given way to arresting visuals—the vibrant, saturated hues of the forest. Fragrant, refreshing scents of pine, cedar, and fir now perfumed the crisp air, a welcome respite from the turpentine smell of sagebrush that had dogged their senses for so long. They were tired, but not too tired to gaze upon the majesty of the scenery.

As they made their way up the winding canyon, between lofty walls of almost perpendicular granite, they traveled across alpine meadows and through ancient groves of gigantic trees towering to unbelievable heights. One will not see these trees today, as the area was heavily logged in the 1870s to supply timber to shore up miles of underground Comstock mineshafts beneath Virginia City. The biggest trees of today are large, but the oldest are only about a hundred and fifty years old, not nearly as large as the ancient ones this expedition had the good fortune to gaze upon.

The canyon turned south again and led through the spacious Dumonts Meadow. Shortly after making it through the meadow, the company came to where the East Fork Canyon narrowed. They encountered a small brook coming out of a smaller canyon, now called Golden Canyon, that opened on the right. The company decided to enter it, probably because it headed west. They had to carefully ascend a slippery slope of almost bare granite in places in order to climb into the canyon. The riders probably dismounted so they could lead their animals up the rocky face and make sure they did not lose their footing. They headed up the canyon, and then stopped to camp beside the brook on the "side of the mountain," as Bidwell described it. Bidwell thought they had traveled twelve miles. Jimmy John thought it was sixteen, while Dawson's log recorded fifteen. It was more like seventeen. The disparity in estimates is understandable because the terrain interferes with distant views. The scale of everything is so large that it distorts a proper sense of distance. They must have been terribly fatigued after a long day of steep climbs and descents and traveling many miles at high altitude. They had penetrated deep into the Sierras and should have felt good about their first day's efforts. Nancy Kelsey recalled that it was her eighteenth birthday on the day they "camped on the summit."[5]

That night, in their mountainside camp, they killed an ox and dried its meat. They were now left with two. Bidwell's memoirs:

> *At this time [the afternoon of October 17] we had but two oxen left, and we had just killed the best of these and were drying meat preparatory to scaling the mountains the next day. The meat was dried to make our loads as light as possible because neither men nor animals were able to carry burdens over the mountains.*[6]

Although their surroundings were stunning, it cannot be emphasized enough how perilous a situation they were in. If a winter storm moved in, which could happen any time, they were doomed. Five years later, at the same time of year, the first of many storms caught the Donner party where it camped near Donner Lake and kept them trapped there for the winter. At least the Donners had emigrant companies ahead of them who realized that they were trapped and knew about where to find them. Relief parties were immediately sent into the mountains to cross the deep snows to bring them help. But in 1841, no one in California was expecting the Bartleson party. Even if they had, no one would have had the faintest idea of where to find them. All the company could do was pray, cross their fingers, and try not to think about such a frightening prospect.

Given the diarists' sketchy descriptions, some readers may wonder if we are accurately describing the path taken by the party into the mountains that day. The answer is simple: the physical terrain guided them. It dictated their route. Besides, their presumed route is entirely consistent with the descriptions and estimated distances recorded by our diarists.

October 18

On October 18, the company would cross a high divide and begin a slow descent to the west.

Bidwell:

> M. 18th. Having ascended about half a mile, a frightful prospect opened before us—naked mountains whose summits still retained the snows perhaps of a thousand years, for it had withstood the heat of a long dry summer, and ceased to melt for the season. The winds roared—but in the deep dark Gulfs which yawned on every side, profound solitude seemed to reign. We wound along among the peaks in such manner, as to avoid most of the mountains which we had expected to climb—struck a small stream descending towards the W., on which we encamped, having come 15 miles. The rivulet descended with great rapidity and it was the opinion of all that we were at least 1 mile perpendicular below the place where we began to descend. The stream had widened into a small valley. Cedars of uncommon size, pines, the most thrifty, clothed the Mountains. (one pine, as it was near our camp, was measured. Though it was far from being the tallest, it was 206 ft. high.) All were pleased to think that we were crossing the mountains so fast.

Jimmy John:

> 18th. Today we crosed the main ridge of the mountains of California in the morning about 10 oclock and descended a deep and narrow rocky valley on the west side of it, covered with tall trees of pine, hemlock, cedar

and fir, some of them a little over 200 feet high and camped in the same valley on the bank of a small stream which we followed from the top of the mountain.

Camping in Golden Canyon on the night of October 17 must have been torture, having to deal with cold, piercing winds. They were camping at seven thousand feet. Crawling from under their blankets on the morning of October 18, they probably gathered their thoughts as they tried to warm themselves by their fires and gulp down their small allowance of meat. To the west, about three miles away, was the upper end of the canyon. It would be their target, and would require climbing another twenty-three hundred feet (a half-mile, according to Bidwell) to its summit of ninety-four hundred feet. Given the oxygen-starved air, it must have been an exhausting climb. Jimmy John mentioned that they reached the summit at ten o'clock in the morning. Near the summit, they crossed what would someday become a section of today's Pacific Crest Trail.

Upon reaching the crest, they found themselves perched upon a rounded ridge above the timberline. They could see sharp-edged granite peaks jabbing skyward in all directions. They must have known that they were at a special place. Indeed, Jimmy John's entry showed that he understood that they had reached the spine of the divide, where the drainage behind them would eventually flow to Carson Lake, and where the drainage ahead would flow to the Pacific Ocean. But the view to their west was still alarming. Countless mountain peaks, ridges, and canyons stretched ahead of them with no end in sight.

On the summit, the winds, which Bidwell described as "roaring," were strong and biting. They would not linger there long. Once over the lip, they tumbled downward along a drainage that led to a small brook that was later named Disaster Creek. The descent was steep, narrow, and treacherous. They had to carefully pick their way through and around rocks and dead trees. During the next four and a half miles, they descended almost three thousand feet, finally staggering into Paradise Meadows. It was a flat, grassy area, nestled in the bottom of a canyon where Disaster Creek emptied into Clark's Fork. They did not remain in the meadow long, but continued westward down the Clark's Fork Canyon for about three miles to where the canyon's bottom widened. There, they stopped to camp, ending a rigorous day of about fifteen miles.

One can reach the estimated location of the company's camp on the night of October 18. It is on the north side of Clark's Fork, on Clark's Fork Road and about six miles east of where it intersects with Highway 108. This intersection is about two and a half miles east of the turnout overlooking the east end of the manmade Donnell Lake. Paradise Meadows is another three miles east on Clark's Fork Road.

October 19

Bidwell:

> T. 19th. Descending along the stream, we found several oak shrubs which confirmed us in the hope, that we were on the waters of the Pacific. But the route became exceedingly difficult—the stream had swelled to a river—could not approach it—could only hear it roaring among the rocks. Having come about 12 miles a horrid precipice bid us stop—we obeyed and encamped. Those who went to explore the route had not time to come to any conclusion where we could pass. We had descended rapidly all day; the mts. were still mantled with forests of towering pines. The roaring winds and hollow murmuring of the dashing waters conveyed in the darkness of the night the most solemn and impressive ideas of solitude. To a person fond of a retired life, this, thought I, would be a perfect terrestrial Paradise, but it was not so to us, when we knew that Winter was at hand, and that Capt. [Joseph] Walker (the mountaineer) had been lost in these very mountains 22 days before he could extricate himself.

Jimmy John:

> 19th. We traveled hard all day and did not get more than 10 miles on account of the way being so rough, rocky and bushy with forests of timber, the largest that I have ever seen, some perhaps 300 feet high. We were obliged to camp this evening on a site of the mountain where there is scarcely any grass for the animals.

Bidwell seemed to know about Joseph Walker struggling over these mountains in 1833. It is a clue that the party had been warned in advance that crossing the Sierras was going to be difficult. It suggests also that they learned about Walker's venture from one or more members of the Fraeb party they met on the Green River. They could have heard Walker describe his trip, or they could even have been members of his 1833 party.

The company stumbled forward near the rocky bed of Clark's Fork, following it downstream about six miles until it flowed into the Middle Fork of the Stanislaus River. Because of their continued descent along the canyon floor, they were now at about fifty-five hundred feet, an elevation hospitable enough to sustain the scrub oaks mentioned by Bidwell. He reported the roaring sound of the Middle Fork as it rushed down the deep canyon and over the boulder-choked riverbed. Despite its ruggedness, the scenery had launched Bidwell into uncharacteristically elegant prose. He must have been upbeat, thinking that they were on the final downslope of their journey. As the expedition continued, the high granite walls of the canyon pressed in more severely. Josiah Belden's memoirs explained how they came to where the canyon was "blocked with immense boulders," compelling them "to leave the track and go on to the ridges."[7] This forced the company to skitter up the canyon's north slope and then travel along its ridge.

At length, the company came to a rocky point above the canyon. Their forward progress was blocked by a deep and precipitous ravine down which Dardanelles Creek plunged into the river. They stopped to camp for the night. High above the river, the location had no grass or water, so Bidwell's memoirs related how some of the men made their difficult way down to the river to quench their thirst. But their strenuous climb to return to camp left them thirstier than they were before.[8]

To reach the location of their October 19 camp, travel east on Highway 108 about two and a half miles beyond the Donnell Lake overlook to Clark's Fork Road. Follow that road a mile to Road 6N06, then turn left and travel three miles to view the location of their camp just to the west of that point.

October 20

Perched high on this rocky point overlooking the river gorge below, the company had to find a way forward. It was on this date, five years later, that the Donner Party would become trapped by the first of a series of heavy snowstorms. They needed to get out of these mountains.

Bidwell:

> W. 20th. Men went in different directions to see if there was any possibility of extricating ourselves from this place without going back. They returned and reported, it was utterly impossible to go down the Creek. One young man [Jimmy John] was so confident that he could pass along the Creek with his horse, that he started alone, in spite of many persuasions to the contrary. Capt. B. also being tired of waiting for the explorers to return, started down the stream, which so jaded his animals that he was obliged to wait all day to rest them, before he was able to retrace his steps. In the mean time the rest of the Company, suffering for water, were obliged to travel. We proceeded directly N. up the mountains about 4 miles, found a little grass and water—here we killed one of the 2 oxen.

They had killed an ox, and were now left with one. Bidwell's sometimes troublesome oxen had probably met their fate by now. It seems surprising that he had not reported in his journal when each of them made the ultimate sacrifice.

Bidwell's and Jimmy John's entries, together with Bidwell's memoirs, explained what happened on October 20. With the company's path obstructed by the deep ravine ahead, two teams of scouts were sent out that morning. Bidwell and Jimmy John were sent to see if they could find a way to cross the deep ravine ahead. A second group was sent north up the mountain to see how far they would have to go to pass around the ravine's upper reaches. The scouts were instructed to fire a gun as a signal if they found a way that was passable for their animals. Sending scouting parties had not been typical of Bartleson; it seemed more like something Ben Kelsey would order. Indeed, Bidwell's memoirs recounted this incident and reported that "Benjamin Kelsey, who had shown himself expert in finding the way, was now, without any election, still recognized as leader, as he had been during Bartleson's absence."[9]

After Bidwell and Jimmy John had gone three-quarters of a mile, Bidwell recalled in his memoirs that he had decided it was impossible to cross the ravine with animals. He claimed that he said to Jimmy John, "Jimmy, we might as well go back; we can't go there." "Yes, we can," Jimmy John argued.[10] Bidwell said Jimmy John was "unmanageable," reporting that he pulled out his pistol and fired it before Bidwell could stop him.[11] The sound of the shot echoed up the canyon. Bidwell raced back to camp to inform the company to disregard the pistol shot and stand fast. When he arrived, Bartleson and seven of his messmates had already mounted their mules and were starting forward toward the ravine. Despite Bidwell's warning to Bartleson that it was not passable, the stiff-necked old man was not about to accept advice from a petulant young upstart like Bidwell. So he and his followers continued on. Ever since Bartleson had rejoined the party four days earlier, he must have chafed under the shadow of disgrace. But as he recovered from his dysentery and gained his strength, it appears he was no longer willing to take a backseat.

The rest of the company heeded Bidwell's warning and chose to not follow the bullheaded Bartleson. Since the company was in desperate need of water for their livestock, they broke camp that morning and headed up the mountainside. With the sound of labored breathing disturbing the morning, the party marched up the steep mountains, moving north and further away from the canyon. After about four miles of travel across creases in the rocky terrain, they had entered a largely bare granite plateau. They stopped to camp at a small basin with grass and water.

Bidwell's memoirs explained that after Bartleson and his men descended into the ravine, they could not go far. Because of the weakened condition of their mules, they had to stay where they were all night to let the exhausted mules recover. They were forced to scramble among the rocks to find grass for their mules and shimmied down to the river to bring water up in cups, boots, and hats. The next morning, according to Bidwell, it took four men pulling and four men pushing each mule to get them, one by one, up to their former campsite. Then they had to return to pick up their belongings and carry them up on their backs.

Shortly after the main company had settled into their new camp high on the plateau, one of Bartleson's men arrived and asked the company to wait until Bartleson and the rest of his men could catch up.[12] Bartleson and his companions had learned no lessons. Eschewing warnings and good sense, the group had made another impulsive decision that backfired.

There are a number of small meadows within a few miles of the area where the company stopped to camp on October 20, and it is impossible to know exactly where they spent the night. Upon leaving the canyon of the Middle Fork of the Stanislaus, the company traveled westward over terrain that is somewhat similar, without distinguishing features. Bidwell recorded very little that was enlightening. Even his mileage estimates had become less accurate and helpful because of the countless twists and turns, coupled with dense forests obscuring the horizon and distant reference points. For the next few days, it will be more difficult to determine their precise route and the locations of their campsites.

As far as Jimmy John was concerned, he would not be seen in the mountains again by anyone in the company. Unlike Bidwell, Jimmy was convinced he could get through the canyon with his horse, and he did. As Bidwell recalled in his memoirs, "[N]obody knows how Jimmy got through that canyon and into the Sacramento Valley. He had a horse with him—an Indian horse that was bought in the Rocky Mountains, and which could come as near climbing a tree as any horse I ever knew. Jimmy was a character. Of all men I have ever known I think he was the most fearless; he had the bravery of a bulldog."[13]

Jimmy John:

> *20th. This morning finding ourselves blocked up in this valley of the creek and surrounded on all sides by high mountains and rock, we thought it best that 2 or 3 men should go on ahead on foot and look out for the way to get through. Accordingly 3 men set out on foot and went down the creek. 2 ventured on back a while after they had started but with some difficulty for having to go down so steep [a] place near the creek that was so difficult that I had my doubts about geting back again, but a short distance from this place I met two of the men returning to camp. They told me they thought it possible and I went on but did not meet the other man. His name was Hoper [Hopper]. He returned some other way and told them that the way was not pasable and they had to turn back a few miles and leave the valley, but [they] did not leave that day on account of my being absent. I went on down the creek a few miles and waited for the company until night, but no one came here. I camped by the side of a frightful looking precipice. My gun fired accidentally as I lit from my horse this evening and frightened the horse so that [he] jumped and knocked my gun into the creek, but I lost no time in getting it dry again.*

As Jimmy John went down the river canyon, struggling through almost impossible conditions, it is incomprehensible that he expected that the rest of the company could follow him. He also mistakenly thought the company would wait in camp for his return. With its history of not waiting for people, the company did it again by leaving him to his own impulses.

In the days to come, Jimmy John would eventually give up trying to rejoin his companions and would find a way out of the mountains by himself. We will follow his solitary trek by means of his daily journal entries. We will notice, however, that he sometimes mentioned things that he could not have known except by learning about them later when he finally rejoined some of his friends. As mentioned in the introduction to this book, this section of Jimmy John's journal appears to be a copy, containing elements that must have been added later.

October 21

Bidwell:

> W. 21st. Our route to day was much better than expected, though in any other place than the mountains, it would be considered horrible. Capt. B. with his 7 or 8 overtook us, but we heard nothing of J. Johns. Distance about 10 miles; could see no prospect of a termination to the mts., mts., mountains!

The company's camp on October 21 had been on a rocky plateau, a wedge-shaped area between the Middle Fork of the Stanislaus River on the south and the North Fork of the Stanislaus River on the north. Most of the ridges on the plateau run southwestward. The creeks closest to the canyons drain into them, while the other creeks run between the parallel ridges and drain southwesterly. Given the terrain, it seems logical that the company would have drifted southwest along the spine of the southernmost ridge to avoid the deep ravines draining into the Middle Fork Canyon.

Once the company broke camp, it left the region of exposed granite and entered an area of tall, dense forests. Ancient and primeval, these forests contained very old pine, fir, and cedar, with trunks exceeding ten feet in diameter and towering three hundred feet high. It is difficult to imagine the immense size of these old-growth trees that are now gone due to the logging that would take place in the late 1800s and early 1900s. Although the party was awed by the scenery, Bidwell's memoirs recalled that they were occupied with more immediate concerns: "The large timber consisting of the firs, pines, including that mammoth of all pines, the sugar pine, and the cedar, were all new and most interesting to us. But we had no time, when nearly starved, to give attention to such objects. Our aim was to make distance on our way to the Pacific."[14] With only one ox left and game being extremely scarce, they had every reason to worry about how much longer it would take to escape this magnificent, but man-starving, landscape.

Because of the absence of distinguishing landmarks in this remote region, and the uncertainty of Bidwell's recorded mileages, we can only estimate that the general location where the company camped on the evening of October 21 was approximately two miles north of the Middle Fork and about eight miles downstream of today's Donnell Lake Dam.

IN THE MEANTIME, Jimmy John began October 21 at the bottom of the Middle Fork Canyon.

Jimmy John:

> *21st. This morning I started down the creek but finding the valley inaccessible, the creek running through a cragged place of rock below, I was obliged to try to get out on one side or the other so I tryed to get out on the north side that I might either return to the camp or strike the Companys trail, but finding it impossible to get out on the north, I went out on the south side and crosed a high spur of the mountain and returned to the creek in the evening where I encamped on its banks. By this time I became hungry having nothing to eat since I left the Company but a few bunches of grapes which I found on the bank of the creek. Here I found plenty of rushes for my horse to eat and eat some myself.*

Coming to where obstructions in the Middle Fork Canyon made it impossible to continue, Jimmy John had to climb out. But it was impossible to climb up on its north side, so he crossed the river and climbed up its south side. After moving downstream along the canyon's south rim, he descended to the river again, to a place that grew rushes. While it is impossible to identify exactly where he climbed out, and where he returned to the river bottom to spend the night, there is a section just east of Beardsley Dam where the river canyon widens slightly into a rush-supporting area. It is also where slopes down the canyon's south wall and up the other side are less severe. It is a likely place where Jimmy John spent the night on October 21.

October 22

Bidwell:

> T. 22d. Descended towards the river about 15 miles—had a tolerable road—arrived within about a mile of the River—could not approach nearer. Here was considerable Oak, some of which was evergreen, and thought to be live oak. 3 Indians came to camp, killed the last ox—let this speak for our situation and future prospects!

Bidwell also mentioned the killing of the company's last ox in one of his memoirs: "[W]e killed our last ox, who was so poor, as nearly all had been for weeks, that he had no marrow in his bones, he was literally only skin and bones."[15] In another memoir, he explained that once their last ox was gone, "we shot and ate crows or anything we could kill, and one man shot a wildcat."[16]

The path of the company on October 22 cannot be plotted with precision, except that they probably moved southwest through dense stands of tall timber. They slowly edged closer to the canyon, but why they did is a puzzle. Almost a mile wide from rim to rim and more than two thousand feet deep, the canyon was a daunting obstacle, especially for horses and mules. They had every reason to continue traveling along one of the ridges in a more westward direction as far as it would take them. Their reasons for not doing so go unexplained.

Jimmy John:

> 22nd. This morning I started down the creek but finding the valley impasable, I made an attempt to get out on the north side which I affected with much difficulty and traveled on a northwest course, hoping that I might cross the Companys trail, but seen no sign of them. I traveled about 14 miles today over a high spur of a mountain. Had nothing to eat except a few grass seeds. This evening I camped on the bank of another creek, with [which] runing through a valley similar to that I left this morning. Here I saw a number of Indian huts but camped behind some rocks to keep from being discovered by them.

With his horse, Jimmy John reported climbing out of the north side of the Middle Fork Canyon, and then traveling northwesterly for about fourteen miles. He finally came to the "bank of another creek." This suggests that in leaving the Middle Fork a few miles downstream of today's Beardsley Dam, he crossed the divide between the Middle and North forks of the Stanislaus by angling west in hopes of intersecting the route he was expecting the company to take. By the end of the day, he had reached a "creek" running through a "valley similar to that I left this morning." The diarists had commonly described the Middle Fork as a "creek." Since the North Fork is similar to the Middle Fork, it is not surprising for Jimmy John to describe it as a "creek" as well. He probably struck the North Fork close to where today's McKays Dam is located.

October 23

Bidwell was restless when the morning of October 23 dawned. The company desperately needed meat, so he decided to go hunting. His previous experiences had evidently not robbed him of his pluck. He would go on foot and alone, heading west along a route that closely paralleled the northern rim of the canyon because he understood that this was the route the company intended to take. His plan to move ahead of the company in order to hunt made sense, as game tended to leave an area when they heard strange sounds. Like Jimmy John, he expected to intercept the company's tracks later in the day.

Bidwell:

> F. 23d. Having no more meat than would last us 3 days, it was necessary to use all possible exertions to kill game, which was exceedingly scarce. For this purpose I started alone, very early in the morning, to keep some distance before the Company, who had concluded to continue as near as possible to the creek on the N. side. I went about 4 miles—met the Indian who came to us last night—obtained a little provisions made of acorns—got an Indian boy to pilot me to his house. He took me down the most rugged path in all nature arrived on the banks of a river at least ¾ of a miles perpendicular from where I started with him—found no more provision, continued down the river—oak in abundance, buckeye, and a kind of maple. The mountains, which walled in the stream, were so steep that it was with great difficulty I scaled them—having in one place come within an inch of falling from a craggy cliff down a precipice nearly a fourth of a mile perpendicular. 4 long hours I labored before I reached the summit—proceeded directly to intersect the trail of the Company. Mts. Covered

with the largest and tallest pines, firs, &c., thick copses of hazel &c.—travelled till dark over hills, dales, crags, rocks, &c., found no trail—lay down and slept.

Years later, Bidwell's memoirs added a few more details to the day:

> The next morning after the killing of our ox, I started ahead of the company to hunt for game. It was especially understood that the route would be west and on the north side of the stream. With that understanding, I gave myself time to reach the place where they would probably camp for the night. Except [for] the banks and bluffs of the Stanislaus River, the country consisted of open hills which were no longer rocky and precipitous. Indians were numerous, and many had visited our camp ere I left in the morning. Following an Indian trail, I descended to the river and went down its banks for some ten miles. In the canyon I met many Indians or rather passed several villages of them. I saw, however, no young men, all were old men, women or children. I think the news of our coming had reached them, and the men had either gone toward our camp or to give news to Indians farther ahead. I lost no time, however, in stopping at these villages. They made no attempt to interfere with me. None had any weapons or clothing that would indicate they had ever come in contact with civilization. At one place I obtained and ate some acorn bread not knowing what it was. The very last flour we had used on Walker River when Captain Bartleson's men overtook us. Anything that would sustain life was now most acceptable.[17]

Struggling up and out of the Middle Fork Canyon, Bidwell intended to intersect the company's tracks by heading north, with the canyon at his back. But just as Jimmy John had experienced, Bidwell was unable to locate the company's tracks. Something had gone wrong. His memoirs added even more detail to his climb out of the canyon and his trek north:

> A most difficult time I had scaling the precipice. Once I threw my gun up ahead of me, being unable to hold it and climb, and then was in despair lest I could not get up to where it was, but finally I did barely manage to do so, and made my way north. As the darkness came on I was obliged to look down and feel with my feet lest I should pass over the trail of the party without seeing it. Just at dark I came to an enormous fallen tree and tried to go around the top, but the place was too brushy, so I went around the butt, which seemed to me to be

about twenty to twenty-five feet above my head. This I suppose to have been one of the fallen trees in the Calaveras Grove of Sequoia gigantea or mammoth trees, as I have since been there, and to my own satisfaction identified the lay of the land and the tree. Hence I concluded that I must have been the first white man who ever saw the Sequoia gigantea, of which I told Fremont when he came to California in 1844. Of course, sleep was impossible, for I had neither blanket nor coat, and burned and froze alternatively as I turned from one side to the other before the small fire which I had built, until morning.[18]

Although Bidwell made no mention of the fallen Sequoia in his journal, he described it in detail in his memoirs. Calaveras Big Trees State Park contains an extensive grove of giant Sequoias, with its southernmost trees found as close as three miles north of the Middle Fork Canyon. It was not only possible, but likely, that Bidwell would eventually stumble across one of these giants. He may have been wrong about being the first white man to see one, however. That honor may belong to Joseph Walker and his trapping brigade. There is strong evidence that they crossed the Sierras approximately five to ten miles north of here in 1833 and encountered Sequoias on the northern side of the Calaveras Big Trees Park.[19]

The reason the company suddenly changed its plans was that one of the Indians visiting them on the morning of October 23 had offered to guide them, and the company agreed to follow. Instead of continuing to march west near the northern rim of the Middle Fork Canyon, as they originally intended, they followed the Indian as he led them south and down the steep slopes of the canyon to its bottom. Here, they spent the night of October 23. Dawson's log entry for that day recorded that they camped on the "river," and he estimated that they had traveled five miles.

Dawson described the day in his memoirs:

One day a stark-naked Indian came into camp, and as he was very friendly, we employed him to pilot us. We were now following a trail, and one day a member of the company, named [Thomas] Jones, went on ahead, expecting the rest to follow. But our new pilot left the trail and struck down a mountain, toward a stream to our left [the Middle Fork], we, of course, following. Jones never came back; and as he was on foot and had no gun, we were anxious as to his fate.[20]

Bidwell later learned that Andrew Kelsey and Thomas Jones had also gone hunting on the morning of October 23. They, too, traveled westward because it was the direction they understood the company would go. It is interesting that Dawson remembered Jones, but did not mention Kelsey or Bidwell doing the same. With the passage of so many years, the failure of Dawson's memory is understandable. What is not so understandable is why the company left these three men without waiting for them. In fact, Nancy Kelsey recounted in her memoirs, "We thought they were dead, but my husband went hunting, discovered their tracks and reported that they were surely alive."[21] Despite that, the company went on, going in a different direction than originally planned. It is unknown who had made the decision to proceed, but it would seem unlikely that Ben Kelsey would decide to leave his missing brother if he believed him to be alive. The decision creates the suspicion that Bartleson, supported by his men, was once again calling the shots.

IN THE MEANTIME, Jimmy John continued his lonely trek west:

Jimmy John:

> *23rd. This morning I crosed on the bank of last night which took me until noon and until nearly night to get out of the other side on account of the deep valley of rocks which it runs through. I was obliged to slide my horse down some places nearly perpendicular for a 100 ft. I camped this night on the side of the mountain by a small spring of water without anything to eat except a few small frogs that I picked up this evening. I gave up all hope of seeing the Company and trying to steer my course into California plains.*

Jimmy John was describing his crossing of the North Fork Canyon. It was deep and difficult, even if it was only about half as deep as that of the Middle Fork Canyon. It took him an entire day to descend to the river, probably near today's McKays Dam, then to cross it and scale the canyon wall on the other side. Alone with his horse, he was now significantly farther west than the company, and had a chance of getting out of these mountains before the company did.

October 24

After spending a miserably cold night near the fallen Sequoia with no blanket or coat, and only a small fire, Bidwell must have been grateful when the sun finally came up on the morning of October 24.

Bidwell:

> S. 24th. Concluded the Company had gone north. I traveled E., found no trail—traveled S.—came to the place where I left the Company yesterday morning, having made a quadrangle in the mts., 8 by 10 miles—took the trail of the Company. They had with great difficulty descended to the river, saw where they staid last night. Distance about 6 miles. Ascended on the S. side of the creek a high precipice. I overtook them; they had traveled to day 10 miles. They had hired an Indian pilot who had led them into the worst place he could find and absconded. 5 horses and mules had given out; they were left. I learned likewise that two hunters (A. Kelsey & Jones) started shortly after I did, and had not returned, part of a horse was saved to eat.

Bidwell's memoirs, adding some new details, provided another account of his efforts to find the company on October 24. Upon leaving the area near the fallen Sequoia:

> I started eastward to intersect the trail, thinking the company had turned north. But I traveled until noon and found no trail; then striking south, I came to the camp which I had left the previous morning. The party had gone, but not where they said they would go; for they had taken the same trail I had followed, into the cañon, and had gone up the south side, which they had found so steep that many of the poor animals could not climb it and had to be left. When I arrived the Indians were cutting the horses to pieces and carrying off the meat. My situation, alone among strange Indians killing our poor horses, was by no means comfortable. . . . That night after dark I overtook the party in camp.[22]

It is impossible to determine Bidwell's precise route on October 24. It is also difficult to determine with certainty the path where the company followed the Indian down to the bottom of the canyon, or where they climbed up its southern side. But an examination of the area reveals a likely place. On the north side of the canyon, about two miles west of today's Beardsley Lake Dam, is a sloping canyon wall that is less severe than other sections. It appears it would have provided a feasible descent to the bottom. The southern canyon wall across from this spot is steep but not so steep that they could not have found a way to climb out with their strongest animals, especially if they scaled the face of the canyon wall by switch-backing up the slope.

When the company camped at the bottom of the canyon that night, their Indian guide disappeared. It seemed to be the crafty Indian's plan to lead them to where it would be difficult for their animals to escape. Why would members of the company allow themselves to be led into such a trap? It was because they were desperate. Any Indian indicating that he knew the way out of these mountains would have been hard to resist.

Once the company ascended the canyon's south rim, it had lost an unspecified number of animals because they were too weak to climb out. The company needed to go west. Considering the terrain, their most logical path was to head west along the relatively flat south rim of the canyon. Bidwell said he caught up to their camp on the evening of October 24, about ten miles distant from their previous camp on the canyon floor.

When Bidwell finally caught up to the company that night, he must have collapsed. He had traveled on foot about forty miles during the previous thirty-six hours through some of the roughest terrain imaginable. One might question Bidwell's judgment from time to time, and he could undoubtedly be reckless. But his toughness and coolheaded ability to follow and catch up to the company are undeniable and worthy of admiration.

The company's campsite on the evening of October 24, when Bidwell finally overtook them, was probably nine miles downstream from the Beardsley Lake Dam and on the top of the southern rim of the canyon. It is a remote and difficult area to access even to this day.

JIMMY JOHN CONTINUED to put more space between himself and the company on October 24.

Jimmy John:

> 24th. Today I traveled about 30 miles in a northwest course, ascended a mountain that took me until afternoon and descended it in the evening to a creek. Here I camped and found a few bunches of grapes.

Because he traveled through homogenous mountain country with no distinctive features, and made a journal entry that did not provide much information, it is difficult to identify the route Jimmy John traveled or where he camped. We do not know what was going through his mind, but it is puzzling that he persisted in heading northwest, since the gradient of the terrain fell toward the west and the ridges he could have most easily traveled down tended to run in that direction as well. Nevertheless, if he had indeed traveled in a northwesterly direction about thirty miles, then the "creek" at which he camped may have been in the canyon of the South Fork of the Mokelumne River, and about four miles northeast of today's Mokelumne Hill, California.

October 25

Bidwell:

> M. 25th. Went about 6 miles & found it impossible to proceed. Went back two miles and encamped,—dug holes in the ground to deposit such things as we could dispense with—did not do it, discovering the Indians were watching us, among them was the old, rascally Pilot. White oak in abundance.

Although Bidwell estimated that the company marched six miles on October 25, he failed to mention the direction they traveled. Since their objective was to head west, it would make sense that they continued along the south rim of the canyon. After only six miles, they found their way blocked. The Middle Fork Canyon had suddenly turned almost due south. To continue west, the company would have had to cross that terrible canyon again. After their recent experience, they were not about to descend into another deathtrap and lose more animals. So they retraced their path, backtracking two miles, and set up camp for the night, probably on top of the canyon's south rim.

Bidwell reported their abortive attempt to bury items they "could dispense with." Dawson's memoirs mentioned it as well: "By this time our animals were failing so fast that we thought we would dig a hole, put our things in it, cover them with soil and build a fire over the spot. . . . But before we had finished digging our pit an Indian was discovered watching us, and the caching was given up."[23]

Bidwell's memoirs described the wary behavior of the Indians they encountered south of the Middle Fork Canyon:

> As we ascended the mountains to the south side of the Stanislaus River, Indians became more numerous, but their attitude towards us did not seem altogether that of friendship. They had evidently some of the implements of civilization, for we saw where trees had been hacked, showing they had axes. The Indians, too, which had cut the horses to pieces had something in the shape of knives or knife blades. But these Indians now betrayed a shyness or an unwillingness to come near us in a friendly manner. Though often seen, they were generally skulking or in flight, and our suspicions were aroused. Some thought best, others not, to stand guard over our horses at night. After a fatiguing day's travel, standing guard during a cold night was anything but a luxury. Still many of us did it.[24]

The Indians' shyness is not surprising. Those whom the company had been encountering since crossing the divide of the Sierra Nevadas had been from the Miwok tribe. It was a large tribe, estimated at approximately nine thousand prior to the Gold Rush. They lived in small villages scattered throughout the foothills and mountains of the Western Sierras, generally between the Consumnes River on the north and the Fresno River on the south. As primitive and isolated as they were, the Miwoks had had previous contact with white men. For example, Lieutenant Gabriel Moraga, a Spanish soldier, led an exploring party from Mission San Juan Batista into Miwok country in 1806. He led his men and a diary-keeping priest across the San Joaquin Valley and into the foothill country near the Stanislaus River. According to the priest, the Indians ran and hid from them. The reason for their fear, the priest learned, was that in earlier years Spanish soldiers had come into their homeland and killed them.[25]

Bidwell's memoirs explained how these Indians came to be horse thieves:

> The Catholic missionaries in California had induced, perhaps taken by force, many Indians inhabiting the region of country lying to the east of the San Joaquin River into the missions near the coast. Some of these Indians, after they had become expert horsemen and learned many of the ways of the Spanish race, had deserted to their native haunts. Precisely how or when they became fond of horseflesh

I know not. Certain it was that they were known before our coming to have subsisted for long years almost entirely upon horseflesh. For this purpose they were in the habit of making raids and sweeping whole ranches of bands of horses. In fact they were the terror of all the ranches between the San Joaquin Valley and the sea coast. Driving away their horses by hundreds, and continually up to the time or nearly so that California came under the Americans, they were known everywhere as the Horse thief Indians.[26]

It is not unexpected that the Miwoks had developed a preference for horses. A horse is much larger than a deer and yields a great deal more meat. Unlike deer, horses can be herded and approached more easily. Since the Californio *rancheros* and soldiers had been sending parties into the foothills and mountains for years to punish the horse thieves and to capture escaped mission Indians, the Miwoks had often suffered at their hands. It explained their wary, standoffish attitude. Armed only with bows, arrows, and spears, they had learned to keep a safe distance from the white man and his firearms.

The famished company had run out of flour nine days earlier. Their all-meat diet did not seem to satisfy them, and they were craving something with starch. Since the company was now camping at an elevation of about four thousand feet, oaks were everywhere. The men had noticed how the Indians gathered acorns from under the oaks and used them for food. But they were unaware of the need to leach the tannic acid out of them. Bidwell's memoirs recalled how, due to their ignorance, they paid an uncomfortable price:

As we advanced the next day [October 25], oak trees began to be abundant and we used acorns for food. Some of them we roasted and others boiled. The bitter acid contained in them soon made us sick. So much so we could not bear to see an acorn, and weak as we were, as far as possible avoided passing under oak trees.[27]

Those who ate the acorns became sick, but none as severely, it appears, as Ben Kelsey. His wife, Nancy, described the incident in her memoirs: "We lived on roasted acorns for two days. My husband came very near dying with cramps, and it was suggested to leave him, but I said I would never do that."[28]

Bidwell knew what it was like to be left behind. Andrew Kelsey, Thomas Jones, and Jimmy John had also suffered the same treatment. But these men were healthy. Bartleson's earlier behavior had prompted the question of what he might do if a member of the company fell terribly ill and became a burden. It is unknown who lobbied for abandoning Kelsey, but the threat has the odious stench of Bartleson's influence.

Nancy Kelsey's memoirs also mentioned a situation in which she found herself. Although she did not specify where it happened, her mention of pine trees suggest it was in this region: "At one time I was left alone for nearly a day, and as I was afraid of the Indians, I sat all the while with my baby in my lap on the back of my horse, which was a fine racing animal. It seemed to me while I was there alone, the moaning of the wind through the pines was the loneliest sound I ever heard."[29]

Very little glue appeared to be holding the company together at this point. Since most were not relatives or bosom friends when they first assembled in Missouri, their bonds would not have been strong to begin with. Their desperate circumstances, coupled with intense hunger, appeared to be infecting them so thoroughly that they were nearing an "each man for himself" state of mind. While their toughness and resolve cannot be questioned, their single-minded focus on surviving was beginning to crowd out the more noble virtues of compassion, sacrifice, and loyalty. We like our heroes to be heroic, and are disappointed when they fall short.

Jimmy John:

> 25th. I left the creek this morning, ascended a high mountain on the north side of the creek with some difficulty. This evening I shot a hawk which had a squirrel in its claws. Did not kill the hawk but made it drop the squirrel. This gave me some relief being nearly all I had to eat since I left the Company. I camped this evening on a small brook where I roasted my squirrel.

It is possible that Jimmy John was describing the crossing of the Mokelumne River Canyon and then climbing up the high mountain on its north side. Beyond that, it is difficult to estimate where he traveled from there on, particularly when he failed to record an estimated distance.

October 26

The sun rose on the morning of October 26, illuminating a beaten-down and disheartened camp. Barely recovered from the improperly prepared acorns, the company set out again. They did not leave Ben Kelsey behind after all. The company's likely course, as suggested by the terrain, was southwesterly along a ridge until they came to a steep slope descending into another ravine. Affected by weakness and malaise, the wrung-out company probably felt it did not have the strength to climb out, so they stopped to camp at its bottom after traveling only three miles.

Bidwell:

> T. 26th. Went S. about 3 miles and encamped in a deep ravine, it was urged by some that we should kill our horses and mules—dry what meat we could carry and start on foot to find way out of the mountains.

The company could not seem to escape the grinding grasp of these mountains. The landscape was so massive and so unending that the party must have felt that they were in danger of being swallowed up. Their reserves of endurance were about exhausted. Debating the killing of their horses and mules for food is evidence of how desperate they had become. Bidwell's memoirs made it clear that they regarded mule meat as a repugnant last resort:

> Some of the meat of one of the mules had been saved in case of emergency for it was evident the meat of the last ox would soon be consumed. When it was gone, most if not all of us refused to touch the mule meat for some time.[30]

Bidwell's memoirs recalled how their attitudes toward their food sources had evolved, their perspectives changing as their circumstances changed:

> I was always so fond of bread that I could not imagine how anyone could live without it. How the people of the Rocky Mountains had been able to live on meat alone was to me a mystery. When our flour began to give out, the idea of doing without bread was painful to me, and by the greatest economy my mess managed to eke out their flour a short time longer than the others. It was bad enough to have poor beef, but when brought to it we longed for fat beef and thought with it we might possibly live without bread. But when poor mule meat

STRUGGLING OVER THE SIERRA NEVADA MOUNTAINS

stared us in the face, we said if we could only have beef, no matter how poor, we could live.[31]

The killing of their horses and mules could have been more about the roughness of the country than the need to eat them. Men on foot were better suited than their animals to descend into and climb out of steep canyons and ravines. The company may now have been looking at their broken-down beasts as anchors around their necks, much as they had once looked upon the wagons.

The place where they spent the night of October 26 was likely in the Knight Creek ravine, another secluded and difficult spot to reach.

Jimmy John:

> 26th. This day I ascended a high ridge. Traveled on a west course until evening and camped on a small brook near some Indian huts. Tonight there came a heavy rain and I suffered much from the want of a shelter.

Jimmy John provided us with nothing by which to gauge his whereabouts.

October 27

A cold and drenching rain arrived during the night of October 26, immersing the company in further misery. Sleep must have been hard to come by as they had discarded their tents long ago and were probably carrying very little under which they could shelter. This was the first rain to bedevil the company since they had experienced a light sprinkle just before reaching the Green River. It is remarkable that the company had managed to travel so long without being hit by storms. The rain also meant snow at the higher elevations. Looking back at the snowclad mountains, they must have thanked their lucky stars that the storm had not arrived a few days earlier; otherwise they would have been snowbound somewhere up there.

Bidwell:

> W. 27th. It commenced raining about one o'clock this morning and continued till noon—threw away all our old clothes to lighten our packs, fearing the rain would make the mountains so slippery as to render it impossible to travel. I have since learned that the Indians in the moun-

tains, here, prefer the meat of horses to cattle, and here in these gloomy corners of the mts. they have been accustomed to bring stolen horses and eat them. Here and there were strewed the bones of horses, so the design of the veteran Indian pilot is apparent in leading us into this rugged part of Creation. As we left this place one of the men, G. Cook, remained concealed to see if the old pilot was among the Indians, who always rushed in as soon as we left our encampments to pick up such things as were left. The old gentleman was at the head of this band, and as he had undoubtedly led us into this place to perish, his crime merited death—a rifle ball laid him dead in his tracks. We proceeded S. about 6 miles. As we ascended out of the ravine, we discovered the high mountains we had passed, were covered with new snow for more than a half mile down from their summits.

Grove Cook had just killed their former Indian guide, the one they were convinced had led them into the bottom of the Middle Fork Canyon for the purpose of trapping their weakest animals. Remaining behind when the company pulled out of camp that morning, Cook lay in wait, hiding. "We had not gone far when we heard the report of a gun," Bidwell recalled. "Cook soon overtook us, laughing, and said that at the crack of the gun the old scamp jumped off the ground with a shriek, and the others ran off."[32]

Jimmy John:

27th. This morning the rain ceased and I started as soon as I could get a little dryer for the rain wet every thing I had. This seemed to be the last high mountain that I had to cross. The land seemed to lower on the west. I traveled about 12 miles today and camped near the foot of the mountain. Found nothing to eat except a few acorns.

Alone and without comrades, Jimmy John must have felt hopeless.

October 28

Climbing out of the Knight Creek ravine, the company probably headed in a southwesterly direction along the next ridge. The day before had been very bad. Today would be worse. After traveling approximately five miles, the foot-weary company came to another daunting barrier—a precipitous canyon through which the South

Fork of the Stanislaus River ran. It may not have been as deep as the Middle Fork Canyon, but it was deep enough. The path they followed down into the canyon was exceedingly steep and treacherous.

Bidwell:

> *T. 28th. Surely no horses nor mules, with less experience than ours could have descended the difficult steeps and defiles which we encountered in this day's journey. Even as it was, several horses and mules fell from the mountain's side and rolling like huge stones, landed at the floor of the precipices. The mountains began to grow obtuse, but we could see no prospect of their termination. We eat the last of our beef this evening and killed a mule to finish our supper.—distance 6 miles.*

Nicholas Dawson's memoirs recalled a difficult descent into a deep canyon. He wrote that they were precariously edging their way

> *along shelves of rock which overhung vast precipices. Here and there great rocks projected over the path and frequently a pack would strike against one of these rocks and over the precipice would go pack and animal, and be lost to us entirely. We all went on foot, leading our animals. Once, I remember, when I was struggling along trying to keep [my mule] Monte from going over, I looked back and saw Mrs. Kelsey a little way behind me, with her child in her arms, barefooted, I think, and leading her horse—a sight I shall never forget. As we neared the stream and were passing the last projecting rock, old Monte struck the rock and would have gone over had I not braced myself and held him hard. I had concocted a plan to get some meat: As soon as I got down the ledge to the stream I took out my knife, and standing to one side asked each one as he came by whether any animal had gone over. "Yes, the Badger had just gone over." I struck up the gulch, and soon found the Badger, struggling and alive. The Badger belonged to Bartleson, and was packed with bed clothes and camp utensils. Others of the party coming up, we lifted the old mule to his feet and removed his pack. He was badly crippled, but made it to camp. Bartleson agreed that we might kill him and eat him. We ate him nearly all that night, for it was the understanding that each should all eat all he wanted. Bartleson made us promise to pay for him when we reached California, and I did pay my portion, but I doubt if the others ever did. I also remember to have payed Chiles 75 cents for the butcher knives with which we purchased the pinion*

nuts. Bidwell and Kelsey, however, never charged us anything for their oxen eaten by us.[33]

Dawson seemed to remember that this experience happened when the Indian guide led them into the depths of the Middle Fork Canyon. But the passage of time can play tricks on a person's memories. His reference to overhanging shelves of rocks causing pack mules to tumble down the precipice sounds like what happened when they descended into the South Fork Canyon. "Badger," it will be recalled, was the obstinate mule Dawson was riding near the Platte River when he experienced his rude encounter with the Cheyenne war party.

The section of the South Fork Canyon that most closely resembles Bidwell's and Dawson's descriptions is about two miles northeast of the old Gold Rush town of present-day Columbia, California. It has extremely steep sides with projecting rock overhangs. Dawson said they descended a "path," suggesting an established Indian trail. With rocks overhanging the trail, it would have been suitable for people on foot, but not for animals, especially ones carrying top-heavy packs. The horses and mules had eaten little the last week because grass was scarce in the high mountains and on the forest floor. They had become stiff and stupid, and descending into this deep canyon was too much to expect of them.

Nancy Kelsey recalled that about this time "one old man gave out, and we had to threaten to shoot him before he would attempt to descend the mountains."[34] Who could that have been? The only "old" men in the company would have been Bartleson and George Henshaw.

With a little scouting, the company could have found an easier path into and out of the canyon if they had gone about four miles further upstream. But exhaustion and inadequate nutrition were probably muddying their thinking. There is no mention of an effort being made to recover the mules. The men may have felt that in their weakened state, it was beyond them to reach the fallen animals or to retrieve the items they carried.

The company undoubtedly watered their remaining animals at the river. Because they had traveled only four miles, and because there was no comfortable place at the bottom of this narrow, boulder-filled chasm on which to bed down, it appears they struggled up the far side of the canyon before setting up camp. When Bidwell mentioned that they "could see no prospect of their [the mountains'] termination," it suggested that they ended October 28 at the top of the canyon's south rim. From there, they would have had a view of the mountains to the west. The best estimate of the company's camp that afternoon would be near Yankee Hill Road, about a mile east of Main Street in Columbia.

Dawson recalled that after crossing the South Fork Canyon, Talbot Green stashed his lead. He wrote that "Green, whose pack of lead, which he clung to most solicitously, had been growing heavier for his weakened animal, took Grove Cook with him, and going off into some gulch secreted or cached it."[35] Green's lead would undoubtedly have great value in California, but at the moment, survival was of paramount importance.

Estimating the company's routes and camp locations since the company entered the Middle Fork Canyon has been particularly challenging. Fortunately, Google Earth has been a resource of inestimable value. Its three-dimensional views of the terrain, coupled with its tools for measuring distances and elevations, have helped separate plausible from implausible routes. While the conclusions are not absolutely certain, all of the projected routes and campsites have been consistent with the terrain and with the diarists' descriptions and distances.

Jimmy John:

> 28th. Today I traveled all day amongst the hills which are covered with oak and long leafed pines and now and then a handsome valley. The acorns here are frequently more than 3 inches long. This night I came to some Indian camps about sunset. I thought that I should be safer at their camps than to camp alone near or in sight of them and accordingly made signs that I wished to stay with them. They did not appear willing at first, but I made signs to them that there was a large company coming on in the morning and that I would start early and the company should not interrupt them and they agreed for me to stay. They gave me some acorn bread and a kind of pine seeds to eat and also a kind of soup made of acorns. They did not appear to be hostile but I seemed a great curiosity to them. I stayed here until morning uninterrupted but kept a good look out, keeping my gun and pistols near me.

It is impossible to know where Jimmy John was at this time.

October 29

During the night of October 28, two horses wandered away, the need to search for them delayed when the company got underway the next morning. In one of his most despairing entries, Bidwell wrote about October 29:

F. 29th. Last night, the Indians stole a couple of our horses. About noon we passed along by several huts, but they were deserted as soon as we came into sight, the Indians running in great consternation into the woods. At one place the bones of a horse were roasting on a fire; they were undoubtedly the bones of the horse we had lost. Traveled no less than 9 miles to day, the night was very cool and had a heavy frost. Although our road was tolerably level to day, yet we could see no termination to the mountains—and one much higher than the others terminated our view. Mr. Hopper, our best and most experienced hunter, observed, that "If California lies beyond those mountains we shall never be able to reach it." Most of the Company were on foot, in consequence of the horses giving out, and being stolen by the Indians, but many were much fatigued and weak for the want of sufficient provision; others, however, stood it very well. Some had appetites so craving that they eat the meat of most of the mule raw, as soon as it was killed, some ate it half roasted, dripping with blood.

There was more to the story about the lost horses. One of Bidwell's memoirs reported that they had actually allowed those horses to stray, and he explained why:

Though often seen, they [the Indians] were generally skulking or in flight, and our suspicions were aroused. Some thought best, others not, to stand guard over our horses at night. After a fatiguing day's travel, standing guard on a cold night was anything but a luxury. Still many of us did it. When the horses of the unwilling ones strayed beyond the line, we were not always careful to turn them back. The result was that two of them one morning were missing. A search till nearly noon failed to discover them, and we began our march. In a few miles, coming in sight of an Indian village, all the Indians, men, women and children were in rapid flight up the steep mountains to the south. On a fire close by the village and scattered around it were parts of the missing horses. The Indians had killed them and were preparing to have a grand feast.[36]

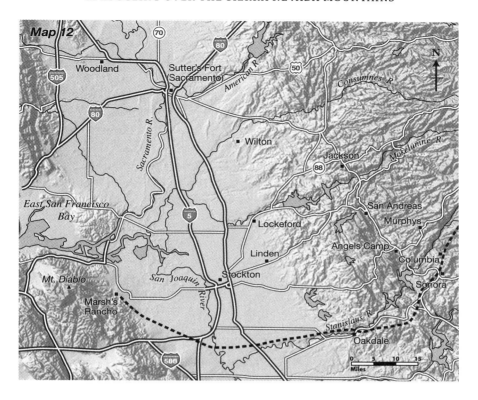

In another of his memoirs, Bidwell was more specific, recounting that one man refused to stand guard that night, "so we let his two horses roam where they pleased. In the morning, they could not be found. . . . [W]e found the horses killed and some of the meat roasting on a fire."[37]

When the company finally left camp late in the morning of October 29, they traveled west. Given the lay of the land, they likely traveled a path of least resistance. This would have taken them through the valley where the present-day towns of Columbia and Sonora are now located. Years later, Bidwell's memoirs confirmed that they "passed through what is now known as Tuolomne County, probably very near the present town of Sonora."[38] Josiah Belden expressed the same belief, writing in his memoirs that they "passed I suppose the neighborhood of where Sonora is now."[39]

More hills lay ahead, although none that looked intimidating. Unknown to them, they were creeping through gold country, a region that would swarm with gold seekers in just a few years. It is supposed that scouts rode to the hilltops to squint into the distance to see what was ahead. According to Bidwell's memoirs, "We could see a range of mountains lying to the west—the Coast Range—[about seventy miles to the west] but could see no valley."[40] The hills ahead concealed the San Joaquin Valley. The distant Coast Range, which they could see, appeared to be a continuation of the mountains through which they were now traveling. They feared that California lay beyond those distant mountains and it frightened them. "[W]e did not even know that we were in California," Bidwell explained.[41] Convinced that they still had a great distance to go, Bidwell recalled in his memoirs that the company was discouraged:

> [T]he Coast Range Mountains . . . rose to view in the blue distance, but we had no knowledge of any intervening valley. . . . it was impossible for any one to say where we were or how far we had yet to travel. It was the opinion of most if not all that we were not yet within five hundred miles of the Pacific Ocean. That the blue range bounding the western horizon was simply the beginning of other and perhaps great ranges beyond. Then came a time of great discouragement, some saying if California lay beyond other ranges of mountains, that we could never live to get there.[42]

With little upon which to hang a rag of hope, the dejected travelers stopped to camp after making only ten miles that day. They may have been disheartened, but did they feel defeated? If only we could have looked into their eyes. There is a saying that no matter how exhausted a man is, his eyes will tell you whether he has cashed in his chips.

The estimated location of their October 29 camp is just west of Jacksonville Road, about four and a half miles south of Jamestown, California.

Jimmy John:

> 29th. I left here early this morning. Saw an Indian dog which I took to be a wolf and shot it and being very hungry took part of it and hung it to my saddle. I had not gone far before I heard the Indians rising the whoop and pursuing me. I was in a bad condition to flee before them, my horse so near worn out that he could scarcely raise a trot and myself nearly famished with hunger and having to pass through a thick growth [of]

brush and over rocky ground, but I got through into a clear place before they overtook me. I lit from my horse to prepare for battle for I had a rifle and four horse pistols well charged. They came within about 100 paces. I thought I could try to deceive them. I raised a yell as loud as I could, beckoning at the same time toward a thick clump of trees that stood near me. They perhaps thought that the company I was telling them of last evening were laying there in ambush for they turned about and fled as fast as their legs could carry them and as they ran I changed my voice as much as I could in order to make [them] think several persons present. I counted 12 of them as they ran and watched them until they were out of sight and then led my horse down a small valley of smooth rocks to prevent them from tracking me and went on in peace until I had an opportunity of roasting my dogmeat which [I] did not relish very well, but being hungry made out to eat it. I travelled about 20 miles today. Camped in hearing of some Indians near a small creek.

It is still difficult to know where Jimmy John was, but it is clear that his difficulties involved more than hunger. Surrounded by danger, he was relying on his wits. His courage is not in question, as Bidwell had remembered him in his memoirs as "the most fearless man" he had ever known.[43]

October 30

When the company arose on the morning of October 30, they had no idea that they were in for a big surprise.

Bidwell:

> S. 30th. We had gone about 3 miles this morning, when lo! to our great delight, we beheld a wide valley! This, we had entirely overlooked between us and the high mountain which terminated our view yesterday. Rivers evidently meandered through it, for timber was seen in long extended lines as far as the eye could reach. But we were unable to reach it to day, and encamped in the plains. Here grew a few white oaks. Traveled today about 20 miles. Saw many tracks of Elk. The valley was wonderfully parched with heat, and had been stripped of its vegetation by fire. Wild fowls, geese, etc., were flying in multitudes.

Shortly after leaving camp, the company probably crossed Slate Creek, a small tributary of the Tuolumne River, and then headed toward a low point in a range of low hills. If that was their route, they would have followed the path of today's Red Hills Road west of the tiny community of Chinese Camp. Proceeding up the ravine, they came to its summit. The San Joaquin Valley, a level plain of great extent that had been previously obscured, now lay before them. It must have taken them by surprise. Although many believed that they still had to cross the distant Coast Range mountains, their spirits must have lifted because the valley meant that there were no deep canyons or steep mountainsides to cross, at least for a while. There would be grass for their animals and, more importantly, as Bidwell observed, there were signs of abundant game—elk and water fowl. Josiah Belden's memoirs recalled where he thought they entered the valley floor: "Finally, we got out of the mountains, striking the plains probably not far from where Knight's Ferry is now. When we got to the plains, we found no water or grass, it having been a dry season. . . . We got on to the plains just at night, and followed down and camped about ten o'clock without water."[44]

Belden's comment indicates that they emerged from the hills about four miles south of where Knight's Ferry was later established along the Stanislaus River. From where they entered the valley, they could not see the river north of them because it flowed through a canyon below the level of the surrounding land.

As the weak and bedraggled company set out across the valley plain, darkness closed in on them. Whatever discipline and cohesiveness remained now unraveled. "All began then to quicken their pace," Bidwell wrote in his memoirs. "Those who had the most strength and the best animals traveled the fastest. Night found us scattered on a line for miles in length. Every one traveled as long as he could and then lay down to sleep."[45]

Bidwell's memoirs further described the situation:

> The evening of the day [October 30] we started down into the valley we were very tired, and when night came our party was strung along for three or four miles, and every man slept where darkness overtook him. He would take off his saddle for a pillow and turn his horse or mule loose, if he had one. His animal would be too poor to walk away, and in the morning would find him, usually within fifty feet. These jaded horses nearly perished with hunger and fatigue.[46]

With members of the company spending the night strung out over four miles, they were scattered between six and ten miles southeast of the present-day town of Oakdale, California.

Dawson recalled spending the night of October 30 camping beside a pond. The valley floor was basically level, but it had small depressions into which rainfall would collect. Water collecting in such depressions are now called vernal pools. The October 27 rainstorm likely created the pond that Dawson's memoirs mentioned:

> [The night] was passed at a nasty puddle of water, with only a lean coyote as supper for the whole crowd. This meat—the worst I ever eat—with the dirty puddle, caused a general anxiety to get to good water; for a person suffers more from thirst than from hunger.[47]

Jimmy John:

> 30th. Today I was followed by 3 Indians. I pointed my gun at them and becned [beckoned] them to go back, which they did. This evening I camped on a small creek in the plain. Saw a few deer and killed a badger which was fat and made me a great feast. Came perhaps 15 miles today.

Jimmy John had finally made it to the valley floor. Considering the different route he took, it is astonishing that he and the company reached the valley floor on the same day, although he reached it approximately fifty miles northwest of them. It is unfortunate that he failed to reveal his thought processes, as it is confounding why he traveled as far north as he did through those mountains. If he had focused more on heading west, he might have emerged from them days earlier.

The small creek where he stopped to camp was probably Laguna Creek. In his next day's entry, he will report that this creek flowed into the Consumnes River, and we can work back to his campsite by using the mileages that he will report. He must have learned the name of the Consumnes River afterwards and included it when he wrote or rewrote this section of his journal.

One can reach his estimated October 30 camp by traveling east on Highway 104 seven miles from where it leaves today's Highway 99. Laguna Creek runs just north of the highway.

October 31

Bidwell's memoirs explained how he caught up the next morning to those who were camped beside the pond described by Dawson:

> When morning came the foremost of the party waited for the others to come up. They had found water in a stagnant pond, but what was better, they had killed a fat coyote, and with us it was anything but mule meat. As for myself, I was unfortunate being among those at the rear and not aware of the feast in the advance. I did not reach it in time to get any of the coyote except the lights [lungs] and the windpipe. Longing for fat meat and willing to eat anything but poor mule meat and seeing a little fat on the windpipe of the coyote, I threw it on the coals to warm it and greedily devoured it.[48]

The differences in Dawson's and Bidwell's recollections are striking. To Dawson, the coyote was "lean," while to Bidwell it was "fat." To Dawson, the coyote meat was "the worst," while Bidwell devoured what was left "greedily." Bidwell had expressed repugnance at the thought of eating mule meat, but was now at the point where he relished a coyote's windpipe and its lungs.

The company was south of the Stanislaus River and west of the edge of the foothills. The Stanislaus River continued to course below the surrounding terrain, so its timber was not visible from a distance. Further downstream, to the northwest, however, the land was lower. It was there that they could see a line of timber. The poor wretches, weak, thirsty, and lagging along on foot, gathered themselves and struggled forward. They were determined to reach that line of timber, praying that it would provide them with relief.

Bidwell:

> S. 31st. Bore off in a N.W. direction to the nearest timber, day was warm, plain dry and dusty, reached timber, which was white oak (very low and shrubby) and finally, the river which we had left in the Mts., joyful sight to us poor famished wretches!!! hundreds of antelope in view! Elk tracks thousands! Killed two antelopes and some wild fowls, the valley of the river was very fertile and the young tender grass covered it, like a field of wheat in May. Not a weed was to be seen, and the land was as mellow and free from weeds as land could be made by plowing it 20 times in the U.S. Distance to day 20 miles.

Bidwell's memoirs related their experiences that day:

We turned directly to the north to reach what seemed the nearest timber. This was at a distance of ten miles or so, which in our weakened condition it took us nearly all day to travel. It brought us to the Stanislaus River at a point not far from the foothills. Here the rich alluvial bottom was more than a mile wide; it had been burned over, but the new grass was starting up and growing luxuriantly though sparsely like thinly sown grain. But what gladdened our eyes most was the abundance of game in sight, principally antelope. Before dark we had killed two of them and two sandhill cranes and besides there was an abundance of ripe and delicious wild grapes. Still we had no idea that we were yet in California, but supposed we had to cross the range of mountains to the west. It was determined to stay one day to hunt game and to rest for a new start.[49]

Nicholas Dawson had his own perspective regarding their crawl toward the river:

The next morning [October 31] we were all very thirsty. We were on a prairie, and no signs of water. To our right, however, apparently three or four miles away, we saw timber, which we hoped lined a watercourse. We set out for it in a devil-take-the-hind-most race. I was on foot; for a short time before [Talbot] Green, for whom I had formed a strong friendship, had asked me to let him ride . . . , as his mule was disabled, and I had agreed, giving him the first bout.

The distance to the timber proved twelve or fifteen miles. Green, on [my mule] Monte, was out of sight ahead, and I toiled on, weary, thirsty, and angry. Watching eagerly, I saw the foremost pass into the timber, and my spirits sank; they would have stopped if there had been a stream there. I went on, however, and finally I and other poor footmen reached the timber. We came upon the advance party, halted and parleying—no water! I sank exhausted to the ground, and was debating whether I should not just remain where I was and die, when I heard a gun fired, and shortly thereafter another. "That is Hopper," I thought, "and when he fires twice there is certain to be meat;" so spirits and body rose, and, the crowd moving on, I followed.

Only a short distance beyond where the crowd had halted, they came to a bluff, and below it lay a low bottom covered with young, green grass and at its farther sides willows and other sure indications of a water course. Across that bottom I made rapid headway, and

> *plunging down the banks beyond, lay down flat over the water and swallowed it; then after raising my head to rest, would go at it again. Shortly after, Hopper came in with a deer on his mule, and reported another killed and ready to bring in. He said there were plenty signs of deer—then there was great rejoicing, and we decided to tarry, kill and eat. Bidwell says there were thirteen deer killed and eaten, and as we remained there two or three days, there must have been some tall eating. We found, also, plenty of what seemed to be the most delicious grapes I had ever eaten.50*

It is impossible to ignore the irony. Dawson had been a member of Bartleson's mess when it suffered no scruples about leaving the rest of the company behind. But here, he expressed anger when his friend Talbot Green rides off on his mule, leaving him to struggle behind on foot.

When the company finally staggered into the wide bottom of the Stanislaus River, they were delighted to find abundant water, grass, wood, grapes and game. Good fortune had finally smiled upon them. Although they believed that they were not yet in California, and thought that they still had to cross the Coast Mountains to the west, this was a delightful place to rest and recuperate before pushing on.

The general area where they camped on October 31 is in the river bottom, on the north side of Highway 108, and about three miles east of the center of Oakdale, California.

Jimmy John:

> 31st. Today I traveled down the creek in a south course and seen plenty of deer. Killed one in the evening which was in good order. Here I camped on the bank of a creek called the Cosameie [Consumnes]. Tonight my horse left me and I remained here 3 nights. Dried some meat. Could find nothing of my horse but seen signs of horses and cattle and also found a Spanish saddle stirrup and saw a small path which crosed the creek and led in a north direction.

Continuing down the small Laguna Creek on October 31, Jimmy John came to where it merged with the Consumnes River. The camp would be on the west side of the river, approximately four miles west of where Twin Cities Road (Highway 108) intersects Highway 99. He would stay there for the next three days, during which time he would not make any journal entries.

Sadly, this is the last we will hear of Jimmy John's remarkable horse. Perhaps the animal had had enough. But it was dangerous country for an unprotected horse, and was probably an unfortunate place for the animal to emancipate himself.

Chapter 16

The Journey Ends

NOVEMBER 1 TO 4, 1841

November 1

On November 1, the company remained in their camp on the Stanislaus River. In light of their recent privations, they were loath to leave the game they found there.

Bidwell:

> Nov. M. 1st. *The Company tarried to kill game; an abundance of wild fowl and 13 deer and antelopes were bro't in. My breakfast, this morning, formed a striking contrast with that of yesterday which was the lights [lungs] of a wolf.*

Nancy Kelsey must have been recounting this day when she reported in her memoirs, "At one place I was so weak I could hardly stand, and I lay on the ground while Mr. Kelsey went out and killed a deer. We were then near Dr. Marsh's ranch."[1]

Joseph Chiles also recalled the day, expressing the joy everyone felt because they were finally at a place with abundant game: "Imagine the wild delight of so many hungry men, one might say starving men, when they reached the Stanislaus River in whose valley was [where] the deer was very abonndant [abundant] and happy were they to find such a camping place and that evening they brought 26 deer into camp and every man wept that night as they feasted."[2]

THE JOURNEY ENDS

November 2

By the morning of November 2, people must have felt partially restored. The group split. Bartleson and his loyal seven stayed behind, purportedly to dry meat. The others resumed their journey, crossing to the north side of the river and then heading west and downstream. The company had lost many of their horses and mules, and the ones they still had were about given out. Many people were on foot because they had no animals to ride. Believing they still had that range of mountains to the west to cross, and thinking that they may have as many as five hundred miles to go, one wonders how they kept going. But as the old adage goes: When you are in the middle of the river, you have no choice but to keep swimming. This is precisely what they were doing.

Bidwell:

> T. 2d. Capt. B. with his 7 remained to take care of the meat he had killed—while the rest of the Company went on. We passed some beautiful grapes, sweet and pleasant. The land decreased in fertility as we descended the stream. Behold! this morning, Jones, who left the Camp to hunt on the 23 d ult. came to the camp. They (he and Kelsey) had arrived in the plains several days before us, and found an Indian, who conducted them to Marsh's house, but he brought bad news; he said there had been no rain in California for 18 months, and that the consequence was, there was little bread stuff in the country. Beef however was abundant and of the best quality—travelled to day 16 miles.

Bidwell's mention of Jones and Kelsey is a reminder how both men, like Bidwell, had gone hunting on October 23. Unable to find the company because it had unexpectedly followed that Indian guide on an unplanned route, the two men had struck west. Although on foot, they had managed to find a quicker way out of the mountains. They encountered Indians who led them to Dr. John Marsh's ranch at the eastern foot of Mount Diablo. The fact that Jones stumbled across the struggling company seems almost miraculous given that the company could have been almost anywhere. But it also could have been shrewd calculating by Dr. Marsh that the company would likely continue following the Stanislaus River as it emerged from the mountains.

This memorable day will be recalled in the memoirs of four of our travelers, and it is amusing to see how they recalled the day's events differently.

First, Josiah Belden's account:

Then we started to follow the [Stanislaus] river down, and after going a little way, we met two of our men who had left the party a number of days before in a canon of the Stanislaus, and had worked their way down on foot ahead of us, and had reached Marsh's ranch at the foot of Mt. Diablo, and had told him of us back in the mountains, and he had furnished them with some Indians and animals and provisions, and fortunately, they just happened to meet us.[3]

Belden's recollection varied from Bidwell's journal by claiming that both Kelsey and Jones found the lost company, in contrast to Bidwell reporting in his journal that it was only Jones.

Bidwell's memoirs recalled the company leaving their camp on the Stanislaus River on November 2:

It was about the first of November, and there was no time to delay if we were going to reach California that fall. Most of the party were ready and anxious to press forward. Captain Bartleson and his men thought otherwise. They said we hadn't yet reached California, we probably still had a long distance to travel, that such a place as we were in could not be found everywhere and they were going to stop and lay in meat for the balance of the journey. Leaving them in camp and crossing the Stanislaus River, we proceeded down the north side of the same and camped. Early the next day the news came that the Indians in the night had attacked them [Bartleson's group] and stolen all their horses. We remained until they came up, carrying on their backs such things as they were able. On the day we had stopped to hunt, two men had been sent ahead to see if signs of settlements could be found. They were gone two days and returned bringing news that they had fallen in with an Indian who conducted them across the valley to the foot of Mount D[iablo] to the ranch of Dr. Marsh. This settled the question that we had actually arrived in California and were not far from San Francisco Bay. It was an occasion of great joy and gladness. We were not only near our journey's end but the men knew just where to go, instead of uncertainty.[4]

After thirty-six years, Bidwell's memory had substantively failed him. He incorrectly recalled that Jones and Kelsey had been sent ahead to find signs of settlements, when the reality was that while in the mountains, they had gone hunting and got separated from the company.

Nancy Kelsey recorded a few brief memories of the day as well: "We were then near Marsh's ranch which was close to what is now Martinez. Mr. Jones, one of the supposed dead men, and one of Dr. Marsh's Indians rode into camp and brought with them some farina for me."[5]

Lastly, we look at Nicholas Dawson's memoirs:

On the day set for our departure [November 2] from this happy valley, some of the animals belonging to members of our mess could not be found. [Ben] Kelsey and his party, containing Bidwell among others, went on down the Stanislaus. We found our animals in a day or two, and followed. We crossed the stream, and finding it heading west, we followed it. We were traveling along, pretty comfortable on the whole, but casting glances of anxiety towards the mountains ahead; when we saw two men approaching transversely to our route. So rare a sight greatly excited our curiosity, and we stopped and waited. As they drew near, someone said, "Why, one of them looks like Jones!" "No it can't be." But it was Jones and an Indian come to find us and pilot us in, if found alive, to Marsh's ranch. Jones story was short. After getting lost from us he had struck westward, had killed with a rock a rabbit, and had subsisted on this until found by some Indians who took him to Marsh's ranch. He had straightway put back, with an Indian guide, to find his comrades. Jones had some provisions, too. We all felt like hugging Jones. We didn't, but those provisions! We must see them. So we camped right there and ate them.[6]

Both Nancy Kelsey's and Nicholas Dawson's recollections matched Bidwell's journal that it was only Jones and an Indian who had found the company trudging along the Stanislaus.

Bidwell recorded traveling sixteen miles that day, while Dawson's log reported that he and his Bartleson group traveled only eight miles. The likely location of the Ben Kelsey camp on November 2 is on the north side of the river, about three miles east of the town of Ripon, California, while Bartleson and his men likely camped beside the river north of the town of Riverbank.

November 3

The company had risen the previous morning thinking that they had not yet reached California. They expected to travel another five hundred miles before reaching their destination. But on the morning of November 3, they awoke to the exhilarating thought that they were in California and would soon reach Dr. Marsh's. They had found a new fountain of energy.

Bidwell:

> W. 3d. We waited till Capt. B. came up, and all started for Marsh's about noon; arrived at the St. Joaquin and crossed it—distance 13 miles found an abundance of grass here. The timber was white oak, several kinds of evergreen oaks, and willow—the river about 100 yds. in width.

California had a Mediterranean climate, something with which the company was unfamiliar. They may not have realized that California's rainfall principally came during the winter and spring months, when it produced annual grasses and a multitude of wild flower species that carpeted the plains with a palette of vibrant colors. As spring and summer advanced, the annual grasses and flowers matured, went to seed, and then shriveled up and turned brown. The company had arrived when the vegetative carpet was, for the most part, dead, dry, and sun-bleached. A few may have recalled Antoine Robidoux's description of California as a "paradise" that was in "perpetual spring." This was not what they were seeing, however.

Even though the land was not wearing its wedding clothes, the company must have felt inexpressible relief that they had finally made it. To their buoyant state of mind, the washed-out landscape should have appeared warm and inviting in comparison to the white salt flats, the sage-covered deserts, and the massive precipices and chasms of the Sierra Nevada Mountains through which they had struggled.

Following Jones and the Indian, the company likely took an Indian trail west until they struck the San Joaquin River, then crossed to its western side. The time of year bestowed an important benefit on the weary expeditioners. Since the snows in the high Sierras from the previous winter had mostly melted, rivers were running at their lowest stages. Coupled with the effects of the recent drought, the San Joaquin River would have been unusually low, making its crossing much less difficult. It is impossible to know where the company crossed, but a review of the elevations of the area, as revealed on Google Earth, provides a clue. An Indian trail approaching the river likely followed the highest ground as it would be a usable route even during wet periods.

Based on these factors, it is estimated that the group crossed the river about three miles east of Interstate 5 and five miles south of its intersection with Highway 205. Durham Ferry would be established at this location in a few years, and its attributes would make it a popular crossing of the river for gold miners when traveling between San Francisco and the gold country.

November 4

Upon leaving the river on the morning of November 4, the company passed through some low areas that, despite the drought, were green, marshy, and full of bulrushes. Josiah Belden commented in his memoirs, "[c]rossing the valley at that time, we saw immense herds of wild horses and elk running over the plain."[7]

It was a long day's travel as they struggled on toward Marsh's ranch. At long last, they would meet the fabled man whose letters had excited so many. Members of the company had undoubtedly brought up his name from time to time during the journey. They must have conjured mental images of an affluent landowner with a prosperous estancia. They had probably imagined him welcoming them and sitting them down at long tables piled high with fresh meats, fruits, and vegetables, fine wines, rich cheeses, cream, and butter. They may have imagined their every need being attended to by numerous servants, and dreamed of sinking into soft mattresses and being covered with thick, down-filled quilts. Indeed, such visions may have played a role in sustaining their long march that day.

After traveling about twenty-five miles, this party of gaunt, greasy, unwashed men (and one woman and child) rounded a hill. The Indian pointed. Ahead was their destination, a small, primitive adobe hut, standing beside a dry creek fringed by willows, sycamores, and a few oaks. Bidwell's journal entry described the day:

> *T. 4th. Left the river in good season and departing gradually from its timber—came into large marshes of Bulrushes. We saw large herds of elk and wild Horses grazing upon the plain. The earth was in many places*

strongly impregnated with salt—came into hills. Here were a few scattering oaks—land appeared various, in some places black, some light clay color, and in other mulatto (between black and white) sometimes inclining to a red soil, but it was all parched with heat, finally we arrived at Marsh's house, which is built of unburnt bricks, small and has no fireplace—wanting a floor and covered with bulrushes. In fact it was not what I expected to find, a hog was killed for the company. We had nothing else but beef, the latter was used as bread, the former as meat. Therefore I will say we had bread and meat for dinner. Several of our company were old acquaintances of Marsh in Missouri, and therefore much time was passed in talking about old times, the incidents of our late Journey, and our future prospects.—All encamped about the house—tolerably well pleased with the appearance of Dr. Marsh, but much disappointed in regard to his situation, for among all his shrubby white oaks, there was not one tall enough to make a rail-cut. No other timber in sight, excepting a few cottonwoods and willows.

Years later, Bidwell's memoirs added more:

Dr. Marsh knew that we were coming, but it would take us two or three days to reach his place, which we did on the evening of the 4th of November, 1841. He seemed delighted to see us and was very communicative and even enthusiastic. Some of our party had known his acquaintance in Missouri and all had a great deal to say. We camped near his house under the large spreading oaks. The country was nearly destitute of grass and the cause of it we learned to be the unprecedented dry season. He killed a hog for us, which was very acceptable. Although no grain had been raised and was consequently scarce, he managed to have a few tortillas made and distributed to us. In return for the kindness extended to us, we opened our treasures consisting of cans of powder, butcher knives, lead and various other useful articles and made the doctor what we considered liberal presents in return. I remember one of the party presented him with a case of surgical instruments. As for money, we had little or none.[8]

Joseph Chiles's memoirs provided his own details:

[Marsh's] house consisted of three small rooms, built of sticks and mud; the furniture, which they considered excellent, consisted of two or three benches, and a rude table, and if the weather was foul, a skin was spread upon the ground inside the dwelling and a skin or two for covering, but if the weather was fair, sleeping was always out of

> doors. Dr. Marsh, although a man of good education, had taken himself an Indian wife and had several children with whom he seemed well pleased. Their living was almost entirely beef which was roasted over a fire out of doors and the hungry travelers thought it was excellent fare.[9]

Dawson wrote that when they arrived, "Marsh was very kind and asked us what we craved the most. We told him something fat. He had a fat hog. This he killed for us and divided it among the messes. We relished it greatly. He also had a small quantity of wheat that he was saving to plant. A part of this he had made into tortillas for us." But their digestive systems had grown unaccustomed to fat and they became sick. As Dawson explained, "they had eaten too much pork."[10] He complained about his difficulties trying to sleep in Marsh's hut that night, writing that "we were much disturbed by fleas, and sick-stomached men trying to get over us."[11]

It would be expected that the new arrivals were sorely disappointed in Marsh's circumstances. After all, his letters had depicted California as an idyllic paradise. It must have been a shock finding him living in such squalor, his house smaller and more primitive than anything they could have imagined. His servants, if you could call them that, were but a few Indians living in grass huts. Because of the drought, Marsh's cattle had likely cropped the grass all the way to the dirt. There was little here but a scene of poverty. The important thing, they had to keep in mind, was that their trip was finally behind them. After five and a half months—174 days—of arduous and dangerous travel, it was completed. Everyone had made it alive, except for George Shotwell.

IT HAD BEEN four days since we last heard from Jimmy John. Having lost his horse, he had remained camping for the last three days on the south bank of the Consumnes River, hunting deer and trying to gather strength. Finally, on November 4, he resumed his efforts.

Jimmy John:

> 4th. This morning I hid my saddle and such things as I could not carry and took with me my saddlebag, pistols and some dried meat. I hid my gun barrel also for I broke the stalk [stock] off it the night I camped here for when I shot the buck it was about to run and being in a hurry

creased him in the neck. He fell but when I approached him, he raised and made battle with me and having nothing else in my hand, I pelted him over the head with my gun. I went down the creek in hopes of finding some settlers but found that [it] turned into a flat tula [tule] swamp. I returned and took the path that led across the creek in a north course. Traveled over a plain about 12 miles and came to a lake where I sit down to rest. I saw an Indian on the opposite side of the Lake. They were afraid of me and went back to their camp. I went down the neck of the Lake and saw their chief approaching me cautiously. I becned to him to come to me which he did. He spoke Spanish which I could not understand. I made signs to him that I wished to go to some settlements. He told me to come to his camp and there would be 2 men there in the evening and they would take me to a house. I stayed here and roasted fish until evening for they were fishing in the Lake with a sein which is near the bank of the Sacrimenta [Sacramento]. About sunset two Indians came on horses and took me and my baggage to Captain Siuter's [Sutter's] house, a distance of 6 miles. Captain Siuter has a fort here made of dobies [adobes] and burned brick, mounted with a few few old cannons and guarded by about 29 men, mostly runaway sailors and Canackers or Owihees [Hawaiians] besides a number of pet Indians which he employs for war parties and who built his fort and farm. He keeps also a harem of Canacker women. This place is called New Helvitia. He has a farm attached to it of perhaps 150 acres in cultivation and also a great number of cattle and horses and mules. This place is situated about two miles from the Sacrimenta river and about the same distance from the mouth of a small river called the American fork of the Sacrimenta.

Upon leaving his camp on the morning of November 4, Jimmy John traveled downstream a few miles until the Consumnes River spread out into a swamp, probably near where it joined the San Joaquin River. The swamp was an impassible barrier, so he returned to camp. After locating the path he had discovered on October 31, he crossed the Consumnes River and followed that path north for about twelve miles until he encountered some Indians on the shore of a lake near the Sacramento River channel. They spoke Spanish and arranged for other Indians to lead him the final six miles north to Sutter's Fort. It seems extraordinarily coincidental that Jimmy John arrived at Sutter's Fort on November 4, the same day that the rest of the company arrived at Marsh's ranch.

November 5 to November 20, 1841

When the company rose after their first night at Marsh's, the doctor's congenial mood had changed. The day before, he was affable and hospitable, and seemed to be genuinely delighted with the company's arrival. But he had a reputation for being greedy and miserly. A graduate of Harvard, Marsh had shown the Mexican authorities his Harvard diploma when he first arrived in California in 1836. He claimed he was a doctor, even though he had never earned a medical degree. Unable to read English, the Mexicans were impressed with his diploma and accepted his word that it was a medical degree. They were delighted to receive him since he would be the only doctor in all of Upper California. With his earnings from practicing medicine, he purchased Los Madános, a seventeen-thousand-acre rancho at the eastern base of Mount Diablo in today's Contra Costa County. He continued to provide medical services to people in the region when called upon, but was known for charging outrageous and unconscionable fees.[12]

Marsh had probably stewed all night about his visitors consuming his livestock and wheat. He awoke in a brooding mood the next morning, no longer able to suppress his tight-fisted temperament. His congeniality had evaporated and his true personality had boiled to the surface. Bidwell's memoirs recalled:

> The next morning [November 5] I rose early, among the first, in order to learn from our host something about California—what we could do, where we could go—and, as strange as it may seem, he would scarcely answer a question. He seemed to be in an ill humor, and among other things he said: "The company has already been over a hundred dollars expense to me, and God knows if I will ever get a real of it or not." I was at a loss to account for this, and went out and told some of the party, and found that others had been snubbed in a similar manner. We held a consultation and resolved to leave as soon as convenient.[13]

With their decision to leave Marsh's squalid circumstances and get away from his sour personality, the company divided and went in different directions. Half of the company decided to return to the San Joaquin River to spend the winter trapping otter, since their pelts would fetch $3 apiece. The other half of the company, fourteen men, decided to go to the Pueblo de San Jose (now the city of San Jose) to see what employment opportunities existed. Only Bidwell remained behind at Marsh's because he thought someone needed to guard the company's belongings.

After the San Jose party had been gone a few days, Michael Nye returned to Marsh's rancho carrying a letter from Mariano Vallejo, the comandante general of Upper California. The letter advised Marsh that the Americans had been arrested and were being held in a jail at Mission San Jose because they were foreigners unlawfully in the country without the proper *cartas de seguridad*, or passports. Vallejo had been told by the Americans that they had come because of Marsh's invitation.[14] Vallejo's letter ordered Marsh to present himself "with the greatest possible promptness."[15]

The Bartleson expedition had arrived in a foreign country beset by tension, intrigue, and suspicion. The Californios were nervous about anyone showing up in their province. The previous year, Isaac Graham, an American saloon owner living near Monterey, together with his American friends (mostly former trappers and escaped sailors), had taunted Governor Alvarado in Monterey by toasting the new Republic of Texas and chanting "California next!"[16] This was when California was populated by an estimated five to seven thousand Mexican Californios, mostly descendants of Spanish soldiers who had been sent at one time or another to protect the Franciscan priests in the early stages of establishing their missions. At the same time, an estimated 300 British and French and 360 Americans now lived there.[17] The Californios may have held the land and power, but they knew that their grip on their fiefdom was precarious. Fearful of an insurrection, Governor Alvarado decided to take no chances and had Graham and his friends rounded up and sent by ship to Mexico as prisoners.[18] The Californios then heard a rumor that a large number of Americans were on their way to conquer their province. In consequence, the Mexican minister of war in Mexico City issued a decree on May 18, 1841, just as the Bartleson expedition was leaving Missouri, to detain and deport any *extranjeros* who arrived in California without passports.[19]

After Vallejo interrogated the Americans, he concluded that they had not come with the intent to conquer. Rather, he decided that they were, according to his own words, "industrious individuals" who could be beneficial to an area that lacked "strong and intelligent workers."[20] He decided to issue them passports in lieu of deportation. Because of Marsh's role in bringing them here, however, he intended to make Marsh vouch for their behavior.

When Nye arrived at Marsh's, Bidwell was asked by Marsh to write down the names of everyone in the company. Marsh took the list with him to Mission San Jose. Vallejo issued the passports and released the men, but only after having Marsh sign as a surety, guaranteeing their good conduct.[21] This was a bone in Marsh's throat, but the shrewd man figured he could turn it into a business opportunity. When he and the Americans had returned to his ranch, Bidwell recalled in his memoirs that Marsh said to them: "Now, men, I want you all to come into the house and I will tell you your fate." Inside, he told them, "You men that have five dollars can have passports and remain in the country and go wherever you please." Thinking they had no choice, the men purchased their passports. As for the men who had no money, they gave Marsh notes and goods of equivalent value.[22]

Nicholas Dawson and Josiah Belden had not been among those returning to Marsh's after being released from jail. Thomas Bowen, an American, had given Dawson a job at his distillery in the redwood forests west of San Jose, and Josiah Belden had traveled to Monterey and became employed as a clerk for shop owner and U.S. consul, Thomas O. Larkin.

Bidwell learned that Marsh had not obtained a passport for him. Stunned, he asked Marsh, "Have you no passport for me?" Marsh responded, "No, you do not need any." Bidwell then asked, "Why, am I not a man?"[23] The conniving Marsh had thought that without a passport, Bidwell would have to "stay at his ranch and make a useful hand."[24] But Marsh had underestimated Bidwell. The furious Bidwell set out for Mission San Jose the next morning, on November 15, determined to get his own passport. As soon as he arrived in the mission village, he, too, was promptly arrested and thrown into jail for lack of the needed document. After languishing in the *calaboose* for three days, Thomas Bowen appeared on November 18 and persuaded Vallejo to issue a passport for Bidwell as well. In their discussions, Bidwell learned from Vallejo that Marsh had obtained the passports "for the asking; they had cost him nothing." At the same time, Vallejo learned from Bidwell that Marsh had charged the men for them, something that angered Vallejo.[25] The poor Americans had been humbugged by Marsh.

By now, Bidwell had added Marsh to his list of men he strongly disliked, calling him "one of the most selfish of mortals."[26] In his March 1842 letter, Bidwell used a few choice words to describe the man: "He is perhaps the meanest man in California. . . . [H]e had already got from them 5 times the value of his pig and bullock in different kinds of articles—powder, lead, knives, etc. . . . There is not an individual in California who does not dislike the man."[27] Bidwell went on to describe how Marsh charged exorbitant fees for his medical services, giving specific examples. In one instance, Marsh charged fifty cows for administering medicine to a boy with a headache. The family was poor, but the boy's mother was clever and she offered to wash the doctor's shirt. Marsh let her do it, and then he learned that she had cleverly charged him twenty-five cows for the service.[28]

The group that had been jailed at Mission San Jose had heard about John Sutter, and they decided to travel to Sutter's Fort. Deeply in debt in his native Switzerland, Sutter had fled his creditors, taking the money he owed them. Leaving his wife and children behind, he sailed for the United States, and then traveled with a wagon party to Oregon in 1838. From there, took a ship to the Sandwich Islands (Hawaii). Then he went to California, arriving at Monterey in 1839. He persuaded the California governor to allow him to explore the Sacramento River. Impressed with the area around the confluence of the Sacramento and American rivers, he obtained ownership of it. He rented three vessels and, with three white men and ten Hawaiian employees, he traveled up the Sacramento River to begin building his settlement. It began with the construction of an adobe brick fort, perhaps inspired by what he had seen when he passed through Fort Laramie, Fort Hall, Fort Boise, and Fort Vancouver during his 1838 trip to Oregon.

Sutter learned that the Russian-American Fur Company was planning to abandon its fur trading posts at Fort Ross and Bodega Bay along the Northern California Coast. He struck a deal with the Russians in which they sold him their livestock, a small launch, and other assets, including forty cannons and a quantity of muskets for the purchase price of $30,000. Sutter was shrewd and he got the Russians to agree that he could pay the price over the next number of years in installments of grain that he intended to produce on his land.[29]

With their passports, Bidwell and his companions were now free to move about without being arrested. So they left Marsh's ranch on November 20 and set out for Sutter's Fort. Because of heavy rains it

*John A. Sutter, circa 1865.
Record No. 001387367. Courtesy of
the California State Library.*

took them eight days slogging through wet, flooded conditions to make the eighty-mile trip. Upon arriving, Bidwell recalled that "Sutter received us with open arms and in a princely fashion." Bidwell recalled, "[O]ur coming was not unexpected."[30] Of course. Sutter had learned about the expedition when Jimmy John staggered into his fort on November 4.

There had been growing alarm among the Californios about the fortress that Sutter was building on the Sacramento River. They were concerned that it would become a magnet attracting large numbers of Americans, and they viewed it as a potential haven for an insurgency. The Californios feared that their province would eventually be overrun by these foreigners. And eventually, it would. Sutter was aware of their unease and felt increasingly under threat. With Sutter's near impregnable fortress nearing completion, the Californios may have been correct that he had ambitions to carve out his own country, independent of Mexico. In fact, Sutter sent a letter to Vallejo's brother-in-law expressing his suspicion that the Californios intended "to drive" him "out of the country."[31] By offering employment to Bidwell and the others when they arrived, Sutter was not only securing the services of men who could help him finish his fort, but also recruiting men who could help defend him and his land if it came down to it.

THIS CONCLUDES THE STORY of the Bartleson party's long journey to California and of the first two weeks after they arrived. They may have reached their destination awkwardly and imperfectly, but they had succeeded in their bold and virtually impossible venture. They had become the first company of American emigrants to make it to California by land. Considering what they had endured and overcome during their five-and-a-half-month-long journey, it is impossible to not appreciate what they had done. They had not always been noble, virtuous, or smart. Their ignorance was astonishing. Their preparations were laughable. Their decisions were frequently inept. Their periodic failures to support each other were disturbing. Yet, somehow, there was enough glue and good sense in most of them to generally hold everything together. It was a classic example of how an epic, heroic venture could be completed by flawed men acting in imperfect ways. Considering the mistakes they made and the hardships they encountered, it was nothing short of a miracle that all of them made it (except for Shotwell). More than anything, they succeeded because of their toughness and unwavering resolve. They would not give up, and just kept going. They were the kind of hardboiled people it would take to open and settle the West.

Their journey was a groundbreaking event, demonstrating once and for all that wagons could be taken further west than previously believed. They proved that an expedition of determined people could make it. Word of the company's success eventually spread, although most of the newspapers ignored it. Wagon parties would head to California—one in 1843, one in 1844, a couple in 1845, and a number of them in 1846. Because of these arrivals, there were enough Americans in California by 1846 that they felt emboldened to rise up and wrest control of the province from Mexico. More wagon parties followed in 1847 and 1848. Then the discovery of gold in 1848 sent an explosive shockwave that reverberated throughout the nation. The earlier trickle into California became an overwhelming flood.

Epilogue

It is natural to be curious about what happened to various members of the Bartleson party after November 20, 1841. This Epilogue will provide a few highlights.

Many in the company looked around and determined that despite its various attributes, California was not for them. They preferred to remain Americans and had no interest in becoming Mexican citizens. So they decided to return to Missouri in the coming spring. One of them was Joseph Chiles. Before he left, he traveled to Napa Valley and met with George Yount, a former neighbor from Independence. Yount had been a Santa Fe trapper and belonged to a trapping brigade that entered California in 1831 by way of the southern route. Yount liked what he saw and stayed, eventually acquiring a rancho in the beautiful Napa Valley. Yount encouraged Chiles to take the southern route back to Missouri and gave him directions.

Chiles's group assembled at Sutter's Fort in April, 1842, after which he added a few others who were still camping on the San Joaquin River. For the most part, the group consisted of members of the Bartleson party who had not seen enough in California to make them want to stay. They marched south through the Central Valley and left the valley through Tejon Pass, south of today's Bakersfield, California. After struggling across the waterless Mojave Desert, they crossed the Colorado River and marched on until they reached Santa Fe. From there they took the Santa Fe Trail to Independence and arrived on September 9, 1842. Those making the overland trip to Missouri in 1842 included Joseph Chiles, John Bartleson, Charles Hopper, John McDowell, Andrew (Gwinn) Patton, Robert Rickman, John Roland, James Springer, Ambrose Walton, and Major Walton.[1] It is not surprising to see Bartleson's name among them, as we recall him declaring on October 16, "Boys! If I ever get back to Missouri, I will never leave there again." True to his word, he lived his final years in Independence and died there in 1848 at sixty-two years of age.

Chiles was different. He had been beguiled by what he had seen in California, being particularly impressed with the beauty of Monterey and the Napa Valley. Noticing how the region badly needed a flour mill, he returned to Missouri for the express purpose of organizing a new wagon party to take to California in the spring of 1843. This time, he took his millwright friend, William Baldinger. Meeting the elusive Joseph Walker at Fort Laramie that year, Chiles managed to hire him to pilot his party the rest of the way. After arriving in California, Baldinger helped Chiles build his flour mill near Napa Valley. Chiles returned to Independence in 1847 to fetch his young children, and in 1848 he guided another wagon party back to California. Sadly, Chiles appears to have been an adherent of Bartleson's perverse values. He took alcohol with him in 1848 and sold it to the Indians along the way. When some in his company were struggling to cross the Sierra Nevadas at Carson Pass, Chiles was perfectly willing, like Bartleson, to leave some of them behind to fend for themselves. He even engaged in extortion by offering to help one of his stragglers on the condition that the man give him his wagon and team of oxen.[2]

Charles Hopper also returned to California, coming back in 1847 and settled on a farm in Napa Valley.[3]

There were a few from the company who left California soon after arriving, but who did not accompany Chiles. Henry Brolaski returned to Missouri by unknown means, and then came back to California during the Gold Rush.[4] George Henshaw, the old invalid, decided he had experienced enough of overland travel and returned east by ship.[5] Jimmy John did not stick around either, and moved to Oregon in the summer of 1842. He remained there the rest of his life.[6]

Nicholas Dawson remained in California about three years and then returned to Arkansas. He returned briefly to California to participate in the frenzied Gold Rush and after collecting about $1,600, he returned east and spent the rest of his life in Texas.[7]

Those who stayed in California included John Bidwell, Josiah Belden, William Belty, Elias Burnett, David Chandler, Grove Cook, Talbot Green, Henry Huber, Ben and Nancy Kelsey, Andrew Kelsey, Samuel McMahon, Michael Nye, John Schwartz, Robert Thomes, and Charles Weber.[8] These men and women played roles of varying significance in the future development of California. Some were involved in the Bear Flag Revolt in 1846 and some became members of John Frémont's California Battalion that defeated the Californios later that year.

A few of the above became very wealthy, which was not that difficult because the region offered limitless opportunities for those willing to take advantage of them. Two factors played important roles in enriching them. The first was the receipt of generous land grants. Unhappy with the neglectful and erratic administration of Governor Alvarado, authorities in Mexican City had appointed Manuel Micheltorena in 1842 to go to California and replace him. When Governor Micheltorena arrived in California with about three hundred soldiers, Alvarado and his Californio compatriots appeared to welcome the new governor's arrival, but in truth they were seething and began plotting an insurrection. Micheltorena needed help and turned to Sutter and the Americans for support. Sutter agreed to cast his lot with the new governor. Most Americans, including Bidwell, did the same out of loyalty to Sutter. But it was more than that. Bidwell briefly met with Micheltorena in Monterey in 1844. When he returned to Sutter's Fort, Bidwell told his friends that they should all support Micheltorena because he was "promising us grants of land."[9] Micheltorena honored his word and busily issued land grants to Americans during 1844 as if he were handing out glass beads.

The second factor that enriched some of the settlers was the discovery of gold in January 1848. A number of the former Bartleson party members were among the first to race into the hills to look for it. Others, eschewing mining, found that providing supplies to the miners was just as lucrative, if not more so. Some engaged in land speculation and became wealthy as land prices in places like San Francisco shot through the roof.

Grove Cook, after being employed by Sutter for a number of years to run his distillery, left Sutter and moved to the San Jose area to purchase Thomas Bowen's distillery. Cook received a land grant in 1844 from the governor and became a wealthy rancher.[10]

After Josiah Belden's stint as a clerk in the store of Thomas Larkin in Monterey, he obtained a large land grant from Micheltorena of twenty-one thousand acres near today's Red Bluff, California. During the Gold Rush, he began selling supplies to the miners.[11]

Henry Huber became prosperous by engaging in land speculation.[12] Talbot Green became a clerk in Thomas Larkin's store in Monterey, then invested in San Francisco real estate and became extremely wealthy selling off his shrewd investments.[13]

Robert Thomes had been a wagon builder in Weston, Missouri, when he left with Bidwell in 1841. His woodworking skills were highly valued in skill-starved California. After first working as a carpenter in San Francisco, he moved to Monterey, where he became a house builder for the locals. Then Micheltorena granted him twenty-two thousand acres in 1844 in what is now Tehama County. Thomes acquired even more wealth during the Gold Rush when he discovered rich deposits along the Feather River.[14]

Charles Weber was never specifically mentioned by any of the diarists or other narrators during the trip, but he became a young man of great significance in the development of California. He left Sutter's employment in the spring of 1842 and moved to San Jose. He formed a partnership with a local blacksmith, an American by the name of William Gulnac. The Californios produced virtually nothing for themselves, buying what they needed off of ships coming from Boston, and paying with hides and tallow. Weber saw the opportunities and took advantage of a number of them. He and his partner built San Jose's first flour mill as well as California's first shoe factory and soap factory. They also started a hotel, bakery, saltworks, and general store. In 1844, Micheltorena gave them a land grant of forty-eight thousand acres butting up against the east bank of the San Joaquin River. Weber bought out Gulnac's interest and founded the town of Stockton. With the discovery of gold, Weber was among the first to go looking for it and found rich deposits. He became enormously wealthy, not only from his gold discoveries, but because his town of Stockton became a major supply point for the miners.[15]

This Epilogue will end with our principal diarist, John Bidwell. From the point of view of the other narrators, Bidwell was rarely mentioned in their description of the trip. When he was, it seemed as if he was not held in high regard. His "snow" adventure near Soda Springs may have branded him as a reckless youngster with poor judgment, a reputation he did not seem to overcome during the rest of the journey. Historians usually refer to him as one of the leaders of the expedition, but it appears that he was treated as anything but. Nevertheless, his high energy, initiative, toughness, and bright intellect were traits that both Marsh and Sutter seemed to recognize. After Sutter hired him, Bidwell explained that early in 1842 Sutter engaged him "to go to Bodega and Fort Ross and to stay there until he could finish removing the property which he had bought from the Russians."[16] Bidwell spent fourteen months at Bodega Bay protecting Sutter's Russian assets and overseeing their movement to Sutter's Fort.

It was while Bidwell was working for Sutter at Bodega Bay that he worked on his lengthy letter iterating the details of their journey. It is unknown who took the letter east. Although it was dated March 30, 1842, it could not have been carried by Chiles or a member of his party because it recited dates and events later than when Chiles and his group had left California. Some authorities believe that it may have been carried east by Lansford Hastings in 1844. The letter was addressed to his friend Elam Brown in Weston, Missouri. "I never wrote it for publication," Bidwell later claimed, but it was published as a pamphlet by an unknown publisher in Weston. The only known copy of the pamphlet was carried to California in 1846 by George McKinstry Jr., and it is in the collections of the Bancroft Library. Bidwell's original trail journal has never been found and is evidently lost to history. His letter encouraged its readers to come to California, but he emphasized the need to bring a passport.

Bidwell may not have liked Bartleson and Marsh, but he admired Sutter a great deal. While Joseph Chiles appeared to have been influenced by the virtue-challenged Bartleson, Bidwell patterned his life after the open-armed hospitality he admired in Sutter. According to Bidwell's memoirs, Sutter was the polar opposite of Marsh, and he praised Sutter's generosity and good-heartedness:

> [Sutter] employed men, not because he always needed them and could profitably employ them, but because in the kindness of his heart it simply became a habit to employ everybody who wanted employment. As long as he had anything he trusted anyone with everything he wanted, responsible or otherwise, acquaintances and strangers alike.[17]

Bidwell was another who received a land grant from Governor Micheltorena. He was still working for Sutter in 1844 when the governor granted him eight thousand acres near today's town of Rio Vista, California. But he sold it and bought another land grant, Rancho Chico, along Chico Creek. Bidwell left Sutter in 1846 to begin developing his new ranch. In 1848, he found gold on the Feather River at a place later called Bidwell's Bar. He became a forward-looking, innovative, and progressive agriculturist. He founded the town of

Chico, and entered politics. He was elected to the first State Senate in 1849 and to Congress in 1864.[18] Later, he unsuccessfully ran as the Temperance Party's candidate for governor of California and for president of the United States. He died in 1900 at eighty years of age. In the end, Bidwell had made a great deal more of himself than his former trail mates ever thought he would.

Notes

Introduction

1. John D. Unruh Jr., *The Plains Across: The Overland Emigrants and the Trans-Mississippi Wesst, 1840–1860* (Urbana: University of Illinois Press, 1993), 120.
2. John Bidwell, *A Journey to California, 1841: The First Emigrant Party to California by Wagon Train* (1843; pamphlet in the possession of Bancroft Library, Berkeley, California; reprint, Berkeley: Friends of the Bancroft Library, 1964).
3. John Bidwell, "California 1841: An Immigrant's Recollection of a Trip Across the Plains" (manuscript in the possession of the Bancroft Library, Berkeley, California); John Bidwell, *Echoes of the Past about California* (Chico, Calif.: Chico Advertiser, 1914; reprint, New York: Citadel, 1962); Doyce B. Nunis, *The Bidwell-Bartleson Party: 1841 California Emigrant Adventure* (Santa Cruz: Western Tanager, 1991).

Prologue

1. William Swilling Wallace, *Antoine Robidoux, 1794–1860: A Biography of a Western Venturer* (Los Angeles: Glen Dawson, 1953), ix.
2. LeRoy R. Hafen, *Broken Hand: The Life of Thomas Fitzpatrick: Mountain Man, Guide, and Indian Agent* (Denver: Old West, 1931; reprint, Lincoln: University of Nebraska Press, 1981), 163–64.
3. Bernard DeVoto, *Across the Wide Missouri* (1947; reprint, New York: Houghton Mifflin, 1998), 23.
4. Robert Morgan, *Boone: A Biography* (Chapel Hill, N.C.: Algonquin, 2008), 135.
5. Louise Barry, *The Beginning of the West: Annals of the Kansas Gateway to the American West, 1540–1854* (Topeka: Kansas State Historical Society, 1972), 271.
6. Ibid., 78, 125.
7. Ibid., 179–80, 204–5, 249, 253.
8. DeVoto, *Across the Wide Missouri*, 8.
9. Barry, *The Beginning of the West*, 262.
10. Ibid., 303; Frances Fuller Victor, *The River of the West: The Adventures of Joe Meek*, vol. 1 (1870; reprint, Missoula: Mountain Press, 1983), 77.
11. Barry, *The Beginning of the West*, 150, 257, 309.

Chapter 1: Dreams of High Adventure

1. Nunis, *The Bidwell-Bartleson Party*, 98.
2. Bidwell, *Echoes of the Past about California*, 5.
3. Barry, *The Beginning of the West*, 310, 315; Robert J. Willoughby, *Robidoux's Town: A Nineteenth Century History of St. Joseph, Missouri* (St. Joseph: St. Joseph Museum, 2006), 15.
4. Bidwell, *Echoes of the Past about California*, 9.
5. Ibid., 12; Nunis, *The Bidwell-Bartleson Party*, 77.
6. Bidwell, *Echoes of the Past about California*, 12.
7. Nunis, *The Bidwell-Bartleson Party*, 77
8. Ibid.
9. Barry, *The Beginning of the West*, 115, 125; Josiah Belden, *Josiah Belden, 1841 California Overland Pioneer: His Memoir and Early Letters*, ed. Doyce B. Nunis (Georgetown, Calif.: Talisman, 1962), 14, 29; Nunis, *The Bidwell-Bartleson Party*, 121n7; Wallace, *Antoine Robidoux*, 39.
10. Barry, *The Beginning of the West*, 295–96.
11. Nunis, *The Bidwell-Bartleson Party*, 101; Bidwell, *Echoes of the Past about California*, 14; Wallace, *Antoine Robidoux*, 39.
12. Edwin Bryant, *What I Saw in California: Being the Journal of a Tour, by the Emigrant Route and South Pass of the Rocky Mountains, across the Great Desert Basin, and through California, in the Years 1846, 1847* (1848; reprint, Crabtree, Ore.: Narrative Press, 2001), 4.
13. Bidwell, *Echoes of the Past about California*, 15; Nunis, *The Bidwell-Bartleson Party*, 78.
14. Nunis, *The Bidwell-Bartleson Party*, 79.
15. Ibid., 78.
16. Bidwell, *Echoes of the Past about California*, 20
17. Nunis, *The Bidwell-Bartleson Party*, 23, 78, 103, 122.
18. Ibid., 78–79.
19. Nunis, *The Bidwell-Bartleson Party*, 104.
20. Ibid., 78; Bidwell, *Echoes of the Past about California*, 20–21.
21. Nunis, *The Bidwell-Bartleson Party*, 79.
22. Bidwell, *Echoes of the Past about California*, 22–23.
23. Nunis, *The Bidwell-Bartleson Party*, 79, 104.
24. Ibid., 142; Helen S. Giffen, *Trail-Blazing Pioneer: Colonel Joseph Ballinger Chiles* (San Francisco: John Howell, 1969), 2.
25. "California and Oregon," *Colonial Magazine* 5 (1841): 229–36, Nunis, *The Bidwell-Bartleson Party*, 275.
26. Transcribed from *Western Atlas*, March 8, 1841, by Dale L. Morgan. From the Dale L. Morgan Research Files at the Huntington Library, San Merino, Calif.
27. Ibid., May 1, 1841.
28. Nicholas Dawson, *Narrative of Nicholas "Cheyenne" Dawson: Overland to California in '41 & '49, and Texas in '51* (San Francisco: Grabhorn, 1933), 2.
29. Ibid., 7.
30. Ibid., 8–9.
31. Ibid., 9.
32. Ibid., 10; Barry, *The Beginning of the West*, 429.

NOTES

33. Barry, *The Beginning of the West*, 429; Nunis, *The Bidwell-Bartleson Party*, 196.

34. Giffen, *Trail-Blazing Pioneer*, 6.

35. Belden, *Josiah Belden, 1841 California Overland Pioneer*, 35–36.

36. Ibid., 36.

37. Hiram Martin Chittenden and Alfred Talbot Richardson, *Life, Letters and Travels of Father Pierre-Jean De Smet, S.J.*, vol. 1 (New York: Francis P. Harper), 1905, 290.

38. Barry, *The Beginning of the West*, 206; DeVoto, *Across the Wide Missouri*, 13–14.

39. DeVoto, *Across the Wide Missouri*, 13.

40. Barry, *The Beginning of the West*, 392, 409.

41. Chittenden and Richardson, *Life, Letters and Travels of Father Pierre-Jean De Smet, S.J.*, 273–74.

42. Barry, *The Beginning of the West*, 428; Nicolas Point, S.J., *Wilderness Kingdom, Indian Life in the Rocky Mountains: 1840–1847, the Journals and Paintings of Nicolas Point, S.J.*, trans. Joseph P. Donnelly, S.J. (Chicago: Loyola University Press, 1967), 6–7.

43. Bidwell, *Echoes of the Past about California*, 10.

44. Nunis, *The Bidwell-Bartleson Party*, 123n20.

45. Dale L. Morgan, Research Files.

Chapter 2: The Gathering at Sapling Grove

1. Nunis, *The Bidwell-Bartleson Party*, 79.

2. Ibid.

3. Ibid., 204.

4. Barry, *The Beginning of the West*, 81.

5. Gregory M. Franzwa, *The Oregon Trail Revisited*, 3rd ed. (St. Louis: Patrice Press, 1990), 87.

6. Barry, *The Beginning of the West*, 426–27.

7. Ibid., 425–26; Aubrey L. Haines, *Historic Sites along the Oregon Trail* (Tucson: Patrice Press, 1981), 30.

8. Ibid., 416, 457.

9. Chittenden and Richardson, *Life, Letters and Travels of Father Pierre-Jean De Smet, S.J.*, 279.

10. Ibid.

11. Ibid., 279; Point, *Wilderness Kingdom*, 24.

12. Point, *Wilderness Kingdom*, 24.

13. Chittenden and Richardson, *Life, Letters and Travels of Father Pierre-Jean De Smet, S.J.*, 279.

14. Point, *Wilderness Kingdom*, 24.

15. Bryant, *What I Saw in California*, 8.

16. National Park Service webpage re, Sapling Grove, http://www.nps.gov/safe/learn/historyculture/loader.cfm?csModule=security/getfile&PageID=2319445.

17. National Park Service webpage re Sapling Grove, http://www.nps.gov/safe/learn/historyculture/loader.cfm?csModule=security/getfile&PageID=2319441.

18. Bidwell, *Echoes of the Past about California*, 21–22.
19. Dawson, *Narrative of Nicholas "Cheyenne" Dawson*, 9.
20. Belden, *Josiah Belden, 1841 California Overland Pioneer*, 37.
21. Dawson, *Narrative of Nicholas "Cheyenne" Dawson*, 9.
22. Point, *Wilderness Kingdom*, 26.
23. Bidwell, *Echoes of the Past about California*, 23.
24. Nunis, *The Bidwell-Bartleson Party*, 13.
25. Ibid., 8.
26. Bidwell, *Echoes of the Past about California*, 15.
27. Nunis, *The Bidwell-Bartleson Party*, 79–80.
28. Bidwell, *Echoes of the Past about California*, 23.

Chapter 3: Sapling Grove to Kansas River Crossing

1. Bidwell, *Echoes of the Past about California*, 22.
2. Dawson, *Narrative of Nicholas "Cheyenne" Dawson*, 10.
3. Nunis, *The Bidwell-Bartleson Party*, 269.
4. National Park Service webpage re Sapling Grove, http://www.nps.gov/safe/learn/historyculture/loader.cfm?csModule=security/getfile&PageID=2319441.
5. Dale L. Morgan, Research Files.
6. Barry, *The Beginning of the West*, 171.
7. Haines, *Historic Sites along the Oregon Trail*, 34.
8. Franzwa, *The Oregon Trail Revisited*, 134.
9. Unruh, *The Plains Across*, 120.
10. Bryant, *What I Saw in California*, 17.
11. J. Quinn Thornton, *Oregon and California in 1848* (1849; reprint, New York: Arno, 1973), 20, 22.
12. Ibid., 30.
13. Ibid., 31.
14. Haines, *Historic Sites along the Oregon Trail*, 40.
15. Charles L. Camp, *James Clyman, Frontiersman: The Adventures of a Trapper and Covered Wagon Emigrant as Told in His Own Reminiscences and Diaries* (Portland: Champoeg, 1960), 74.
16. Chittenden and Richardson, *Life, Letters and Travels of Father Pierre-Jean De Smet, S.J.*, 280.
17. Barry, *The Beginning of the West*, 474; Haines, *Historic Sites along the Oregon Trail*, 40.
18. Ibid., 428.
19. Point, *Wilderness Kingdom*, 26.
20. Belden, *Josiah Belden, 1841 California Overland Pioneer*, 37.
21. Chittenden and Richardson, *Life, Letters and Travels of Father Pierre-Jean De Smet, S.J.*, 280.
22. Thornton, *Oregon and California in 1848*, 33–36.
23. Barry, *The Beginning of the West*, 429; Giffen, *Trail-Blazing Pioneer*, 5.
24. Nunis, *The Bidwell-Bartleson Party*, 182.
25. Giffen, *Trail-Blazing Pioneer*, 6.
26. Ibid., 6, 8.
27. Nunis, *The Bidwell-Bartleson Party*, 160; James Shebel, *Weber! The Ameri-*

can Adventures of Captain Charles M. Weber (Lodi, Calif.: San Joaquin Historical Society, 1993), 3, 12.

Chapter 4: Organizing and Departing

1. Nunis, *The Bidwell-Bartleson Party*, 104.
2. Point, *Wilderness Kingdom*, 26.
3. Ibid.
4. Ibid.
5. Thornton, *Oregon and California in 1848*, 21.
6. Chittenden and Richardson, *Life, Letters and Travels of Father Pierre-Jean De Smet, S.J.*, 276.
7. Bidwell, *Echoes of the Past about California*, 27–28.
8. Dixon Ford and Lee Kreutzer, "Oxen: Engines of the Overland Emigration," *Overland Journal* 33, no. 1 (spring 2015): 16.
9. Ibid., 18.
10. Barry, *The Beginning of the West*, 166.
11. Chittenden and Richardson, *Life, Letters and Travels of Father Pierre-Jean De Smet, S.J.*, 280–81.
12. Barry, *The Beginning of the West*, 208–9.
13. Stephen E. Ambrose, *Undaunted Courage: Meriwether Lewis, Thomas Jefferson and the Opening of the American West* (New York: Simon and Schuster, 1996), 42.
14. Point, *Wilderness Kingdom*, 28.
15. Chittenden and Richardson, *Life, Letters and Travels of Father Pierre-Jean De Smet, S.J.*, 282.
16. Camp, *James Clyman, Frontiersman*, 73.
17. Chittenden and Richardson, *Life, Letters and Travels of Father Pierre-Jean De Smet, S.J.*, 284.
18. Ibid., 284–85.
19. Barry, *The Beginning of the West*, 421; George E. Hyde, *The Pawnee Indians* (1951; reprint, Norman: University of Oklahoma Press, 1974), 203.
20. Barry, *The Beginning of the West*, 423.
21. Ibid.
22. Ibid.
23. Chittenden and Richardson, *Life, Letters and Travels of Father Pierre-Jean De Smet, S.J.*, 286.
24. Bidwell, *Echoes of the Past about California*, 25–26.
25. Chittenden and Richardson, *Life, Letters and Travels of Father Pierre-Jean De Smet, S.J.*, 286; Point, *Wilderness Kingdom*, 28.
26. Barry, *The Beginning of the West*, 289.
27. Bryant, *What I Saw in California*, 26, 28, 31.
28. Chittenden and Richardson, *Life, Letters and Travels of Father Pierre-Jean De Smet, S.J.*, 286–87.
29. DeVoto, *Across the Wide Missouri*, 75.
30. LeRoy R. Hafen, *Broken Hand: The Life of Thomas Fitzpatrick; Mountain Man, Guide and Indian Agent* (1931; reprint, Lincoln: University of Nebraska Press, 1981), 168.
31. Dawson, *Narrative of Nicholas "Cheyenne" Dawson*, 10.

32. Point, *Wilderness Kingdom*, 26.
32. Bidwell, *Echoes of the Past about California*, 28.
33. Ibid.
34. Nunis, *The Bidwell-Bartleson Party*, 105.
35. Ibid., 162.
36. Haines, *Historic Sites along the Oregon Trail*, 43.

Chapter 5: Across a Sea of Grass

1. Haines, *Historic Sites along the Oregon Trail*, 44.
2. Bryant, *What I Saw in California*, 13.
3. John C. Frémont, *Report of the Exploring Expedition to the Rocky Mountains in the Year 1842, and to Oregon and North California in the Years 1843–44* (1845; reprint, Santa Barbara: Narrative Press, 2002), 9.
4. Bryant, *What I Saw in California*, 25, 29.
5. Candace Savage, *Prairie: A Natural History* (Vancouver: Graystone, 2004), 64–70.
6. Bryant, *What I Saw in California*, 40.
7. Frémont, *Report of the Exploring Expedition*, 10.
8. Bryant, *What I Saw in California*, 32.
9. Hyde, *The Pawnee Indians*, 64.
10. Ibid., 180–81, 197–201, 228–29.
11. Ibid., 202, 364.
12. Barry, *The Beginning of the West*, 759.
13. Michael E. LaSalle, *Emigrants on the Overland Trail: The Wagon Trains of 1848* (Kirksville, Mo.: Truman State University Press, 2011), 71–72.
14. Barry, *The Beginning of the West*, 437–38; Rufus B. Sage, *Rocky Mountain Life, or, Startling Scenes and Perilous Adventures in the Far West, during an Expedition of Three Years* (1846; reprint, Lincoln: University of Nebraska Press, 1982), 32–33, 57.
15. Frémont, *Report of the Exploring Expedition*, 10.
16. Bryant, *What I Saw in California*, 33.
17. Ibid., 36.
18. Ibid., 41.
19. Chittenden and Richardson, *Life, Letters and Travels of Father Pierre-Jean De Smet, S.J.*, 287.
20. Point, *Wilderness Kingdom*, 30.
21. Joseph Williams, *Narrative of a Tour from the State of Indiana to the Oregon Territory in the Years 1841–2* (n.d.; reprint, New York: Cadmus Book Shop, 1921), 25–29.
22. Ibid., 29.
23. Ibid., 31.
24. Ford and Kreutzer, "Oxen," 15.
25. Williams, *Narrative of a Tour*, 33.
26. Ibid., 34.
27. Ibid., 32.
28. Ambrose, *Undaunted Courage*, 168.
29. Bryant, *What I Saw in California*, 42.
30. Camp, *James Clyman, Frontiersman*, 82.

31. Nunis, *The Bidwell-Bartleson Party*, 223.
32. Camp, *James Clyman, Frontiersman*, 83.
33. Hyde, *The Pawnee Indians*, 139.
34. Ibid., 140.
35. Ibid., 202, 364.
36. Williams, *Narrative of a Tour*, 34.
37. Barry, *The Beginning of the West*, 432.
38. Sage, *Rocky Mountain Life*, 52.
39. Point, *Wilderness Kingdom*, 30.
40. Frémont, *Report of the Exploring Expedition*, 12.

Chapter 6: Along the Platte River

1. Point, *Wilderness Kingdom*, 30.
2. Williams, *Narrative of a Tour*, 34.
3. Haines, *Historic Sites along the Oregon Trail*, 63.
4. LaSalle, *Emigrants on the Overland Trail*, 95.
5. Dawson, *Narrative of Nicholas "Cheyenne" Dawson*, 11–12.
6. Point, *Wilderness Kingdom*, 31.
7. Nunis, *The Bidwell-Bartleson Party*, 80.
8. Mike Tyson.
9. Belden, *Josiah Belden, 1841 California Overland Pioneer*, 38.
10. Ibid., 39.
11. Nunis, *The Bidwell-Bartleson Party*, 198.
12. Point, *Wilderness Kingdom*, 30.
13. Nunis, *The Bidwell-Bartleson Party*, 105.
14. George E. Hyde, *Red Cloud's Folk: A History of the Oglala Sioux Indians* (1937; reprint, Norman: University of Oklahoma Press, 1975), 5–29; John H. Moore, *The Cheyenne* (Malden, Mass.: Blackwell, 1996), 18, 32, 89.
15. Moore, *The Cheyenne*, 93.
16. Hyde, *The Pawnee Indians*, 180–81; Moore, *The Cheyenne*, 87.
17. Hyde, *The Pawnee Indians*, 184–86.
18. Thornton, *Oregon and California in 1848*, 66.
19. Hafen, *Broken Hand*, 184.
20. Williams, *Narrative of a Tour*, 35.
21. Ambrose, *Undaunted Courage*, 152.
22. Nunis, *The Bidwell-Bartleson Party*, 108.
23. Ibid., 214.
24. Dawson, *Narrative of Nicholas "Cheyenne" Dawson*, 13.
25. Frémont, *Report of the Exploring Expedition*, 176–77.
26. LaSalle, *Emigrants on the Overland Trail*, 92.
27. Frank G. Roe, *The North American Buffalo* (Toronto: University of Toronto Press, 1951), 78.
28. Frémont, *Report of the Exploring Expedition*, 17.
29. Camp, *James Clyman, Frontiersman*, 85.
30. Francis Parkman, *The Oregon Trail: Adventures on the Prairie in the 1840's* (n.d.; reprint, Santa Barbara: Narrative Press, 2001), 54.
31. LaSalle, *Emigrants on the Overland Trail*, 132.
32. Bidwell, *Echoes of the Past about California*, 30.

33. Nunis, *The Bidwell-Bartleson Party*, 81.
34. Point, *Wilderness Kingdom*, 32.
35. Ibid., 32.
36. Camp, *James Clyman, Frontiersman*, 85.
37. Haines, *Historic Sites along the Oregon Trail*, 74.
38. Ibid., 76, 80.
39. Point, *Wilderness Kingdom*, 26.
40. Williams, *Narrative of a Tour*, 37.
41. Ibid., 37.
42. Bidwell, *Echoes of the Past about California*, 31–32.
43. Bryant, *What I Saw in California*, 48.
44. Bidwell, *Echoes of the Past about California*, 30.
45. Bryant, *What I Saw in California*, 59.
46. Bidwell, *Echoes of the Past about California*, 31.
47. Belden, *Josiah Belden, 1841 California Overland Pioneer*, 36.
48. Nunis, *The Bidwell-Bartleson Party*, 222–23.
49. Ibid., 81.
50. Unruh, *The Plains Across*, 185, 410–13, 517n86.
51. Merrill J. Mattes, *The Great Platte River Road: The Covered Wagon Mainline via Fort Kearney to Fort Laramie* (Lincoln: Nebraska State Historical Society, 1969), 82; Unruh, *The Plains Across*, 516n75.
52. Unruh, *The Plains Across*, 308.
53. Hyde, *Red Cloud's Folk*, 49.
54. Mattes, *The Great Platte River Road*, 287; Sage, *Rocky Mountain Life*, 76.
55. LaSalle, *Emigrants on the Overland Trail*, 111–12.

Chapter 7: Fort Laramie and Beyond

1. Nunis, *The Bidwell-Bartleson Party*, 81.
2. Williams, *Narrative of a Tour*, 38.
3. Sage, *Rocky Mountain Life*, 90.
4. Nunis, *The Bidwell-Bartleson Party*, 108.
5. William E. Hill, *The California Trail: Yesterday and Today: A Pictorial Journey along the California Trail*, 2nd ed. (Boise: Tamarak, 1993), 113; Mattes, *The Great Platte River Road*, 404.
6. Williams, *Narrative of a Tour*, 38.
7. Mattes, *The Great Platte River Road*, 426–27.
8. Thornton, *Oregon and California in 1848*, 107.
9. Camp, *James Clyman, Frontiersman*, 89.
10. Parkman, *The Oregon Trail*, 84.
11. Mattes, *The Great Platte River Road*, 451.
12. Haines, *Historic Sites along the Oregon Trail*, 112.
13. Hyde, *The Pawnee Indians*, 231.
14. Barry, *The Beginning of the West*, 1029–32; Hafen, *Broken Hand*, 300–301; Haines, *Historic Sites along the Oregon Trail*, 112.
15. Haines, *Historic Sites along the Oregon Trail*, 112.
16. Mattes, *The Great Platte River Road*, 480–81.
17. Hyde, *Red Cloud's Folk*, 45–46.
18. Haines, *Historic Sites along the Oregon Trail*, 136.

19. Mattes, *The Great Platte River Road*, 482.
20. Barry, *The Beginning of the West*, 285; Hafen, *Broken Hand*, 146.
21. Haines, *Historic Sites along the Oregon Trail*, 136–37; Mattes, *The Great Platte River Road*, 481.
22. Ibid., 133.
23. Ibid.
24. Frémont, *Report of the Exploring Expedition*, 47–48.
25. Parkman, *The Oregon Trail*, 69–70.
26. Hafen, *Broken Hand*, 147; Mattes, *The Great Platte River Road*, 483.
27. Frémont, *Report of the Exploring Expedition*, 48; Mattes, *The Great Platte River Road*, 483.
28. *Californian*, 28 October 1848.
29. Camp, *James Clyman, Frontiersman*, 90.
30. Bryant, *What I Saw in California*, 68; Parkman, *The Oregon Trail*, 65.
31. Honoré-Timothée Lempfrit, *His Oregon Trail Journal and Letters from the Pacific Northwest, 1845–1853*, trans. Patricia Meyer and Catou Lévesque (Fairfield, Wash.: Galleon, 1983), 86.
32. Haines, *Historic Sites along the Oregon Trail*, 144.
33. Mattes, *The Great Platte River Road*, 487.
34. Ibid., 486.
35. Ibid., 487.
36. Ibid., 490–91.
37. Francis Parkman, *The Journals of Francis Parkman*, vol. 2, ed. Mason Wade (New York: Harper and Brothers, 1947), 448.
38. Zenas Leonard, *Adventures of Zenas Leonard, Fur Trader*, ed. John C. Ewers (Norman: University of Oklahoma Press, 1959), 8–9.
39. Hafen, *Broken Hand*, 141–43.
40. Ibid., 160.
41. Nunis, *The Bidwell-Bartleson Party*, 135n10.
42. Frémont, *Report of the Exploring Expedition*, 62.
43. Haines, *Historic Sites along the Oregon Trail*, 156.
44. Mattes, *The Great Platte River Road*, 482.
45. Bryant, *What I Saw in California*, 67.
46. Parkman, *The Oregon Trail*, 127–28.
47. Richard Martin May, *A Sketch of a Migrating Family to California in 1848* (Fairfield, Wash.: Galleon, 1991), 14–15.
48. DeVoto, *Across the Wide Missouri*, 317.
49. Hyde, *Red Cloud's Folk*, 53–54; Parkman, *The Oregon Trail*, 95–96.
50. Bryant, *What I Saw in California*, 67.
51. Ibid.
52. Parkman, *The Oregon Trail*, 93.
53. Hyde, *Red Cloud's Folk*, 52; Parkman, *The Oregon Trail*, 84.
54. DeVoto, *Across the Wide Missouri*, 120–21.
55. Riley Root, *Journal of Travels from St. Josephs to Oregon* (1850; reprint, Oakland: Biobooks, 1955), 15.
56. Dawson, *Narrative of Nicholas "Cheyenne" Dawson*, 13.
57. Frémont, *Report of the Exploring Expedition*, 67.
58. Hill, *The California Trail*, 123.

59. Nunis, *The Bidwell-Bartleson Party*, 82.
60. Ibid., 211–12.

Chapter 8: Crossing North Platte, Up the Sweetwater

1. Nunis, *The Bidwell-Bartleson Party*, 223.
2. Stegner, *The Gathering of Zion: The Story of the Mormon Trail* (1964; reprint, New York: McGraw-Hill, 1971), 148–49.
3. Thornton, *Oregon and California in 1848*, 122.
4. Bryant, *What I Saw in California*, 78.
5. Ibid.
6. Nunis, *The Bidwell-Bartleson Party*, 212.
7. Haines, *Historic Sites along the Oregon Trail*, 199.
8. Ibid., 211–12; Franzwa, *The Oregon Trail Revisited*, 258.
9. Haines, *Historic Sites along the Oregon Trail*, 206.
10. DeVoto, *Across the Wide Missouri*, 126.
11. Nunis, *The Bidwell-Bartleson Party*, 233.
12. Ibid., 212, 233.
13. Haines, *Historic Sites along the Oregon Trail*, 209.
14. Chittenden and Richardson, *Life, Letters and Travels of Father Pierre-Jean De Smet, S.J.*, 297.
15. Point, *Wilderness Kingdom*, 32.
16. Ibid., 34.
17. Williams, *Narrative of a Tour*, 40.
18. Ibid.
19. Dawson, *Narrative of Nicholas "Cheyenne" Dawson*, 13.
20. Bidwell, *Echoes of the Past about California*, 30.
21. Root, *Journal of Travels*, 17.
22. Nunis, *The Bidwell-Bartleson Party*, 82.
23. Williams, *Narrative of a Tour*, 41.

Chapter 9: Over South Pass, On to the Green River

1. Williams, *Narrative of a Tour*, 41.
2. Ibid.
3. Bidwell, *Echoes of the Past about California*, 35.
4. Nunis, *The Bidwell-Bartleson Party*, 82.
5. Dawson, *Narrative of Nicholas "Cheyenne" Dawson*, 13.
6. Bryant, *What I Saw in California*, 88.
7. Camp, *James Clyman, Frontiersman*, 100.
8. Williams, *Narrative of a Tour*, 41.
9. Chittenden and Richardson, *Life, Letters and Travels of Father Pierre-Jean De Smet, S.J.*, 299.
10. Charles Kelly and Dale Morgan, *Old Greenwood: The Story of Caleb Greenwood, Trapper, Pathfinder and Early Pioneer* (Georgetown, Calif.: Talisman, 1965), 106; George R. Stewart, *The Opening of the California Trail* (Berkeley: University of California Press, 1953), 60.
11. Nunis, *The Bidwell-Bartleson Party*, 108.
12. Chittenden and Richardson, *Life, Letters and Travels of Father Pierre-Jean De Smet, S.J.*, 299; Point, *Wilderness Kingdom*, 34.

NOTES

13. Bidwell, *Echoes of the Past about California*, 35.
14. LeRoy R. Hafen, *The Mountain Men and the Fur Trade of the Far West*, vol. 3 (Glendale, Calif.: Arthur H. Clark, 1966), 137; David J. Wishart, *The Fur Trade of the American West, 1807–1840: A Geographical Synthesis* (Lincoln: University of Nebraska Press, 1979), 143.
15. Bil Gilbert, *Westering Man: The Life of Joseph Walker* (1983; reprint, Norman: University of Oklahoma Press, 1985), 181. The records of the transaction with Abel Stearns are in the Stearns papers at the Huntington Library at San Marino, California.
16. Williams, *Narrative of a Tour*, 42.
17. Dawson, *Narrative of Nicholas "Cheyenne" Dawson*, 13.
18. Chittenden and Richardson, *Life, Letters and Travels of Father Pierre-Jean De Smet, S.J.*, 294; Point, *Wilderness Kingdom*, 34.
19. Nunis, *The Bidwell-Bartleson Party*, 82.
20. Williams, *Narrative of a Tour*, 42.
21. Nunis, *The Bidwell-Bartleson Party*, 108–9.
22. Dawson, *Narrative of Nicholas "Cheyenne" Dawson*, 10–11.
23. Point, *Wilderness Kingdom*, 34.
24. Ibid., 35.
25. Chittenden and Richardson, *Life, Letters and Travels of Father Pierre-Jean De Smet, S.J.*, 300; Point, *Wilderness Kingdom*, 34.
26. Point, *Wilderness Kingdom*, 34.
27. Barry, *The Beginning of the West*, 436.
28. Ibid.
29. Dawson, *Narrative of Nicholas "Cheyenne" Dawson*, 14.
30. Gilbert, *Westering Man*, 183.
31. Ibid., 191–97.
32. Hafen, *The Mountain Men*, 131–39.
33. Point, *Wilderness Kingdom*, 35.
34. Nunis, *The Bidwell-Bartleson Party*, 109.
35. Ibid.
36. Augusta Fink, *Monterey County: The Dramatic Story of its Past* (Santa Cruz: Western Tanager, 1972), 72–73.
37. Haines, *Historic Sites along the Oregon Trail*, 262.
38. Ibid., 262, 280.
39. Williams, *Narrative of a Tour*, 43.

Chapter 10: Along the Bear River

1. Williams, *Narrative of a Tour*, 42.
2. Nunis, *The Bidwell-Bartleson Party*, 135n10.
3. Williams, *Narrative of a Tour*, 43.
4. Point, *Wilderness Kingdom*, 35.
5. Camp, *James Clyman, Frontiersman*, 100–101.
6. Chittenden and Richardson, *Life, Letters and Travels of Father Pierre-Jean De Smet, S.J.*, 300.
7. Dawson, *Narrative of Nicholas "Cheyenne" Dawson*, 14.
8. Williams, *Narrative of a Tour*, 44.
9. Dawson, *Narrative of Nicholas "Cheyenne" Dawson*, 14.

10. Camp, *James Clyman, Frontiersman*, 101.
11. Williams, *Narrative of a Tour*, 44.
12. Belden, *Josiah Belden, 1841 California Overland Pioneer*, 40.
13. Nunis, *The Bidwell-Bartleson Party*, 110.
14. Belden, *Josiah Belden, 1841 California Overland Pioneer*, 40.
15. Point, *Wilderness Kingdom*, 35.
16. Nunis, *The Bidwell-Bartleson Party*, 110.
17. Dawson, *Narrative of Nicholas "Cheyenne" Dawson*, 14.
18. DeVoto, *Across the Wide Missouri*, 146; Richard K. Brock, *Emigrant Trails West: A Guide to the California Trail: From the Raft River to the Humboldt Sink*, 4th ed. (Reno: Trails West, 2000), 76.
19. Gilbert, *Westering Man*, 122–38.
20. Nunis, *The Bidwell-Bartleson Party*, 143.
21. Ibid., 83.
22. Chittenden and Richardson, *Life, Letters and Travels of Father Pierre-Jean De Smet, S.J.*, 296.
23. Shebel, *Weber!*, 3, 15.
24. Point, *Wilderness Kingdom*, 35.
25. Ibid., 26.
26. Chittenden and Richardson, *Life, Letters and Travels of Father Pierre-Jean De Smet, S.J.*, 296.
27. Bidwell, *Echoes of the Past about California*, 40; Nunis, *The Bidwell-Bartleson Party*, 111.
28. Nunis, *The Bidwell-Bartleson Party*, 84.
29. Ibid., 111.
30. Ibid., 84.
31. Dawson, *Narrative of Nicholas "Cheyenne" Dawson*, 15.
32. Nunis, *The Bidwell-Bartleson Party*, 158–59.
33. Ibid., 111–12.

Chapter 11: Across the Great Salt Lake Country

1. Dawson, *Narrative of Nicholas "Cheyenne" Dawson*, 15.
2. Ibid., 15–16.
3. Nunis, *The Bidwell-Bartleson Party*, 112.
4. Dawson, *Narrative of Nicholas "Cheyenne" Dawson*, 16.
5. Ibid., 14, 16.
6. Nunis, *The Bidwell-Bartleson Party*, 111.
7. Ibid., 110.
8. John S. Galbraith, *The Hudson's Bay Company as an Imperial Factor, 1821–1869* (Berkeley: University of California Press, 1957), 108.
9. Dawson, *Narrative of Nicholas "Cheyenne" Dawson*, 16.
10. Belden, *Josiah Belden, 1841 California Overland Pioneer*, 40.
11. Dawson, *Narrative of Nicholas "Cheyenne" Dawson*, 16–17.
12. Ibid., 17.
13. Nunis, *The Bidwell-Bartleson Party*, 112.

NOTES

Chapter 12: Languishing North and West of Salt Lake

1. Dawson, *Narrative of Nicholas "Cheyenne" Dawson*, 18.
2. Ibid., 17.
3. Belden, *Josiah Belden, 1841 California Overland Pioneer*, 41.
4. Nunis, *The Bidwell-Bartleson Party*, 85.
5. Ibid., 198.
6. Ibid., 142.
7. Ibid., 142–43.
8. Bryant, *What I Saw in California*, 122–23.
9. Ibid., 122–23, 126–27.
10. Dawson, *Narrative of Nicholas "Cheyenne" Dawson*, 17.
11. Nunis, *The Bidwell-Bartleson Party*, 86.
12. Ibid., 86, 112.
13. Ibid., 86.
14. Ibid.
15. Dawson, *Narrative of Nicholas "Cheyenne" Dawson*, 18.

Chapter 13: Ignorant Wanderings

1. Nunis, *The Bidwell-Bartleson Party*, 86, 112.
2. Dawson, *Narrative of Nicholas "Cheyenne" Dawson*, 17.
3. Ibid., 18.
4. Nunis, *The Bidwell-Bartleson Party*, 112–13.
5. Dawson, *Narrative of Nicholas "Cheyenne" Dawson*, 18.
6. Ibid., 17.
7. Ibid., 18.
8. Nunis, *The Bidwell-Bartleson Party*, 113.
9. Ibid.
10. Ibid., 113–14.
11. Ibid., 87.
12. Ibid., 114.
13. Ibid., 88.
14. Ibid., 198.
15. Ibid., 115.
16. Ibid.
17. Ibid., 88.
18. Dawson, *Narrative of Nicholas "Cheyenne" Dawson*, 19.
19. Nidever, *Life and Adventures of George Nidever*, 32; John C. Ewers, ed., *Adventures of Zenas Leonard, Fur Trader* (Norman: University of Oklahoma Press, 1959), 71.
20. Brock, *Emigrant Trails West*, 126.
21. Nunis, *The Bidwell-Bartleson Party*, 115–16.
22. Ibid., 88–89.
23. Brock, *Emigrant Trails West*, 116.

Chapter 14: Will the Humboldt Ever End?

1. Nunis, *The Bidwell-Bartleson Party*, 116.
2. Ibid., 88, 116.

3. Brock, *Emigrant Trails West*, 170.
4. Nunis, *The Bidwell-Bartleson Party*, 116.
5. Ibid.
6. Ibid.
7. Dawson, *Narrative of Nicholas "Cheyenne" Dawson*, 19.
8. Nunis, *The Bidwell-Bartleson Party*, 116–17.
9. Belden, *Josiah Belden, 1841 California Overland Pioneer*, 42.
10. Nunis, *The Bidwell-Bartleson Party*, 90.
11. Ibid., 89.
12. Dawson, *Narrative of Nicholas "Cheyenne" Dawson*, 19.
13. Ibid., 19–20.
14. Nunis, *The Bidwell-Bartleson Party*, 117.
15. Ibid., 90.
16. Ibid., 90, 117.
17. Dawson, *Narrative of Nicholas "Cheyenne" Dawson*, 20.
18. Ibid., 20–21.
19. Nunis, *The Bidwell-Bartleson Party*, 90.
20. Ibid., 117; Bidwell, *Echoes of the Past about California*, 56.
21. Michael J. Gillis and Michael F. Magliari, *John Bidwell and California: The Life and Writings of a Pioneer, 1841–1900* (Spokane: Arthur Clark, 2003), 22.

Chapter 15: Struggling over the Sierra Nevada Mountains

1. Doyce B. Nunis, ed., *Josiah Belden 1841 California Overland Pioneer: His Memoir and Early Letters* (Georgetown, Calif.: Talisman, 1962), 43.
2. Nunis, *The Bidwell-Bartleson Party*, 90.
3. Ibid., 117–18.
4. Belden, *Josiah Belden, 1841 California Overland Pioneer*, 42–43.
5. Nunis, *The Bidwell-Bartleson Party*, 198.
6. Ibid., 90.
7. Belden, *Josiah Belden, 1841 California Overland Pioneer*, 43–44.
8. Nunis, *The Bidwell-Bartleson Party*, 91.
9. Bidwell, *Echoes of the Past about California*, 58.
10. Ibid., 58–59.
11. Nunis, *The Bidwell-Bartleson Party*, 91.
12. Ibid., 90–91, 118.
13. Ibid., 118.
14. Ibid., 92.
15. Ibid., 91.
16. Ibid., 119.
17. Ibid., 92.
18. Ibid., 119.
19. Scott Stine, *A Way across the Mountain: Joseph Walker's 1833 Trans-Sierran Passage and the Myth of Yosemite's Discovery* (Norman, Okla.: Arthur H. Clark, 2015), 186–88.
20. Dawson, *Narrative of Nicholas "Cheyenne" Dawson*, 23.
21. Nunis, *The Bidwell-Bartleson Party*, 198.
22. Ibid., 119.
23. Dawson, *Narrative of Nicholas "Cheyenne" Dawson*, 22.

24. Nunis, *The Bidwell-Bartleson Party*, 93.
25. "The Gabriel Moraga Expedition of 1806: The Diary of Frey Pedro Munoz." *Huntington Library Quarterly* 9, no. 3 (May 1946): 232.
26. Nunis, *The Bidwell-Bartleson Party*, 94.
27. Ibid., 93.
28. Ibid., 198.
29. Ibid.
30. Ibid., 93.
31. Ibid.
32. Ibid.
33. Dawson, *Narrative of Nicholas "Cheyenne" Dawson*, 23–24.
34. Nunis, *The Bidwell-Bartleson Party*, 198.
35. Dawson, *Narrative of Nicholas "Cheyenne" Dawson*, 25.
36. Nunis, *The Bidwell-Bartleson Party*, 93.
37. Ibid., 120.
38. Ibid., 94.
39. Belden, *Josiah Belden, 1841 California Overland Pioneer*, 44.
40. Bidwell, *Echoes of the Past about California*, 62.
41. Ibid.
42. Nunis, *The Bidwell-Bartleson Party*, 94.
43. Ibid., 118.
44. Belden, *Josiah Belden, 1841 California Overland Pioneer*, 44.
45. Nunis, *The Bidwell-Bartleson Party*, 94.
46. Bidwell, *Echoes of the Past about California*, 63.
47. Dawson, *Narrative of Nicholas "Cheyenne" Dawson*, 25.
48. Nunis, *The Bidwell-Bartleson Party*, 95.
49. Ibid.
50. Dawson, *Narrative of Nicholas "Cheyenne" Dawson*, 25–26.

Chapter 16: The Journey Ends

1. Nunis, *The Bidwell-Bartleson Party*, 198.
2. Ibid., 143.
3. Belden, *Josiah Belden, 1841 California Overland Pioneer*, 44.
4. Nunis, *The Bidwell-Bartleson Party*, 95–96.
5. Ibid., 198–99.
6. Dawson, *Narrative of Nicholas "Cheyenne" Dawson*, 27.
7. Belden, *Josiah Belden, 1841 California Overland Pioneer*, 45.
8. Nunis, *The Bidwell-Bartleson Party*, 96.
9. Ibid., 143.
10. Dawson, *Narrative of Nicholas "Cheyenne" Dawson*, 30.
11. Ibid.
12. George D. Lyman, *John Marsh, Pioneer: The Life Story of a Trail-Blazer on Six Frontiers* (New York: Charles Scribner's Sons, 1930), 224–28.
13. Bidwell, *Echoes of the Past about California*, 68–69.
14. Alan Rosenus, *General Vallejo and the Advent of Americans* (Berkeley: Heyday/Urion, 1995), 37.
15. Ibid., 40.
16. Fink, *Monterey County*, 75–76.

17. Bidwell, *Echoes of the Past about California*, 73; Rosenus, *General Vallejo and the Advent of Americans*, 35.
18. Fink, *Monterey County*, 76.
19. Rosenus, *General Vallejo and the Advent of Americans*, 37.
20. Ibid., 41.
21. Ibid., 40.
22. Bidwell, *Echoes of the Past about California*, 72.
23. Nunis, *The Bidwell-Bartleson Party*, 94.
24. Rosenus, *General Vallejo and the Advent of Americans*, 40.
25. Bidwell, *Echoes of the Past about California*, 73.
26. Ibid., 68.
27. Nunis, *The Bidwell-Bartleson Party*, 69.
28. Lyman, *John Marsh, Pioneer*, 228.
29. Bidwell, *Echoes of the Past about California*, 77; John A. Sutter Jr., *The Sutter Family and the Origins of Gold-Rush Sacramento*, ed. Allen R. Ottley (1943; reprint, Norman: University of Oklahoma Press, 2002), 85.
30. Ibid., 75.
31. Rosenus, *General Vallejo and the Advent of Americans*, 46.

Epilogue

1. Barry, *The Beginning of the West*, 458.
2. LaSalle, *Emigrants on the Overland Trail*, 449–55.
3. Nunis, *The Bidwell-Bartleson Party*, 158.
4. Ibid., 135n4.
5. Barry, *The Beginning of the West*, 458; Nunis, *The Bidwell-Bartleson Party*, 259, 261.
6. Ibid., 160.
7. Ibid., 145; Dawson, *Narrative of Nicholas "Cheyenne" Dawson*, 45.
8. Nunis, 260–68.
9. Ibid., 107
10. Ibid., 259–60.
11. Ibid., 127.
12. Ibid., 262.
13. Ibid., 261.
14. Ibid., 203.
15. Shebel, *Weber!*, 33–37.
16. Nunis, *The Bidwell-Bartleson Party*, 97.
17. Bidwell, *Echoes of the Past about California*, 81.
18. Gillis and Magliari, *John Bidwell and California*, 163, 188.

Bibliography

Ambrose, Stephen E. *Undaunted Courage: Meriwether Lewis, Thomas Jefferson, and the Opening of the American West.* New York: Simon and Schuster, 1996.
Anderson, William Wright. "Diary of William Wright Anderson From St. Joseph, Missouri, to Oregon City in the Year 1848." Typescript, Manuscripts Department, Lilly Library, Indiana University, Bloomington.
Bancroft, Hubert Howe. *History of California.* 7 vols. San Francisco: History Company, 1886.
Barry, Louise. *The Beginning of the West: Annals of the Kansas Gateway to the American West, 1540–1854.* Topeka: Kansas State Historical Society, 1972.
Belknap, Keturah. "History of the Life of My Grandmother, Kitturah Penton Belknap; as copied from the original. Typewritten transcription of her journal." Washington State University, Pullman, cage 1680, no. 132.
Bidwell, John. "California 1841: An Immigrant's Recollection of a Trip across the Plains." MS, Bancroft Library, University of California, Berkeley.
———. *Echoes of the Past about California.* Chico, Calif.: Chico Advertiser, 1914. Reprint, New York: Citadel, 1962. Originally published in *Century Illustrated Monthly Magazine* (November, December 1890) and *Out West* (1904).
———. *A Journey to California, 1841: The First Emigrant Party to California by Wagon Train.* 1843. Reprint, Berkeley: Friends of the Bancroft Library, 1964.
Brandon, William. *The Men and the Mountain: Frémont's Fourth Expedition.* New York: William Morrow, 1955.
Brock, Richard K., ed. *Emigrant Trails West: A Guide to the California Trail, from the Raft River to the Humboldt Sink.* 4th ed. Reno: Trails West, 2000.
Bryant, Edwin. *What I Saw in California: Being the Journal of a Tour, by the Emigrant Route and South Pass of the Rocky Mountains, across the Continent of North America, the Great Desert Basin, and through California, in the Years 1846, 1847.* 1848. Reprint, Crabtree, Ore.: Narrative Press, 2001.
Camp, Charles L., ed. *James Clyman, Frontiersman: The Adventures of a Trapper and Covered Wagon Emigrant as Told in His Own Reminiscences and Diaries.* Portland: Champoeg, 1960.
Chambers, W. L., and Harry L. Wells. *History of Butte County, California.* 1882. Reprint, Berkeley: Howell-North, 1973.
Chittenden, Hiram Martin, and Alfred Talbot Richardson. *Life, Letters and Travels of Father Pierre-Jean De Smet, S.J.* Vol. 1. New York: Francis P. Harper, 1905.

Conrotto, Eugene L. *Miwok Means People: The Life and Fate of the Native Inhabitants of the California Gold Rush Country*. Fresno: Valley Publishers, 1973.
Cornwall, Bruce. *Life Sketch of Pierre Barlow Cornwall*. San Francisco: A. M. Robertson, 1906.
Dary, David. *The Oregon Trail: An American Saga*. New York: Alfred A. Knopf, 2004.
Dawson, Nicholas. *Narrative of Nicholas "Cheyenne" Dawson (Overland to California in '41 and '49, and Texas in '51)*. San Francisco: Grabhorn, 1933.
DeVoto, Bernard. *Across the Wide Missouri*. 1947. Reprint, New York: Houghton Mifflin, 1998.
———. *The Year of Decision: 1846*. 1942. Reprint, New York: St. Martin's, 2000.
Ewers, John C., ed. *Adventures of Zenas Leonard, Fur Trader*. Norman: University of Oklahoma Press, 1959.
Farquhar, Francis. *History of the Sierra Nevada*. Berkeley: University of California Press, 1965.
Fink, Augusta. *Monterey County: The Dramatic Story of Its Past*. Santa Cruz: Western Tanager, 1972.
Ford, Dixon, and Lee Kreutzer. "Oxen, Engines of the Overland Emigration." *Overland Journal*, 93, no. 1 (spring 2015): 4–29.
Franzwa, Gregory M. *Maps of the California Trail*. Tucson: Patrice Press, 1999.
———. *Maps of the Oregon Trail*. 3rd ed. St. Louis: Patrice Press, 1990.
———. *The Oregon Trail Revisited*. 3rd ed. Gerald, Mo.: Patrice Press, 1983.
Frémont, John C. *Report of The Exploring Expedition to the Rocky Mountains in the Year 1842, and to Oregon and North California in the Years 1843–44*. 1845. Reprint, Santa Barbara: Narrative Press, 2002.
Galbraith, John S. *The Hudson's Bay Company as an Imperial Factor, 1821–1869*. Berkeley: University of California Press, 1957.
Giffen, Helen S. *Trail-Blazing Pioneer: Colonel Joseph Ballinger Chiles*. San Francisco: John Howell, 1969.
Gilbert, Bil. *Westering Man: The Life of Joseph Walker*. 1983. Reprint, Norman: University of Oklahoma Press, 1985.
Gillis, Michael J., and Michael F. Magliari. *John Bidwell and California: The Life and Writings of a Pioneer, 1841–1900*. Spokane: Arthur H. Clark, 2003.
Hafen, LeRoy R. *Broken Hand: The Life of Thomas Fitzpatrick: Mountain Man, Guide and Indian Agent*. 1931. Reprint, Lincoln: University of Nebraska Press, 1981.
———. *The Mountain Men and the Fur Trade of the Far West*. Vol. 3. Glendale, Calif.: Arthur H. Clark, 1967.
Haines, Aubrey L. *Historic Sites along the Oregon Trail*. Tucson: Patrice Press, 1981.
Hansen, Barbara Julia. "Wagon Train Governments." Master's thesis, History Department, University of Colorado, 1962.
Hastings, Lansford W. *The Emigrants' Guide to Oregon and California*. 1845. Reprint, Bedford, Mass.: Applewood, 1996.
Hill, William E. *The California Trail: Yesterday and Today: A Pictorial Journey Along the California Trail*. 2nd ed. Boise: Tamarack, 1993.
History of Holt and Atchison Counties, Missouri. St. Joseph, Mo.: National Historical Company, 1882.

BIBLIOGRAPHY

Holmes, Kenneth L., ed. *Covered Wagon Women: Diaries and Letters from the Western Trails, 1840–1849.* Vol 1. 1983. Reprint, Lincoln: University of Nebraska Press, 1995.

Horn, Hosea B. *Horn's Overland Guide from the U.S. Indian Sub-Agency, Council Bluffs, on the Missouri River to the City of Sacramento, in California.* 1852. Reprint, Ann Arbor, Mich.: Books on Demand, 2008.

Hunt, Rockwell. *John Bidwell: Prince of California Pioneers.* Caldwell, Idaho: Caxton Printers, 1942.

Huntington Library. "The Gabriel Moraga Expedition of 1806: The Diary of Fray Pedro Munoz." *Huntington Library Quarterly* 9, no. 3 (May 1946).

Hyde, George E. *The Pawnee Indians.* 1951. Reprint, Norman: University of Oklahoma Press, 1974.

———. *Red Cloud's Folk: A History of the Oglala Sioux Indians.* 1937. Reprint, Norman: University of Oklahoma Press, 1975.

Kelly, Charles, and Dale Morgan. *Old Greenwood: The Story of Caleb Greenwood, Trapper, Pathfinder and Early Pioneer.* Georgetown, Calif.: Talisman, 1965.

Korns, J. Roderic. "The Salt Lake Cutoff." *Utah Historical Quarterly* 19 (1951): 248–68.

LaSalle, Michael E. *Emigrants on the Overland Trail: The Wagon Trains of 1848.* Kirksville, Mo.: Truman State University Press, 2011.

Lavender, David. *Westward Vison: The Story of the Oregon Trail.* Lincoln: University of Nebraska Press, 1963.

Lempfrit, Honoré-Timothée. *His Oregon Trail Journal and Letters from the Pacific Northwest, 1845–1853.* Translated by Patricia Meyer and Catou Lévesque. Edited by Patricia Meyer. Fairfield, Wash.: Galleon, 1983.

Lewin, Jacqueline A., and Marilyn S. Taylor. *The St. Joe Road: Emigration Mid-1800s: A Travelers' Guide from the Missouri River to the Junction of the St. Joe and Independence Roads.* St. Joseph, Mo.: St. Joseph Museum, 1992.

Logan, Sheridan A. *Old St. Jo: Gateway to the West, 1799–1932.* 2nd ed. Edited by Alberto C. Meloni. St. Joseph, Mo.: St. Joseph Museum, 2002.

Lyman, George D. *John Marsh, Pioneer: The Life Story of a Trail-Blazer on Six Frontiers.* New York: Charles Scribner's Sons, 1930.

Mattes, Merrill J. *The Great Platte River Road: The Covered Wagon Mainline via Fort Kearney to Fort Laramie.* Lincoln: Nebraska State Historical Society, 1969.

May, Richard Martin. *A Sketch of a Migrating Family to California in 1848.* Fairfield, Wash.: Galleon, 1991.

McCartney, Laton. *Across the Great Divide: Robert Stuart and the Discovery of the Oregon Trail.* New York: Simon and Schuster, 2003.

McLynn, Frank. *Wagons West: The Epic Story of America's Overland Trails.* New York: Grove, 2002.

Meldahl, Keith Heyer. *Hard Road West: History and Geology along the Gold Rush Trail.* Chicago: University of Chicago Press, 2007.

Moore, John H. *The Cheyenne.* Malden, Mass.: Blackwell, 1996.

Morgan, Dale, ed. *Overland in 1846: Diaries and Letters of the California-Oregon Trail.* Vol. 1. Lincoln: University of Nebraska Press, 1963.

Morgan, Robert. *Boone: A Biography.* Chapel Hill, N.C.: Algonquin, 2008.

Nidever, George. *Life and Adventures of George Nidever, 1802–1883.* Edited by

William Henry Ellison. Berkeley: University of California Press, 1937. Reprint, Santa Barbara: McNally and Loftin / Tucson: Southwest Parks and Monuments Association, 1984.

Nunis, Doyce B., ed. *The Bidwell-Bartleson Party 1841, California Emigrant Adventure*. Santa Cruz: Western Tanager, 1991.

———. *Josiah Belden 1841 California Overland Pioneer: His Memoir and Early Letters*. Georgetown, Calif.: Talisman, 1962.

Olson, James C., and Ronald C. Naugle. *History of Nebraska*. 3rd ed. Lincoln: University of Nebraska Press, 1997.

Parkman, Francis. *The Journals of Francis Parkman*. Vol. 2. Edited by Mason Wade. New York: Harper and Brothers, 1947.

———. *The Oregon Trail: Adventures on the Prairie in the 1840's*. N.d. Reprint, Santa Barbara: Narrative Press, 2001.

Point, Nicolas, S.J. *Wilderness Kingdom, Indian Life in the Rocky Mountains: 1840–1847, the Journals and Paintings of Nicolas Point, S.J.* Translated by Joseph P. Donnelly, S.J. Chicago: Loyola University Press, 1967.

Porter, William. Original diary, in the possession of one of Porter's great-grandchildren. Typescript available at http://oregonpioneers.com/porter.htm.

Preuss, Charles. *Exploring with Frémont: The Private Diaries of Charles Preuss, Cartographer for John C. Frémont on His First, Second and Fourth Expeditions to the Far West*. Translated and edited by Erwin G. Gudde and Elisabeth K. Gudde. Norman: University of Oklahoma Press, 1958.

Pritchard, James A. *The Overland Diary of James A. Pritchard from Kentucky to California in 1849*. Edited by Dale L. Morgan. Denver: Old West, 1959.

Rosenus, Alan. *General Vallejo and the Advent of the Americans*. Berkeley: Heyday/Urion, 1995.

Robertson, James R. "A Pioneer Captain of Industry in Oregon." *Quarterly of the Oregon Historical Society* 4 (1903): 150–67.

Rohrbough, Malcolm J. *Days of Gold: The California Gold Rush and the American Nation*. Berkeley: University of California Press, 1997.

Root, Riley. *Journal of Travels from St. Josephs to Oregon*. 1850. Reprint, Oakland, Calif.: Biobooks, 1955.

Russell, Osborne. *Journal of a Trapper, 1834–1843*. Ed. Aubrey L. Haines. Lincoln: University of Nebraska Press, 1965.

Sage, Rufus B. *Rocky Mountain Life, or, Startling Scenes and Perilous Adventures in the Far West, during an Expedition of Three Years*. 1846. Reprint, Lincoln: University of Nebraska Press, 1982.

Savage, Candace. *Prairie, a Natural History*. Vancouver B.C.: Greystone, 2004.

Schmidt, Earl F. *Who Were the Murphys: California's First Irish Family*. Murphys, Calif.: Mooney Flat Ventures, 1992.

Shebel, James. *Weber! The American Adventure of Captain Charles M. Weber*. Lodi, Calif.: San Joaquin Historical Society, 1993.

Smith, Clarence, and Wallace Elliott. *Illustrations of Napa County, California: With Historical Sketch*. 1878. Reprint, Fresno, Calif.: Valley Publishers, 1974.

Smith, Edward. Original journal. In possession of the Fresno City and County Historical Society, Fresno, California.

Stegner, Wallace. *The Gathering of Zion: The Story of the Mormon Trail*. 1964. Reprint, New York: McGraw-Hill, 1971.

BIBLIOGRAPHY

Stewart, George R. *The California Trail: An Epic with Many Heroes*. New York: McGraw-Hill Book Co., Inc., 1962.

———. *The Opening of the California Trail*. Berkeley: University of California Press, 1953.

Stine, Scott. *A Way across the Mountain: Joseph Walker's 1833 Trans-Sierran Passage and the Myth of Yosemite's Discovery*. Norman: Arthur H. Clark, 2015.

Sutter, John A. *New Helvetia Diary*. San Francisco: Society of California Pioneers, 1939.

Sutter, John A., Jr. *The Sutter Family and the Origins of Gold-Rush Sacramento*. Edited by Allen R. Ottley. 1943. Reprint, Norman: University of Oklahoma Press, 2002.

Thornton, J. Quinn. *Oregon and California in 1848*. Vols. 1–2. 1849. Reprint, New York: Arno, 1973.

Tobie, H. E. "Joseph L. Meek: A Conspicuous Personality." *Oregon Historical Quarterly* 40 (1939): 243–64.

Tortorich, Frank, Jr. *Gold Rush Trail: A Guide to the Carson River Route of the Emigrant Trail*. Pine Grove, Calif.: Wagon Wheel Tours, 2006.

Unruh, John D., Jr. *The Plains Across: The Overland Emigrants and the Trans-Mississippi West, 1840–1860*. Urbana: University of Illinois Press, 1993.

Vestal, Stanley. *Joe Meek: The Merry Mountain Man*. 1952. Reprint, Lincoln: University of Nebraska Press, 1963.

Victor, Frances Fuller. *The River of the West: The Adventures of Joe Meek*. Vols. 1–2. 1870. Reprint, Missoula, Mont.: Mountain Press, 1983, 1985.

Wallace, William Swilling. *Antoine Robidoux, 1794–1860: A Biography of a Western Venturer*. Los Angeles: Glen Dawson, 1953.

Webb, W. P. *The Great Plains*. Boston, 1931.

Williams, Joseph. *Narrative of a Tour from the State of Indiana to the Oregon Territory in the Years 1841–2*. New York: Cadmus Book Shop, 1921.

Wishart, David J. *The Fur Trade of the American West, 1807–1840: A Geographical Synthesis*. Lincoln: University of Nebraska Press, 1979.

Willoughby, Robert J. *Robidoux's Town: A Nineteenth Century History of St. Joseph, Missouri*. St. Joseph, Mo.: St. Joseph Museum, 2006.

Wyoming Recreational Commission. *Wyoming: A Guide to Historic Sites*. Casper: House of Printing, 1976.

Newspapers

Daily Missouri Republican, St. Louis, April 20, 1841, and May 19, 1841.

The Western Atlas and Saturday Evening Gazette, St. Louis, March 8, 1841, and May 1, 1841.

Acknowledgments

Materials for this book came from a variety of libraries, archives, collections, and books. I am indebted to all of them for the value of their contributions. I wish to express my thanks for the help of Loren Pospisel at the Chimney Rock State Historical Site and Visitor Center, of Robert Manasek at the Scotts Bluff National Monument, of Patricia Keats at the Society of California Pioneers, of Kathleen Correia at the California State Library, of Lisa Marine at the Wisconsin Historical Society, of Nancy Sherbert at the Kansas State Historical Society, of Maddie McDermott at the Jesuit Archives, Central District, and of Caitlin Eckard at the Jackson County Historical Society.

I thank Ken Guddal, owner of the E. S. Paxson painting, for graciously allowing me to use the wonderful image of his painting on the cover of the book.

I thank Tom Willcockson at Mapcraft for his excellent maps and my eagle-eyed copyeditor, Fred Kameny, for his superb work.

Lastly, but most importantly, I express my deepest gratitude to Chris Crochetière at BW&A Books for her talents and expert advice in designing and producing this beautiful book.

Index

Page numbers in *italics* refer to illustrations.

alcohol, 92, 149, 156, 208, 212
Alcove Spring, 79–80
alkali, 150, 176, 184, 190, 328, 331; animals affected by, 150, 172, 262; in dust clouds, 99, 171; in water, 172, 305, 318, 320, 325
Alkali Slough, 172
Alvarado, Juan Bautista, 396, 403
American Board for Foreign Missions, 13
American Fur Company (AFC), 92, 109, 110–11, 114, 138, 152, 179; Fort Laramie bought and sold by, 144, 146, 149, 150; Oglala trade with, 145–46; Rocky Mountain Fur Company vs., 111; supply trains of, 14, 27, 36, 62
Anderson, William, 99
antelope, 85, 88, 101–3, 109, 132, 136, 139, 142, 184, 198, 202, 214, 222, 224–25, 228, 244, 255, 269–70, 283, 291, 296, 318, 382–83, 386; speed of, 86, 89, 265
Antelope Valley, 339
Apache Indians, 77
Applegate, Jesse, 49
Arapahoe Indians, 13, 77, 141, 145, 212
Arikara Indians, 78
Arkansas, 12
Ash Hollow, 127–29, 130
Ashley, William, 11–12, 48, 63
ash trees, 127, 129, 132

Baker, James, 29, 210, 211
Baldinger, William, 402
Baldridge, William, 19, 21, 26
Baptists, 13
Barnett, Elias, 324–25, 333
Bartleson, John, 25, 31, 153, 189, 236, 293, 328–29, 354–55, 373, 374, 387, 388; alcohol carried by, 208, 212; Bidwell rebuked by, 240; Bidwell's dislike of, 56, 291, 292, 299, 313, 319, 322, 323–24, 405; as elected captain, 55, 66, 235; final years of, 401–2; Hopper and, 240, 265–66, 267, 268, 271–72, 285–86, 294–95, 325; Indian encounters and, 102, 105, 297–98; Marsh and, 21, 26, 41, 186, 211; misjudgments by, 241, 247, 250, 253–54, 255, 264, 272, 276, 278–79, 286–87, 292, 294–95, 299, 304, 306, 313, 319, 321, 324, 325–26, 330, 333, 346, 355, 363, 368–69, 384, 400; in Sierra Nevada Mountains, 341–44; Williams and, 91, 195, 237
Battle Creek, 212, 243–44, 256
Beardsley Dam, 358, 360
Bear Flag Revolt, 403
Bear Lake, 215, 221, 226
Bear River, 202, 215, 219–47, 251, 252–53
Beaver Basin, 239
Beer Springs, Idaho, 230
Belden, Josiah, 4, 26, 52, 170, 171, 230, 272, 324, 330, 388, 391; California-Oregon split recalled by, 232; as California resident, 3, 397, 402, 403; Cheyenne viewed by, 104, 105;

Belden, Josiah, (*continued*)
  Great Salt Lake region recalled by, 259; on scouting mission, 345; in Sierra Nevada Mountains, 342, 353, 377, 380; as young adventurer, 26–27, 38, 124–25
Belty, William, 313–14, 402
Bidwell, John, 20, 54, 73, 80, 86–90, 116, 140–42, 286, 293, 295–97; accurate estimates by, 74, 161; alcohol viewed by, 208, 212; Bartleson disliked by, 56, 291, 292, 299, 313, 319, 322, 323–24, 405; at Bear River, 219–45; at Big Sandy Creek, 201–6; at Big Springs, 280–82; at Blacks Fork, 214–18; buffalo described by, 109, 113, 114, 121, 122, 123–24, 185–90, 198; buffalo extinction feared by, 114–15; as California resident, 3, 15, 402–6; California-Oregon split recalled by, 231–33; camp routines recalled by, 65–66; Cheyenne encounter described by, 102–4, 105, 110; court martial recalled by, 120; deforestation noted by, 147; De Smet and Fitzpatrick credited by, 14, 61, 66, 105, 236; expedition planned by, 19–23; at expedition's outset, 31, 33–38, 40, 42, 43, 44, 45, 52, 55, 56–57, 59; fishing trip by, 237–41; flora noted by, 67, 124, 132, 157, 158, 225, 353, 357; at Fort Laramie, 144, 146; Fraeb's company and, 205, 206, 207, 211, 212, 213; geological features noted by, 133, 134, 135, 137, 138–39, 161, 163, 226; in Great Salt Lake region, 246–47, 250–73, 276–77, 279–82; at Green River, 204–10; at Humboldt River, 300–317, 326, 328–39; at journey's end, 390–92, 395–99; Kansa massacre recalled by, 60; memoirs of, 3–4, 19, 121; mineral deposits noted by, 95, 99, 144, 170, 183, 229–30; naming errors by, 79, 85, 218; at North Platte River, 159, 164, 165, 167, 170, 171, 172, 194; organizational meeting recalled by, 55–56; oxen and, 75–76, 91, 118, 119, 287–91, 299, 320–22, 329, 354, 359; pack animals and, 284–85; Pawnees viewed by, 71, 77, 78, 81–82; along Platte River, 94–131; Red Vermillion crossing recalled by, 69; self-aggrandizement by, 15, 58; shooting accident recounted by, 125, 126, 146; Shoshone encounter and, 297–300; in Sierra Nevada Mountains, 341–46, 350–80, 382–84; slow pace noted by, 244; at Stanislaus River, 386–89; strengths of, 15, 365; at Sweetwater Creek, 176–98; weather noted by, 85, 87, 92–93, 95–96, 109, 110, 111, 128, 174, 228–29, 270, 319, 351, 371; Western Emigration Society cofounded by, 18–19; Williams and, 83, 84; as young adventurer, 15–16, 39, 153, 241
Bidwell Pass, 278
Bidwell's Bar, 405
Big Blue River, 79, 80, 81
Big Meadows, 320
Big Sandy Creek, 201–6
Big Springs, Nev., 280–81
Big Timber Creek (La Bonte Creek), 159, 161, *162*
Bitter Cottonwood Creek, 157
Bitterroot Mountains, 14, 27
Blackfeet Indians, 238, 239, 241, 298
Black Hills, 106–7, 129, 130, 144, 154, 155, 164
Black Hills Gap, 157
Blacks Fork, 213–15, 217–18
Black Vermillion Creek, 77, 80, 117
blue lupine, 124
Blue Spring Hills, 255, 258
Bodega Bay, Calif., 405
Bonneville, Benjamin, 202, 234
Bonneville Salt Flats, 276
Bowen, Thomas, 397, 403
Boxelder Creek, Colo., 73
Box Elder Creek, Wyo., 164
Bridger, Jim, 11, 63, 213, 215
Bridger Creek, 223
Brigham's Peak (Grindstone Butte; Knob Hill), 163

INDEX

Brolaski, Henry, 27, 256–57, 402
Brown, Elam, 42, 405
Brown's Hole, Utah, 212
Bruff, J. Goldsborough, 149, 179
Bryant, Edwin, 6, 17, 76, 80, 81, 121–22, 278; antelope described by, 86; Indians viewed by, 62, 71, 155, 156; prairie described by, 85–86; rivers described by, 77, 79, 172; rough terrain described by, 49–50
buffalo, 109, 175; as danger, 121, 171; as food source, 91, 122, 198, 212, 227, 267; hunting of, 23, 27, 37–38, 39, 57, 60, 62, 78, 90, 102, 106, 108, 111–15, 123, 124, 129, 130, 145, 158, 159–62, 165, 170, 174, 176, 183–92, 195, 197–98, 201, 206, 210, 224; oxen mingling with, 118–19; skins of, 12, 48, 51, 68, 92, 106, 113–15, 142, 144
"buffalo chips," 121–22
buffalo grass, 87, 124
Bull Bear (Oglala chief), 144–45, 155–56, 178
burials, 126–27, 142
Burnett, Elias, 402
Bush Creek, 81

Cache Valley, 215, 221, 233, 242, 244, 246–47
cactus, 87
California: development of, 15; emigration to, 2–3, 22–23, 39, 49, 401–6; under Mexican rule, 18, 19, 213, 396–400; mythology of, 16–18
Camp, Charles, 5
Campbell, Robert, 11, 144
Canada geese, 87
Carlin Canyon, 306–7
Carson, Kit, 79
Carson Lake, 329, 333, 335, 345, 351
Carson Pass, 332, 402
Carson River, 328, 329, 331–34, 344, 348
Castle Rock, 138, 139
Catholics, 14, 27, 67, 236
Cayuse Indians, 14
Cedar Creek, 133
Cedar Springs, 258, 259, 269

cedar trees, 125, 127, 129, 132, 229, 258, 268
Central Valley, 401
Chalk Buttes, 163
Chandler, David, 27, 402
Cheyenne Indians, 77, 111, 119, 126, 141, 178, 209, 256, 298; emigrants' and trappers' encounters with, 101–7, 109–10, 212, 235, 256, 374; migration of, 13, 106; Sioux displacement of, 130–31, 145
Chief Smoke, 156
Chiles, Joseph B., 4, 22, 77, 117, 235, 278, 325, 373; as adventurer, 52–54; at journey's end, 386, 392–93; late start by, 52, 55, 59, 66–68, 74–76; Nancy Kelsey recalled by, 275; oxen and wagons of, 209, 231; return to Missouri by, 212, 401–2, 405; Walker and, 212, 234, 306, 402
Chimney Rock, 133, 136–37, 139
Chippewa Indians, 106
cholera, 127
Christian Advocate, 13
Chugwater Creek, 155
Clark, William, 11, 108
Clark's Fork, 351, 353
Cleasons, William, 29
Clover Valley, 290
Clyman, James, 60, 86, 114, 139, 221, 224, 295; Fort Laramie described by, 149; Great Pawnee Trail noted by, 89–90; at Kansas River, 51; at North Platte River, 129; South Fork crossing recalled by, 117; as trapper, 11, 48, 63
Coast Range Mountains, 378, 380
Cocrum (Richard Fillan; R. Phelan), 154, 217
Colorado River, 199, 207, 401
Columbia River, 232, 256, 304, 310
Comanche Indians, 77
Conner Springs, 256, 258
Consumnes River, 367, 381, 384, 393, 394
Continental Divide, 196, 198–99, 221
Cook, Grove, 26, 292, 325, 372, 402, 403
Corral Creek, 301

| 431 |

Cottonweed Creek, 157
cottonwood trees, 95, 101, 142, 147, 157, 205, 392
Courthouse Rock, 133–34, 137
Coyote Rock, 138
Cranne Rock, 184
Cross Creek, 59
Crow Indians, 13, 141
Cumberland Gap, 219
Curry, George, 130–31

Dardanelles Creek, 353
Dawson, Nicholas "Cheyenne," 53, 112, 212, 272, 274, 275, 279, 282, 284–85, 289, 306; at Bear River, 224, 233, 236, 239–40, 250, 253, 255; camp routines recalled by, 65; Cheyenne encounter with, 101–6, 107, 374; at expedition's outset, 26, 37, 39, 44, 45–46, 47, 49–50, 51, 56; final years of, 402; Fitzpatrick viewed by, 65; food scarcity recalled by, 189, 198, 267; in Great Salt Lake country, 257, 261–62, 263; at Humboldt River, 322, 324–25, 326, 328, 329, 330, 333–34; at journey's end, 397; log maintained by, 4, 74, 81, 82, 86, 89, 90, 92, 100, 108, 111, 121, 123, 141, 165, 170, 193, 201, 214, 217, 286, 295, 319, 330, 336, 349, 362; rough terrain recalled by, 160, 223, 280, 373–74; in Sierra Nevada Mountains, 362–63, 366, 373–74, 375, 381–84, 389, 393; Snake Indians recalled by, 207, 208–9; as young adventurer, 24–25, 27, 38
Dead Camel Mountains, 333
Deep Creek, 244
Deep Sand Route, 185
Deer Creek, 164–65
Delaware Indians, 13, 34, 60
De Smet, Pierre-Jean, 28, 51, 52, 62, 68, 98, 174, 211, 232, 240; Bartleson viewed by, 235; Bear River descent described by, 222–23; at expedition's outset, 30, 35, 42, 43, 44; Fitzpatrick and, 14, 29, 202–3; Flatheads and, 27–28, 42, 66, 178, 207, 229; geological features noted by, 163; Iroquois conversions viewed by, 61; Kansa Indians and, 59–60; as marriage officiant, 217; non-Catholics and, 236–37; Pawnee encounter recalled by, 81–82; rock signing recalled by, 179; skepticism toward California of, 58; Sweetwater River described by, 180–81; weather noted by, 110; Williams and, 84

Devil's Backbone (Rock Avenue), 174
Devil's Gate, 180–81, 184
DeVoto, Bernard, 63, 178
Disaster Creek, 351
dogs, 83–84, 116–17
Donner party, 79, 278, 312, 349–50, 353
Donner Pass, 326, 332
Donner Springs, 278
drought, 390, 391, 393
Dumonts Meadow, 349
Dunmore, John Murray, earl of, 12
Durham Ferry, 391

Eagle Canyon, 124
East Fork Canyon, 348, 349
East Humboldt Range, 290, 293
elk, 86, 379, 391
Elm Grove, Kan., 46, 47–48, 49, 52
Emigrant Canyon, 315
Emigrant Trail, 214, 222
Eugene Mountains, 318

Farnham, Thomas Jefferson, 18
Feather River, 404, 405
Ferris Mountains, 181
Fillan, Richard (Cocrum; R. Phelan), 154, 217
fires, 72, 100–101, 229, 244
Fitzpatrick, Thomas, 29, 45, 82, 90, 112, 163, 177, 179, 233–34; Cheyenne encounter and, 101–2, 103–4, 105; criticisms of, 150–51; departure of, 152, 186, 232; De Smet's expedition led by, 14, 27, 29, 30, 42–43, 44; DeVoto's view of, 178; expertise and experience of, 63, 65, 73, 74,

98, 105–6, 161, 199, 215, 235, 237, 250; at Fort Laramie, 156; Fraeb's company and, 206; as fur company partner, 111, 145–46; as Indian Agent, 141; joint expedition led by, 27, 55, 57, 58, 59, 66, 76–79, 98, 121, 138, 159, 173, 196–97, 200, 202–3, 206, 210, 214, 218–21; precautions urged by, 126, 129, 185, 189, 223, 230, 239, 241, 257, 299; reputation of, 62–64, 106, 107, 108; Sioux encounter with, 212–13; straying oxen and, 120; as trail guide, 64, 117, 124, 128, 130, 165–66, 199, 200, 224; as trapper, 11; Williams's view of, 91
Flathead Indians, 14, 27–28, 42, 66, 178, 207
Fool Chief, 51, 59–60, 61
Fort Boise, Idaho, 398
Fort Bonneville, Wyo., 202
Fort Bridger, 213, 215, 224
Fort Hall, Idaho, 2, 178, 212, 234, 236, 250, 256–57, 300, 306, 345, 398
Fort Kearny, Neb., 99, 150
Fort Laramie, Wyo., 107, 140, 143–50, 152, 173–74, 178, 212, 398
Fort Osage, Mo., 13
Fort Platte, Neb., 146
Fort Ross, Calif., 398
Fort Vancouver, Wash., 256, 398
Forty-Mile Desert, 326
Fourche Boise Creek, 164
Fox Indians, 13
Fraeb (Frapp; Trapp), Henry, 205, 206, 207, 210–13, 233, 239, 256, 352
Franklin, Mo., 13
Franzwa, Gregory M., 5, 74, 223–24
Frémont, John C., 71, 179, 294, 295, 362; at Big Blue River, 79; at Black Vermillion Creek, 77; California Battalion led by, 403; Fitzpatrick and, 64; flora noted by, 87, 154; at Fort Laramie, 147; as "Great Pathfinder," 40; hide-trading companies described by, 114; Humboldt River named by, 233; at Little Blue Creek, 86, 90; Pawnees described by, 93; at Rock Creek, 82; rough terrain described by, 160–61; sites named by, 77, 79, 82, 233, 335; at South Pass, 6
Fresno River, 367
Frye, Amos, 29, 210, 211
fur trade, 11–12, 14, 32, 41, 63, 106, 179, 221

Geddes (alias Talbot Green), 25–26, 55, 325, 375, 383, 402, 403–4
geese, 87
Gillis, Michael J., 340
Glass, Hugh, 11
gnats, 112
Golden Canyon, 349, 351
Gold Rush, 2, 179, 312, 320, 400, 402, 403, 404; cholera during, 127; environment affected by, 114, 147, 154–55, 314; Indian encounters during, 332; routes used during, 118, 161, 305, 311, 326
Goose Creek, 234, 306
Goshute Valley, 295
Graham, Isaac, 396
Grand Island, Neb., 48, 94, 99
Grant, Richard, 235–36, 257
Gratten Massacre (1853), 142
Gravely Ford, 309
Gray, John, 29, 39, 89, 104, 112, 168, 178, 192, 195, 211, 224; Fraeb's company found by, 205, 206; at Green River rendezvous, 179, 190–91, 210
Gray, Mrs., 217
greasewood, 183
Great American Desert, 86
Great Pawnee Trail, 89–90
Great Salt Lake, 233–34, 252, 253, 255, 263, 268, 277, 295
Great Stone Face, 184
Green, Talbot (alias of Paul Geddes), 25–26, 55, 325, 375, 383, 402, 403–4
Greenhorn's Cutoff, 307
Green River, 153, 191–92, 196, 198–210, 212–14, 217–18, 223, 230, 231, 239, 265, 282, 352, 371; trappers' rendezvous at, 27, 178–79, 190, 203
Greenwood, Caleb, 202, 326
Greenwood's Cutoff (Sublette's Cutoff), 202–3

Grindstone Butte (Brigham's Peak; Knob Hill), 163
grizzly bears, 159, 163, 174, 175
Gros Ventre Indians, 63
Grouse Creek Mountain Range, 271, 272–73
Gulnac, William, 404

Haines, Aubrey L., 5
Hall Springs, 278
Hams Fork, 214, 215, 217–18
Harris, Black, 11, 48
Harrison Pass, 301
Hastings, Lanford, 294, 295, 405
Hastings Cutoff, 295
Henderson, Paul, 5
Henshaw, George, 20–21, 402
Hensley (expedition member), 22
hickory wood, 67–68
Hopper, Charles, 324–25, 326, 356, 401; Bidwell's misadventure recalled by, 240–41; as California resident, 402; as hunter, 25, 81, 89, 112, 333, 376, 383–84; scouting trip by, 265–68, 271–72, 285–86, 294–95
Horse Creek, 140–41, 176, 202
horses: diet of, 36, 157, 358, 374; exhaustion of, 312, 364, 376, 380, 387; as food source, 364, 367–68, 370–71, 372, 376, 377; hunting with, 106, 112, 171, 224; Indian warriors on, 37, 298; oxen vs., 58–59, 205, 286–87, 319; as pack animals, 207, 209, 256, 257, 273–74, 281, 284–85; picketing of, 65, 70–71, 145; speed of, 58; straying of, 71, 376–77; theft of, 60, 77, 93, 102, 218, 271, 367–68, 372, 376–77, 388; trade in, 33, 206, 207, 208, 256, 268; wild, 17, 132, 391
Horseshoe Creek, 158
Hoye Canyon, 339
Huber, Henry, 402, 403
Hudson Bay Company (HBC), 233, 236, 257, 299, 300
Huet, Charles, 29
Humboldt, Alexander von, 233
Humboldt Mountains, 317, 320
Humboldt River, 233, 257, 264, 270, 272, 276, 285, 295, 300–40

Humboldt Sink, 290, 309, 320, 324, 325, 329, 331, 332, 335, 342
Huntington Creek, 302

Ice Slough, 186
Idaho, 14
Illinois, 12, 13
Indian Creek, 160
Indian grass, 72
Independence, Mo., 13, 32
Independence Landing (Wayne City Landing), Mo., 31–32
Independence Rock, 176–78, 184, 191
Independence-Westport Road, 34
Indiana, 12, 13
Indian Knolls, 262
Indian Territory, 12–13, 34, 37, 60, 156
Iowa, 12, 13
Iroquois Indians, 27, 61

jackrabbits, 86
Jail Rock, 134
Jasper Pass, 286, 289, 295
Jesuits, 14, 27, 67
John, James (Jimmy), 3, 4, 53, 79, 88–89, 91, 102, 127, 268–80, 283–84, 286, 293, 295–98; at Bear River, 219–45; bears noted by, 158, 159, 163; at Big Sandy Creek, 201–6; buffalo noted by, 109, 113, 115, 120, 158, 183–87, 189, 192, 198; Cheyenne noted by, 103, 105, 111; flora noted by, 132, 157, 244; at Fort Laramie, 144, 146–47, 160–65; geological features noted by, 133, 139, 162, 164, 176, 179–80, 231; at Grand Island, 99; in Great Salt Lake region, 246–47, 250–66; at Green River, 206–18; at Humboldt River, 301–32, 335–40; at journey's end, 393–94, 399; late start by, 52, 66–67, 68, 74, 76; at North Platte River, 167, 169–71, 173, 174; omissions by, 73, 80, 90, 93, 100, 108, 112, 121–22, 269; in Oregon, 402; Pawnees recalled by, 77, 78, 81–82; shooting accident recounted by, 125–26; in Sierra Nevada Moun-

tains, 342, 344, 346–47, 349–52, 354, 356–61, 363, 365–72, 375, 378, 379, 381, 384–85; Sioux noted by, 153, 155; at South Fork, 115–16, 117; straying oxen recalled by, 122–23; at Sweetwater Creek, 176–98; at Warm Springs, 289–91; weather noted by, 85, 87, 96–97, 99, 128, 129, 136, 139, 140, 142, 270; youthfulness of, 54, 153
Johnson, David H., 340
Johnson, Thomas, 34, 62
Johnson, William, 61
Jones, J. M., 210, 211
Jones, Thomas, 362–63, 364, 368, 387, 388–89, 390
juniper trees, 100

Kansa Indians, 13, 34, 51, 57, 59–62, 75, 77
Kansas, 14
Kansas River, 45, 50–52, 80
Kearney, Stephen Watts, 64, 99
Kelly, William, 149
Kelsey, Andrew, 363–64, 368, 402
Kelsey, Benjamin, 38, 39, 273–74, 297, 354, 363, 370, 374, 388–89; at California-Oregon split, 231–32; as California resident, 403; illness of, 368–69; Indians intercepted by, 300; as leader, 325–28, 330, 332–41, 344, 346; wagons abandoned by, 284
Kelsey, Isaac, 95, 97
Kelsey, Nancy A., 4, 39, 51, 182, 217, 232, 233, 348, 349, 363, 368, 369, 373, 374, 386, 389; as California resident, 402; Chiles's admiration for, 275; Dawson criticized by, 105; Shoshone encounter recalled by, 300; in Utah, 245
Kelsey, Samuel, 38, 217
Kelsey family, 26, 37
Kentucky, 12
Keyes, Sarah, 79–80
Kickapoo Indians, 13, 14
Kiowa Indians, 77
Knight Creek, 371, 372
Knight's Ferry, 380

Knob Hill (Brigham's Peak; Grindstone Butte), 163

La Bonte Creek (Big Timber Creek), 159, 161, 162
Laguna Creek, 381
La Prele Creek, 163–64
Laramie Mountain Range, 140, 143, 154, 165
Larkin, Thomas O., 397, 403
Lassen, Peter, 319
Lassen Meadows, 318–19, 320
Lee, Jason, 13, 61
Lempfrit, Honoré-Timothée, 149
Leonard, Zenas, 150–51, 309
Lewis, Meriwether, 11, 108
lightning, 72, 87, 118–19, 229
Little Antelope Valley, 340, 344
Little Blue River, 81, 85–86, 91
Little Colorado Desert, 199
Little Mountain, 244, 254, 255
Little Muddy Creek, 218, 219, 220–21
Little Sandy Creek, 198, 200–201
Little Snake River, 212, 256
Little Vermillion Creek (Red Vermillion Creek), 69, 80
Locomotive Springs, 262
Long, Stephen H., 86
Lost Creek, Kan., 67
Louisiana Purchase (1804), 11
Lower Humboldt Drain, 325
Lupton, Lancaster P., 146

Malade River, 250, 251, 253
malaria, 17
Maps of the Oregon Trail (Franzwa), 5, 6, 74, 223–24
Marsh, John, 25, 42, 335, 396, 397, 404, 405; Bartleson and, 21, 26, 41, 186, 211; California ranch of, 386–93, 398; duplicity of, 395, 398; as entrepreneur, 21–22
Mason Valley, 337
Mast, William, 29, 153
Mattes, Merrill, 5
May, Richard, 155
McDowell, John, 401
McKays Dam, 360, 363
McKinstry, George, Jr., 405

McMahon, Samuel, 402
McPherson, John, 149
Mengarini, Gregorio, 28, 88, 126, 167–68
Methodists, 13, 34
Mexico, 18, 19, 213, 396–400
Micheltorena, Manuel, 403, 404, 405
Middle Fork Canyon, 357, 358–59, 361, 362, 363, 366, 372, 373, 374
Mill Canyon, 345
Miller, Alfred Jacob, 145, 155
Minnesota, 106
Mission San Jose, 397, 398
Missouri, 12
Missouri River, 95, 108, 144
Miwok Indians, 367–68
Mojave Desert, 401
Mokelumne River, 366, 369
Montana, 14, 27, 28, 66
Monument Point, Utah, 262
Moraga, Gabriel, 367
Morgan, Dale, 5
mosquitoes, 17, 112, 182, 200–201, 227
Mount Diablo, 387, 388, 395
Mount Wilson, 337
Muddy Creek, 165
mules: diet of, 36; disadvantages of, 58–59; as food source, 370–71; speed of, 58, 98
Murray, Charles, 17

Napa Valley, 401, 402
National Park Service, 5
Newell, Robert (Doc), 12
Nez Perce Indians, 14, 27
Nidever, George, 309
North Fork Canyon, 363
North Platte River, 123, 124, 127, 129, 131–33, 138, 140–43, 154, 157, 159, 160, 164–71, 182
Nye, Michael, 21, 41, 396, 397, 402

oak trees, 50, 77, 79, 352, 353, 359, 360, 366, 379, 392
Ogden, Peter Skene, 42, 233
Oglala Indians, 129, 144–46, 155
Ohio, 12, 13
Old Spanish Trail, 206
Omaha Indians, 78

Oneida Narrows, 242
Oregon-California Trails Association, 6
Oregon Territory, 13, 48–49
Oregon Trail, 6, 49, 90, 99, 154, 181, 199, 224
Osage Indians, 77
Osgood Mountains, 315
Otoe Indians, 13, 78
Overton, William, 22, 26, 325
Owl Springs, 273, 274, 284
oxen, 33–34, 174–75, 205, 222, 289, 309, 341–42; digestive system of, 36, 59, 160–61, 172–73, 259, 318; exhaustion of, 150, 173, 259, 267, 273, 274, 275, 280, 306, 313, 346; as food source, 59, 191, 267, 269, 288, 290–91, 319, 321, 328–29, 349, 354, 374; impulsiveness of, 83–84; as pack animals, 284–85, 286–87, 312; slowness of, 58, 98, 287, 312, 320–21, 323, 326; straying by, 67, 69, 70–71, 75–76, 87, 118–20, 122–23, 125, 256, 260, 284, 287–89, 292, 299
Oyster Ridge, 219

Pacific Crest Trail, 351
Pacific Springs, Wyo., 196, 199
Paden, Irene, 5
Paden, William, 340
Paiute Indians, 290, 309, 317, 323, 328
Palisades Canyon, 307
Palmer, Joel, 117–18
Papin (Pappan), Joseph, 51, 68
Papin (Pappan), Louis, 51, 68
Paradise Meadows, 351, 352
Parker, Samuel, 13, 155
Parkman, Francis, 114, 140, 148–49, 150, 155, 156
Patton, Andrew (Gwinn), 25, 325, 401
Pawnee Indians, 57, 69, 93, 111, 118, 126, 141, 209; bellicosity of, 60–61, 62, 71, 75–78, 81–82, 108; buffalo hunting by, 90, 130; Cheyenne vs., 104, 107; Fort Kearny site purchased from, 99; missions among, 13; Sioux vs., 130, 145
Payton, Henry, 52, 211
Pequop Mountains, 279–80, 286

INDEX

Phelan, R. (Cocrum; Richard Fillan), 154, 217
Pierre's Hole, Idaho, 14
Piga (trapper), 29
Pilot Mountains, 275, 276–77, 278, 295
Pilot Peak, 275
Plains Indians, 37, 64, 130, 141
Platte Purchase, 16
Platte River, 12, 73, 91, 94–131
Plum Creek, 108
Point, Nicholas, 28, 39, 51–52, 179, 203, 207, 209, 210–12, 220, 232; Bartleson admired by, 56; buffalo noted by, 186; camp routines recalled by, 65, 119; Cheyenne encounter recalled by, 102, 105, 235; De Smet's departure recalled by, 35; discipline stressed by, 57; dogs described by, 116–17; flora described by, 93; Kansa Indians and, 59–60, 61; non-Catholics and, 236–37; Pawnees recalled by, 82; pests recalled by, 182; Platte River described by, 94
Poison Springs, 172, 174
Ponca Indians, 78
Potawatomie Indians, 13, 67
prairie dogs, 86, 123, 124
Presbyterians, 13
Preuss, Charles, 137, 140
Promontory Mountains, 258, 260
pronghorn antelope, 86
Prospect Hill, 176
Pumpkin Creek, 133, 134

Rabbit Springs, 273
Raft River, 234, 306
Raft River Mountains, 262–63, 270
Rattlesnake Pass, 180
Rattlesnake Range, 181
rattlesnakes, 124, 182
Red Cloud (Smoke warrior), 156
Red Earth Country, 162
Red River carts, 30
Red Springs, 158
Red Vermillion Creek (Little Vermillion Creek), 69, 80
Reed, James, 79
Register Cliff, 154

Rickman, Robert, 22, 26, 52, 325, 401
Robidoux, Antoine, 16–18, 140, 390
Robidoux, Joseph, 16, 80, 140
Robidoux Pass, 140
Rock Avenue (Devil's Backbone), 174
Rock Creek, 82
Rocky Crossing, 251
Rocky Mountain Fur Company (RMFC), 63, 111, 145, 206, 233–34
Rocky Mountains, 36, 40, 298; fur trapping in, 11, 29, 34, 48, 63, 78, 208, 211
rocky mountain spotted fever, 182
Rocky Ridge, 190
Rodriguez Flat, 345
Rogers (member of De Smet's expedition), 29, 210, 211
Roland, John, 401
Romaine, W. G., 29, 30, 39, 59, 112, 174, 211, 224; at Green River rendezvous, 178, 179, 190–91, 210
Root, Riley, 158, 190
Rosebud Springs, 271
Rowland-Workman party, 2
Ruby Mountains, 294–96, 301, 302
Russian-American Fur Company, 398

Sac Indians, 13
Sacramento River, 335, 342, 344, 394, 398, 399
Sage, Rufus B., 5–6, 78, 92, 137
sagebrush, 129, 160, 183, 200, 244, 320
St. Joseph, Mo., 80
St. Mary's Mission, 67
Salt Creek, 256
Salt Wells, 260, 262
Sandy Creek, 85
sandhill cranes, 87
San Joaquin River, 334–35, 367, 390–91, 395, 401, 404
San Joaquin Valley, 367–68, 378, 380
Santa Fe, N.M., 13, 21, 33
Santa Fe Trail, 13, 33, 34, 48, 49, 401
Sapling Grove, Kan., 1, 15, 18, 31–43
Schwartz, John, 402
Scott, Hiram, 138
Scotts Bluff, 138
Scott Spring, 75

Secret Creek, 294
Secret Pass, 294, 295, 306
Sedgwick Peak, 239
Sequoia trees, 362
Shawnee Indian Mission, 34, 62
Shawnee Indians, 13, 34, 60, 77
Sheep Mountain, 163
Shibley Springs, 277, 278
Shoshone Indians (Snake Indians), 13, 141, 155, 209, 210, 247, 297–300, 313, 316, 317; Sioux vs., 199–200; trade with, 195, 207, 239, 264; Western branch of, 265, 270, 282–83, 300
Shotwell, George, 27, 125–26, 127, 393, 400
Shunganunga Creek, 50
Sibley, George, 36
Sierra Nevada Mountains, 234, 328, 329, 331, 332, 336, 338–85, 390, 402
Silver King Valley, 348
Silver Zone Pass, 278, 279
Simpson, George, 153
Simpson's Gulch, 204
Sioux Indians, 13, 77, 78, 106, 129–30, 141, 142, 145, 178, 256; along Battle Creek, 145; at Fort Laramie, 155–56, 209; at Independence Rock, 212–13; Snake Indians vs., 199–200; U.S. Army vs., 143
Slate Creek, 379
Slinkard Creek, 340
smallpox, 60, 78
Smith, Edward, 114
Smith, Jedediah, 11, 42, 63
Smith Creek, 301–2
Smith's Fork, 225
Smith Valley, 338–39
Snake Indians. *See* Shoshone Indians
Snake River, 206, 231, 233, 234
snakes, 73, 124, 182, 320
Snodgrass Creek, 347–48
snow geese, 87
Soda Lake, 184
Soda Springs, Idaho, 83, 229–30, 232–33, 404
Soldier Creek, 52, 55–56, 59
Sonoma Mountains, 315
South Dakota, 106–7, 129, 144, 155

South Fork Canyon, 374–75
South Pass, 12, 63, 199, 212
Spaulding, William, 13–14
Specht, Joseph, 29
Split Rock, 184
Spring Canyon, 124, 127
Spring Creek, 160
Springer, James, 401
Spruce Mountain Ridge, 286
Stanislaus River, 353, 355, 357, 360, 361, 367, 372–73, 380, 382–83, 386–89
Steamboat Springs, Idaho, 230
Stearns, Abel, 206
Stephens-Murphy party, 326
Strawberry Creek, 190
Sublette, Milton, 11, 63, 151
Sublette, William, 11, 48, 63, 144, 145, 151, 176, 178
Sublette's Cutoff (Greenwood's Cutoff), 202–3
Sublette's Trace, 48–49
Sunflower Munitions Works, 49
Sutter, John A., 394, 398–400, 403, 404–5
Sutter's Fort, 394, 398–99, 401, 403, 405
Sweetwater River, 12, 174, 176–98, 212, 259, 305
switch grass, 72

Table Rock, 138
Tejon Pass, 401
Tenmile Springs, 263, 267
Thirty-Two Mile Creek, 91
Thomas Fork, 225
Thomes, Robert H., 4, 21, 31, 35, 292, 402, 404
Thornton, J. Quinn, 6, 50, 52, 57, 107, 139, 171
Thousand Springs Creek, 276, 306
Three Crossings Route, 185
ticks, 182
Toano Range, 278, 295
tobacco, 76, 104, 145, 208, 313
Townsend, John, 32
Toyn Creek, 301
Trails West, 6
Trapp (Fraeb; Frapp), Henry, 205,

206, 207, 210, 211–12, 213, 233, 239, 256
Trinity Range, 320
Truckee River, 326, 331, 332
trumpeter swans, 87
Tunnel Springs, 275

Uinta Mountains, 218
Utah, 245

Vallejo, Mariano, 396–97
Vasquez, Louis, 213
Vieux, Louis, 69–70
volcanoes, 163, 171, 229

wagon breakdowns, 82–83, 87, 215, 220, 221
Wagon Hound Creek, 162
Wakarusa River, 49–50
Walker, Joseph, 42, 66, 153, 233, 250, 257, 311, 335; Chiles's expedition led by, 211, 234, 306, 402; elusiveness of, 186, 211–12, 236; in Great Salt Lake region, 234; as trader, 206; Paiute encounter with, 290, 309; in Sierra Nevada Mountains, 352, 362
Walker, William, 13
Walker Lake, 343, 344
Walker River, 331, 335, 336–39, 340, 344, 361
Walton, Ambrose, 401
Walton, Major, 401
Warm Creek, 290, 291
Warm Springs, 154, 289, 290–91, 295, 306
Wayne City Landing (Independence Landing), Mo., 31–32
Weber, Charles M., 3, 52, 53, 54, 66, 77, 236, 402, 404

Wellington Hills, 338–39
Western Emigration Society, 18–19, 22
Weston, Mo., 16, 31
Weston Creek, 244, 246
Westport, Mo., 13, 34
Whirlwind (Oglala Sioux chief), 155
White, Elijah, 107, 178, 213
Whitman, Marcus, 13–14
Whitman, Narcissa, 13–14
Williams, Joseph, 108, 187, 192, 194, 200, 207–8, 216, 217, 223, 227; De Smet's view of, 237; geological features noted by, 137, 138; on guard duty, 119; Indians noted by, 93, 105, 195; late start by, 81, 83; as marriage officiant, 95, 97; self-righteousness of, 84, 91, 220, 228; sermons by, 90, 125–26, 188
Williams, Miss, 95, 97
Williams, Richard, 38, 95, 97
Williams family, 37
Willow Springs, 175
willow trees, 95, 101, 122, 174–75, 192, 200, 207, 222, 226, 238, 252, 255, 290, 302, 305, 307, 308, 309, 319, 321, 322, 335, 383, 390–92
Wilson Canyon, 338
Wind River Mountains, 184–85, 193, 194, 199, 200
Wisconsin, 12
Wislizenus, F. A., 36, 45, 48, 64, 120, 145
wolves, 86, 174, 175, 192
Wyandotte Indians, 13
Wyeth, Nathaniel, 82, 151
Wyoming, 6, 12

Yount, George, 301

About the Author

Michael E. LaSalle is a retired attorney who graduated from University of California, Davis, Law School in 1970. During his many years practicing law, he found himself constantly drawn to the history of the Far West, especially to the era of the covered wagon and the emigrant trails. In 2011, Truman State University Press published his book *Emigrants on the Overland Trail: The Wagon Trains of 1848*. He lives near Hanford, California.